CW01238791

POWER AND POLITICS IN TUDOR ENGLAND

Power and Politics in Tudor England

Essays by G.W. Bernard

Jeremy
with best wishes
George

Ashgate

Aldershot • Burlington USA • Singapore • Sydney

© G.W. Bernard, 2000

All rights reserved. No part of this publication may be reproduced, stored in a retrieval system, or transmitted in any form or by any means, electronic, mechanical, photocopying, recording, or otherwise without the prior permission of the publisher.

The author has asserted his right under the Copyright, Designs and Patents Act, 1988, to be identified as the author of this work.

Published by
Ashgate Publishing Limited
Gower House
Croft Road
Aldershot
Hants GU11 3HR
England

Ashgate Publishing Company
131 Main Street
Burlington
Vermont 05401-5600
USA

Ashgate website: http://www.ashgate.com

British Library Cataloguing-in-Publication data

Bernard, G.W.
   Power and politics in Tudor England
   1. Power (Social sciences) – England – History   2. Upper class – England – History   3. Great Britain – Politics and government – 1485–1603
   I. Title
   942'.05

Library of Congress Cataloging-in-Publication data

Bernard, G.W.
   Power and politics in Tudor England / G.W. Bernard.
      p.   cm.
   1. Great Britain – Politics and government – 1485–1603.   2. Power (Social sciences) – England – History – 16th century.   3. England – Social conditions – 16th century.   4. Tudor, House of.
   I. Title.
   DA315.B38 2000
   942.05–dc21

00-034848
CIP

ISBN 0 7546 0245 1

Typeset in Times by N^{2}productions and printed on acid-free paper and bound in Great Britain by Antony Rowe Ltd, Chippenham.

Contents

Acknowledgements		vi
1	Introduction	1
2	The continuing power of the Tudor nobility	20
3	The fall of Wolsey reconsidered	51
4	The fall of Anne Boleyn	80
5	Elton's Cromwell	108
6	Court and government	129
7	The downfall of Sir Thomas Seymour	134
8	Amy Robsart	161
9	Architecture and politics in Tudor England	175
10	The Church of England *c.* 1529–*c.* 1642	191
11	History and Postmodernism	217
Index		231

Acknowledgements

In preparing this collection, and especially for their comments on the introduction, I should wish to thank Peter Gwyn, Mark Stoyle and Greg Walker. And I should want to thank once again all those whose encouragement and advice is recorded in the notes for the individual essays.

* * *

Chapter 2 is a substantially reworked development of 'The Tudor nobility in perspective', from G.W. Bernard (ed.), *The Tudor Nobility* (Manchester University Press, 1992), pp. 1–48, and also draws on G.W. Bernard, *The Power of the Early Tudor Nobility: a study of the fourth and fifth earls of Shrewsbury* (Harvester, 1985).

Chapter 3, 'The fall of Wolsey reconsidered', *Journal of British Studies*, xxxv (1996), pp. 277–310, is reproduced with the permission of the University of Chicago Press © 1996 by the University of Chicago. All rights reserved.

Chapter 4, 'The fall of Anne Boleyn', *English Historical Review*, cvi (1991), pp. 584-610, is reproduced by permission of Oxford University Press.

Chapter 5, 'Elton's Cromwell', *History*, lxxxiii (1998), pp. 587–607, and Chapter 10, 'The church of England *c.* 1529–1642', *History*, lxxv (1990), pp. 183–206, are reprinted with the permission of the Historical Association.

Chapter 7, 'The fall of Sir Thomas Seymour', in G.W. Bernard (ed.), *The Tudor Nobility* (Manchester University Press, 1992), pp. 212–40, is reprinted with the permission of Manchester University Press.

Chapters 1, 6, 8, 9 and 11 are published for the first time.

1
Introduction

At the heart of the essays in this volume lies an interest in the nature and expression of power, defined quite straightforwardly as the ability to take and to enforce a decision. My first researches focused on the power of the nobility in Tudor England, a choice of subject that was in itself a critique of the then dominant emphasis – it is sufficient to cite Sir Geoffrey Elton here – on the institutions of central government as the key to the location and the effective operation of power. Yet much writing on the politics of early modern continental countries suggested rather the continuing importance of noblemen, despite the myth of rising royal absolutism; it seemed worth exploring the sources to determine more fully the role of the nobility in England. Chapter 2 here offers my latest reflections on this subject, drawing on my *The Power of the Early Tudor Nobility* (1984), an introductory essay to *The Tudor Nobility* (1992) and a paper in *History Review* (1995), but developing and expanding the arguments there in several places.

My claims are multiple. The nobility remained powerful, socially, economically, politically and ideologically. That power was generally applied in the service of the monarchy and the monarch's policies. In consequence, historians have tended to underestimate it, since noblemen were not normally opponents of the Crown: they did not see themselves as having a duty to rebel. The nature, extent and limits of noble power are explored in detail in Chapter 7 on the downfall of Sir Thomas Seymour: the depositions made in connection with his trial illustrate these themes with a remarkable richness of detail. Chapter 8, treating Amy Robsart, apart from the fascination of a mysterious death, may also be read as an exploration of the ambitions of a courtier-noble, Robert Dudley. In moments of crisis, rare though they were, the power of the nobility, indeed of individual noblemen, could, nonetheless, be crucial. The loyalty shown by George Talbot, fourth earl of Shrewsbury, against the Pilgrimage of Grace in autumn 1536 saved Henry's break with Rome and associated religious policies. Tudor monarchs were not omnipotent, and there were significant limits to royal power. Nor were the nobility the only brakes: taxpayers lower down the social scale effectively prevented the development of financial demands at the monarch's whim when they refused the Amicable Grant in 1525, a sequence of events I studied in *War, Taxation and Rebellion in Early Tudor England* (1986).

That background of local power, of government depending on informal as well as formal relationships between local elites and kings, counsellors and courtiers, in short a sort of unwritten convention among the ruling classes, is important too in the proper understanding of high politics, the theme of several of the essays here, notably those which take issue with the fashionable notion of 'faction'. The idea of faction has become commonplace in writing on Tudor political history. In Sir Geoffrey Elton's textbook, *Reform and Reformation* (1977), struggles between factions serve as an organising framework for the narrative. Elton had, in one of his earliest articles published in 1951, explained the fall of his hero Thomas Cromwell in 1540 as the victim of a plot by a conservative faction led by the third duke of Norfolk and Stephen Gardiner, bishop of Winchester;[1] he later substantially developed such a factional interpretation under the influence of his pupil David Starkey.[2] Eric Ives is another historian who has been emphasising the role of faction: in an Historical Association pamphlet, *Faction in Tudor England* (1979, revised 1987), in his biography of *Anne Boleyn* (1986), and in recent essays on 'Henry the Great?', and 'Henry VIII: the political perspective'.[3] If Elton, Starkey and Ives have been the most eloquent and influential exponents of factional ideas, these are widely, sometimes unconsciously, shared. In *English Reformations* (1993), for example, Christopher Haigh draws heavily on the swirl of faction to account for what he sees as shifts in religious policy.

Historians who emphasise faction are engaged in an attempt to characterise early Tudor politics as essentially a conflict – a contest for power, for influence, for favours and for policies. Perez Zagorin offers a characteristic description: Henry VIII's court was 'a perilously unstable world in which power and honours were always at risk'; 'every shift of royal policy in these years was attended with factional intrigue and the possibility of disgrace and death for those on the wrong side'.[4] For David Starkey, faction is 'the name given to the groups formed by courtiers and councillors the better to pursue their restless struggles for power and profit'.[5] Ives has claimed that 'the faction battle was endemic, inherent in the realities of kingship, court and royal personality, a never-ceasing groundswell of competition to secure favour, office, wealth and influence': 'what has to be recognised is how constant the element of faction is throughout the reign' of Henry VIII.[6] Such struggles could be between equals or groups of equals competing for office or for decisive influence, or between a leading minister or a royal favourite on the one hand and those who disliked his power and tried to bring him down on the other. This view of politics as factional struggle tends to diminish the position of the king. It is usually accepted that the personal decisions of the monarch were important – as Ives concedes, 'policy was what the king decided' – but what appear on the face of it to have been the personal decisions of monarchs are seen by the factional school of historians as in reality the result of factional manipulation. 'The object of a faction,' says Ives, 'was ... to influence the king as he made his decision and hence to be rewarded with the duty to implement it. Instead of Henry VIII governing according to his own autonomous will, government emerged from the shifting political and individual context around him'. 'The more contentious the issue, the more the full battery of tactics might be tried: restricting access to the king, the claque, the innuendo, the bribe, the diversion. These brought Wolsey down, Anne Boleyn down, Cromwell down and the Howards and Gardiner'.[7] Monarchs are seen as vulnerable in a variety of ways to such factions. What mattered was the manipulation of the king. Factions might seek to control members of the privy chamber, the close body servants of the king, who saw him more often and for longer than anyone else, and so could press for favours and policies for the faction to which they belonged. Factions might seek to use the king's bed, by introducing the king to attractive young women who would then further the interests of the political factions who sponsored them. Malicious charges might be brought against enemies, or attention drawn to what was true but damaging. Sometimes such struggles were purely about office, purely personal; sometimes they might acquire an ideological flavour from divisions over religion or over policies, especially foreign alliances. Such is the model of political explanation that has become so fashionable in the past generation.

But these notions have also been vigorously challenged by several historians, including Peter Gwyn in his study of Cardinal Wolsey, *The King's Cardinal* (1990), Greg Walker, most recently in *Persuasive Fictions* (1996), and by myself in several of the essays reprinted here. A very different view of politics is offered, one in which Henry VIII was very much in charge, ruling as well as reigning, and in which factional interpretations are simply unnecessary. By looking *in depth* at events – in the way I have tried to do for the falls of Anne and Wolsey in Chapters 3 and 4[8] – and at the relationship of king and minister – as in Chapter 5 on 'Elton's Cromwell' – very different conclusions impose themselves.

It is worth adding here that while examination of particular events is vital, and often illuminates much more than the events themselves, a broad understanding of the nature of power demands the exploration of ideas and attitudes as well as events. Chapter 2 on the nobility includes a discussion of attitudes to nobility, in particular contemporary reflections on how inequality of wealth could be reconciled with God's order for the world. The nobility, I contend, derived enormous sustenance from the widely-voiced conviction that such a hierarchical society was both just and necessary. Chapter 9 on architecture explores how far Tudor buildings can be understood as reflections of power and so illumine our understanding of Tudor society. But while ideas and architecture – and literature and art – should be no less part of the political historian's scope than specific events, care must be taken not simply to read into them pre-formed interpretations from the world of politics, narrowly defined.

Although some factional historians have responded to criticism by reasserting or in small ways recasting their claims,[9] the most fashionable response has been to concede that those of us who have criticised them have shown up the crudity of their explanatory model but that we are ourselves guilty of similar over-simplification. 'I understand your irritation with those who reduce Henry VIII to the status of a hosepipe, which squirts in different directions depending on who is holding the nozzle. But surely it is possible to construct a more sophisticated account of the origins of policy than in effect reversing this simplistic metaphor and saying that the nozzle was self-directed'.[10] But my claim that Henry VIII was the driving force in the politics and policies of his reign is not an attempt 'to construct a more sophisticated account of the origins of policy' but rather what my study of the evidence has led me to conclude, and my criticism of factional historians is not that their approach is unsophisticated or simplistic, but that it is not supported by the evidence, their theories too often being erected on a literal reading of a single remark drawn out of context. By and large the advocates of 'faction' have been less careful, and less inclined to explain from where they have taken their evidence and to justify their deployment of it, than those of us who have emphasised the role of the king. Too often literary sources, especially Polydore Vergil's *Historia Anglica*, George Cavendish's *Life of Wolsey*, William Tyndale's *Practice of Prelates*, and John Foxe's *Acts and Monuments*, have been relied upon heavily, and above all unthinkingly, by factional historians. Evanescent gossip reported as such by foreign ambassadors has been seized upon as the key to the mysteries of the politics of the reign, even though it is contradicted in the same letter. All this is not to say that those sources are valueless, only that they must be read critically, and never in isolation. And if they are read aright, it is my contention that the sources do point to the dominant role of Henry VIII.

Several historians have tried to reconcile that claim with the arguments of the factional historians. It is not an either/or dichotomy, they claim: these two interpretations can be combined perfectly satisfactorily. Felipe Fernandez-Armesto, for example, notes 'the current debate over the structure of government rages between supporters of the old, pre-Eltonian view of decision-making controlled – albeit capriciously – by an unreconstructed "strong monarch", and opponents who see the crown as embedded in a court environment in which the pressure of contending factions determined policy': he then goes on roundly to assert that 'these opposing camps can be reconciled: most court structures have a powerful decision-maker at their core and factions struggling to control access to him'.[11] Jim Alsop, reviewing Greg Walker's collection of essays, declared that 'there remains room for powerful (not necessarily dominant) factions *and* a strong, self-confident sovereign who needed to be counseled, petitioned, cajoled, and at times manipulated'. 'It is a pity', he continued, 'that the 1950s debate over the responsibility for the royal supremacy, "king or minister", has been succeeded by an equally sterile "king

Introduction 5

or faction?"'.¹² Whether the debate has been 'sterile' is perhaps not a judgment a participant should make, but the subject – the way in which power was exercised – is surely of fundamental importance. Neither Fernandez-Armesto, in a preface, nor Alsop, in a review, had the opportunity of offering further and detailed illustrations of how what might be considered logically contradictory propositions – that Henry VIII was manipulated by factions and that Henry VIII was a dominant king – could be reconciled. Two historians have, however, attempted to do that, and their efforts rather confirm any such attempts are to follow a will-o'-the-wisp.

John Guy, who has on occasions, especially in his study of *The Public Career of Sir Thomas More* (1980), adopted a strongly factional interpretation, recently put forward what appears to be an attempt to combine both approaches.¹³ In places the king is still weak or led. Henry VIII 'was relatively manipulated by women and intimates'; he was 'less attentive to mundane affairs of state' than his father or Elizabeth I; 'the young Henry intervened less in politics before 1527 (possibly 1525)'; and he allowed Cromwell to make the running in religious policy in the mid and late 1530s until 1539, at which time 'the king had resumed command of his religious policy', a comment that implies that he had earlier relinquished command of it for a time. But in other places Guy says of Henry, 'yet always he was king'; 'his voice was dominant in politics; his merest whisper could dictate the fundamental decisions of the reign'; 'he always retained the right to have the last word'; in summer 1527 'Henry personally seized the initiative from an absent Wolsey in soliciting support and orchestrating the debate' over the divorce; 'the king might intervene or change his mind at will'. If Guy concedes an ultimate superiority to the king – 'it was the king who ruled and not his ministers', 'what mattered in Henrician politics was the king's unqualified trust' – and follows the claims I made in *War, Taxation and Rebellion* in calling the relationship between Henry and Wolsey a partnership, nonetheless he sees Wolsey as winning the king's favour by being the most earnest and readiest to advance his pleasure, and as maintaining his position by settling policy with the king before he consulted other councillors. Guy also sees faction in operation generally, with noblemen and councillors and advisers jostling between themselves in a variety of ways: Henry VII's councillors against Wolsey in the first years of the reign; Wolsey against noblemen and other councillors in the 1520s; Cromwell against his enemies in the 1530s. Guy offers a factional interpretation of the fall of Anne Boleyn, 'the putsch of 1536'. 'When Henry repudiated Anne Boleyn in the spring of 1536, Cromwell was deft enough to obtain the evidence to destroy both Anne and her court allies in order that Henry might marry Jane Seymour. But he also took the opportunity to drive his own political opponents from court on the grounds that they had plotted to restore Princess Mary to the succession'. Thereafter Cromwell's power was 'sustained by factional politics rather than the king's unqualified trust'; efforts were made to topple Cromwell in the Pilgrimage of Grace; Cromwell's evangelical religious policies were challenged by 'Cromwell's enemies'; and in 1540 Henry 'threw Cromwell to the wolves', presumably meaning his factional enemies; Cromwell was executed in 1540 'a victim of faction politics'. Each of these quoted sets of claims is on its own a plausible description, but I do not see how they can all be true: the attempt to pick and mix ends in contradiction and confusion. This simply serves to show that if you attempt to combine factional and non-factional approaches, you end up with a muddle.

A similarly fruitless attempt was made by Steven Gunn. To the question who, king or ministers, was in charge, Gunn, exploring what he terms the structures of Tudor politics, answers 'it all depends': some of our sources say that Henry was manipulated, others suggest that he was dominant.[14] But that shirks the issue. It is an answer answerless to the great conundrums of the reign of Henry VIII: it seems to say that all sources are equivalent, even that all historians' arguments are of equal value. The flaw is that while source criticism is essential, it is not in itself sufficient. Gunn takes as the point of departure of his essay historians' sharply differing views of the fall of Anne, but his method does not enable him to offer any view of his own. Examining in turn ambassadors' letters, Lancelot de Carles's verse life of Anne, the indictments, Sir William Kingston's letters from the Tower, Cromwell's letters, and so on, as types of source, entertains more than it enlightens. Yet if one is to say anything definite about Tudor politics, one does have to come to a decision on, say, the fall of Wolsey or the fall of Anne Boleyn. And trying instead to accept 'both the king's position as initiator and arbitrator of policy and the possibility of independent initiative and lobbying from those around him' does not lead Gunn to a more nuanced interpretation than one that sees Henry as in command of his counsellors. If it means that Henry was manipulated by his lobbying counsellors, then he was not initiator or arbitrator; if it means that he did determine policy, then any lobbying must have had very clear limits. Gunn's essay is inconclusive.

Another attempt to reconcile these interpretations has been made by C.S.L. Davies (in private correspondence). Davies at first accepts that Henry was in charge, that there is no question but that Henry was ultimately responsible for policy, and that he took a keen personal interest in policy-making, especially in religious policy, and he concedes that such policy may have been rather more consistent than is often allowed. But almost immediately he raises doubts that undermine what he has just conceded. Did Henry always know which way he was going, was he really that consistent, is it possible to believe in anybody being *totally* impervious to influence from those around them? The faction debate, he claims, pushes everything into an either/or dichotomy and approaches everything too mechanically.

Yet in any political situation, influence flows in every direction; the leading figures have strong views of their own, and are able to enforce them, but that does not exclude the point that they are nonetheless open to influence, that it is possible to affect the navigation by leaning a bit on the tiller; nobody makes decisions in a vacuum, multilateralism is inherent in any decision-making process.

Henry VIII '*is* plainly somebody who needs to be persuaded, ... he has strong views, prejudices, which have to be overcome, but ... he is singularly lacking in any creative input, reactive not pro-active, reluctant to make up his mind completely, finally'. And Davies seizes on what he sees as evidence that different religious groups did manoeuvre round Henry, that they did have some input into the finished product, that Henry's position did vary, though within certain limits, according to circumstances; that contemporaries (foreign observers, Thomas Cromwell, Thomas Cranmer, Norfolk, Gardiner) felt the king was open to influence; that participants and other observers did see a religious struggle taking place, a struggle to determine just where Henry would come down; that if religious policy was broadly consistent, nonetheless the wobbles en route were significant; that policy was influenced by Henry's perceptions of events, which in turn depended on how and by whom information was processed. In short, the king's volatility meant that 'he reacts to circumstances, which leaves room for a certain degree of presentation'. Davies denies that this reasoning makes him a factional historian. Indeed, he has here subtly shifted the subject under debate. What he is defending is not the factional historians' claims that Henry was *manipulated* by factions, but rather the much more reasonable proposition that Henry, like all rulers, was open to *influence*, though Davies seems to verge on saying that Henry was more vulnerable to influence, because of weaknesses of character, than most rulers. And when in a recent published essay he writes of 'the way in which the religious future of the country came to hang on the outcome of attempts to turn Henry against his current queen',[15] his argument has further evolved from a would-be neutral stance (a king who is both dominant and influenced) to what is almost wholly an endorsement of the factional position – exactly what Elton, Starkey, Guy (in factional mode) and Ives would claim.

To claim, as I do, that Henry was very much the dominant force in the politics and policy-making of his reign is not to claim that he could do whatever he liked. That would be a caricature of the arguments of those who have made that case. My argument is directed against those historians who have claimed that Henry was *manipulated* by factions. It is not my claim that Henry was somehow totally immune from influence. Rather, the influences upon Henry are best explored in different ways. We know less about his early and adolescent years than would be necessary to make confident claims, and too often, influences must be inferred from actions and outcomes. But manifestly Henry grew up and was greatly influenced by contemporary chivalric attitudes, as his love of jousting and his zealous, if intermittent and strategically cautious, pursuit of war suggests; and that chivalric culture was also reflected in Henry's friends and closest companions in the 1510s. Henry was obviously influenced by religion, attached to the mass, interested in theology, but sympathetic to Erasmian criticisms of 'traditional' religion and to the need for purifying reformation. Once adult, Henry's attitudes, like most men's attitudes, were largely formed, and they would, like most men's attitudes, not easily be changed. What 'influenced' the mature Henry VIII was not the supposedly manipulative genius of Wolsey or Cromwell or whoever, but rather the interplay between Henry's attitudes and the hard facts of the situations in which Henry found himself. Henry did shift from defence of papal authority against Luther in 1521 to repudiation of the usurped power of the bishop of Rome after 1533. But from the start Henry's papalism was more conditional than that formulation would suggest: he was already capable of asserting his authority in grandiose terms. And it was the growing realisation that the pope would not grant him his divorce that led Henry inexorably towards the break with Rome, not the insinuations of some scheming courtier. Reginald Pole, who spurned the king's offer of the archbishopric of York on condition that he assisted the king in his divorce, recalled how he had grasped in late 1530 that 'there was butt one gate open to enter in to the kynges fauor att that tyme which was by fauoreng the mattier off dyuorse'.[16] On the subsequent development of religious policy, my claim is that what happened – the formulations of faith, the dissolution of monasteries, the ending of pilgrimages – essentially reflected the king's wishes and was more consistent than is usually allowed. That in turn makes it unnecessary to see the more radical aspects of policy – the dissolution, the pulling down of shrines – as the work of radical councillors, and the retention of old practices, notably the mass, as the work of conservatives. Both were rather the preference of the king, more or less successfully imposed.[17] It is very hard to show in any detail that Henry changed his opinion or his policy on the divorce or on the royal supremacy or on religion. The timing of developments reflects external matters, not fluctuations in Henry's mind. Do those historians who claim that Henry was open to persuasion really believe that he could have been persuaded to change his mind on the divorce after 1527 or on the royal supremacy after 1534?

To claim that Henry was dominant is not, however, to say that he was all-powerful. In the years of the divorce, Henry found that some bishops were less willing to support him than others, John Fisher of Rochester least of all. Gradually the king could put pressure on them to acquiesce, and take advantage of vacancies to appoint those more sympathetic to his concerns. For all that, from the mid-1530s on, it seems unlikely that any bishop wholly agreed with Henry's religious policy. Some tried to defend pilgrimages and images, and probably secretly regretted the break with Rome, though they firmly supported the king's refusal to abandon the mass and adopt the Lutheran Confession of Augsburg. Others welcomed the break with Rome and attacks on idolatry, but would have wished to go much further. What is plain is that none of them altered Henry's course – there was no reconciliation with Rome, no safeguarding of pilgrimages, no reprieve for monasteries; but there was also no justification by faith, no Confession of Augsburg, no change to the mass. Not only did none of the churchmen change Henry's policy, but there is little evidence that any of them tried to persuade the king to do so. From time to time – in 1536, 1537 and 1540, for example – bishops and theologians were asked to give their opinions on various matters of contention, which they did forcefully and seemingly freely. But once the formal debates were over, it is much harder to show any attempt to persuade or influence the king, except when the king explicitly asked for comments. At the end of 1537, for example, the king asked Cranmer to comment on his marginal comments on the Bishops' Book: Cranmer did so vigorously; but there is not much evidence that at other times Cranmer ever sought to convince the king, let alone succeeded in doing so. Bishops well knew which of their colleagues were conservatives and which radicals (though they would have had to allow for individual ambiguities and contradictions), but they were not modern-style campaigning politicians, and if they sought to influence the king, it was no doubt by private prayer. There simply is no evidence that they did any more or went any further. In their dioceses, of course, they could prevent or encourage reforming ideas, practices and preachers, though at some risk of being denounced by those of opposite persuasions as subverters of the king's 'middle way'. But that hardly counts as influencing the king.

Secular noblemen and councillors were much less likely than bishops to have influence over religious policy. Noblemen doubtless had views, though they were not graduates in theology, and for the most part they kept them to themselves. Conservative nobles may have grumbled in private or lamented the state of the world to Chapuys, the imperial ambassador, but there is little to suggest that they tried to change the king's policies by argument or by manipulation – and there is certainly nothing to show that those policies changed. It was not the nobility or the gentry who began the rebellions in the north of England in 1536. The king's councillors might appear more plausible as men who influenced the king, but once again it is hard to show that they tried or ever succeeded in deflecting his purpose. Much of such a case rests on the unargued assumption that policies such as the break with Rome, the dissolution of the monasteries, the dismantling of pilgrimage shrines could not have been Henry's policy – because he was too stupid to have thought of them or too conservative to have willingly agreed to them – and that he must therefore have been manipulated and influenced into adopting them. But if those policies were fully Henry's, his councillors appear more as partners and executors than as authors. Sometimes councillors may have been enthusiastically behind those policies because they sincerely believed in them, sometimes they may have followed orders fearfully or reluctantly, sometimes they may simply have convinced themselves that the policies of the moment were indispensable and obviously right, as apparatchiks always do, only to be found enforcing opposed policies with equal conviction and rectitude in a later reign.

It is possible occasionally to gain some glimpses of these relationships between king and councillors: what they reveal is very different from what the factional historians suppose. Where the king's counsellors might persuade him to change his mind was over tactics and timing, not over the broad lines of policy. A nice example is how the council persuaded the king that his passionate desire to exempt at least some ringleaders from the general pardon that his commanders were likely to be compelled to grant to the Pilgrims of Grace was quite unrealistic.

> Albeit we thought the graunting of suche a free pardon shuld not be honorable for us, but a meane to put theise rebelles in great pride, and an occasion to cause others to attempt like rebellions herafter, *yet giving place to thadvice of our counsail therein* we haue not only sent suche a pardon to our said cousin [the duke] of Norff[olk] as is free and general to be neuertheles retayned in his handes and in no wise graunted vnto them vnles very extremytie shall enforce the same.[18]

Henry yielded – but to the military realities of the rebellion, rather than any factional manipulation.

In autumn 1538, when Henry Pole, Lord Montagu and Henry Courtenay, marquess of Exeter, were arrested and convicted of treason, Lord Delaware also fell under suspicion. The king's councillors were evidently quickly persuaded of his loyalty and did not want to hold him in the Tower. But they were fearful of the king's reaction. On 1 December they wrote to Henry VIII. Their salutation, 'our most bounden dueties right humbly remembered to your most excellent maiestie', might at first seem mere convention; their insistence that 'we your most humble subiectes and obedient seruantes have this present daye employed all our most diligence, industrie and actiuitie' no more than a statement of the obvious; but when they went on to defend their actions 'most humbly prostrate at your maiesties fete', and implored the king 'not to be offended therewith but to pardone vs', it is clear that they were anxiously hoping that the king would approve of what they had done. On trying out 'the veray bottom and pith of suche thinges as the Lorde Lawarre hath ben detected to have offended your maiestie', they could 'as yet … fynde no sufficient grounde to committe hym to pryson into your graces Towre'. They had ordered him to made a written declaration, and not to talk to anyone else under suspicion, but they informed the king that 'we fynde as yet no sufficuent mater agenst hym'. Accordingly, 'havyng respect aswell to your mercyfull clemencye as also to your graces honor that wold not have hym vpon a weak grounde (wherof he myght clere hym self afterward) to be extremely handled we have respyted his emprisonment'. This letter was signed by Audley, the dukes of Norfolk and Suffolk, Cromwell, the earls of Sussex, Hertford and Southampton. It is not written in the language of factional manipulation – and the signatories, including the supposed factional rivals Norfolk and Cromwell, are hard to turn into a faction along the lines favoured by factional historians.[19] Moreover, despite the council's evident unwillingness, Delaware *was* imprisoned the very next day,[20] suggesting that the king was not amused by his councillors' actions, though Delaware's subsequent release without trial, on a hefty bond, suggests that the councillors may well have been right on the substantive point of Delaware's innocence.[21] But the impression left is very much that of the nervous courtiers of a tyrant, struggling to uphold the due process of law, but fearful of the royal wrath.

A similar impression is left by developments at the very end of the reign. The fall of the Howards – the third duke of Norfolk and his son the earl of Surrey – is often seen as the work of the rising Seymour faction, who subsequently doctored the dying king's will on order to establish themselves as dominant after Henry VIII died. But there is no need to invoke factional intrigue – what Ives sees as 'a characteristic struggle between alliances of courtiers and ministers seeking to persuade the king to act in their favour' – to explain the fall of the Howards. They fell simply because of what the young earl of Surrey had foolishly done, quartering his family arms with those of the king, asserting his family's claims to control Prince Edward if he were still a minor after Henry's death, actions that followed on incompetence and irresponsibility displayed in the most recent military campaign in France. As Ralph Houlbrooke has neatly put it, Surrey was thus 'the victim of his own arrogance, impetuosity, overwheening ambition and lack of judgment'.[22] It was perhaps harsh to hold that to be treason, but it was understandable that Henry VIII should take it to be so. That it was the king, and not any political faction, that pressed the charges against the Howards emerges from the way in which the duke of Norfolk was treated. Both Norfolk and his son were convicted of treason. Surrey was duly executed on 19 January. Norfolk was condemned by act of attainder which received the royal assent on 27 January; he was due to be executed the next day. But then Henry VIII died. If Norfolk was the victim of some factional coup spearheaded by the Seymours because they saw him as a political obstacle to their ambitions, there was every reason why he should have been put to death. He had already been convicted. If some legal technicalities arising from the king's death created problems, it would have surely have been possible to have secured (say) another act of attainder in parliament. Yet Norfolk was not executed. His life was spared and he remained in the Tower for the whole of Edward VI's reign. Does that not suggest that it was Henry, rather than the Seymours or anyone else, who had taken so hostile a view of the Howards' behaviour?

Ten years earlier it was Henry VIII himself who refused to allow Norfolk to return home in April 1537. Norfolk had been sent north in January, and (from the king's point of view) his efforts to restore the king's rule after the rebellions of the previous year had been remarkably successful. Now Norfolk wanted to come back. Henry, however, was not yet convinced that the north was fully pacified and wrote at length reproving Norfolk for seeking to leave. In the letter the king marvelled that he 'woll make soo lyght of matiers that be soo weightie' and assured him if he thought that 'youe be stayed of our presence ... without greate groundes therunto moving vs, youe take the matier amysse and torment yourself without cause'. Norfolk, he insisted, was wrong to think that absence from the king's presence would harm any of his suits before the king. 'This writen from oure mouthe', the king continued, 'is more thenne sufficient to cause youe to quiet yourself for this tyme'. Henry was intending to go to the north himself by Michaelmas and he reminded Norfolk of his earlier offer to 'serve vs there without remuneration tyll the tyme of wynter and soo lenger if we shuld thynke it so convenient'. He made it quite plain that he wanted Norfolk to stay in the north. And from that revealing phrase – 'this writen from oure mouthe' – we can imagine Henry dictating this letter (and, dare one extrapolate, many others) to his secretary, Thomas Wriothesley, in whose hand the surviving draft is written. Norfolk was not being held in the north by some faction anxious to keep him from the king, however much Norfolk might have harboured doubts. He had been sent to the north, and was now being told to remain there, as serious and as heavy a responsibility as any nobleman could have. And his instructions came personally and directly from the king.[23]

Nor is it the case that Henry was so weak a king that he could be insulted to his face without reproach. Here the interesting example often cited has been Sir George Throckmorton. As Elton tells it:

> What then are we to make of the scene, some time around 1533, when Sir George Throckmorton, a knight of the reformation parliament who had consistently opposed the crown's bills touching religion and the church, was summoned to the royal presence to explain himself? Being told, mildly enough, that the king was sorely troubled about his marriage to his brother's widow, Sir George riposted that marriage to Anne Boleyn would come to trouble him similarly, 'for it is thought you have meddled with the mother and the sister' – relations which created the same canonical impediment as that alleged to exist in the Aragon marriage. Here was a man of neither standing nor significance, with a record of opposition, accusing the king to his face of multiple adultery as well as hypocrisy: surely the royal wrath struck him dead? What Henry VIII actually said, in some embarrassment, was only 'never with the mother', a reply so naively revealing as to infuriate Cromwell, who, standing by, interjected, 'nor never with the sister either, so put that out of your mind'.[24]

On the face of it Henry looks a weak king, humiliated by a mere Warwickshire knight and rescued from complete disaster only by Thomas Cromwell. But we must stand back and reflect more carefully upon the source. We know about all this because Sir George made a deposition in October 1537. We do not know exactly why he was under suspicion then. It may have been because of the activities of his brother Michael, in service with the exiled Cardinal Reginald Pole who had denounced Henry as a tyrant and called upon Charles V and Francis I to combine and depose the schismatic king of England. It may have been because it was just then that the authorities had learned something new and damaging about him: a few years earlier Sir George Throckmorton had publicly opposed the break with Rome in parliament, and it is not at all surprising that anything discovered against him should have been taken seriously. Sir George evidently decided to make a clean breast of things, and gave a lengthy account of his earlier dissent, claiming that he had then been blinded by false counsels and that he had now seen the error of his ways. It was from his statement that Elton and other historians have drawn the tale, now familiar from retelling, of how Sir George told Henry that he had meddled both with Anne's mother and sister. But those historians who have retold it (including myself) have been insufficiently attentive to the detail. When these are carefully examined, great doubts are raised as to whether Sir George ever spoke to the king's face the words so often quoted. What Sir George recalled was not the interview he had with the king but rather a conversation he had had with a friend, Sir Thomas Dingley. Sir George declared how some years ago he met Dingley and how they discussed 'the parliament mattiers'. Dingley was surprised that the Act of Appeals and others had passed 'so lytly': he had, he continued, heard how Sir George had spoken much. Sir George admitted it: 'And I said true yt ys, I haue spoken some thinge yn thact of appeylys'. He added that thereupon 'the kinges grace dyd sende for me and spake with me yn dyuers mattiers', incidentally offering a picture of an ever-vigilant king, responding at once to any hint of criticism of royal policy in the House of Commons. The syntax of Sir George's deposition is then a little unclear; some of it is addressed directly to the king ('yor grase'), some of it refers to the king in the third person ('his grace'); and the tenses sometimes switch from past to present: the deposition we have is evidently an edited version. Sir George continued, 'and that I parseyue hys gracys concyens ys troubled'. What troubled the king's conscience, Sir George recalled, was 'that he hath maryd hys brothers wyfe and he thynketh god ys not pleysyd therwith'. Henry had presumably repeated to Sir George his standard justification for the divorce. But Sir George then recalled how he had told Dingley what he had replied to the king.

> And I seyd to hym [Dingley] that I tolde yor grase [the king], I feyred if ye did marye quene Anne, yor consyens olde [= would] be morys troubled at length, for that hyt ys thought ye haue medyled bothe with the modere and the syster. And his grase seyd never with the moder And my Lorde Privey Seyle [Cromwell] standyng by seyd: nor never with the sister nether, and therfor putt that out of yor mynde. And thys ys all I seyd to hym or he to me or wordes myche lyke to the same effect to my remembrance, as god schall juge me at my moste nede.

What is striking here is that what Sir George is admitting is that he told this tale to Dingley: he told Dingley that he spoke these words to the king. But nothing here is evidence that Sir George actually said all this to Henry. Referring to his words, Sir George protested that 'I thowth no harme to yor grase yn the speking of theym'. He went on, 'for that I ever spake thiyes wordes to hym [Dingley] or to any other man was to lamente what I thouth olde folowe of the mariage to yor grase and to yor reyme in tyme to come'. And he then declared 'the verye yntente wherapon I spake yt', namely 'I thynke yn my consiyens a pon a proude and vayne gloryouse mynde, as who seyth, they that I dyd tell yt to shulde note me to be a mane that durst speake for the commen welthe'.

In other words, summoned by the king after speaking out in parliament, Sir George had been intimidated and humiliated. Henry had repeated his justification of the divorce. Sir George, understandably, did not then stand up for his convictions. Desperate to avoid losing face, or perhaps, as he said, simply keen to be noted 'a mane that durst speake for the commen welthe', on returning from the king he boasted to his friends, especially to Sir Thomas Dingley, that he had spoken to the king the famous remarks about meddling with Anne's mother and sister. But he had not done so at all – and the king knew nothing of Sir George's supposed riposte. A few years later, in 1537, reports of what Sir George had then told Dingley and others evidently came to light – we do not know how – and he made his abject submission. Petrified, Sir George pleaded that 'seing thies wordes were spoken so long agoo and to no yll intent as I shall be saved at the days of dome And that it woll please your hyghnes to accept me into yor favor and mercy without the which I did not desire to live. Written with the moste sorowfullest hart and by the most vnhappie man that ever I thinke did live in this worlde'. But in the eyes of the authorities, Sir George's statement was thought insufficient, and in a remarkable set of interrogatories, he was pressed further on what he thought he had been saying. The tone of these interrogatories make it plain that his reflections on the king's sexual conduct were deemed wholly unacceptable, indeed seditious; it is revealing that the words themselves were not repeated. Did he think in his conscience that those words were true or not? If he said that he thought they were true, what documents or proofs did he have to lead him to think so? If he said that he did not reckon them true, did he not think 'that suche wordes spoken of any man were very sclaunderous and dymynisshing a manes good name and fame, moche more a princes?' Sir George's claim that he had simply sought to be seen as a 'defender of the commen weale' was then challenged. 'Where as he rekeneth that by spekyng of the said wordes he shulde haue ben counted to be a defender of the commen weale, howe dothe he take that the same shulde make any thing for the common weale? Or what did that make to the allowing or reproving of the statutes that were than in hande?' Had Sir George not been intending to stiffen opposition to the bills that the king was then putting through parliament? And was it 'expedient for the quiete of a commen weale' that the king's subjects 'shulde reken hym to be suche a greate offender ageinst god and his lawes as he rekened hym to be'? A pair of questions probed further. Did he think that a man who laboured to persuade the people to have a good opinion of their prince did the duty of a true subject? Did he reckon that 'a man that studies to bring the people to haue an yll iudgement and opinion of their prince dothe contrarie to the duetie of a trewe subiect or no'? And was it not dangerous to make people think ill of the king? The final question asked 'whether he dothe not reken that yll opinion conceyved by subiectes of their prince mynissheth there love towarde the same, and wante of love bringeth forth disobedience and the same bredeth sedicion and sedicion bringeth the prince into perill of his person and his crowne'.

All that makes the accepted version of the story - that Sir George had told the king to his face that he had meddled with Anne's mother and sister - most implausible. It is very hard to suppose that Henry would have allowed such remarks to pass without response in 1533 while later treating reports that they had been uttered so seriously. Moreover Sir George did not defend himself by saying that he had said these words to the king directly and that the king had not minded. Appealing to the king for mercy for the service he had done the king in the past, and not 'for thies lewde and vndyscrete wordys' which (he insisted) had meant no harm, Sir George remembered 'how good and gracyous lorde ye were to me at Grafton to pardone and forgyfe me al thynges paste consarnyng the parliment'. Sir George then added the phrase 'as al other spekyng and lewde demenor mysvsyd to yor hyghnes yn tyme paste'. That would suggest that on earlier occasions Throckmorton had spoken out against the king – but that the king had personally pardoned and forgiven him. If that pardon had included forgiveness for the telling of the story of Henry's meddling with Anne's mother and sister, then Sir George would surely have said so here. That he did not do so, but referred to 'al other spekyng and lewde demenor mysvsyd to yor hyghnes', suggests that the 'lewde and vndyscrete' words that were under investigation in 1537 had only recently come to light and had not been admitted by Sir George when he had earlier been forgiven by the king (or perhaps had been spoken after that earlier pardon).

Where had Sir George got the story from? He was a Warwickshire gentleman, not a prominent courtier, so what he told Dingley was not based on personal knowledge of the king's behaviour. Nor was Sir George a canon lawyer, so it is unlikely that he would have independently grasped just why any sexual relationship between Henry and Anne Boleyn's sister, let alone her mother, would have been so damaging to the king's case for an annulment. As his deposition reveals, Sir George owed the story to someone more familiar with the court and well versed in canon law, friar William Peto, provincial minister of the Observant Franciscans at Greenwich. At Easter 1532 Peto had preached defiantly in the king's presence against the divorce. Henry berated him for it afterwards in the garden, and a few weeks later had him placed under arrest at Lambeth Palace. It was at that time Peto asked Sir George to see him. Peto told Sir George about 'a longe commynycacyon that was between yor grase [the king] and hym [Peto] yn the garden after the sarmone', and how Peto had outlined to the king his objections to the divorce. Peto, Sir George continued, 'ferdere seyd that he dyd shewe yor grase that ye coude never marye Quene Anne for that it was seyd ye had meydld with the moder and the dowter'. That Peto should have remonstrated with the king in this way is entirely consistent given the fiery tone of his sermon. The story of Henry's alleged meddling with Anne's sister and mother was vivid and damaging. Is it fanciful to suppose that, warned off by the king for daring to oppose the Act of Appeals in the Commons, Sir George later should have boasted privately to his friends that he, Sir George, had spoken these words to the king's face? On such a view modern historians been taken in by Sir George's boasting.[25]

What is important is to read letters alertly for what they reveal of the king's actions. Probably in early September 1535 Stephen Vaughan, the king's agent in the Low Countries, wrote to Cromwell. Cromwell, replying, informed him 'that being absent from the courte yor lettres addressed vnto me chaunced amongst others to com to the handes of the kinges highnes who in myn absence bothe opened and redde them and at my repaire ayen to the courte delyuered them vnto me willing me to answer you in this wise folowing ...'.[26] A king who would open and read letters addressed to one of his ministers and then instruct him on how to reply was no cipher.

It is remarkable how closely Henry followed diplomatic negotiations. Stray remarks might superficially suggest that Henry was lazy or inefficient – and it is on such quotations that factional historians build their edifice – but careful reading quickly disposes of any such interpretation. For example, on 10 November 1524, Louis de Praet, the imperial ambassador, wrote that 'the king has never taken less interest in affairs than he does at present', and that it was therefore important that Cardinal Wolsey should receive his pension, 'for in truth he does everything here'. That appears very clear and seems good evidence for the view of Wolsey as *alter rex*, manipulating the monarch. Yet earlier in the very same letter, de Praet described how he had been with Henry at the beginning of the month. The king had spoken bitterly and in detail about the military campaign then being waged in Italy by the duke of Bourbon (the French nobleman in rebellion against the king of France and thus a potential ally for Henry in any war against the French), had blamed the imperialists for not giving more support, and had then drawn de Praet aside to ask for two detailed favours from Emperor Charles concerning the bishopric of Malta and the duke of Milan.[27] This is no idle monarch neglecting public affairs. Henry often saw ambassadors himself – for example, on at least seven occasions between June and November 1523 – and such interviews were often lengthy. Henry might be in the country hunting, but he always took a close and eager interest in important events: in autumn 1524, seeing letters in Thomas More's hand, Henry interrupted him before he could begin to say what letters he was bringing, and guessed, wrongly, whom the letters were from, and then 'he fell in meryly to the redyng of the lettres ... and all the other abstractes and wrytynges'.[28]

Such vignettes of Henry's style of ruling are precious glimpses – particular moments vividly illuminated, yet more widely revealing and suggestive. There are no doubt more to be found. Beyond that, the most fruitful way to take understanding of Tudor politics further will lie in deeper explorations of the making of policy. An examination of diplomacy and of the making of war will allow a richer evaluation of the relative role of king and advisers. A reconsideration of the divorce and break with Rome will permit a reappraisal of the 'king or minister' debate. A close analysis of the evolution of religious policy, especially in the later years of Henry VIII's reign, will offer much scope for the detailed teasing out of influences. And much can be learned from attempting to set policy, especially religious policy, in the context of longer periods. Chapter 10 on 'The church of England c. 1529–c. 1640' extends the theme of royal power into the field of religion and into the early Stuart period, presenting the church of England as a 'monarchical church', the character of which cannot be understood without grasping the roles of successive monarchs; successive rulers, it is claimed here, pursued what were in many respects very similar policies.

Of course such explorations, particularly on the vexed question of 'faction', touch on more philosophical questions about the nature of historical truth. How can we know what we believe we know about the past, and with what degree of confidence do we make claims to knowledge? By what criteria do we critically assess our sources? Such issues underlie my exploration of the Amicable Grant of 1525. Factional historians have seemed to me so determinedly to seek to argue the opposite of what was said in the documents that I have felt compelled to observe with Trollope's Mrs Harold Smith that 'we are so used to a leaven of falsehood in all we hear and say, nowadays, that nothing is more likely to deceive us than the absolute truth'. In recent years several writers, usually not themselves historians, that is authors of historical books and articles in historical periodicals, but rather philosophers, or perhaps more accurately commentators on the activities that historians pursue, have been casting doubt on the possibility of objective truth in history. Like, I suspect, most practising historians, I have had little sympathy for such notions. But I have felt it necessary to articulate my reasons for rejecting them, and I present them here in Chapter 11, originally written as a lecture given to first-year students on an Approaches to History course, warning them against the seductive temptations of the postmodernist heresy. My experience is that of an historian, not a philosopher; my defence for venturing into these deep waters is that the study of all rigorous intellectual disciplines raises questions about the nature of knowledge and that it is proper for practitioners of them to offer their answers and responses, even if they are not formally trained philosophers. It would be reassuring to think that what is being attacked here is a straw man, but the quotations with which Chapter 11 begins sadly suggest that it is not. It would be reassuring to suppose that these notions are the now defunct modish philosophical cul-de-sacs of earlier times – 1968? the 1970s? – but again that would be complacent. My quarrel is not so much directly with certain philosophers but with those who have presented their thought as a direct challenge to the study of history, and, at a different level, with the naive nihilism or relativism so often – unthinkingly – voiced by students. If these are essentially philosophical questions, my concern with them has arisen directly from my efforts to understand the politics of Tudor England, and that explains why I have included this essay in this collection.

Notes

1. G.R. Elton, 'Thomas Cromwell's decline and fall', *Historical Journal*, x (1951), pp. 150–85 (reprinted in G.R. Elton, *Studies in Tudor and Stuart Politics and Government* (Cambridge, 4 vols, 1974–93), i. pp. 189–230).
2. G.R. Elton, *Reform and Reformation* (1977).
3. E.W. Ives, 'Henry the Great?', *The Historian* (1994), xliii (1994), pp. 3–8; 'Henry VIII: the political perspective', in D. MacCulloch (ed.), *The Reign of Henry VIII: Politics, Policy and Piety* (1995), pp. 13–34.
4. P. Zagorin, 'Sir Thomas Wyatt and the court of Henry VIII: the courtier's ambivalence', *Journal of Medieval and Renaissance Studies*, xxxiii (1993), pp. 120–21.
5. D. Starkey, 'From feud to faction: English politics c.1450–1550', *History Today* (November 1982), pp. 16–22; idem, *The Reign of Henry VIII: Personalities and Politics* (1985).
6. Ives, 'Henry VIII: the political perspective', p. 30.
7. Ibid., p. 33.
8. See also Gwyn, *King's Cardinal*, pp. 159–72, for the fall of Buckingham; G. Walker, 'The "expulsion of the minions" of 1519 reconsidered', *Historical Journal*, xxxii (1989), pp. 1–16, reprinted as 'Faction in the Privy Chamber? The "expulsion of the minions", 1519', in *Persuasive Fictions: Faction, Faith and Political Culture in the Reign of Henry VIII* (1996), pp. 35–53.
9. E.g. E.W. Ives, 'Anne Boleyn and the early Reformation in England: the contemporary evidence', *Historical Journal*, xxxvii (1994), pp. 389–400 esp. 397–400.
10. I owe this formulation to T. Reuter.
11. 'Introduction' to Folio Society edition of G.R. Elton, *England under the Tudors* (1997), p. xviii.
12. *Sixteenth Century Journal*, xxix (1998), p. 268.
13. J. Guy, 'Henry VIII and his ministers', *History Review*, xxiii (1995), pp. 37–40.
14. S.J. Gunn, 'The structures of politics in early Tudor England', *Transactions of the Royal Historical Society*, 6th series, v (1995), pp. 59–90 (cf. C. Haigh, 'Religion', *Transactions of the Royal Historical Society*, 6th series, vii (1997), p. 296).
15. C.S.L. Davies, 'The Cromwellian decade: authority and consent', *Transactions of the Royal Historical Society*, 6th series, vii (1997), p. 194.
16. Public Record Office [hereafter PRO] SP1/116 ff. 56–57v (*Letters and Papers, Foreign and Domestic, of the Reign of Henry VIII*, ed. J.S. Brewer, J. Gairdner and R.H. Brodie (1862–1392) [hereafter *LP*], XII i 444).
17. G.W. Bernard, 'The making of religious policy, 1533–1456: Henry VIII and the

search for the middle way', *Historical Journal*, xli (1998), pp. 321–49; idem, 'The piety of Henry VIII', in N.S. Amos, A. Pettegree and H. van Nierop, (eds), *The Education of a Christian Society* (Aldershot, 1999), pp. 62–88.
18. PRO SP1/112 ff. 97–97v (*LP*, XI 1236; *State Papers of Henry VIII*, i. 521). [My italics.]
19. BL Cotton MS, Titus B i. ff. 70–70v (*LP*, XIII ii 968).
20. *LP*, XIII ii 982.
21. *LP*, XIII ii 1112, 1117.
22. R.A. Houlbrooke, 'Henry VIII's wills: a comment', *Historical Journal*, xxxvii (1994), pp. 891–9.
23. PRO SP1/118 ff. 61–63 (*LP*, XII i 863). Norfolk had similarly wanted to return home from the Scottish borders and been refused permission by Henry and Wolsey in autumn 1523 (Gwyn, *King's Cardinal*, pp. 568–9).
24. G.R. Elton, 'Tudor Government: the points of contact. III The Court', *Transactions of the Royal Historical Society*, 5th series, xxvi (1976), p. 220 (reprinted in his *Studies in Tudor and Stuart Politics and Government* (4 vols, 1974–91), iii. 47–8).
25. PRO SP1/125 ff. 202–206 is original confession (*LP*, XII ii 952 (1)); PRO SP1/125 ff. 207–209v is fair copy (*LP*, XII ii 952 (2)); PRO SP1/125 f. PRO SP1/125 ff. 211–211v (*LP*, XII i 953) are the 'Interrogatories to be ministred to Sir George Throgmerton, wherupon he maye be examined'. For Peto, see N. Harpsfield, p. 203.
26. BL Harleian MS, 283 f. 18 (*LP*, X 376: probably misdated in calendar).
27. *Cal. State Papers, Spanish, Further Supplement*, pp. 407, 403–4.
28. BL Cotton MS, Galba B viii ff. 132–132v (*LP*, IV i 882).

2
The continuing power of the Tudor nobility[1]

That the sixteenth century was a period of fundamental transformation in the fortunes of the English nobility is one of the most enduring of historical myths. Were not nobles powerful only in the Middle Ages? And did not the Middle Ages come to an end in the sixteenth century, defeated by the mortal blows of the renaissance and reformation? Had not the Wars of the Roses been the self-defeating last gasp of a warring and factious nobility? Was not the Tudor century a time of strong government, with determined rulers such as Henry VII and able ministers such as Thomas Cromwell establishing a 'new monarchy' or a 'revolution in government' at the expense of the nobility? Was there not a 'crisis of the aristocracy'? Were not nobles now reduced to the status of ornaments of an enhanced royal court while the Tudors relied on new men, drawn from social categories below the nobility, to rule the localities? Were not all these changes a 'good thing', since the nobility were obviously self-seeking while kings were the fathers of their people, ruling not for themselves but for the good of all?

More subtly than such caricatures, but in essentially the same vein, Steve Gunn has recently characterised the sixteenth century as a period experiencing a fundamental shift from a culture based on honour, lineage and locality to one based on obedience, civil society and the nation, or in other words, from values associated with noble power in a decentralised society to those associated with royal power in a centralised state. Was the peerage as a group, as he suggested, 'losing much of its prescriptive right to influence within government'? Were noblemen being deprived, by the development of a small privy council staffed largely by professional administrators, of 'access to the decision-making machinery of government'? Was the natural power of noblemen in the localities 'no longer as great as it had been'? Was there a decline in the power that landholding brought the nobility corresponding to the decline in the manors that noblemen held at the end of the sixteenth century? Did they spend recklessly as a consequence in order 'to reassure themselves, and continue to exert the influence over their inferiors which went with visible magnificence'? Did the Crown watch over the relationship between nobles and gentry more closely than before? Did noble households decline, and with them the influence they gave? Were noblemen losing influence over their tenantry? Were noblemen themselves more dependant on royal favour and on the favour of those influential in court and council? Did their role in war diminish? It sounds a formidable catalogue.[2]

Yet, however tenacious the notion of a declining nobility in Tudor England has proved to be, it is nonetheless seriously misleading. Its first fault is the assumptions that it makes about the Middle Ages. It usually implies a romantically exaggerated view of all-powerful medieval barons, and takes as typical of medieval England the disruption of the mid-twelfth-century anarchy and the mid-fifteenth-century Wars of the Roses. But the nobility were never as dominant as this model supposes. It was never true that the north knew no prince but a Percy: the earls of Northumberland were both matched in the north by other noble families and considerably dependent on the Crown for local office, notably the wardenship of the East Marches.[3] Historians who make claims that the power of the Tudor nobility was declining often fail to compare their Tudor evidence with evidence such as this for an earlier period: the comparison is all too often with an idealised, nostalgic and schematic vision of the Middle Ages. Yet it was never the case that tenants unthinkingly followed their noble leaders into the field. There are many fifteenth-century instances of tenants' reluctance: among the most striking are two from 1471. Trying to persuade the gentry of Yorkshire to support Edward VI, who had landed there in the hope of recovering the throne, Henry Percy (c. 1449–89), fourth earl of Northumberland, found (according to the official history of Edward IV's restoration), 'many gentlemen, and other, whiche would have be araysed by him, woulde not so fully and extremly have determyned them selfe in the kyng's right and qwarell as th'erle wolde have done hymselfe'. All that Northumberland could do was to stop any open hostility to Edward VI: he could not cajole the gentry into action on Edward's side. When later that year Richard Nevill (1428–71), first earl of Warwick, implored Henry Vernon of Haddon to support him, writing in his own hand, 'Henry I pray you ffayle not now as ever I may do ffor yow', Vernon nonetheless refused, and also refused the appeals for help he received from Edward IV and George Plantagenet (1449–78), duke of Clarence.[4] A century earlier, John of Gaunt (1340–99), duke of Lancaster, one of the greatest of all English magnates, was unable on several occasions to impose his will on his affinity or to protect the interests of his own retainers against those of independent local gentlemen.[5] If, as such examples suggest, the medieval nobility was never overweeningly powerful, then its Tudor standing must look less exceptional, less different. Such instances warn against the danger of exaggerating the extent of the medieval dominance of nobles over lesser men and going on to prove a Tudor decline by contrasting medieval exaggeration with Tudor realities.

But, it might be countered, Tudor nobles did lose their influence in central government. That suggestion again mistakes the nature of the earlier role of the nobility. Noblemen, in K.B. McFarlane's words, were not aspirants for office, they were counsellors.[6] As such they were involved in the most important decisions that governments took, for example over war, or royal marriage plans, but they were not, except for a few individuals, much interested in taking part in the day-by-day work of executive government. Of course it was not uncommon for councillors and diplomats who were specially close servants of kings to achieve ennoblement: for example, Giles Daubeney, Willoughby de Brooke and Charles Somerset under Henry VII. But they should not be seen as 'a new style of service aristocracy' and part of 'a major realignment of relations between king and nobility'.[7] They were usually preoccupied with service at court and in council and were therefore not personally concerned in the government of the localities. But usually they tried to convert the possibly ephemeral royal favour which they enjoyed into something more permanent – a landed patrimony which their family would enjoy for generations.[8] New nobles were very often the founders of landed families, and their interests can therefore be seen as essentially similar to those of landed families of ancient lineage.

Did the nature of the royal court change in the Tudor century, especially under Henry VIII, and were any such changes intended to diminish noble power? As monarchs allegedly became more powerful and government more centralised, did those who had regular personal contact with them gain at the expense of others? Was high politics increasingly a question of who was influential in the king's privy chamber? Did groups of courtiers and politician-administrators squabble over policies and the fruits of office? And were noblemen increasingly excluded, no more than ornaments if they attended the court, or reduced to impotent provincial obscurity if did not?

A fundamental difficulty with such a line of argument is that all this was not obviously novel. Kings had always had courts – or households. At a most basic level kings had to be housed, clothed and fed, in a style appropriate to their position. Those of their servants whose task it was to organise such matters clearly held important posts. Kings could not rule alone: they always depended on others to give advice and to implement policies. Many of those involved in such duties at court would be influential, and would do well for themselves, but this phenomenon has a long history. Oderic Vitalis complained in the early twelfth century that Henry I raised up new men from the dust. Literary satires of the court first date from the same period, especially the reign of Henry II. That the court was an amoral free-for-all was noted by Chaucer: 'And therefore, at the kynges court, my brother/Ech man for hymself, ther is noon other'.[9] Those historians who believe that it was only in the Tudor century, and especially in the reign of Henry VIII, that politics became court-centred have been misled by the sudden abundance of sources such as ambassadors' letters, full of gossip about who was in and who was out of favour. It is not possible to document court politics in the same detail in earlier periods, but occasional scraps of evidence suggest that something very similar was already happening.[10]

But how important was the court from the perspective of noblemen? Clearly attendance at court was crucial for courtier magnates, men on the make who were rising through royal favour. In a minority or period of weak government access to the king might also be seen as unusually significant. Thomas Seymour, Protector Somerset's brother, clearly thought so, intriguing with members of the privy chamber, and sending the young King Edward money. But although that irritated Somerset, it did not win Seymour the leading position he sought. The young king had the good sense not to support Seymour's schemes.[11] Later, in October 1549, after the rebellions in the West Country and East Anglia had finally been defeated, Protector Somerset lost the support of virtually all his fellow councillors, noblemen and administrators alike: the fact that Somerset had the young king with him did not help.[12] Perhaps the political importance of access to the monarch and to the court, even in a royal minority, can be overstated. When Edward VI died in 1553, the duke of Northumberland attempted to divert the succession away from Mary, and have Jane Grey, to whom he had married his son, crowned queen instead. The unsuccessful makers of that coup were largely courtier- and administrator-magnates: they were defeated by the provincial nobles and gentry, especially Thomas (d. 1584), Lord Wentworth, Henry Radcliffe (d. 1557), earl of Sussex, and John Bourchier (d. 1560), earl of Bath, whom Mary rallied to her cause.[13] At the end of Elizabeth's reign, Robert Devereux (d. 1601), second earl of Essex, a courtier-magnate lacking in landed endowments, succeeded for a while in building a nationwide following held together by little more than his influence over royal patronage, but once that influence was removed by the queen, he found he had no solid resources of his own to mount a credible rebellion.[14]

It is most unlikely that nobles held, as a kind of badge of their status, any clearly defined theory of 'aristocratic conciliarism', any idea that it was the duty of noblemen to come together and revolt against would-be absolutist kings and ministers. They were not as a group keen on disorder, which after all would disrupt the agrarian economy on which their wealth rested. They rarely joined rebellions, usually doing so only in desperate self-defence, provoked by some personal injustice. Disputed successions and civil wars horrified most noblemen. It is revealing how many noblemen avoided getting involved in the divisons of 1469–71, 1483–85, and indeed in 1487, when few noblemen fought either for the pretender Lambert Simnel or for Henry VII. Hardly any noblemen were interested in the cause of Perkin Warbeck in the 1490s. When the Cornish rebelled against taxation in 1497, only one nobleman, James Tuchet (1463–97), Lord Audley, tried to make use of the troubles. When there was widespread refusal of the Amicable Grant in 1525, noblemen, far from fanning the flames of revolt, instead did what they could, at considerable risk, to persuade men to agree to make a grant, and, in East Anglia, to put down a small-scale rising against it.

In 1536 the Pilgrimage of Grace, a large rebellion involving as many as 30,000 men in the north of England protesting against Henry VIII's religious policies, especially the dissolution of the monasteries, threatened Henry's throne. Any assessment of the role of the nobility at that time must begin with George Talbot (1468–1538), fourth earl of Shrewsbury. If the rebels had moved south in large numbers – as Cornishmen had moved east as far as Blackheath in the tax rebellion of 1497 – and if they had secured support along the way, then the pressure on Henry VIII might have become overwhelming. But the Pilgrims did not succeed in moving further south than Doncaster. That was not because they were so attached to their own regions that they did not dare to think of leaving them. It was rather because they faced the formidable opposition of the earl of Shrewsbury, whose loyalty to Henry VIII was crucial to the failure, in the end, of the Pilgrimage of Grace. Shrewsbury's estates were centred on Sheffield, and extended southwards through Derbyshire to Nottinghamshire. If the Pilgrims were to move south, they would have to move through Shrewsbury's area of influence. But Shrewsbury was wholly loyal. He mobilised his servants, tenants and friends at once, raising 3654 men within a week. He deterred Lord Hussey from joining the rebels in Lincolnshire. He marched north to Doncaster to save that town from the rebels. He halted the momentum of the rebels' advance. Outnumbered, he (and the duke of Norfolk) twice made a deal with the rebels, promising concessions if they disbanded and returned home, and worked to divide the rebels' leaders, trying in particular to win over Lord Darcy. In short, Shrewsbury held a firm base in the north Midlands and South Yorkshire for the king. That may have been in spite of his own preferences: he does not seem to have been very sympathetic to Anne Boleyn, and his will and elaborate chantry chapel in what is now Sheffield Cathedral show that he remained a conservative in religion. But he and his family had owed a great deal to royal favour, he held many offices on Crown lands, and he displayed that instinctive loyalty to the Crown that characterises the service nobility of late medieval and early modern England. Shrewsbury's loyalty, firmly and boldly displayed, kept his own area free from rebellion. It stiffened the commitment of other noblemen – Edward Stanley (1509–72), third earl of Derby in Lancashire, George Hastings (1488–1544), first earl of Huntingdon and Thomas Manners (d. 1543), first earl of Rutland, in adjacent areas in the east Midlands, and Thomas Howard (1473–1555), third duke of Norfolk, whom Henry VIII sent northwards to join Shrewsbury. Shrewsbury's action moreover deprived the Pilgrims of the hope that they would receive support from great nobles and weakened their claim that such great men were not being consulted by the government in the making of policy. If the rebels had pressed on and resorted to military force, they would have found themselves fighting the very noblemen whose counsel they had been urging should be heeded by the king. Shrewsbury's role was thus crucial: 'which way he was inclined, it was thought verily the game were likely to go', as the chronicler Holinshed would later put it. It is scarcely an exaggeration to say that in October 1536 the fate of Henry VIII and of the break with Rome lay in the hands of the fourth earl of Shrewsbury. That strikingly illustrates the crucial nature of noble power in Tudor England; and incidentally shows once again that in that society power was not only to be found at the royal court.[15]

But was Shrewsbury's behaviour during the Pilgrimage of Grace untypical of the nobility? Some historians have seen other noblemen, notably Lord Hussey (d. 1537), Lord Darcy (d. 1537) and Thomas and Ingram Percy, younger brothers of Henry Percy (1502–37), sixth earl of Northumberland, as prominently involved,[16] but recent studies question such interpretations. Certainly Hussey and Darcy had long been sympathetic to Catherine of Aragon, and they were very hostile to the break with Rome. In early 1536 they (according to Elton) hoped that the overthrow of Anne Boleyn by a conservative faction at court would put matters to rights, but when Thomas Cromwell trumped that conservative plot, they then had no alternative – so this line of reasoning goes – but to stir up rebellion in the country. In support of such an argument, there is an interesting letter by the imperial ambassador Chapuys dated 30 September 1534. Darcy had said to one of Chapuys's servants that what was happening was so outrageously contrary to God and to reason that he could not count himself a good man or a good Christian if he agreed to it. In the north he knew that there were 16 earls and other great gentlemen – not 1600, as the editors of *Letters and Papers* erroneously state – who shared his opinions. Darcy said that with Charles V's assistance, he would raise the banner of the crucifix and put 8,000 men in the field. Lord Hussey had personally told Chapuys that there should be an insurrection of the people which would be joined immediately by the nobility and the clergy. All that is certainly treasonable, and it shows that Darcy and Hussey were willing to contemplate rebellion, but whether it proves that they started the Pilgrimage of Grace in 1536 is much less sure. Hussey insisted that Charles V should make war *first* – 'prelablement' – before any insurrection; Darcy similarly linked the raising of the banner of the crucifix to Charles's assistance.[17] Hussey and Darcy seem to have been taken by surprise in October 1536. That they were regarded by Henry and Cromwell as responsible and eventually executed does not necessarily prove that they instigated the troubles. It would obviously be useful if the government could make the rebellion look as if it was the work of a small, partisan and treasonous minority, rather than the expression of resentments widely held by the northern nobility, gentry and common people. How far have modern historians who have seen Hussey and Darcy as instigators of revolt fallen for the government's propaganda? Neither seems very convincing in such a role. Hussey was a first-generation peer, a sometime courtier and administrator in the last years of Henry VII's reign, who never regained his earlier influence after that king's death. In 1536 he was an old man, living on his estates at Sleaford. He did make efforts to resist the rising, planning for a general rendezvous of loyalists, but such plans were overtaken by events. Possibly he failed to grasp the strength of the rebellion at first and then found himself facing serious threats from the rebels. His tenants stopped him making preparations to attack the rebels gathered at Lincoln: they would not fight the rebels, though they would protect him from them. Quite probably Hussey sympathised with the demands of the rebels; quite possibly he hoped to act as a mediator between the rebels and the king, perhaps by serving as a link between them and a great nobleman such as the earl of Shrewsbury. But that does not amount to starting or furthering the rebellion. If Hussey had wished to launch a rebellion, why did not more happen in south Lincolnshire, near his residence at Sleaford? Louth, Caistor and Horncastle were a very long way from Hussey's estates. And his difficulties in raising troops and deterring rebels were matched by those confronting the unequivocally loyal Lincolnshire gentleman John Harrington, showing that the initiative in the rebellion may well have come from below.[18]

What of Lord Darcy? His conversations with Chapuys may well have been treasonable. He did not immediately mobilise men in the way that the unquestioned loyalist the fourth earl of Shrewsbury did in October 1536. Withdrawing to Pontefract Castle may have been tactically unwise. At an early stage Shrewsbury asked Darcy's son Sir Arthur how many men his father might make and received the answer 5000 – if abbeys might stand.[19] When Darcy sent out a letter prohibiting all assemblies except meetings of gentlemen and household servants, that could be construed as impeding loyalists who wished to serve the king.[20] There is a mysterious and arguably suspicious letter charging the recipient addressed simply as 'cousin' to come to him at once to discuss certain 'urgent and weyghty causes'.[21] And Darcy yielded Pontefract Castle to the rebels without a fight. Shrewsbury and Henry VIII evidently thought that he could and should have stopped the rising.

But none of that is as damning as it might at first glance seem. Darcy was not an especially powerful nobleman. Another first-generation peer, he exercised authority in the West Riding of Yorkshire largely because he held several royal offices, including the post of constable of Pontefract Castle. He lacked independent and long-established personal influence. It is therefore quite plausible to suggest that he could not have done much more than he did to stop the rebellion. When his son Sir Arthur declared that his father could make 5000 men provided abbeys might stand, he was not bargaining, but simply being realistic.[22] The rebellion in Yorkshire did not begin in the areas in which Darcy was influential: it seems rather to have spread from Lincolnshire, across the Humber, and flared up in the East Riding, notably at Beverley, before moving westwards. It is highly credible that Pontefract Castle was bereft of ordnance: reports by undoubted loyalists from the castles at Nottingham, Huntingdon and Stamford similarly lamented the lack of ordnance.[23] Darcy's son's children were threatened by the rebels. Darcy may well have felt much more under pressure than some modern historians have been prepared to recognise. Henry Clifford (1493–1542), eleventh lord Clifford and first earl of Cumberland, a more powerful magnate, nonetheless was besieged by the rebels in his castle at Skipton, and succeeded in holding out only because the castle itself with its massively thick walls and ample supplies (unlike Pontefract, it was in use as a residence) was much more defensible. Of course, Darcy did not react as firmly against the rebellion as the earl of Shrewsbury did. He probably could have fled from Pontefract. No doubt Darcy sympathised with the grievances of the commons. Perhaps, like Hussey, he appealed to Shrewsbury in the hope that the involvement of a greater nobleman would shield him from criticism.[24] And it is possible that even after he had yielded Pontefract to the pilgrims, he still never saw himself as a rebel, striving instead to moderate the fury of the Commons by acting as their spokesman and voicing their grievances in an orderly fashion.

The sixth earl of Northumberland did very little. If he went to meetings held by the rebels at York on 28 November and 9 December, there is nothing to suggest that he played a leading role. Indeed he spoke in defence of Henry VIII and Cromwell. His brothers Sir Thomas and Sir Ingram were more directly involved, but they seem to have got caught up in events not of their devising. Sir Ingram then made use of the commotions as a cloak for his feud with Sir Reynold Carnaby, a great favourite of the earl, no doubt trusting that a general royal pardon to the rebels would absolve him from penalties for his misconduct. But that is a long way from making him a leader of rebellion. Neither brother took part in rebel meetings at York or Pontefract. And there is little to connect the Percys with Robert Aske. So once again any attempt to see the Pilgrimage as a noble-inspired rebellion founders on close scrutiny.[25]

What of the northern rising of 1569? Was that an authentic rebellion of 'feudal' earls? What such a view presupposes is that there was a definite anti-noble policy on the part of the Elizabethan government. That is unconvincing. What made the government stop giving important responsibilities to Thomas Percy (1528–72), seventh earl of Northumberland, and to William (1500–1563), Lord Dacre, was not any hostility to magnates but rather well-founded doubts about their competence in the case of Northumberland (well illustrated by the military campaign of 1557) and fears about their lack of enthusiasm for the new religious settlement. If Northumberland, Dacre, Henry Clifford (1517–70), second earl of Cumberland, Charles Neville (1542/3–1601), sixth earl of Westmorland, and other northern nobles were unhappy it was not because they were excluded from court, but because they would have wanted the queen and her ministers to follow different policies. In 1567 Northumberland became a catholic again. Increasingly these discontented northern nobles looked to the succession to resolve their grievances: the arrival in England of Mary Queen of Scots in May 1568 was a catalyst of intrigues, also involving the fourth duke of Norfolk. The government mishandled the situation, summoning Northumberland and Westmorland to London: their rebellion began more as a means of resisting arrest than as a carefully planned conspiracy. The rebellion had, it has been argued, emerged from weeks of discussion, vacillation and dissension, and was not the result of careful planning. If its roots lay in alienation from the government, especially over religion, it was a hurried, ill-prepared and, above all, defensive rebellion. Northern gentry were associated from the start, indeed often took the initiative. It was not a 'feudal' revolt – tenants, servants and friends of the earls were only a small proportion of those who took part, and only a small proportion of the earls' tenants were mobilised.[26]

More broadly, looking back over earlier centuries, and forward to the seventeenth century, it is worth noting that what is now a generation of revisionist scholarship has played down the role of constitutional ideas in the opposition to John, Henry III and Richard II, and Charles I, not least because those rulers are no longer seen as holding to a programme of royal absolutism, but rather as striving, like all capable rulers, to increase their power, or, more simply, to get their own way.[27] The flaw in a monarchical system of government is the accession of a weak ruler. If in consequence government is palpably bad – exceptionally incompetent, disastrously unsuccessful in war, corrupt and one-sided – then noblemen would indeed be likely to express their anger and to press for reform. Noblemen would do so reluctantly, compelled to do so to defend their own interests. Nor would they do so alone: many lesser men would feel as critical as they were. The demands that nobles and non-nobles alike would make might include the appointment of noblemen to particular offices, and in particular as royal councillors. Declarations in past crises might be invoked in support of such claims. But this was not a continuous tradition of aristocratic protest, even though that might well, in such circumstances, be what many would claim. Such claims, however, were rather somewhat rough and ready efforts by men dealing with grave political problems to solve them. In so far as they drew on any ideas, it was not some sophisticated political ideology, but rather a much less tangible, though undoubtedly real, sense of what was right and what was wrong. Theories, in so far as they were invoked at all, tended to be used retrospectively to validate decisions taken and actions done in the heat of the moment, instinctively, to deal with immediate challenges.

If noblemen were not continuous exponents of any theory of aristocratic protest, nor were they normally opposed to royal ministers. Recent writing on Tudor politics which has misleadingly presented it as a constant clash of factions has in turn exaggerated the frequency and depth of noble hostility to royal ministers. Noblemen were not as a rule resentful of royal ministers. It is not fair to say that 'new men in government were always resented by baronial families, however short their own pedigrees were' or to describe the Tudor nobility as 'the group most strenuously opposed to ministerial power'.[28]

An interesting test case is the attitude of the nobility to Cardinal Wolsey, since it is often claimed that noblemen hated Wolsey and schemed to bring him down, finally succeeding in 1529. But it is hard to find much evidence of that alleged hostility. Often John Skelton's verse is cited in support, but as Greg Walker has shown, Skelton's treatment of the nobility was determined more by his overall satirical intentions than by any detailed knowledge of what noblemen wanted or any deep conviction as to how noblemen should behave.[29] Peter Gwyn's masterly study of *The King's Cardinal*, has examined in great detail the relations between every nobleman and Wolsey in these years and found very little to support the traditional view. Wolsey did not exclude the third duke of Norfolk from involvement in government: he served in Ireland in 1520 and on the Scottish borders in 1523 and 1524; he was involved, as ambassadors' letters show, in making decisions at the highest level; he vigorously pursued the Amicable Grant in 1525 and watched over the risk of social unrest in 1528. Charles Brandon, duke of Suffolk, very much the creation of the king, is often presented as the leader of a hostile aristocracy, motivated by anticlericalism, against Wolsey: however, that claim rests largely on an excessively free translation of a remark by Chapuys, the imperial ambassador.[30]

And if, far from being the Crown's natural opponents, noblemen were in fact the trusted servants of the Crown, then the Crown did not need any 'antibaronial' policy. It is mistaken to see kings as set against the greater nobility. M.L. Bush has shown how what appears to be a consistent policy against noblemen of royal blood was no more than unrelated but understandable responses to occasional problems.[31] What is often cited as evidence for such a policy is the fate of individual nobles who fell foul of the law in particular instances. But they had usually done enough to make their punishment, while sometimes harsh, inevitable. The third duke of Buckingham, executed for treason in 1521, had unwisely been listening to the prophecies of a Carthusian monk that his family would one day ascend the throne, and even more provocatively had been outspokenly criticising the king and Wolsey when speaking to his servants, some of whom betrayed him.[32] His fate is not good evidence that kings were trying to destroy or to curb the nobility as a whole. The execution of Henry Courtenay (1498–1538), marquess of Exeter, and Henry Pole (d. 1538), Lord Montagu in 1538, at first glance looks like the brutal destruction of noblemen of royal blood. But closer examination prompts questions about the timing. If Henry VII had been bent on their elimination, why had he not acted sooner? Why had he shown Henry Courtenay such favour, promoting him marquess of Exeter in 1525? Henry had clearly changed his mind. What prompted that was the break with Rome, and in particular the opposition of Reginald Pole, Montagu's younger brother, who in exile took an ever more hostile stand against the king. He sent him a violent diatribe, *De*

Unitate, denouncing Henry as a tyrant, in 1536. He attempted, as papal legate to Francis I and Charles V, to stir those rulers into taking military action against Henry VIII. Not surprisingly, Henry was both angry and fearful. He failed to have Pole assassinated. His family in England, including his mother, Margaret Plantagenet (d. 1541), countess of Salisbury, the duke of Clarence's daughter, did nothing: indeed Margaret may even have been critical of her son. The marquess of Exeter was one of many noblemen who served loyally against the rebels during the Pilgrimage of Grace in 1536. But then the king learned from his servant Hugh Holland how Sir Geoffrey Pole had warned his brother Reginald of the plots to assassinate him. Ruthlessly interrogated – and driven to the point of attempting suicide – Sir Geoffrey revealed conversations in which his elder brother, Lord Montagu, and the marquess of Exeter had voiced sympathy for the Pilgrims of Grace, denounced newly-appointed bishops as heretics and criticised the treason laws. Exeter had complained of the knaves ruling about the king and said that he hoped to give them a buffet one day. Such private grumbling was in no sense a conspiracy, much less a rebellion, but, fearing invasion, Henry VIII treated it as treason. Maybe that was to show excessive caution, but Henry was undoubtedly fearful of what Reginald Pole in exile might yet do. Above all this episode emphatically does not prove that Henry wished to destroy the nobility as a class.[33]

Although not of the blood royal, the Percys earls of Northumberland are often regarded as overmighty subjects whom the Tudors pursued. It has already been suggested that the Percys were not that overmighty: now it is necessary to ask whether the crown sought to reduce their power. Of course, if they were by no means as powerful as has sometimes been supposed, then there would have been correspondingly less need to reduce their power. It has recently been implied that Henry VII's purpose in obliging the fourth earl of Northumberland to carry out the collection of unpopular taxation in 1489, in the course of which he was murdered, was to test his loyalty to the king, to tarnish his reputation as a good lord and to divide him from his tenants and servants by associating him with unpopular royal policies.[34]

One historian has even gone so far as to say that Henry VII actually engineered the earl's death to deal with the threat that he supposedly posed.[35] All that seems far-fetched. It would have been a desperately risky strategy. Taxation was, after all, necessary, and it was not uncommon for great noblemen to act as in effect royal agents in its local administration, especially in times of difficulty when there was resistance. That subsequently 'only' six rebels were executed and some 1500 were pardoned after the disturbances[36] is not evidence of collusion between king and tax protestors. That seems rather a characteristic, and sensible, way of dealing with such resistance.[37] After the protests against the Amicable Grant in 1525, some five hundred individuals were indicted in king's bench but the cases were not pursued: in effect they were let off. But in no sense is that evidence of collusion between king and tax protestors intended to weaken the local standing of noblemen who were seeking acquiescence in the grant.[38]

What of Henry Algernon Percy (1478–1527), fifth earl of Northumberland? The first two Tudor kings never appointed him warden of the east and middle marches. Does that show that they wished to undermine the traditional power of the Percys on the borders? Or was it rather simply a judgement that he personally was not best suited for what was undoubtedly a demanding responsibility? Interestingly, his son, the sixth earl of Northumberland, was at once appointed warden in 1527 and he served in the defence of the northern borders in 1532–33, when fear of Scottish invasion was great, acting as de facto president of the northern council. That makes it hard to see Crown policy as consistently directed against the Percys. Nor were the various steps taken to deal with the sixth earl's financial difficulties intended by the Crown to weaken his standing. Rather, the aim was to save the earl from his own gullibility, and to protect him from his creditors.[39] The beneficiaries from the earl's generosity were not courtiers but rather favourites he had chosen himself, especially Sir Thomas Arundell and Sir Reynold Carnaby. When in 1536 the earl made Henry VIII his heir and then in the year of his death in 1537 exchanged his lands for a royal pension, he was not the victim of royal avarice: he was rather trying to thwart his half-brothers and his estranged wife. Would Henry have granted the Percy lands to the earl's half-brother, Sir Thomas Percy, in due course, had Sir Thomas not got caught up in the Pilgrimage of Grace and suffered execution for treason?[40]

Did the extent of the power of the nobility in the regions of England change in the sixteenth century? Noble power in the localities had always been variable. Some nobles owned but a few manors, others dominated their 'country'. Much depended on personality, on the powers of leadership displayed by particular noblemen. But in the Tudor century noblemen, with their estates consolidated around their principal residences, remained the general supervisors of regions. In effect the country was divided into spheres of influence that could be displayed on maps; in some senses England was a federation of noble fiefdoms. It was not just well-established families such as the Talbots earls of Shrewsbury or the Stanleys earls of Derby that enjoyed such power. Newly created noblemen such as John Russell (d. 1555), first Lord Russell, later first earl of Bedford, could be endowed with concentrations of land, offering them the scope to build up comparable local dominance. It is misleading to suggest that the Russells were advanced 'with the firm understanding that they were to be the Crown's agents, never an independent territorial power': the massive grants of former monastic land that Russell received in the late 1530s were made in perpetuity and were regionally concentrated in the south-west. Moreover the timing is significant. In 1538 the marquess of Exeter fell, as we have seen, on suspicion of treason. Here was an opportunity for the Tudor government to replace that noble patrimony by something else: but far from eliminating noble power, the Crown, in endowing Russell, revived it.[41] And, more generally, no Tudor government attempted to create a class of intendants – legally trained officials appointed by the crown – to rule the localities.

Nor did the Tudors take a different approach to those regions bordering on Scotland and Wales, aiming at diminishing the role of noblemen. There is a tendency for historians studying Marcher lords to assume that the greatest problem and concern for English kings was the threat that the power of such lords allegedly posed to their tenure of the throne, and to suppose that 'the rule and defence of these remote frontiers were of central significance to the development of the modern state'. Of course, that could be true at certain moments, especially at times of a disputed succession or civil war, but it is mistaken to suppose that when, say, Henry VIII considered the north of England, his first concern was whether the Percys would launch a rebellion against him. That was not likely. Marcher society was neither a threat to the Crown of the Tudors nor a significant influence on the political culture of the Tudor state: it was too poor and too remote from the centre of royal power in London. The Tudors did not need and did not seek deliberately to reduce the power of Marcher lords. But were northern noblemen dealt glancing blows arising from the supposed ideologically-driven imperialistic ambitions of Tudor monarchs to set up a 'Britain' which the kings of England would dominate? Did any such ambitions necessitate the subordination or the elimination of Marcher lords? To speak of 'Tudor strategies of incorporation and assimilation' and to claim that 'the Tudors had a collective view of the dominions which they ruled', seeing them 'as one unit which they attempted to weld together into an English nation-state', is to read far too much consistency of purpose and coherent practice into the Scottish policies of Henry VIII and Protector Somerset in the 1540s, and to ignore English rulers' attitudes and actions (or lack of action) for most of the rest of the century. While all power is in a broad sense unitary in ambition, nonetheless policy towards Scotland (and Ireland) was far more reactive than claims for imperialistic ambitions would allow. The belief in a constantly aggressive English imperialism directed against the Scots, the Welsh, the Cornish and the Irish was rather the consolation of those who saw themselves as victims, or who at particular times actually became victims, rather than a fair description of English royal policy. No doubt from the vantage points of Scotland, Wales, Cornwall and Ireland, the rulers of England and, perhaps more importantly, English cultural influences would always have looked more threatening, more aggressive, more purposeful and more consistent than they really were. While England was the wealthiest and most populous part of the British Isles, giving its kings a comparative advantage over other rulers, those who ruled England had never been strong enough to dominate the whole archipelago: neither the Romans, nor the Anglo-Saxons, nor the Normans attempted, let alone managed, to subdue the whole area. The power of English rulers was always potentially sufficiently great to inflict considerable immediate damage, especially when focused on particular targets, and then to compel some sort of political recognition. English power as exerted by Edward I had proved just about strong enough to subdue Wales, though far from totally, as the 1400s showed. In Ireland, however, the English were long unable to establish control beyond the pale. And measured against Scotland, English power was just not sufficiently overwhelming and sustainable – under Edward I and his successor, under Henry VIII and Protector Somerset – to convert military successes into lasting political dominance.

But if the achievement of 'Britain' was not an active ambition of English rulers, then that necessarily qualifies claims about the role of Marcher lords whose powers were supposedly being limited in the interests of an imperial policy.[42] Much more immediate a concern than any 'British' aspirations were recurrent threats of Scottish invasion and much more urgent was the need to strengthen border defences to withstand the Scots. Disunity would weaken those defences, so the Crown tried hard to minimise disputes between northern lords. Above all, the Crown was anxious that key posts – the wardenries of the East, Middle and West Marches – were held by able and hard-working noblemen. At that personal level there might be doubts about the suitability of particular individuals, and noblemen might sometimes be criticised for incompetence or even arrested on suspicion of disloyalty. But when a nobleman was passed over or dismissed, what happened next revealed not some fundamental reform of the system of military administration in the borders, but just the appointment of another nobleman whom the king hoped would prove more competent and more reliable. After William, Lord Dacre (1500–63), was arrested and tried in 1534 for treasonable dealings with the Scots, and dismissed as warden of the West Marches even after he had been acquitted, he was simply replaced by the first earl of Cumberland, in much the same way that his Dacre ancestor had been built up by the Crown in the 1460s.[43] Tudor governments thought less in structural terms than one might suppose, and when they did embark on institutional reform, it was often because at the moment of doing so they could find no suitable capable nobleman with whom to work. The development of regional councils – the council of the north, the council of the Marches – in the sixteenth century illustrates that well. Regional councils were as much an administrative convenience for local litigants as an instrument of royal government, and their introduction and development can often be linked to the chance absence of a suitable adult nobleman to supervise a region. The considerable development of the council in the north from 1537 reflects the lack of competent adult noblemen, untainted by involvement, however unwilling, in the Pilgrimage of Grace. It is significant that Lancashire was excluded from the jurisdiction of the council of the north – this was where the earl of Derby held sway.[44]

Of course, much of the detailed donkey work of local government was done by the gentry, serving as JPs and on commissions, but that was not a novelty of the Tudor age, but went back to at least the fourteenth century. More delicate tasks, however, such as the great military survey of 1522, were often entrusted to special commissions including leading noblemen. County studies, both fashionable and practically convenient approaches for graduate students in search of a PhD topic, may give a disproportionate weight to gentry families compared to noblemen whose estates in a single county may not have been that great but whose influence may have stretched across several counties. Relations between noblemen and gentry remained various: they did not undergo a sea-change. Noblemen might no longer issue indentures and pay fees to retainers, but they continued to employ significant numbers in their service. Noble households were being rivalled by the universities and the inns of court as centres of gentry education, but the greatest noble families continued to maintain them. Nobles continued to exercise patronage on their estates and to spend much of their time on their patrimonies. Noblemen did not habitually use force locally in pursuit of their interests or to impose their authority on neighbouring gentry, but in so far as they did, they were still well capable of doing so at the end of the sixteenth century, as Gilbert Talbot (1552–1616), seventh earl of Shrewsbury, notoriously did when sending his men to destroy Sir Thomas Stanhope's weir in 1593.

Several historians have cited that dispute – but rarely much else – in support of the claim that noble power was declining at the end of the sixteenth century at the expense of gentry who enjoyed favour at court. One example is an adequate basis for such a generalisation. Moreover this example, carefully scrutinised, does not support it. It was not because he lacked influence at court that Shrewsbury did not achieve all his aims. A remark by Thomas Sackville (1527–1608), Lord Buckhurst, one of the members of the council to whom Shrewsbury appealed for help, has been misconstrued. Writing of John and Michael Stanhope, brothers of Sir Thomas Stanhope with whom Shrewsbury was in dispute, Buckhurst told the earl that 'the continuall presens of thes two brethren in court, with the nere place that they have with her Majestie, and that which is above all the rest, the especial favor which hir Highnes doth beare unto them, will alwaies prevaile with so great advantage against you'. That might seem conclusive. But it must be noted that Shrewsbury had recently been at court and spoken to the queen himself: a little later she would inform him of her continuing affection. Shrewsbury was not some marginalised backwoods squire. As Buckhurst's letter shows, he did have friends at court who could watch over his interests and advise him what to do. What damaged him was not his absence from court and the presence at court of the brothers of his local rival, but quite simply that what he wanted and what he was doing was outrageous. Warning him that the Stanhopes were favoured by queen and council, Buckhurst wrote that consequently it would be hard for Shrewsbury to win his dispute against them, 'except your caus be marvelous plain and just'. The defect of Shrewsbury's cause was that it manifestly was not just. And his methods further weakened it. Elizabeth was especially displeased that fishermen and merchants had been bullied by Shrewsbury's servants into signing a petition against the weir in contention. So Shrewsbury failed to get the council to order the destruction of the weir, built across the Trent some fifteen years earlier by Sir Thomas Stanhope. But that did not stop him. In January 1593 he successfully thwarted the ambitions of the Stanhopes in parliamentary elections in Nottinghamshire. And then in the spring, his men took matters into their own hands and destroyed the weir. The earl was leniently treated: if his men were fined in Star Chamber, he himself was not tried or punished. His local power remained considerable, as the Stanhopes, for all their court favour, were very well aware.[45]

Noblemen, as we have seen, continued to have the ability 'to make men', to raise forces to do down a neighbour, to mobilise against a rebellion. The fourth earl of Shrewsbury raised 3654 men on horseback within a week to resist the Pilgrimage of Grace.[46] More importantly still, noblemen one way or another supplied and commanded armed forces in military campaigns in France or on the northern borders. Some historians have seen as a fundamental transformation the change from the early Tudor period, in which the Crown contracted with noblemen and greater gentry to raise their servants, tenants and friends under contract, and the reign of Elizabeth, when the Crown appointed them as lord lieutenants to raise the county militia. But the difference was more apparent than real: the responsibility for raising and for leading armed forces still rested upon the nobility. True, it was the Crown who appointed lord lieutenants; but in any given county there was not a great deal of choice. And it is more accurate to see the lord lieutenancy as a formalisation of the existing regional powers and responsibilities of the nobility. This is at once obvious if one thinks of alternative possibilities – such as a standing army staffed by professional officers and administered by men with no landed interests – that, revealingly, were never attempted in Tudor England.

Many historians have argued that the military role of the nobility declined sharply at this time. That is misleading. The sixteenth century was a period of internal peace. Compared to the Hundred Years' War, English military intervention overseas was limited. So it is not surprising that inventories from the early seventeenth century list outdated weapons and armour. But when wars were fought or feared, noblemen were still highly prominent. The large-scale campaigns in France in 1513 and 1544 were led by noblemen, as were virtually all armies and navies raised in this period. Noble commanders were not figureheads but actively involved in the laborious tasks of supplying armed forces and making tactical decisions. Of course, non-noble technical experts gave advice, but that was no novelty. Noble families whose lands lay near frontiers, such as the Dacres in Cumbria, devoted a great deal of their energies and resources to war and defence. When internal conflict returned to England in 1642, noblemen were much involved on both sides in raising men and in commanding fortified strongpoints. Maybe in the very long run the 'military revolution' would ultimately diminish the role of noblemen in war: gunpowder should in theory have eroded the effectiveness of knights on horseback. But cavalrymen responded to the challenge posed by well-trained infantry equipped with strengthened artillery by fighting in groups, fighting at greater speed and riding lighter horses, styles of combat which were developed by changes in the practice of tournaments. And in England in the Tudor century there just was not any extended experience of fighting that might have led to more substantial changes in the technology of warfare which in turn would have affected the role of the nobility.[47]

But what of noble finances? The central issue in this most heated of historical debates in the 1950s and 1960s was the economic fortunes of the nobility. Was there a 'crisis of the aristocracy', to use Lawrence Stone's term? Did noblemen's incomes fall as their expenditure rose? Did, as R.H. Tawney claimed, the gentry acquire wealth and status at the expense of the nobility? It soon became evident that there were very serious weaknesses in such arguments, and efforts to demonstrate them statistically ran into the sand.

Statistical approaches involve the identification of a group for measurement. If the intention is to measure trends in the wealth and income of the nobility, it seems at first reasonable to follow Lawrence Stone in the *Crisis of the Aristocracy* and define the nobility as the parliamentary peers. The problem, however, with such a definition is that there was no regular recruitment into the parliamentary peerage on consistent principles. Without new creations, the number of peers would inevitably fall, through the workings of biology, whenever peers died without leaving male heirs. For such reasons, among others, monarchs could and did create new peers. In the sixteenth century, several courtiers and administrator-politicians built up their fortunes and, as we have seen, sought to convert what might be temporary royal favour into lasting landed endowments for their families: ennoblement ratified their efforts. But the incidence of creation of peers varied greatly. Many peers were created by Henry VIII and in the minority of Edward VI, relatively few under Elizabeth, considerably more under James I. 'Parliamentary peers' was thus a changing, not a constant, category. To compare the parliamentary peers of 1602 with those of 1558 is not to compare like with like. Furthermore the parliamentary peers were not necessarily the largest landowners: there was a rough but by no means exact and unvarying relationship between title and landed wealth. And there were very considerable variations in wealth and income within the peerage between the richest duke and humblest country lord, variations that further undermine the validity of treating the peerage as a group in this way.

Statistical analysis depends upon aggregation. But that is reliable only when the statistics which are being aggregated are produced according to clear and consistent and continuous procedures. That is not the case when estimates of noblemen's incomes have to be made from a variety of sources. Rentals, valors, tax assessments, inquisitions post mortem, marriage contracts, and materials prepared for legal cases may all be informative up to a point, though each requires very sensitive analysis. But simply to add up everything that these disparate sources yield is to make an act of faith: errors do not necessarily cancel each other out. Nor is it acceptable to take the numbers of manors noblemen owned as proxies for their wealth and income, and simply add them up, as if one manor was much the same as any other. But manors were far too diverse in size and in economic value for that to be a precisely meaningful exercise.

Statistical approaches often build in that which they seek to prove. At first sight the claim that a sample of parliamentary peers held only 71 per cent of the manors in 1602 that they had held in 1558 seems compelling evidence that the nobility was in decline. (63 families in 1559 held 3390 manors or 54 each; 57 families in 1602 held 2220 manors or 39 each.) But when it is remembered that but for the inclusion in the total for 1558 of the estates of the earls of Northumberland and Westmorland, who crashed in unsuccessful rebellion in 1569 and lost most of their lands as a result, the proportion of manors held by the peers in 1602 would be similar to that in 1558, it is clear that what such figures reflect is political miscalculation by two peers, not the inexorable financial decline of a class.[48]

It remains quite unproven that the nobility as a whole suffered a financial crisis in the sixteenth century. The only convincing method of throwing light on that question is to study systematically the wealth and income of individual families over a long period. That has been attempted most recently for the Radcliffes earls of Sussex, and that evidence suggests that noble families could readily hold their own, given due care and attention to their estates.[49] That reinforced the conclusions of earlier studies of the Stanleys earls of Derby, and of Henry Percy (1564–1632), ninth earl of Northumberland.[50] It has also become evident that debt was by itself not compelling evidence of economic troubles but rather a common feature of aristocratic life. Spectacular collapses such as that of Richard Grey (d. 1524), third earl of Kent, were quite possible, but they were rare and the result of an individual's inadequacy, not the failings of a whole social class.[51] Whatever difficulties some families may have experienced – and this is not to minimise the anguish that individual noblemen, their families and their descendants consequently suffered – they were brief and particular.

The broadest economic and social trends in this period ought in theory to have favoured, rather than harmed, the interests of the largest landowners. This was not an age of agrarian depression. Population grew in the sixteenth century. That meant greater demand for land, and for the food and clothing materials that were produced on the land. There were significant innovations in farming practices, leading to an increase in agrarian productivity. Who benefited from such developments? In the long run, the largest landowners stood to gain the most. Of course, this was also an age of inflation, and inflation might erode the value of rents. Raising rents was a slow process, since lands were characteristically let out on long leases with little provision for rent reviews, or on customary, that is to say theoretically unchangeable, terms. But over time it does seem to be the case that rents and revenues from lands rose, as the magisterial survey that Eric Kerridge conducted on the estates of the earls of Pembroke most notably shows.[52] It may be that the Crown did not do very well on its vast estates, but given the extent of the Crown lands, and the difficulty of effective central monitoring, that is not surprising and should not be taken as evidence that noblemen, with more compact holdings and, generally, fewer responsibilities to distract them, were not prospering. Moreover the rising agrarian productivity may have had important social effects. An estate that in 1540 supported one gentlemen could by 1640 support more: certainly there were more gentlemen than there had been in 1540. But if that can be seen as 'the rise of the gentry', it was not at the expense of the nobility and greater landowners, who also benefited greatly overall, though with obvious individual exceptions, from these trends. If any social group suffered at the expense of nobility and gentry it was the church. The effect of the sales of the lands of the dissolved monasteries and chantries was to reinforce the local power of those, by definition already wealthy, who were in a position to acquire them. And if instead of staring in close detail at the parliamentary peerage in one reign, the reign of Elizabeth, one stands back, and looks at the fortunes of the nobility over a much longer time span, then it becomes even more difficult to see this period as a turning point or as in any way exceptional. Julian Cornwall, studying the social structure of early Tudor England, remarked that 'individually most of the nobility were men of great wealth'; historians of the nobility on the later seventeenth and eighteenth centuries emphasise the great wealth of great families, to which countless grand country houses still bear vivid testimony.[53]

* * *

Moreover it is unlikely that there was any change in the dominance of aristocratic values over Tudor England. What ambitious and successful non-nobles aspired to was the ownership of a landed estate. Humanist thought challenged the nobility less than might be supposed, offering an emphasis on virtue that might easily be combined with a belief in a hierarchical society. By criticising noblemen for behaving badly, writers such as Thomas Elyot and Lawrence Humfrey were implying that they ought to behave better than other men, and consequently that when noblemen were indeed virtuous, virtues glittered more brightly in them than in others. Hierarchy was thus inherently good. In the Tudor century there were no alternative models: not the enlightenment rhetoric of all men being born equal, nor the new liberalism or socialism of the late nineteenth and twentieth centuries, with their emphasis on redistribution of wealth to produce a more just society. The ideological pre-eminence of noble values in sixteenth-century England both reflected and immeasurably reinforced the social and political standing of the nobility.[54]

Obviously Sir John Fitzherbert was correct to answer the question 'howe and by what maner doo all these great estates and noblemen and women lyue, and maynteyne theyr honour and degree?' by saying, 'by reason of their rentes, issues, reuenewes, and profyttes that come of their maners, lordshyps, landes and tenementes to theym belongynge'.[55] And yet this does not explain why noblemen were allowed to possess so unequal a share of lands and resources in money and men. Their power did not rest – indeed given the inadequacy of the means of repression available to the nobility, could not rest – on force alone. Ultimately it had to rest on consent. Men who obeyed their masters may have obeyed because they feared that they would be punished if they did not, but at the same time most obeyed because they had been told, and very largely had accepted, that it was morally right that they should obey.[56] In the context of medieval towns 'much willing submission' has been noted, 'most of all by those who according to our standards were most unjustly treated'.[57] The issue of noble privileges was aired in contemporary literature. But almost always criticisms of nobility gave way to vigorous justifications, a triumph that both reflected and reinforced noble power. The nobility drew enormous strength from the common acceptance of the belief that its inherited position conferred a special and privileged place upon it.

There are obvious difficulties in considering contemporary attitudes to nobility. The views expressed in what is overall a very small number of books cannot be taken as definitive. They were not written by noblemen. That they were representative of those who thought about the matters with which they deal must be taken on trust. That these attitudes reflected and influenced the outlook of kings, administrators and noblemen, and percolated through society, may only tentatively be suggested. Some of the works cited below were dedicated to noblemen. Some noblemen did collect books: most notably, perhaps, in this period, Henry, lord Stafford.[58] But it is not easy for the early and mid-Tudor periods to show connections and interactions between ideas and politics, between intellectual interests and political ideals, as has been attempted, for example, for the earl of Arundel in the 1620s.[59] It would be foolhardy to point to any specific instance in the lives of the fourth and fifth earls of Shrewsbury in which attitudes counted. And yet such a minimalist approach, which might undermine any study of the history of ideas, does leave large questions unanswered. It is misleading to suppose that what cannot be shown precisely cannot be evaluated at all.

Criticisms of nobility were expressed – not least by rebels, or potential rebels. Richard Fulmerston reported to Somerset from Bath in May 1549 that he had heard 'lewde and unfyttinge talke', such as 'why shulde oone manne have all and another nothing'.[60] Edmund Dudley devoted some space in the *Tree of Commonwealth* to the refutation of the arrogant messenger who contrasted worldly inequality with the natural equality of men.[61] Laurence Humfrey believed 'there be neither fewe, nor those altogether euel, that think this nobilitye ought to be banished and not borne in the commen wealth'; it was 'muche doubted ... whether nobles oughte to be borne in a wel ordred and christianlike state'.[62] The extent of class conflict, even of class consciousness, was not great: certainly there was nothing on the scale of late eighteenth-century Languedoc where seigneurs lived in fear of their peasants, seeing their pigeons strangled and their places in church taken by dissident tenantry.[63] But it should not be supposed that noble privileges were unquestioned.

Criticisms of nobility were implicit in discussions of the definition of nobility and of what constituted true nobility. The problem here was that in theory the nobility were the virtuous, while in fact nobility was derived from birth, inheritance, wealth and favour. Clearly there was in early Tudor society, as in any society, no visible connection between virtue and nobility.[64] The ideal was a nobleman at once virtuous in his actions and rejoicing in ancient lineage. Humfrey thought that 'the hawtiest, worthiest and honourablest nobilitye is that whyche with the renoume and fame of auncestrye hath coupled excellent chrystyan and farre spred vertue'.[65] Nobility solely dependent on ancient lineage was generally criticised. 'For the onely noblenes of birth and lignage, there is no honour nor prayse to be gyuen vnto a man,' argued *The Boke of Noblenes*.[66] The emphasis that Elyot gave to education in *The Governor* tended to undermine any belief in the sufficiency of good birth.[67] A major source of criticism of nobility was the medieval Christian tradition. 'Everyone came of Adam and Eve', noted Rastell's ploughman, who then asked the old question, 'for when adam dolf and eue span who was then a gentylman'.[68] The arrogant messenger whose subversive arguments were outlined by Dudley in his *Tree of Commonwealth* took this line further:[69]

> He will tell you that ye be the childeren and righte enheritors to Adam aswell as thei. Whie should thei haue this great honours, royall castelles and manners, with somotche landes and possessions, and ye but poore cottyges and tenementes? He will shew also how that Christ bought you as derely as the nobles with one maner of price, which was his precioues Bloude. Whie then should ye be of so poore estate and thei of higher degre, or whie should you do them somotche honour and reuerence with croching or knelyng and thei take it so highely and stately on them? And percase he will enforme you how conserning your soules and theres, which make you all to be men or els ye were all but beestes, god creatyd in you one maner of noblenes without any diuersitie and that your soules be as precious to god as theires. Why then should thei haue of you so greate auctoritie and power to commytt you to prison, and ponishe and iudge you?

The Booke of Noblenes observed that all men had the same celestial father.[70] Humfrey pointedly remarked that it was Joseph the carpenter and Mary the humble maid that Jesus had chosen for his parents. Nor had he borne arms.[71] All in all, Christian ideals made it difficult to argue that vice or virtue corresponded to differences in social status: if the first chapter of the first gospel was devoted to a genealogy of Christ, tracing his royal descent from King David, and if Saint Paul, Roman citizen, might be regarded as noble, nonetheless the Bible made no explicit reference to nobility.[72] Arguments supporting equality might also be drawn from parallels with the body. Dudley was eloquent: 'loke when our glorious garmentes be don off, and we nakyd, what differens is then between vs and the poore laborers. Peraduenture a more foolle and shamefull karcase'.[73] Rastell's ploughman told the knight 'thy blood and the beggars of one colour be, Thou art as apt to take sekenes as he'.[74] That we were all born the same way was a commonplace: 'Beginne we not all our life with wrallyng, and cryes?'[75] After death everyone would be powder and dust: once buried there was no difference between nobles and others.[76] (The notion of 'fame' that would outlive the decay of the body seems to have developed later in the century.) There were also complaints that noblemen were misusing their privileges – enclosing, engrossing, enhancing rents – but most often (with the interesting exception of Rastell's ploughman) such criticisms tended to be expressed as censure of wicked individuals who had failed in their duty and who were called upon to reform, and not as a fundamental critique of the social order. Nonetheless the force of this questioning of the nobility may be measured by the volume of efforts devoted to justifying it at a time when Humfrey believed that men neither wrote nor spoke freely of the state of the nobility.[77] Did those who set down these criticisms of the nobility neutralise the supposedly radical implications of their insistence that true nobility came from virtue? Did they usually go on to claim that, in empirical fact, virtue was most fully displayed by members of the traditional ruling class?[78] But the claim that virtue was the source of true nobility was hardly novel, and therefore should not be seen as so radical. And if writers such as Elyot and Humfrey admitted that nobles began life with the advantage of the example of their illustrious forbears,[79] they did not believe that noblemen were always virtuous. Indeed, they often castigated noblemen precisely for not behaving as virtuously as they ought. What did undermine their criticisms of nobility was first, that the very fact of criticising noblemen for behaving badly tended to imply that nobles ought to behave better than other men, that they were somehow intrinsically or potentially superior, that when they were virtuous, their virtues glittered more brightly than in other men,[80] and secondly, that the emphasis placed on virtue, and on learning, as a sign of true nobility, was easily compatible with the defence of an hierarchical society at the apex of which noblemen – virtuous noblemen – were still properly to be found.[81] Moreover, however much early Tudor writers were prepared to cajole noblemen who fell short of the highest standards and to report the radical arguments of critics, ultimately they defended nobility with vigour.

Nobility was a singular grace of God, asserted Humfrey.[82] God 'hath ordeyned dyuers estates and degrees in his people and creatures' wrote

Fitzherbert.[83] Edmund Dudley declared that God had set an order between man and man, and man and beast.[84] More specific biblical justification was offered by the knight in Rastell's dialogue who cited Noah's curse, referring to the malediction of Canaan son of Ham who had seen the nakedness of his father Noah and to the blessing of Noah's sons Shem and Japheth who were to be served by Canaan. Canaan's posterity became commoners, Shem and Japheth were the ancestors of noblemen and gentlemen.[85] Parallels were drawn from the body to justify inequality. Rebellion by the commons was seen as the contention of 'the vyler partes of the bodie' with the 'fiue wittes'.[86] Parallels were also drawn from the natural world. Humfrey declared 'howe muche men passe beastes, so muche the nobles to excell the rest'.[87] Elyot argued that bees, cranes, red deer and wolves all had governors and leaders.[88] Gradation was implied in a view of the world that ranked fire, air, water and earth. Considerable emphasis was placed on blood. Some men, and races, were seen as superior to others. Elyot wrote of 'Irisshemen or Scottes, who be of the same rudeness and wilde disposition that the Suises and Britons were in the time of Cesar'.[89] Rastell's knight noted that artificers made things for lords 'because comenly they haue lytell wyt'.[90] 'As it becometh neither the Man to be Governed of the Woman, nor the Master of the Servant,' wrote William Thomas, 'even so in all other Regiments it is not convenient the Inferior should have power to direct the Superior'.[91]

In France there was a greater emphasis on racial criteria for nobility. Some writers argued that those qualities which placed a man in society were transmitted hereditarily and that therefore the children of nobles and those of *roturiers* had inherently different capacities. Much was made of the mysterious potency of *sang* and *semence* and no little ingenuity was deployed in parrying obvious objections. In the later sixteenth century it became common to see the French nobility as descendants of warrior Franks, while the *roturiers* were the posterity of the vanquished Gaulois Gauls.[92] No such clear cut racial theory evolved in England: the 'Norman Yoke' theme does not seem to have been used in this way.[93] Mythical or quasi-historical origins of nobility were discussed, however, and were used to justify nobility. Elyot told how in the beginning people had everything in common and were equal but they had agreed to give their possessions to men 'at whose vertue they meruailed' whom they regarded as fathers. 'Of those good men were ingendered good children who were brought up in virtue, strove to equal the virtue of their ancestors, and so retained the favour of the people.'[94] A different kind of justification of nobility was the contention that the social order depended on hierarchy, and, as a corollary, that rebellions, the aim of which was to produce equality, were the greatest of evils, leading to anarchy. 'Wherfore yf we shuld dystroy enherytaunce, We shuld dystroy all good rule and ordynaunce.'[95] The Doctor in *A Discourse of the Commonweal* of this realm of England asked 'what ship can long be safe from wreck where every man will take upon him to be a pilot; what house well governed where every servant will be a master or teacher?'[96] Elyot praised 'the discrepance of degrees, wherof procedth ordre'. Without order there would be chaos. 'Where there is any lacke of ordre needes must be perpetuall conflicte.' Without government and laws the stronger would force the weaker to be their servants. Equality would be destroyed. Worse would ensue – manslaughters, ravishments, adulteries and other enormities – unless those who sought equality 'coulde perswade god or compelle him to chaunge men in to aungels'.[97] Without the spur of poverty, men would do no work. A crucially important extension of such attacks against rebellions was to point out, as Cheke did, 'how can ye keepe your owne if ye keepe no order, your wife and children, how can they be defended from other mens violence, if ye will in other things breake all order, by what reason would ye be obeyed of yours as seruauntes, if ye will not obey the king as subiectes, howe would ye haue others deale orderly with you, if ye will vse disorder against all others?' In an hierarchical society only those at the very bottom had no one to obey them. 'The existing social order was accepted as natural, immutable: its property-orientated, patriarchal, authoritarian character in fact harmonising with much of the peasant's own experience in relation to his family and land holding.'[98] Moreover noblemen provided support and employment for those around them: the Doctor in *A Discourse* noted that spending on building and trimming of houses provided revenues for carpenters, masons and labourers. 'The household worked as part of the local, and to some extent national, economic system, providing a major stimulant in the market economy.'[99] Nobility was then defended because it was ordained by God, paralleled in the body and natural world, sanctified by blood, demonstrated by myth and history, necessary if social order and prosperity were to be maintained, advantageous to society and reckless to overturn.

At the same time the apparent harshness of inequality was mitigated by the tacit or explicit recognition of the possibility of social mobility. If Humfrey attacked 'lewde cutters and roysters who in theyr vtter behauiour, apparayle, practises & talke, counterfaite a maner nobility', he nonetheless defended new nobles who 'by theyr owne vertue and commendacion of wisedome... atteynde to this higher room, as many at this day both singulerly learned and guyltles and sincere in life'.[100] *The Institucion of a Gentleman* vigorously defended the 'vngentle gentle'. 'Suche as worthynes hath broughte vnto honor' should be defended from the charge of being upstarts: 'no man oughte to contempne or dispise that man whom virtue hathe set vp more hygher then his parentes wer before him'.[101]

What moralists taught, the day-to-day manifestations of hierarchy reinforced. Even if sumptuary legislation failed to impose appropriate clothing for different ranks in society, the successive acts and proclamations did publish the hierarchy and a man's dress did broadly correspond to his social status.[102] The extreme deference adopted in ceremonies or in the addressing and writing of letters to the great also reinforced hierarchy. Royal letters, proclamations and parliamentary statutes usually distinguished noblemen from the rest.[103]

Of course, the nobility survived, and, in short, the fundamental values of early Tudor society were aristocratic. In two important respects the justifications of nobility triumphed. First, the poor turned to resignation, receiving advice from Humfrey to pray to God 'the stout auengeour of the poore', or waiting, as did Rastell's ploughman 'tyll god wyll send/ A tyme tyll our gouernours may intend/ Of all enormytees the reformacyon/ ... / For the amendment of the world is not in me'.[104] Secondly, noble values permeated lower levels of society. Popular culture, based on mythical, medieval and chivalric societies, was imbued with aristocratic values which, however much modified by this 'sinking', influenced even the uneducated and the poor.[105] At a higher level, ambitious men were constantly striving to be accepted as gentlemen, and then to establish their families within the gentry. Prosperous yeomen sought the trappings of gentility. Courtiers such as Sir William Compton built up a landed inheritance that would serve as a power base for his heirs and lead to a title of nobility for his grandson, testifying eloquently to the attractions of the noble way of life to ambitious men in early Tudor England.[106] Royal administrators did the same. Lawyers 'as soon as they were able ... acquired the lands and interest of the country gentleman'. The objectives of common lawyers were 'nowhere more obvious than in the widespread refusal of families to forge continuing links with the profession'. There were few legal or administrative dynasties: such careers were 'lucrative careers for individuals'.[107] Few lawyers, or merchants, who could afford to set themselves up as gentry (and of course not all could) failed to do so. Once advanced, such social climbers had a vested interest not only in raising the drawbridges but also in defending nobility and gentility as such. 'Quel meilleur signe de la vigueur de la noblesse que "la trahison de la bourgeoisie"?'[108] Such aspirations survived well into the nineteenth century and beyond.[109]

* * *

In conclusion, the nobility remained in Tudor England what it had long been and would long remain, the most powerful and the most influential segment of society. If the finances of individual families might sometimes fluctuate, nonetheless the fortunes of the nobility in general, both financially and in a broader sense, remained strong in the Tudor century. Noblemen continued to wield considerable local power, acting on behalf of the Crown as in effect general supervisors of the regions in which they held land. The values of this society remained aristocratic. But in asserting the importance of the nobility, historians should not exaggerate it, as some historians of the seventeenth- and eighteenth-century nobility have recently done. Noblemen needed to offer leadership in order to realise their power, and their relationships with their inferiors were not one way. Noblemen did not habitually rebel against the Crown or join in factions to manipulate rulers. That relationship between Crown and nobility was one of co-operation not conflict; nobles served the Crown loyally far more often than not, and they worked with, not against, royal ministers. If there was not a constant *identity* of interest, there was certainly a considerable *community* of interest, and the government of England is best characterised as a partnership between the Crown and the landed classes. That did not change in the Tudor century.

Notes

1. I should like to thank Mr C.S.L. Davies, Mr P.J. Gwyn, Mr H. James, the late Jennifer Loach, Dr S.J. Payling, Mr T.B. Pugh and Professor K.M. Sharpe for their comments on an earlier essay on the nobility on which I have drawn in preparing this chapter.
2. S.J. Gunn, 'Off with their heads: the Tudor nobility 1485–1603', in J.S. Moore (ed.), *The House of Lords: a Thousand Years of British Tradition* (1994), pp. 52–65.
3. M. Weiss, 'A power in the north? The Percies in the fifteenth century', *Historical Journal*, xix (1976), pp. 501–9; M.A. Hicks, 'Dynastic change and northern society: the career of the fourth earl of Northumberland, 1470–89', *Northern History*, xiv (1978), pp. 78–107. J.A. Tuck, 'The emergence of a northern nobility', *Northern History*, xxii (1986), p. 17, exaggerates the power of the Percys. For earlier brief but salutary scepticism see M.L. Bush, 'The problem of the far north: a study of the crisis of 1537 and its consequences', *Northern History*, vi (1971), pp. 40 n. 1, 41–2.
4. S. Walker, 'Autorite des magnats et pouvoir de la gentry en Angleterre a la fin du moyen age', in P. Contamine, *L'etat et les aristocraties: XIIe–XVII siecles. France, Angleterre, Escosse* (Paris, 1989), pp. 189–211; *Historical Manuscripts Commission, xxiv, Rutland*, i pp. 3–4; J. Bruce (ed.), *History of the Arrivall of Edward IV in England*, Camden Society i (1838), p. 6; J.S. Davies (ed.), *An English Chronicle*, Camden Society lxiv (1856), p. 65; cf. C. Ross, *Edward IV* (1975), p. 154; A.J. Pollard, *North-Eastern England during the Wars of the Roses: Lay Society, War and Politics 1450–1500* (Oxford, 1990), pp. 308–13; T.B. Pugh, *Henry V and the Southampton Plot* (Gloucester, 1988), pp. 14, 20–21. Further instances may include the reluctance of the gentry of Brecon to support the duke of Buckingham in October 1483 (T.B. Pugh, *The Marcher Lordships* (Cardiff, 1963), pp. 240–41; C. Rawcliffe, *The Staffords, Lords Stafford and Dukes of Buckingham 1394–1521* (Cambridge, 1968), p. 34; R. Horrox, *Richard III: a study in service* (Cambridge, 1989), pp. 162–4) and the report that instead of joining Richard Nevill, earl of Warwick, in 1470, men 'left their gathering and sat still' for fear of facing defeat at the king's hands (J.G. Nichols (ed.), 'The Chronicle of the Rebellion in Lincolnshire, 1470', *Camden Miscellany i Camden Society*, old series, xxxix (1847), pp. 5, 12; Pollard, *North-Eastern England*, pp. 307–8; but cf. P. Holland, 'The Lincolnshire Rebellion of March 1470', *English Historical Review* iii (1988), p. 865 n. 2, who suggests that there was insufficient time for mobilisation).
5. Walker, 'Autorite de magnats', p. 91; S. Walker, *The Lancastrian Affinity*

1361–1399 (Oxford, 1990), pp. 139–41, 160–62, 166, 221, 232–4, 250, 260–61.
6. K.B. McFarlane, *The Nobility of Later Medieval England* (Oxford, 1973), p. 120.
7. S.J. Gunn, 'The courtiers of Henry VII', *English Historical Review*, cviii (1993), pp. 23–49; Gunn, 'Off with their heads', pp. 52–65; Gunn, 'Sir Thomas Lovell (c. 1449–1524): a new man in a new monarchy', in J.L. Watts (ed.), *The End of the Middle Ages?* (Stroud, 1998), pp. 117–54. See also D. Luckett, 'Crown patronage and political morality in early Tudor England: the case of Giles, Lord Daubeney', *English Historical Review*, cx (1995), pp. 578–95.
8. See also below, Chapter 9.
9. G. Walker, 'Continuity and change in the royal court in late medieval and renaissance England', in C.D. Baschiera and J. Everson (eds), *Scenes of Change: studies in cultural transition* (Pisa, 1996), pp. 193–210, at p. 199.
10. L. Harf-Lanener, 'L'enfer de la cour: la cour de Henri II Plantagenet et la Mesnie hellequin', in P. Contamine (ed.), *L'etat et les aristocraties: XIIe–XVII siecle. France, Angleterre, Escosse* (Paris, 1989), pp. 51–78; R. Horrox, *Richard III: a Study in Service* (Cambridge, 1989), p. 251.
11. See Chapter 7 below.
12. G.W. Bernard, *The Power of the Early Tudor Nobility: the Fourth and Fifth Earls of Shrewsbury* (Brighton, 1985), pp. 61–2.
13. J. Loach, *Edward VI* (1999), pp. 170–79.
14. M. James, *Society, Politics and Culture* (Cambridge, 1986), pp. 416–65. P.E.J. Hammer, 'Patronage at court, faction and the earl of Essex', in J. Guy (ed.), *The Reign of Elizabeth I: Court and Culture in the Last Decade* (Cambridge, 1995), pp. 56–86.
15. Bernard, *The Power of the Early Tudor Nobility*, pp. 30–58; R. Holinshed, *Chronicles* (6 vols, 1807–8 edn), iii. 800.
16. M.E. James, 'Obedience and Dissent in Henrician England: the Lincolnshire Rebellion, 1536', *Past and Present*, xlviii (1970), pp. 3–78 (reprinted in *Society, Politics and Culture*, pp. 188–269); G.R. Elton, 'Politics and the Pilgrimage of Grace', in B. Malament (ed.), *After the Reformation* (Pennsylvania, 1980), pp. 25–56 (reprinted in G.R. Elton, *Studies in History* (4 vols, Cambridge, 1974–91), iii. 183–215); R.B. Smith, *Land and Politics in the England of Henry VIII: the West Riding of Yorkshire 1530–46* (Oxford, 1970), ch. v.
17. Vienna, Haus-, Hof- unds Staatsarchiv, Karton 6, Korrespondenz, Berichte, 1534, ff. 64–65v (PRO PRO31/18/3/1 ff. 328–330v; *Calendar of State Papers, Spanish*, V i. no. 257, pp. 608–11; *LP*, VII 1206). I am grateful to the British Academy for grant enabling study in Vienna.
18. Bernard, *The Power of the Early Tudor Nobility*, pp. 32–4.
19. PRO SP1/117 f. 191 (*LP*, XII i 783).
20. PRO SP1/107 ff. 85, 88 (*LP*, XII i 605, 606).
21. PRO SP1/110 f. 45 (xvii) (*LP*, XI 687).
22. I owe this suggestion to R.W. Hoyle.
23. *LP*, XI 588, 615, 621, 808 (but cf. 846).
24. Bernard, *The Power of the Early Tudor Nobility*, pp. 36–8.
25. R.W. Hoyle, 'The fall of the House of Percy', in Bernard (ed.), *The Tudor Nobility*, pp. 198–9.
26. S.E. Taylor, 'The crown and the north of England 1559–70: a study of the rebellion of the northern earls, 1569–70, and its causes', University of Manchester PhD thesis (1981).
27. J.C. Holt, *Magna Carta* (Cambridge, 1965); C. Russell, *The Causes of the English Civil War* (Oxford, 1990), esp. pp. 131–55; K. Sharpe, *The Personal Rule of*

Charles I (1992); D. Carpenter, 'King, magnates and society: the personal rule of Henry III', 1234–1258', *Speculum*, lx (1985), pp. 39–70; 'What happened in 1258?', in J. Gillingham and J.C. Holt (eds), *War and Government in the Middle Ages: Essays in Honour of J.O. Prestwich* (Woodbridge, 1984), pp. 106–19.

28. M.T. Clanchy, *England and its Rulers 1066–1272* (1983), pp. 214–15. Was it not conventional for fallen ministers to be charged with having disdained the nobility of the realm, as Thomas Cromwell was? (*LP*, XV 498 (60)).

29. G. Walker, *John Skelton and the Politics of the 1520s* (Cambridge, 1988); 'John Skelton, Cardinal Wolsey and the English nobility', in Bernard, *The Tudor Nobility*, pp. 111–33.

30. P. Gwyn, *The King's Cardinal* (1990), pp. 549–98; see Chapter 3 below, pp. 56–7.

31. M.L. Bush, 'The Tudors and the royal race', *History*, clxxxiii (1970), pp. 37–48.

32. See especially *LP*, III i 1283a; cf. Gwyn, *The King's Cardinal*, pp. 159–72.

33. I hope to publish on the Poles at greater length elsewhere.

34. S. Cunningham, 'Henry VII and rebellion in north-eastern England, 1485–1492: bonds of allegiance and the establishment of Tudor authority', *Northern History*, xxxii (1996), pp. 42–74, at p. 47.

35. M.E. James, 'The murder at Cocklodge', *Durham University Journal*, lvii (1964–65), pp. 80–87.

36. Cunningham, 'Bonds', p. 69.

37. Cf. M.J. Bennett, 'Henry VII and the northern rising of 1489', *English Historical Review*, cv (1990), pp. 34–59; M.A. Hicks, 'Dynastic change and northern society: the career of the fourth earl of Northumberland 1470–89', *Northern History*, xiv (1978), pp. 78–107.

38. G.W. Bernard, *War, Taxation and Rebellion in Early Tudor England: Henry VIII, Wolsey and the Amicable Grant of 1525* (Brighton, 1986), pp. 138–40.

39. See for another illustration, G.W. Bernard, 'The fortunes of the Greys, earls of Shrewsbury, earls of Kent, in the early sixteenth century', *Historical Journal*, xxv (1982), pp. 671–85.

40. Gwyn, *King's Cardinal*, pp. 220–25; Hoyle, 'The fall of the House of Percy'.

41. J.A. Youings (ed.), *Devon Monastic Lands, Devon and Cornwall Record Society*, new series i (1955), pp. 4–7; *LP*, XIV i 1354 (12, 13); D. Willen, *John Russell, First Earl of Bedford: One of the King's Men* (1981), pp. 30–31, 62–6.

42. Pace S.G. Ellis, *Tudor Frontiers and Noble Power: the Making of the British State* (Oxford, 1995), a somewhat strained attempt to link disparate themes, esp. pp. ix, 7, 209; idem, 'A crisis of the aristocracy? Frontiers and noble power in the early Tudor state', in J.A. Guy (ed.), *The Tudor Monarchy* (1997), pp. 330–40. See important criticisms by David Loades, *History Today* (August 1996), pp. 58–9.

43. R.W. Hoyle, 'Faction, feud and reconciliation amongst the northern English nobility, 1525–1569', *History*, lxxxiv (1999), pp. 590–613.

44. C. Haigh, *Reformation and Resistance in Tudor Lancashire* (Cambridge, 1975), pp. 103–4.

45. J.R. Dias, 'Politics and Administration in Nottinghamshire and Derbyshire, 1590–1640', University of Oxford D.Phil. thesis (1973), pp. 174, 263, 292–8; W.T. MacCaffrey, 'Talbot and Stanhope: an episode in Elizabethan politics', *Bulletin of the Institute of Historical Research*, xxxiii (1960), pp. 73–85, esp. 85; K.M. Sharpe, 'Crown, parliament and locality: government and communication in early Stuart England', *English Historical Review* ci (1986), p. 332 (reprinted in K. Sharpe, *Politics and Ideas in Early Stuart England* (1989), pp. 182–206); C. Haigh, *Elizabeth I* (1988), pp. 88–9; J.E. Neale, *The Elizabethan House*

of Commons (rev. edn, 1963), pp. 59–63; G.R. Batho, 'Gilbert Talbot, seventh earl of Shrewsbury (1553–1616): the "great and glorious earl"?', *Derbyshire Archaeological Journal* ciii (1973), p. 26; *Historical Manuscripts Commission, Bath, v, Talbot, Dudley and Devereux Papers, 1553–1569* (1980), pp. 103, 108, 110, 111, 115.

46. PRO SP1/110 ff. 67 (*LP*, XI 930).
47. G. Parker, *The Military Revolution: military innovations and the rise of the west 1500–1800* (Cambridge, 1988), pp. 1–2, 7, 10–11, 24, 26–9, 41–5, 57–8, 69, 147; I. Roy, 'England turned Germany? The aftermath of the Civil war in its European context, *Transactions of the Royal Historical Society*, 5th series, xxviii (1978), p. 134; H. Watanabe-O'Kelly, 'Tournaments and their relevance for warfare in the early modern period', *European Studies Quarterly*, xx (1990), pp. 451–63; S.J. Gunn, 'Tournaments and early Tudor chivalry', *History Today* (July 1991); M. Vale, *War and Chivalry: Warfare and Aristocratic Culture in England, France and Burgundy at the End of the Middle Ages* (1981), pp. 104–5, 126, 130, 172, 174; cf. S. Anglo, *TLS*, 25 September 1981, p. 1103.
48. For further discussion see C. Thompson, *The framework of 'The Crisis of the Aristocracy, 1558–1641'* (Wivenhoe, 1986) and *The Counting of Manors: Professor Stone's Reply Confuted* (Wivenhoe, 1990). See also reviews of Stone, *Crisis*, by D.C. Coleman, 'The "Gentry" controversy and the aristocracy in crisis, 1558–1641', *History*, li (1966), pp. 165–78, and J.P. Cooper, *TLS*, 7 April 1966, pp. 285–8.
49. S. Doran, 'The finances of an Elizabethan nobleman and royal servant: a case study of Thomas Radcliffe, 3rd earl of Sussex', *Bulletin of the Institute of Historical Research*, lxi (1988), pp. 286–300.
50. B. Coward, 'A "crisis of the aristocracy" in the sixteenth and seventeenth centuries?', *Northern History*, xviii (1982), pp. 54–77; G.R. Batho, 'The finances of an Elizabethan nobleman: Henry percy, ninth earl of Northumberland (1564–1632)', *Economic History Review*, 2nd series, ix (1956–7), pp. 433–50.
51. Bernard, 'The fortunes of the Greys, earls of Kent, in the early sixteenth century', pp. 671–85.
52. E. Kerridge, 'The movement of rent 1540–1640', *Economic History Review*, 2nd series, vi (1953–54), pp. 17, 24–5, 28.
53. J.C.K. Cornwall, *Wealth and Society in Early Sixteenth-Century England* (1988), pp. 143–4; J.V. Beckett, *The Aristocracy in England 1660–1914* (Oxford, 1986).
54. The following pages are drawn from my *Power of the Early Tudor Nobility*, pp. 185–93.
55. J. Fitzherbert, *Surveyinge* (1539), f. 2.
56. Cf. M.E. James, 'The concept of order and the northern rising, 1569', *Past and Present*, lx (1973), p. 82 (reprinted in *Society, Culture and Politics*, pp. 270–307).
57. S. Reynolds, *An Introduction to the History of English Medieval Towns* (Oxford, 1977), p. 138.
58. Staffordshire Record Office, D (W) 1721/1/10, after p. 434.
59. K.M. Sharpe, 'The earl of Arundel, his circle and the opposition to the duke of Buckingham, 1618–28', in idem, *Faction and Parliament: Essays on Early Stuart history* (Oxford, 1978), pp. 209–45.
60. *Historical Manuscripts Commission, Marquess of Bath*, iv. 109.
61. D.M. Brodie (ed.), *The Tree of Commonwealth: a Treatise Written by Edmund Dudley* (Cambridge, 1948), pp. 88–92; cf. T. Starkey, *Exhortation to unitie and obedience* (rept. Amsterdam, 1973), f. 23v.

62. L. Humfrey, *The Nobles or Nobilitye* (1563), sig. B vi–vi^v.
63. O.H. Hufton, 'Attitudes towards authority in eighteenth-century Languedoc', *Social History*, iii (1978), pp. 281–302.
64. Cf. G.E. Aylmer, 'Caste, ordre (ou statut) et classe dans les permiers temps de l'Angleterre moderne', in R. Mousnier (ed.), *Problemes de stratification sociale* (Paris, 1968), p. 142; S. Anglo, 'The courtier: the renaissance and changing ideals', in A.G. Dickens (ed.), *The Courts of Europe: Politics, Patronage and Royalty 1400–1800* (1977), pp. 34–53, esp. pp. 37–8; C.C. Willard, 'The concept of true nobility at the Burgundian court', *Studies in the Renaissance*, xiv (1967), pp. 33–48.
65. Humfrey, *Of Nobilitye*, dedication.
66. *The Booke of Noblenes*, trans. J. Larke (?1550), sig. A vi (but cf. sig. A ii^v and A iii).
67. T. Elyot, *The Boke named the Gouernour*, ed. H.H.S. Croft (2 vols, 1880), book i esp. chs xiii–xxiii.
68. J. Rastell, *Of Gentylnes and Nobylyte* (repr. Oxford, 1950 for 1949), sig. A vi^v; B i.
69. Dudley, *Tree of Commonwealth*, pp. 81, 88–9.
70. *The Booke of Noblenes*, sig. B i.
71. Humfrey, *Of Nobilitye*, sig. K viii^v; L i.
72. A. Murray, *Reason and Society in the Middle Ages* (Oxford, 1978), pp. 328–9.
73. Dudley, *Tree of Commonwealth*, pp. 81–4.
74. Rastell, *Of Gentylnes*, sig. B i.
75. *The Booke of Noblenes*, sig. B iii^v; cf. Dudley, *Tree of Commonwealth*, pp. 81–4; *The Courtyer of Count Baldessar Castilio*, trans. T. Hoby (1561), sig. C iii^v; Humfrey, *Of Nobilitye*, sig. R v^v.
76. Humfrey, *Of Nobilitye*, sig. B i–ii^v.
77. C.S.L. Davies, *Peace, Print and Protestantism* (1976), pp. 32–3; Humfrey, *Of Nobilitye*, sig. A vii^v–viii.
78. As claimed by Q. Skinner, *The Foundations of Modern Political Thought* (Cambridge, 2 vols, 1979), i. 236–8, 259.
79. E.g. Elyot, *Governor*, p. 14.
80. Humfrey, *Of Nobilitye*, sig. K iv^v; L ii^v.
81. Cf. Murray, *Reason and Society*, pp. 274–5.
82. Humfrey, *Of Nobilitye*, sig. D iv.
83. Fitzherbert, *Surveyinge*, Prologue, f. 1; cf. Elyot, *Governor*, i. 4–5.
84. Dudley, *Tree of Commonwealth*, pp. 90–91.
85. Rastell, *Of Gentylnes*, sig. B iv^v; cf. Genesis, ix. 21–7.
86. J. Cheke, *The Hurt of Sedition: how grievous it is to a common welthe* (1549: 1563 edn cited), sig. B iii–iii^v.
87. Humfrey, *Of Nobilitye*, Dedication, sig. A iv^v.
88. Elyot, *Governor*, ii. 120.
89. Ibid., i. 88–9.
90. Rastell, *Of Gentylnes*, sig. A ii.
91. Cited by J. Strype, *Ecclesiastical Memorials*, ii. app. X p. 65.
92. A. Jouanna, *L'idee de race en France au XVIeme siecle et au debut du XVIIeme siecle (1498–1618)* (Paris, 3 vols, 1976), esp. pp. 1, 19, 113–17, 287; A. Devyver, *Le sang epure: les prejuges de race chez les gentilshommes francais de l'ancien regime (1560–1720)* (Brussels, 1973), esp. chs. 1–3; and for an earlier period J. Martindale, 'The French aristocracy in the early middle ages: a reappraisal', *Past and Present*, lxxv (1977), pp. 4–45.
93. C. Hill, 'The Norman Yoke', in *Puritanism and Revolution* (1958), ch. 3.

94. Elyot, *Governor*, ii. 27–8 (and cf. ii. 186); cf. *The Boke of Noblenes*, sig. A vii; Rastell, *Of Gentylnes*, sig. B i^v.
95. Rastell, *Of Gentylnes*, sig. B iv.
96. M. Dewar (ed.), *A Discourse of the Commonwealth of this Realm of England*, attributed to Thomas Smith (Virginia, 1969), pp. 31, 52.
97. Elyot, *Governor*, ii. 186.
98. Cheke, *Hurt of Sedition*, sig. I i^v; M.E. James, *Family, and Civil Society: a Study of Society, Politics and Mentality in Durham Region 1500–1640* (Oxford, 1974), p. 38.
99. *A Discourse*, p. 84; cf. Rastell, *Of Gentylnes*, sig. C i^v–ii; R.G.A.K. Mertes, 'The secular noble household in medieval England, 1350–1550', University of Edinburgh PhD thesis (1981), pp. 315–16.
100. Humfrey, *Of Nobilitye*, sig. F i; H i; cf. K iii^v–iv.
101. *The Institucion of a gentleman*, sig. C iiii–D i^v.
102. N.B. Harte, 'State control of dress and social change in pre–industrial England', in D.C. Coleman and A.H. John (eds), *Trade, Government and Economy in pre–industrial England: essays presented to F.J. Fisher* (1976), pp. 132–65.
103. E.g. *Tudor Royal Proclamations*, i. nos. 86, 116, 118, 193, 215, 293.
104. Humfrey, *Of Nobilitye*, sig. C vii^v–viii; Rastell, *Of Gentylnes*, sig. C ii^v.
105. J.P. Cooper, 'General introduction', in idem (ed), *New Cambridge Modern History vol. iv. The Decline of Spain and the Thirty Years' War 1609–1648/59* (Cambridge, 1970), pp. 28–9 (reprinted in *Land, Men and Beliefs*, pp. 127–8).
106. G.W. Bernard, 'The rise of Sir William Compton, early Tudor courtier', *English Historical Review*, xcvi (1981), pp. 754–77.
107. E.W. Ives, *The Common Lawyers of Pre-Reformation England: Thomas Kebell: a case study* (Cambridge, 1983), pp. 16, 330–65, 380, 418.
108. F. Billacois, 'La crise de la noblesse europeen (1550–1650): une mise au point', *Revue d'histoire moderne et contemporaine*, xiii (1976), pp. 258–77, esp. 274. Cf. in a different context C.R. Lucas, 'Nobles, bourgeois and the origins of the French Revolution', *Past and Present*, lx (1973), pp. 84–126, and much other research on eighteenth-century French society. Cf. also A.J. Fletcher, *A county community in peace and war: Sussex 1600–1660* (1975), p. 22.
109. M. Wiener, *English culture and the decline of the industrial spirit 1850–1980* (Cambridge, 1981); F.M.L. Thompson, 'The making of the English upper class', paper read at the Institute of Historical Research, University of London, 14 January 1983.

3
The fall of Wolsey reconsidered[1]

In the autumn of 1529 Cardinal Thomas Wolsey, who had served as Henry VIII's principal minister for a decade and a half, fell from power. On 17 October he surrendered the Great Seal, thus formally resigning as Lord Chancellor, the position he had held since 1515. A few days earlier, on 9 October, he had been indicted in the court of King's Bench for offences under the fourteenth-century statute of praemunire (which restricted papal powers within England) and on 22 October he was to acknowledge his guilt in an indenture made with the king. Nevertheless he was not utterly destroyed. He remained Archbishop of York, and was allowed to set off for his diocese in early 1530.

The fashionable explanation for these events is to see Wolsey as the victim of faction, a notion briefly asserted or implied in much current writing, and substantially elaborated by Professor E.W. Ives. For J.J. Scarisbrick, Wolsey was 'the victim of an aristocratic putsch': 'there can be no doubt that for long an aristocratic party, led by the dukes of Norfolk and Suffolk, had been hoping to "catch him in a brake" and dispossess him, and that they looked to Anne Boleyn as their weapon ... it was an aristocratic faction that led the way'. For David Starkey, 'Boleyns, Aragonese, nobles ... sank their fundamental differences and went into allegiance against him. Together they worked on Henry's temporary disillusionment with his minister, and the pressure coupled with Anne's skilful management of her lover, was enough to break the trust of almost twenty years and destroy Wolsey'. John Guy wrote of 'the aristocratic coup which displaced Wolsey as Henry VIII's chief minister' ... 'an aristocratic backlash par excellence'. Christopher Haigh sees Anne Boleyn as scheming with Norfolk, Suffolk and her father against Wolsey, and refers to Wolsey's 'enemies' and 'the aristocratic conspirators and their allies'. For J.S. Block 'Norfolk, together with Charles Brandon, duke of Suffolk and the Boleyn family were [sic] the hub around which turned aristocratic opposition to Cardinal Thomas Wolsey'; 'the moment of truth for the Boleyn faction had arrived'.[2]

But it has, however, been E.W. Ives who has elaborated the notion of Wolsey's downfall as the work of faction in the greatest detail, especially when dealing with the events of 1529. For Ives, 'faction drove Wolsey from office' He sees Wolsey's 'rivals' as forming 'an alliance whose target was an individual' – Wolsey – 'which operated by seeking to put pressure on the ruler' – Henry VIII – 'and which sought to exploit the mechanisms of the court'. Their success was for Ives the culmination of what he sees as long years in which Wolsey's position had never been secure. There had been 'a crisis every year or two' and the pattern of Wolsey's rule was of his 'overcoming substantial opposition from various quarters' in 1515, 1516, 1517, 1519, 1525, 1527. 'The final pressure on Wolsey began in January 1529', Ives claims, 'as a consequence of Anne Boleyn's turning against him'. Ambassadors reported 'that powerful groups were plotting against Wolsey'; 'from New Year 1529, one can see these people chipping away at Wolsey's position'. Then, at the end of July, says Ives, the faction struck against Wolsey – but they failed to persuade Henry until the end of August or early September; even at that point, according to Ives, Henry was reluctant to let his minister go, and ensured that Wolsey's fall ended in a soft landing, losing his position as Lord Chancellor but retaining his archbishopric of York.[3] Ives's argument has been influential. It has recently been described as 'the fullest and ultimately most convincing account of this hotly debated episode'.[4] S.J. Gunn, who earlier in places adopted an interpretation similar to that which will be put forward here, in particular in questioning any view of the duke of Suffolk as the leader of an aristocratic grouping, nonetheless still saw Norfolk, Rochford and Anne Boleyn as joining in clear opposition to Wolsey in late 1528, and wrote of how Norfolk, Suffolk and Rochford grew from critics of the cardinal to 'a clear group of rivals'. And Gunn now appears to endorse Ives's interpretation: 'The chronology of long-drawn-out humiliation ... can most plausibly be explained by the successive waves of pressure on the king from Wolsey's enemies ... We cannot enter Henry's mind at the moment of Wolsey's dismissal to discover conclusively whether it was the king's own frustration at the faltering divorce campaign or the urgings of Wolsey's rivals that contributed more to Henry's decision to break with his minister; but Eric Ives argues strongly that key details of the events of 1529 and even some of the king's own words and actions firmly indicate the latter'.[5]

Ives's argument offers an immediate coherence and it has proved persuasive. It is because his claims have already been so influential that this discussion will concentrate on them, questioning his interpretation and above all his use of evidence. It will follow Ives in examining what happened in 1529 in detail, since no attempt at a factional explanation of the fall of Wolsey can make sense if it fails to account for the events of that year. Further, if the claim of this paper, that the evidence just does not bear out Ives's interpretation, is upheld, then his broader case for faction is seriously undermined. But it is vital first to reiterate the conclusions of other recent work whose thrust is to call into question the factional nature of politics in general during the long period of Wolsey's ascendancy. The most important argument has been to emphasise the leading role played by Henry VIII himself. Wolsey has been presented not as a manipulating politician but as 'the king's cardinal', a tirelessly hard-working and loyal servant of the king. Wolsey was therefore not involved in recurring struggles against those supposedly closer to the king than he was. Courtiers such as Sir William Compton, groom of the stool, were undoubtedly keen on their own enrichment, but there is little sign that they ever influenced policy. The 'expulsion of the minions' in 1519 was not an attempt by an anxious Wolsey to send influential courtiers away from the king but rather an exercise in disciplining and educating boisterous young men at court by entrusting them with significant responsibilities, not least in Calais. Nor did Wolsey face continuing opposition from the nobility. The third duke of Norfolk rather worked closely with him in the government of the realm. John Skelton did not write his satires against Wolsey at the duke's command, as was once supposed. Norfolk was much involved in crucial negotiations with Scotland in 1524. He vigorously pressed the Amicable Grant in Norfolk in 1525; and neither he nor the duke of Suffolk ever attempted to exploit the resistance to the Amicable Grant against the Cardinal. It is thus misleading to present the politics of Wolsey's ascendancy as those of a running battle between Wolsey and his supposed enemies. It would be fairer to see Wolsey, noblemen such as Norfolk and Suffolk, and courtiers and administrators as working together to govern the realm and to serve the king. In such circumstances factional opposition to the king's chief minister would be quite inappropriate, since that would be indirectly to challenge the Crown. And, at the level of those involved in government and royal service (as opposed to tax-payers or those upset by a particular policy), there is little convincing contemporary evidence of any opposition to or criticism of Wolsey while he enjoyed the king's favour during the 1520s.[6]

Why then have other historians taken the notion of faction so seriously? Largely because they have been misled by certain types of sources, especially literary sources and ambassadors' letters, which they have read with too little critical attention but rather accepted unquestioningly at face value. Both literary sources and ambassadors' letters may often prove illuminating, but both risk leading astray those who rely on them too credulously. Literary sources were often written long after the events they claim to describe and their authors might be too readily influenced by stereotypes and the need to tell a dramatic and a moral tale. Ambassadors' letters are undoubtedly one of our most important sources, but they need careful handling, especially when they are reporting gossip about the fluctuating fortunes of politicians and courtiers. What they say cannot be dismissed out of hand, but may not always be true. When ambassadors report what men and women actually did, that may be a safer guide than their remarks about factional plotting, especially when letters written to and by the king and his principal ministers and advisers give a different impression. An example from each of these types of evidence showing how Ives has been misled offers a fruitful point of departure for this study of the politics of 1529.

The literary source is the life of Wolsey written by his gentleman usher,

George Cavendish, on which Ives places much weight in elaborating his interpretation. Yet Cavendish was somewhat wide-eyed in his reactions to political events. What he tells us must be considered sensitively and, in particular, related to the aims and interests of the king, which he tends to neglect. Cavendish treated Wolsey's fall at length. Ives highlights a section in which Cavendish wrote how Henry Norris, chief gentleman of the bedchamber, brought a message from Henry VIII to Wolsey in late October 1529, after Wolsey had been disgraced. Henry had said to Norris that while his dealing with Wolsey might seem ungenerous, 'it is for no displeasure that he beryth you, but oonly to satysfie more *the myndes of some whiche he knowyth be not your frendes* than for any indynacion'.[7] Ives takes this at face value: for him, not only is the story true, but Henry's words should be treated as a sincere expression of his regret that he has had to treat Wolsey harshly in order to satisfy Wolsey's enemies. For Ives, this sentence shows that what Henry had done was 'in part a response to third parties, to ... the political circles of the day'. It proves that Henry was being manipulated. It shows that Henry did not really want to bring Wolsey down: instead he was having 'secret and frendly communication with Wolsey' at the same time as Wolsey was being prosecuted at law.[8] But Ives may simply be following Cavendish in misunderstanding what was happening. If Henry said what Norris, according to Cavendish, said he did, it may well be that Henry was simply wishing to deflect the responsibility for Wolsey's fall away from himself, a very human action, or possibly a shrewd political gesture if Henry wished to retain the option of Wolsey's services in the future. Henry may well have been lying.

Ives has similarly been misled by the inability of an ambassador fully to grasp the role of the king. That weakens Ives's exposition of what he sees as the acceleration of factional pressures on Wolsey in early 1529. Ives makes a good deal of a letter sent by Inigo de Mendoza, the imperial ambassador, on 4 February 1529. Here Mendoza describes how Anne Boleyn had begun to suspect that Wolsey was delaying her marriage with Henry as long as he could for fear of losing his power the moment she became Queen. That suspicion had led her, Mendoza continued, to form an alliance with her father, Thomas Boleyn, Lord Rochford, and the dukes of Norfolk and Suffolk to try to see whether they could jointly ruin the Cardinal. But Ives has not done justice to the whole letter. In a later passage, referring to Henry's desire for an annulment of his marriage to Catherine of Aragon, Mendoza said that he had heard that Henry had pressed so hard on the two legates, Wolsey and Campeggio, to have the queen's case tried in London, that they had sent their secretaries to Rome about the matter. The king was so blind with passion, Mendoza continued, that there was nothing that he would not do or promise in order to obtain his object. Mendoza's letter, read in full, suggests that it was Henry, rather than Anne Boleyn, who was setting the pace in threatening the legates. Wolsey, Mendoza said, was no longer received at court as graciously as before, and now and then the king uttered certain angry words about him. True, Mendoza attributed that to the work of Anne and her friends, though noting that they had made no impression on the king except for these effects. But Mendoza may well have underestimated the independent anger of the king. And even taken at face value, Mendoza's letter makes it quite plain that the initiative was coming from the king. This is no 'dual dynamic' with both monarch and some 'faction' combining against Wolsey: what mattered was the attitude that Henry took.[9] Interestingly, at much the same time the French ambassador, Jean du Bellay, noted that 'monseigneur le legat en est en grant peine, car la chose en est si avant que, si elle ne vient a effect, le roy son maistre, s'en prendra a luy'.[10]

The heart of Ives's argument lies in his portrayal of events in mid-1529. He moves on to argue that 'in June and July they [Anne Boleyn and her allies] had put together a carefully prepared attempt at a coup against Wolsey'. The end of the legatine trial of the marriage between Henry and Catherine of Aragon offered a propitious moment. 'A carefully worked out attack which focused on his [Wolsey's] vulnerability to praemunire was launched against the minister at the end of July'. 'They launched the coup immediately [after the legatine court] only to find Henry unwilling to throw Wolsey to their mercy, and Wolsey adept enough to bribe his way out of trouble'. They wanted, Ives claims, to see Wolsey arrested and interrogated, and a parliament called to deal with him: but, he says, they succeeded only in securing a parliament. 'Their direct assault in July was blocked.'[11]

As a scheme this sounds superficially plausible. But Ives can offer very little evidence for these vital assertions. He cites a number of papers prepared by Thomas Lord Darcy, listing offences allegedly committed by Wolsey.[12] But nothing in them explains their status or just why they were prepared. They are full of very personal grievances, and suggest very little consultation with others. In attempting to construct an elaborate circumstantial case upon Darcy's articles, Ives is building on very uncertain foundations. Moreover in support of his claim that Darcy took the lead against Wolsey by compiling this set of articles, Ives cites a passage in Edward Hall's *Chronicle*. But he curiously misreads it. What Hall wrote was 'when the nobles and prelates perceuied that the kings favour was from the Cardinal sore minished, euery man of the Kynges Counsaill beganne to laye to him suche offences, as they knewe by hym'. That unquestionably means that it was *after* it was clear that Wolsey's standing in the king's eyes had dwindled that the king's councillors began to accuse Wolsey of having committed offences. It is a crucial difference. This passsage from Hall suggests that it was the king who lost confidence in Wolsey and that it was that loss of royal confidence which prompted councillors to criticise him. Hall does *not* say that the councillors launched a coup against Wolsey, nor that they compiled articles which led to the king's losing his trust in Wolsey. Hall's account simply does not support Ives's interpretation; indeed it appears to offer a very different view, of the king taking the initiative and stimulating his councillors into action. In such a climate an aggrieved individual such as Darcy may have put together his own very particular set of complaints: if the chief minister was about to fall, there might be hope of redress. But that hardly makes him a member, let alone a leading member, of a faction.[13] It is conventional for historians at this point to adduce also the complaints made by John Palsgrave, the schoolmaster, against Wolsey, linking them with those drawn up by Darcy, and thus creating an impression of a wave of denunciation of the Cardinal at that time.[14] But Palsgrave's charges were clearly prepared long before 1529. It has been suggested that they must have been written before Wolsey became bishop of Winchester (since that see is not mentioned in a list of his dignities) and before an identifiable captured Scot who is mentioned died in 1528; on that basis *c.* 1526 was proposed, the year in which Palsgrave was dismissed from the duke of Richmond's northern council, which would have given him a grievance. But the text of his notes seems very much a commentary on the specific events of the years 1521 to 1523. That list of Wolsey's dignities offers a further clue. It has Wolsey accepting '... the bishopric of Bath ... and the bishopric of Durham' in a passage that appears to be emphasising his pluralism. Wolsey was bishop of both sees simultaneously for a very short period, between 21 March 1523 and 2 May 1523, when John Clerk was appointed to Bath and Wells. On 15 April 1523 a parliament met. Palsgrave's notes make no explicit mention of a parliament. His references to taxation do, however, seem to fit the circumstances of 1523: he has Wolsey demanding 28 fifteenths (the long-established parliamentary tax, involving a set sum to be paid by each locality every time it was granted, and thus yielding the predictable sum of roughly £29,000 on each occasion), amounting to some £826,000, very close to the £800,000 which Edward Hall says Wolsey sought. These circumstantial details, and the curious form of Palsgrave's notes, prompt the speculative suggestion that they are partly notes of a speech or speeches that Wolsey made in parliament in 1523 justifying his activity as king's minister so far, and partly satirical renderings of those speeches, possibly delivered, but more likely simply Palsgrave's private work. But they have no direct connection with the events of 1529, and particularly with Darcy's charges, despite their placing in the calendar of *Letters and Papers of Henry VIII* adjacent to Darcy's.[15]

In support of his claim that Wolsey's enemies launched a coup against him in the summer of 1529, Ives then cites the duke of Suffolk's protest at the legatine trial. There are three surviving versions of this. According to Cavendish, Suffolk asserted that 'It was neuer ... mery in Englond whilest we had Cardynalles among vs'; according to Hall, Suffolk said 'by the Masse, now I see that the olde saied sawe is true, that there was neuer Legate nor Cardinall, that did good in Englande'; according to Chapuys, the imperial ambassador, Suffolk had declared 'that it was very true what he had always heard say, that never had legate been to the profit of England and that they had not been nor would be anything but evil and damage' ('quil estoit bien vray ce quil avoit tosioures ouy dire que jamays legat ne fust au prouffit dangleterre et quil ny firent ne feroint oncques que mal et dommaige').[16] Much misunderstanding and unprofitable speculation about Suffolk as a proto-Protestant anti-clerical has arisen from the excessively free translation of Chapuys's further comments given in the Calendar of State Papers, Spanish. This has Chapuys say 'I need scarcely observe that if these sentiments of the Duke gain ground with the King and with the people of this country, there will be a door wide open for the Lutheran threat to creep into England'. What Chapuys wrote was simply 'Si cela se demeure voila la porte ouverte pour entrer lutherens' – if things remain like this, here is the door open for Lutherans to enter. The Calendar goes on to refer to 'innumerable people in the country who would follow the Duke's advice'; but once again what Chapuys more modestly said was that 'cuyde quil en y a innumerables que sil navoint autre craincte que de la melediction du Pape seront bien de cest aduis' – there are countless who would be of this opinion if they had no fear other than that of excommunication by the pope.[17] It would thus be mistaken to draw on Chapuys's comments as evidence of Suffolk's opinions as independent of the king's or influencing him; modern historians who have done so have been victims of the mistranslation in the Calendar. Moreover if, as some suppose, Suffolk had indeed been leading a lay anti-clerical attack on Wolsey, one might reasonably expect to find such attitudes reflected in what he said and did later. But there is no evidence that Suffolk at any other time in his life expressed any significant independent views on religion or ecclesiastical organisation, much less any systematic Lutheran or even simply anti-clerical views. His latest biographer describes his religious views as remaining 'on the conservative side of ambiguity'.[18]

That reinforces the argument for seeing him not as a leader of a faction hostile to Wolsey, but as a loyal servant of the king, here executing royal instructions, which is how both Cavendish and Hall present him. In Cavendish's account, Henry went to the legatine court; his learned council called on the legates to pass judgment; Campeggio refused and adjourned the court; 'with that stept forthe the Duke of Suffolk frome the kyng And *by his commaundement* [my italics] spake thes wordes with a straight and hault countenaunce'.[19] According to Hall, Campeggio adjourned the trial till October; reports reached the king, who realised that 'he should then haue no ende' and complained to the dukes of Norfolk and Suffolk, and 'other nobles of his counsaill', how he was delayed; he willed them at the next session to require the legates to make an end of the cause, saying he would accept any judgment they gave. 'The noble menne desired them to make an ende ... but they answered that they could sit no more till October whiche answere sore displeased the noble menne, *whiche the king had sent thether*, in so much that Charles Duke of Suffolke, seeyng the delay, gaue a great clappe on the Table with his hande and said' the words already quoted; and then all the temporall lords 'departed to the King'.[20] Cavendish and Hall both clearly present Suffolk as acting on royal instructions, not independently. That must also dispose of any efforts to shore up the factional interpretation of politics by putting together a 'mixed' model that seeks to combine royal initiative with independent noble-led attacks on Wolsey. Such a model might be thought to be conceptually contradictory: either the king was in charge or he was not, and if he was in charge, then factions would be unlikely, since they would have little chance of success. But its main weakness is that this is not what the evidence shows. None of the sources state that it was criticism of Wolsey by noblemen and courtiers that persuaded a reluctant king to make a fuss; rather, the king is presented as giving them the lead throughout. Ives notes a recent treatment of these events, in which Suffolk is seen as loyally shadowing the king's disenchantment with Wolsey, speaking 'not in terms of passionate personal outrage' but making 'a considered royal statement against papal intransigence'; but Ives rejects this explanation because, he says, 'Henry became disenchanted with Wolsey only in September'.[21] But that is to allow preconceptions based on an interpretation – as we shall see, a misinterpretation – of later events to colour his understanding of this event. And it is worth reflecting on the circumstances of the legatine trial. By late July it was clear that Campeggio would not agree to find for the king, not least given the vigorous and public opposition of Catherine of Aragon. The adjournment of the court was to be expected – and indeed was foreseen by Wolsey, who treated it as a standard practice. Henry could not have imagined that Campeggio would be intimidated by his presence, or by the declaration of Suffolk, into passing judgement for the king. But what took place before the legates was a strikingly theatrical and polemical declaration of the king's purposes. It was a carefully stage-managed royal threat against papal authority in England. And if the anti-legatine sentiments were indeed those of the king, then that would suggest that Henry was seriously annoyed with Wolsey.[22]

Ives, however, believes that what he sees as a factional attack on Wolsey at the end of July did not succeed. He claims that Wolsey bribed his way out of trouble, offering Henry £1200. Such a suggestion suffers from a lack of proportion. If Ives's portrayal of events were correct, then so small a sum could hardly have been expected to deflect the king from giving credence to the complaints that Norfolk and Suffolk were making against Wolsey. Moreover the case for seeing this transaction as a bribe is technically obscure, if not flawed. It was rent due to the king from Wolsey's officers in Durham – Wolsey had been bishop of Durham – which had not been paid on time. Wolsey excused himself and offered various arrangements to make amends, which were complex since the king had granted the sum in question to Lord Rochford. In no sense could this be seen as a bribe.[23] Ives, nonetheless, argues that what he sees as the coup against Wolsey at the end of July failed, suggesting that Wolsey remained in favour with the king. For Ives, the next stage came when Henry and Wolsey differed over foreign policy. The faction opposed to Wolsey seized on Henry's disagreement with Wolsey at the end of August/beginning of

September and cranked up into action once more, achieving much greater, but still not total, success. Ives builds up this speculative edifice upon a letter by the French ambassador, du Bellay, written on 22 October. Du Bellay reported that Wolsey had been dismissed from his residence and that all his goods had been placed in the king's hands. 'Oultre les pilleries dont on le charge et les brouilleries semes par son moyen entre les princes chrestiens, on luy mect encores tant d'aultres choses suz qu'il est du tout affole'. Ives reads that sentence as reflecting the manifold accusations that the faction was making against Wolsey. These, he says, were based on the book of articles drawn up in July, itself based, he adds, on Lord Darcy's careful work. The faction wanted these accusations to be turned into a parliamentary act of attainder against Wolsey: failing that, they would serve as excellent propaganda against him. Du Bellay's letter went on to say that 'ilz prennent pour lese-majeste qu'il ayt guarde la legation plus de dix ans contre les lois du pays'. Ives sees this as a more moderate line of attack against Wolsey – though he does not explain why lese-majesty should be thought a lesser charge than pillaging. Du Bellay continued his report by saying that Wolsey was given the choice 'de respondre devant le Roy ou le parlement'. Ives makes a great issue of this choice. Answering before parliament, meant, according to Ives, answering his factional enemies and dealing with the many accusations against him, while answering before the king meant, according to Ives, responding in King's Bench to what Ives sees as the lesser charge of offences against the law of praemunire. For Ives it is not then surprising that Wolsey should have preferred to submit to the king's mercy rather than to face judges in parliament chosen by the lords, as du Bellay put it. Once more for Ives, the king is resisting the pressures against Wolsey and trying to secure the lesser of the punishments. All this makes far too much of du Bellay's letter, and in particular it introduces categories and motives which are absent from it. This approach oddly minimises the severity of the law of praemunire: it could be argued against Ives that offences against this law were more serious, and carried greater penalties, than the miscellany of charges listed in Lord Darcy's articles, always supposing that it was indeed that list that was brought against Wolsey at this time. Since that list in any case included offences under the law of praemunire, it is even odder to distinguish the general charges from that of praemunire in particular. If praemunire charges were serious, then Ives's case that Henry was being moderate and trying to shield Wolsey from the worst of the factional onslaught collapses. Indeed if Hall's account is correct, then it may have been the king's councillors who informed Henry in October that Wolsey had broken the laws of praemunire and provisors.[24] Although Ives earlier refuses to see Suffolk as acting on royal instructions at the legatine trial, he does see Thomas More, the new Lord Chancellor, as 'deliberately and on instructions, setting out to forestall an attack on the cardinal' in parliament in the following month. Here More is an ally of the king acting against the faction opposed to Wolsey. For this speculation –

that this was a response by the king to 'pressure from Anne and her allies to abandon his lenient treatment of Wolsey' – there is not a shred of evidence. The notion that More – and through him the king – were somehow trying to protect Wolsey does not survive a reading of More's speech to parliament. More's description of Wolsey as 'the great wether which is of late fallen' does not sound like someone trying to limit criticism of Wolsey. And Ives's view of More is inconsistent. Very soon he treats More, as we shall see, as a member of the anti-Wolsey faction.[25]

That faction had not, for Ives, wholly succeeded. Wolsey had been dismissed, but he had not been utterly ruined. What the faction now sought, says Ives, was to secure some public condemnation of and confession by Wolsey so that he could never return to his former position. Here Ives calls as evidence a petition signed by 17 men. He links it with a remark in Hall's *Chronicle* that 'duryng this Parliament was brought doune to the commons, the boke of Articles whiche the Lordes had put to the kyng agaynste the Cardinall'. It seems from the context of Hall's remark that the Lords in question means the House of Lords, but Ives claims that Hall was referring to the lords of the king's council and that this book of articles was the collection of articles first prepared by Lord Darcy in July. That is possible, but there is no direct evidence. The purpose of presenting, or reviving, these articles, says Ives, was 'to extort a confession from Wolsey as the price he had to pay to secure a resolution of his problems'. 'Forcing Wolsey to admit a range of offences against the Crown much wider than anything he had confessed at common law, and drawing that admission to the attention of the Commons, was as near as his enemies could get to such a formal parliamentary censure'. 'The one thing which no desire by Henry to restore his old friend to power could over-ride was a condemnation in parliament'. It is far from clear that this was so, but in any case what Hall's *Chronicle* suggests is that the book of articles was shown to the Commons for information rather than for action.[26] Moreover the signatories of the petition are more of a problem for Ives than he admits. He says that 'the possibility must be that the list of the December signatories is the list of the faction which for at least six months had been trying to bring the cardinal down'. That this is too simple is shown by Ives's almost immediate adjustment: the December list 'is an aggregate of the faction which had failed in July and other groups and individuals who had joined subsequently'. Ives then indulges in speculative ruminations about 'grand faction': 'the coming together of disparate groups and individuals to pursue one single objective – the removal of Wolsey'. Yet the signatories are an odd collection for a faction. Ives himself has just had More as an ally of the king against the faction as late as November. Ives recognises that 'supporters of Anne and Catherine may seem strange bedfellows', and then launches into circumstantial explanations of why Catherine's supporters might have been offended by Wolsey's encouragement of the divorce and supposed leniency towards heretics. Yet instead of seeing this list as a faction, it would make much more sense to see it as a list of all those currently influential in the king's counsels, not then as evidence of the existence of a faction, but rather, and simply, as a list of royal servants. It is difficult to see who was excluded, apart from churchmen, hardly surprising for what was an attack on the church as well as Wolsey. Twelve noblemen signed it: the dukes of Norfolk and Suffolk, the earls of Shrewsbury, Northumberland and Oxford, the marquesses of Exeter and Dorset, and Lords Darcy, Rochford, Mountjoy, Sandys and Fitzwalter. Those noblemen who did not sign, hardly constitute a pro-Wolsey faction. The earls of Derby and Essex were, as was usual, away from court, the earl of Worcester was young, Lord Stafford, son of the third duke of Buckingham, executed for treason in 1521, had yet to recover his family's fortunes. Lords Bergavenny and Lisle are perhaps more surprising absentees yet it is hard to see their omission as politically significant. The remaining signatories were important office-holders: Sir Thomas More, Lord Chancellor; Sir William Fitzwilliam, Treasurer of the Household; Sir Henry Guildford, Comptroller of the Household; Anthony Fitzherbert, Justice of the Common Pleas; and Sir John Fitzjames, Chief Justice of King's Bench. It is difficult to find anyone of comparable standing who was absent. If this is, then, just a list of leading noblemen and office-holders, then yet another piece of evidence cited by Ives in favour of the existence of faction melts away. It is worth comparing this list with that of the witnesses of the grant of 8 December creating Thomas Boleyn, viscount Rochford, Anne Boleyn's father, earl of Wiltshire. Here Archbishop Warham was included. Apart from that the names are very similar: the dukes of Norfolk and Suffolk, the marquesses of Exeter and Dorset, the earls of Oxford and Shrewsbury, and Lords Lisle, Sandys and Bergavenny, from the nobility, and Sir William Fitzwilliam, Sir Henry Guildford from the office-holders. As the list ends with the phrase 'et al' there may have been more. But once again it is difficult to see the presence of Lisle and Bergavenny in this list as any more significant than their absence from the list of signatories of the articles against Wolsey. And it appears ever more probable that witnesses and signatories were simply obtained from as many of the noblemen and leading office-holders as possible: efforts to find political meaning in the composition of such lists are thus searching for something which is not there.[27]

Repeatedly these criticisms of Ives's arguments have alluded to the role of Henry VIII. For Ives, in his study of Wolsey's fall, Henry was a fundamentally weak man, manipulated by factions. His agreement to what a faction wanted was essential, but he was persuadable, and his agreement would be, as it were, the final straw. That picture was amplified in Ives's recent general reflections on 'Henry the Great'. 'The faction battle was endemic, inherent in the realities of kingship, court and royal personality, a never-ceasing groundswell of competition to secure favour, office, wealth and influence'. Ives concedes that 'policy was what the king decided', but argues that 'the object of a faction was … to influence the king as he made his decision and hence to be rewarded with the duty to implement it. Instead of Henry VIII governing according to his own autonomous will, government emerged from the shifting political and individual context around him'.[28] Yet the evidence for the events of 1529 suggests a very different Henry VIII, a king knowing what he wanted, unable immediately to overcome delays and refusals from the papacy, yet preparing the way for more decisive action in the future. It is the purpose of the next section to review the events of 1529, and the fortunes of Wolsey, from the perspective of the king. What this will crucially show is that Ives is mistaken in thinking that Wolsey was still high in the king's favour as late as August 1529,[29] a mistake that fatally weakens his argument and narrative. It will also appear that it was the king, not Anne Boleyn or anyone else, who was taking the lead.

As early as summer 1527 the king's desire for an annulment of his marriage with Catherine of Aragon had created tensions in his relations with Wolsey, which had only been resolved by Wolsey's assiduous efforts to secure the divorce by means of a decretal commission that would enable him to pronounce finally on the matter in England.[30] Tensions remained: in August 1528 the king reportedly used the most terrible language to Wolsey.[31] And by early 1529 it was plain that things were not going well between them. Mendoza, the imperial ambassador, reported in January that the king was beginning to inculpate the cardinal, who, the king said, did not fulfil his promises.[32] A fortnight later (in a letter already discussed above, since Ives sees it as evidence of the emergence of a faction), Mendoza noted that Wolsey was not being received by the king as graciously as before, and that now and then the king uttered certain angry words about him. Moreover the king had pressed the legates very hard to have the queen's case tried in London. The king was so blind with passion that there was nothing he would not do to obtain his object.[33] Henry was becoming impatient and angry at the delay in securing his divorce, and he was beginning to blame Wolsey. At much the same time du Bellay, the French ambassador, picked up a similar report: Wolsey was in great difficulty, the matter had gone so far that if it did not take effect – that is, if there was no annulment – the king would fall out with him.[34] In the light of such evidence, it is hard to agree with Ives that it was not until the end of August that Henry lost confidence in Wolsey.

Moreover Wolsey's position did not improve. In these early months of 1529 Henry received repeated reports from Rome that his cause was increasingly hopeless. Many of Henry's agents cast doubt upon the loyalty of Cardinal Campeggio. At first sight that might not seem greatly to affect Wolsey's position. But Campeggio's agreement would be indispensable if Wolsey and he were jointly to pronounce on the king's marriage. Doubts about Campeggio's reliability cast a shadow over Wolsey, not least since the broad plan of having the matter resolved by the two legates was one to which Wolsey was deeply committed.[35] On 9 January Francis Bryan, whom the king had sent to Italy, reported his encounter with Governor Umberto de Gambara of Bolgona: who 'sware many grett othes, that and yf he were in my Lord legates place, he wold have gevyn jugement on your syde long or thys tyme; and also he sayd, he marvalys, why that my sayd Lordes legattes dud not geve jugement with Your Grace, for he sware to me that he knew well that they had commyssyon of the Pope to juge your cause; and furthar he sayd, that whatsoever they dyd juge for Your Grace, that he was sure the Pope wold afferme yt'. This is just what Henry would have wanted the legates to do. It is worth noting that Bryan was very much the king's diplomat, writing to the king as well as to Wolsey. Moreover he was clearly working at the king's command, not at Anne Boleyn's. Any suggestion that Anne was influencing the king's actions not just in the general sense that he was passionately in love with her, but in the more specific sense of directing day-to-day policy in response to news from Rome, is undermined by Bryan's closing remarks, at the end of a pessimistic letter: 'sir I wold have wryttyn to my mystres that shalbe [i.e. Anne] but I wyll not wryte unto hyr, tyll I may wryte that shall plese hyr most in this worlde'. Bryan manifestly saw Henry, not Anne, as in charge.[36] On 26 January Bryan wrote directly to Henry expressing further doubts about Campeggio: 'and, Sir, yt ys here in every mannys mowthe, that Cardynal Camegyus ys, hart body and sowle, good Imperyall, and that men recon, for your purpose, ther could not have ben sent a wors'. The pope was and would remain 'good Imperyall'.[37]

In late March Stephen Gardiner's letter to the king, significantly more pessimistic than that sent at the same time to Wolsey, arrived; Bryan wrote at the same time saying that the pope would do little for the king.[38] It may have been in response to these letters that Henry berated Campeggio, as Campeggio reported in early April: the king, he wrote, seemingly sympathised with Lutheran-inspired attacks on church property in Germany and criticised wickedness at Rome.[39] It is worth remarking on the independent and vigorous action of the king. Meanwhile Bryan once more wrote ominously and pessimistically to Henry. He and Henry's agents in Rome, Gardiner, Peter Vannes and Casale, had done as much as they thought could be done; but the king would see clearly that the pope would do nothing for him. Ominously Bryan added, 'and who so ever hath made Your Grace beleve, that He wold do for You in thys cause, hath not, as I thynke, doone Your Grace the best servyce'. Bryan added how sorry he was to write such news, 'but yf I shuld not wryte thys, I shuld not do my dewtye. I wold to God my former letter myght have ben lyes, but I feryd ever thys ende'. It is not clear whether Bryan's target was Campeggio or Wolsey: it seems more probable that it was Campeggio. Interestingly again for any assessment of Anne Boleyn's role, Bryan, adding that he was writing 'to my cosyn Anne', told the king that 'I dare not wryte to hyr the trauthe of thys, bycause I do not know, whether Your Grace wylbe contentyd that she shuld know hyt so shortly or no; but I have sayd to hyr in my letter, that I am sure Your Grace wyll make hyr prvvy to all our newys' – although Bryan had, of course, made it possible for the king to hide the bad news from her if he wished.[40] Probably before he received this letter Henry had written to Bryan defending Campeggio against earlier warnings. In early May Bryan responded by telling Henry bluntly, 'and where as Your Grace wrytys unto us, that the Cardinall Camegges says he ys your sarvant, and that he wyll do for Your Grace in all thynges; Sir, hys fayre wordys that he says to Your grace ys, bycause he wold have the Bysshopryke of D[urham]'. Bryan assured Henry that Campeggio 'hath wrytten hether to the pope, that he ... neuer promysed nothyng to Your Grace particularly, but in generall wordys, and byddys the Pope trust therto, for he never dyd nor never wyll doo, and bad the pope styke fast Hym self, for of hym he sayd he shuld be sure. Sir, all that ys tolde You there, that the pope wyll doo for your Grace yn thys cause, I insure you they tell you the glosse, and not the texte'. Again Bryan did not wish to write directly to Anne: 'I dare not wryte vnto my cosyn Anne the trawthe of thys matter, bycause I do not knowe Your Graces plesur, whether I shall so doo or noo'.[41] Once more Bryan's care in allowing Henry to keep Anne in the dark if he so chose is highly suggestive about the limited extent of Anne's influence. Clearly, but for Anne, there would have been no efforts to secure a divorce from 1527, and therefore the fact of Henry's passion for Anne was crucial. But it does not follow from that that Anne influenced the policies and procedures of the campaign for the divorce. There is very little evidence that could be adduced in support of any such claims, and Bryan's letters on the contrary rather strongly suggest that she played little independent part in suggesting ways of pursuing the divorce. And it would be hard to show that Anne came to suspect Wolsey before the king did and that she influenced him against the Cardinal. Henry's increasing doubts about Wolsey may well have emerged rather from his growing concern over Campeggio.

For at some point Bryan also told the king how Francis I, king of France, had cast doubt upon Campeggio's loyalty. Francis had asked Bryan about the progress of Henry's divorce, and added 'well, there be somme, that the King my brother doeth trust in that matier, that wold it shuld never take effect', intending Campeggio, it seems, a deduction that Francis had apparently made from his conversation with Campeggio when that legate had been on his way to England in autumn 1528. Our knowledge of Bryan's report comes not from any surviving letter from Bryan, but from the account that the duke of Suffolk gave of the 'secrete charge' Henry VIII had given him in May 1529. By then Henry was becoming increasingly suspicious of Campeggio and sent Suffolk to pursue Bryan's report directly with Francis I. Francis confirmed what he had told Bryan. What happened next shows that Henry VIII had begun to mistrust not just Campeggio but Thomas Wolsey. Suffolk, after asking Francis about Campeggio, went on, astonishingly, to ask Francis's opinion about Wolsey's devotion to the king's cause. Francis was opaque. When he had seen Wolsey,

> as farr as I could perceyve in hym, he wold the devorce shuld goo furth and take effect, for he loved not the Quene. But I will speke frankly ... as He that no lesse entendith in his good mynd and hert the avauncement of the Kinges good purpos in this matier than he doith hym self. Myn advyse shalbe to my good brother, that he

shall have good regarde, and not to put so moche trust in no man, wherby He may be disceyved, as nigh as He can. And the best remedy for the defence therof is to loke substauncyally upon his matiers Hym self, as I here say He doithe, whiche I am not a litell glad of.

Francis went on, Suffolk added, to say that Wolsey 'had a mervelous intelligence with the Pope, and in Rome, and also with the Cardinal Campegius. Wherfor, seyng that he hath such intelligence with theym, whiche have not mynded to advaunce your matier, He thinketh it shal be the more nede for Your Grace to have the better regarde to your said affeyre'. In effect Francis was reinforcing the suspicion which was already in Henry's mind and which had prompted him to send Suffolk to consult with the French king. There is no sign that Suffolk was here acting independently or as a leader of a faction; he wrote regularly to Henry (only once to Wolsey, whom he assumed that the king would make privy to the letters he wrote direct to the king) and he began his crucial report of his interview with Francis by referring to the 'secrete charge that Your Grace gaue me in commaundement to disclose unto Hym'.[42]

Wolsey found out about all this - most likely, as he said, from the French ambassador. He complained to the king that Suffolk had put him out of favour with Francis by some of his conversations. In front of Wolsey, the king asked Suffolk if it were true; Suffolk said he had not spoken of it. But Suffolk, we know, *had* indeed spoken of it and, in a letter to Henry, said that he had done so at Henry's bidding. It is difficult to avoid concluding that here Henry and Suffolk deliberately staged this scene together to deceive Wolsey.[43]

It was becoming abundantly clear that Cardinal Campeggio would not settle the king's matter in England, and in particular would not allow the legatine trial which opened in May to pronounce in the king's favour. Moreover it was increasingly likely that the next stage would be the advocation – or transfer – of the case to Rome. That prospect was anathema to the king. In late June and July his servants did all they could to make it plain to the pope what the consequences of such an advocation would be. Their threats have not received the attention they deserve in any discussion of Wolsey's fall. They strongly suggested that it would be Wolsey who would pay the price of papal refusal to satisfy the king.

On 22 June Wolsey wrote to Vannes and Casale that 'ye may constantly affirme vnto hys holynes that if he shuld at any personnys persute graunt the seid advocacion he shuld not oonly therby lose the king and devocion of the Realme from hym and the see apostolique but also vtturly distrowe me for euer'.[44] Of course this could be taken as mere bluster, but it is worth pausing to note that the destruction of Wolsey and, ultimately, the break with Rome did indeed ensue after the advocation. A few days later Wolsey warned Casale that the advocation of the case would cause his ruin: it would risk losing the king, and depriving Wolsey of his authority, reputation and, indeed, his very life.[45] On 25 June Stephen Gardiner, back in England, wrote to Vannes on similar lines.

'This advocation of the cause is gretly pondred and considred here, not oonly with the Kinges Grace, but also with al other nobles of the realme: for in cace the Pope, as God forbydde, shulde advocate the said cause, not only therby the Kinges Grace and al his nobles shulde decline from the Pope and See Apostolique, but also the same shulde redounde to my Lord Cardinalles, our common masters, utter undoing'.[46] Once again it might be noted that these threats proved not idle but prophetic. On 9 July Benet and Casale, in Rome, reported to Wolsey how they had showed the pope the scandal and ruin which the advocation would cause: 'immensa et manifesta scandala, ingens dedecus summam infamiam, excidiumqr irreparabile ...'.[47] On the same day Benet, writing alone, gave Wolsey a longer account of his meeting with the pope. Benet had spoken directly to Clement, warning him that Wolsey

> most humblely besought hys holines to beleve thes vndowztly to folowe that yff hys holynes schuld at the labors of the cesarians advoke the cause he schuld not alonly to offend the kynges hyznes whych hetherto hathe byn a stay a help and a defens of the see apostolike but also by reason of this inuiry without remedy shal alienat hys maiesty and royuame with other from the deuocion and obediens of the see apostolique. Thys I shewed hys holynes that yor grace dothe evidently perceve to folowe yn case hys holynes shuld inclyne to the cesarians desyre on thys behalfe; ye furdor I seyd that yor grace most clerly perceveth also by that acte the churche of yngland vtterly to be dystroyed and lykewyse yor person. And that thes yor grace with wepyng teres most lamentablely committed vnto me to schew to hus holynes.[48]

Once more the pope was being warned that the advocation would lead to the alienation of the king and his kingdom from Rome, and to the destruction of the church of England and of Wolsey's person. And the picture of Wolsey most lamentably and 'with wepyng teres' instructing Benet to show all this to the pope reinforces the claim that these were substantial, not empty, threats, not least since they succinctly state what was in fact to happen. A few days later Benet, Casale and Vannes reported that they had left nothing undone to warn the pope of the dangers that any advocation would provoke: 'scandalum tumultum infamiam quie ex hac aduocatione proueniret assidue declaramimus ecclesiae ruinam iacturam et regni Angliae at Franciae'.[49] Wolsey repeated his warnings when writing to Benet, Casale and Vannes on 27 July. The king was resigned to the advocation. Rather than 'thus to stand contynually in the suspence and doubte of the said advocacion ... it hath ben thought convenient to studie and excogitate some other waies and meenes here for remedy of the Kinges cause ... better it shall be to begin betimes to the experimenting and actual execution of the said other waies and meanes'. As for any advocation, which would involve the citation of the king to the court of Rome, under pain of interdiction and excommunication, 'the dignitie and prerogative roiall of the Kinges crowne, wherunto al the nobles and subgettes of this Realme wol adhere and strike to the deth, may not tollerate nor suffer that the same be obeid'. If the king ever came to the court of Rome, 'he would do the same with suche a mayne and army roial, as should be formidable to the Pope and al Italy'. To summon the king to the court of Rome was 'no more tollerable than the hole amission of his said astate and dignitie roial, and that may ye wel assure the Pope'. If the Pope could not satisfy the king, and that quickly, 'surely ye see not but it wolbe a meane to aliene this Realme from the obedience of that See'.[50] Wolsey's warning that Henry might break with Rome and seek other means of gaining his divorce could hardly be more plainly expressed. And that Wolsey might himself prove to be a victim of such alternative methods was confirmed by Catherine of Aragon who, according to Mendoza, had written that the king's disappointment and passion at not being able to carry out his purpose were such that the Cardinal would inevitably be the victim of his rage.[51]

All this shows that Henry was losing confidence in the ability of Wolsey to secure his divorce, and that well before the adjournment of the legatine trial at the end of July. It is worth noting that Wolsey repeatedly saw his own destruction as a consequence of the advocation of the divorce to Rome. Wolsey never spoke of any faction or any rivals or any opponents in England; he would rather be a victim of the king's anger at the pope's unwillingness or inability to grant Henry the divorce.

It is clear that Wolsey's position as the king's chief minister was already undermined by the end of July. Yet Ives persists in seeing relations as rosy throughout August. Indeed it is central to his interpretation that 'Henry became disenchanted with Wolsey only in September'. 'Correspondence between Henry and Wolsey after Blackfriars [that is, end of July] shows *no sign of strain* [my italics]: Henry expresses recognition and approval of Wolsey's efforts; as late as 28 August Henry sought prior confidential advice from the cardinal before broaching diplomatic matters to the council'. 'It was a month later [that is, one month after the end of the legatine trial] before the king lost confidence in him – and that as a result of the cardinal's miscalculation of the diplomatic priorities' when Wolsey pointed out the bad faith of the French.[52] Yet, quite apart from the compelling evidence that Wolsey's position was already weakened before the summer, Ives's claims here show a fundamental misunderstanding of what the letters to and from Wolsey in August and September reveal.

It is striking that Wolsey was no longer in charge of business. The last payment 'by my lord Cardinal's warrant' recorded in the Treasurer of the Chamber's accounts is dated 18 July. The last surviving letter Wolsey wrote to English diplomats abroad is dated 27 July; there is nothing later, and no reference to anything later in letters that English agents sent from abroad. It is true that Wolsey was consulted by the king on several points, but that is very different from his former co-ordinating and directing role. Wolsey was throughout reacting to specific requests for advice: he was never acting on his own initiative.[53] There is a new and anxious humility of tone in his letters, as he offered the king what he repeatedly described as 'my poore opinion'.[54]

Wolsey no longer saw ambassadors as quickly and as regularly as he had previously done. Towards the end of August Guillaume du Bellay and Langey (who had served as link between Francis I and his mother in the negotiations that had led to the treaty of Cambrai) arrived from France, to join Jean du Bellay, in order to secure from Henry VIII various letters, deeds and securities relating to the emperor's debt to Henry in 1522.[55] But it was a long time before they met Wolsey. That was a marked departure from past practice. Jean du Bellay had seen Wolsey 'longuement' on his arrival in England in May; Wolsey had similarly met Johann le Sauch, Margaret's ambassador, in June.[56] But in August Wolsey was no longer involved. He did not meet the new imperial ambassador, Eustace Chapuys, who arrived at the end of August. Chapuys indeed remarked in his first despatch, on 1 September, that 'le roy de quelque temps en sa n'a permis que l'on s'adresse a luy, ne les ambassadeurs ausy'.[57] Not till mid-September did du Bellay see Wolsey again.[58] Wolsey was clearly no longer the chief minister he had been.

It is also more likely than not that Henry deliberately avoided seeing Wolsey. Ives (following Neil Samman's thesis) disagrees,[59] but the evidence does not bear him out. At first, it appears that Henry was indeed preparing to meet his minister. On 1 August Gardiner informed Wolsey that Master Treasurer [Brian Tuke] 'moved the kinges highnes howe yor grace is mynded to receyve him and his trayne at the More and defraye his charges wherewith his highnes was wel content'.[60] But on 4 August Gardiner wrote that where Wolsey in his recent letter had said 'howe glad ye wolde be to receyve the kinges highnes at the More', the king responded that 'synnes his determination to go thither he was aduertised howe at Rikemansworth and other townes aboute the more certain this yere and of late have had the swet [the sweating sickness] the oonly name and voyce wherof is so terrible and fearful in his hignes eeres that he dare in noowise approche vnto the place where it is noysed to have been and therfor his highnes wil not goo thither but in the stede of that goo to Titennehanger and take suche chere of yor grace there as he shuld haue had at the More mynding according to his former gists [travelling plans] to departe from Barnet vpon Saterday come sevenight and after dyner to goo that night to Titenhanger and there to be Sondaye al daye and Monday after brekefast to departe'.

Ives reads this as meaning that Henry was in no way fobbing Wolsey off, simply rearranging their meeting to take place at Wolsey's house at Tittenhanger, rather than The More. But Gardiner continued that he told the king he thought Tittenhanger 'to lytel to receyve his highnes wherunto his highnes answred that yor grace as he doubted not ye woold removing for the tyme with yor company to Saynt Albuns it shulde serue for the which he wolde tary there'. In other words, while Henry was indeed intending to come to Wolsey's residence at Tittenhanger, he trusted that Wolsey would go away with his servants to St Albans. The offhand tone, and the presumption that not just

Wolsey's servants but Wolsey himself would move – 'yor grace ... removing for the tyme with yor company' – are deeply revealing. Henry was quite clearly not intending to see Wolsey.[61] The sources cited by Samman, on whom Ives relies to show that he did, fail to substantiate that claim. Samman refers to three documents. The first is a letter from the earl of Northumberland acknowledging receipt of a letter from Wolsey dated 14 August at Tittenhanger.[62] But since the king was intending to arrive there after dinner, that letter could easily have been written earlier in the day, not least since it was a response to instructions from the king sent two days earlier,[63] and it does not in itself prove that Henry and Wolsey were together at Tittenhanger on 14 August. The second is a grant issued under the Great Seal, that is by Cardinal Wolsey as Lord Chancellor, dated 16 August at Tittenhanger.[64] But Henry could easily have left as planned after breakfast that day, and such a grant could have been drawn up later, after his departure, It does not in itself prove that the two men met. Finally Samman cites the comptroller's accounts. These record various payments made at Tittenhanger on 14 and 15 August. The payments for 16 August were made at Woburn. But they do not state that Henry was present, much less that he met Wolsey.[65] There is then no definite evidence that any meeting took place at Tittenhanger. Moreover Gardiner's earlier letter to Wolsey from Barnet on 12 August, conveying the king's decision about the Scottish nobleman the earl of Angus who was on the point of returning to Scotland, gives not the slightest hint that a meeting between Henry and Wolsey would be taking place in two days time.[66] It is of course quite likely that Henry did go to Tittenhanger. Apart from the expenditure recorded in the comptroller's account, there is Wolsey's later reference, not noted by Samman, to 'soch determinacion as was taken at the kinges highnes being at Tytynhanger', according to which Wolsey later had a long discussion with John Clerk, bishop of Bath and Wells, about the papal advocation of the divorce. It would be possible to see this as showing that Henry and Wolsey met then, but that is not a necessary reading. Wolsey does not say that he was present: indeed the somewhat impersonal rendering hints that this was a decision to which he was not a party.[67] The evidence, then, is patchy, yet there is nothing at all definite to confirm the claim that Henry met Wolsey at Tittenhanger, but rather some circumstantial detail which suggests that he did not.

Wolsey's continuing eagerness to meet the king appears in his response to a letter from Gardiner dated 30 August: Wolsey ended his reply 'yf my comyng thether may any thyng further the kinges highnes vpon knowlege of hys graces pleasure I shall not fayle with good hert and diligence to repair thither as well to see and vysyt his grace as also to provide my poor cownsell for the ... oof his affeyre somoche as may ...'.[68] That proved unavailing. A little later Wolsey, according to Gardiner's reply, had written that he had certain things to show to the king 'which Your Grace thinkith [not] convenient to be committed to wrytyng'. Wolsey, evidently desperate to see the king, had declined to set out his opinions in writing, but asked to come in person. But Henry clearly did not want to see Wolsey: and reacted strongly, almost brutally, instructing Gardiner to tell Wolsey to set down whatever he wanted to say in writing:

> I as [sure] your Grace that at the reding therof His Hig[nes] semed to me somwhat altered and moved after su[che] sorte as the obscure signifie of newes, appering be [...] of importaunce doth require. Whereupon His Highnes, as in that seire of further knowlege, troubled, et frustra tamen conjiciens, what it is that Your Grace, the weyes being sure, and without feare of interception, shuld, that notwithstanding, not thinke convenient to be put in wryting; knowing also right wel, that Your Grace is not wont to spare any labours paynes in wryting, whenne the case soo requiring; musing and merveling, therfor, more and more, what the matier shulde be; willed me [to send his servant to Wolsey with all haste] to desire Your Grace incontinently, by letters of Your Graces owne hande, to be directed unto his Highnes handes [to tell Henry what was in his mind].[69]

Not until about 19 September did Wolsey see the king again, on the occasion of Campeggio's formal leave-taking.[70] Chapuys, the imperial ambassador, noted how the king had not wished to see Wolsey and how it was only thanks to Campeggio that he had been able to obtain that permission.[71] That Henry should throughout August and September have been so reluctant to see Wolsey casts doubt on Ives's claims that their relations remained good.

Wolsey was evidently concerned that Gardiner was not doing the best for him. On 29 August Brian Tuke, evidently responding to doubts expressed by Wolsey, wrote that in his communications with Gardiner 'I assure yor grace I founde hym suche on as towardes yor grace he shulde be and a man neither mynded to medle with many thinges but to deal with one thing suche as he shal fortune to be appointed vnto, ne mynded to write more in his letters to yor grace then shal be to the purpose thinking that like a wise man to be the best way'.[72] Gardiner was a little offhand with Wolsey; on 30 August he acknowledged Bonner's arrival with Wolsey's opinions: 'wherin me semith Your Grace hath taken very excessive paynes and laboures, with gret study, and busynes of mynde, to depech so moch matier by writing, and instructions, in soo lytel tyme'. Gardiner would inform the king, but 'for spedy speking with the King, and to speke at laysure, I reckenne gret difficulte; and as for this night I am ought of hope, by reason the Kinges Highnes is out on hunting and usith, as Your Grace knoweth, to cumme in very late'.[73]

If Henry no longer wanted to see Wolsey and if Wolsey was no longer running business, why then was he not dismissed immediately? The explanation is that Wolsey could still perform useful service to the king. On technical matters relating to the divorce and to foreign policy, his actions and advice remained valuable.

Wolsey was needed to persuade his fellow Cardinal Campeggio to keep secret what he had learned about the king's great matter. Henry was very concerned that Campeggio might reveal matters relating to the divorce.

Campeggio had offered the king a pollicitation – a promise, but not a binding promise – not to tell the pope the king's secrets.[74] Wolsey was asked to find out from Campeggio just how much he had already told the pope.[75] Wolsey was also engaged in working out how Catherine of Aragon could be restrained from making matters worse for the king. But he was acting under instructions, as his assurance to Gardiner makes clear: 'For as hys grace by the aduyse of hys councell there shall thynke best to be don and shall most aduayalles and agreable to hys plasure so shall I endeavour mysaelf to persuade the legat and such of the quenes cownsell...'.[76] The king asked him to cajole Campeggio into restraining Catherine of Aragon: the 'kinges highnes desirith your grace to instruct Campegius what wordes he shal use to the q[ueen] moving and persuading her to be content to procure such thing be comprised in the said aduocation irritate the kinges highnes and his nobles'.[77]

Wolsey would later use 'all meanes and persuasions that I can imagyn' to persuade Campeggio to persuade the queen.[78] Wolsey also discussed with John Clerk, bishop of Bath and Wells, and a member of the queen's council, what advice he should give her on how to proceed. As the king had never taken part as an aggrieved party, but all had been done ex officio, he argued that the queen on her side should also not 'make a partie' against the king: she should be content 'no ferder to procede ne processe in the cowrt of Rome ... to successe and forbere for hir harte'. But, as Wolsey acknowledged, the queen listened more to strangers and imperials than to any of her English council. Clerk agreed to do all he could to persuade her not to take the matter further. Wolsey had made plain to Clerk 'the great daunger that maye ensue and arrise to the quene and hir cownsellors in case the king shuld be cyted or any processe made against his highnes in the court of Rome'. Clerk said that if the queen were wilful he would not remain on her council.[79] At this point Wolsey saw 'ryght good hope and apparaunce that the quene wilbe inducyd to good conformyte'.[80] Later Wolsey was joined by other members of the queen's council. But it was clear to them that the queen would not agree – and in any event the matter was soon taken out of her hands by the pope. Wolsey was also asked for advice over the papal inhibition or 'letters citatorial' preventing the matter from being dealt with further in England. Wolsey offered suggestions which the king found 'very pleasaunt, agreeable, and acceptable' and for which he sent his 'most harty thankes'. Henry 'having great trust and confidence in Your Graces dexteritie and [...], doubteth not but that Your Grace, by good handeling [of the] Cardinal Campegius, and the Quenes Counsail, ... the execution of those letters citatorial, also on your [...], and to cause them to be content the same inbition [be] doon and executed by vertue of the Popes [brief] to Your Grace'.[81] Wolsey accordingly here again worked with Campeggio and Clerk: but Clerk feared what he termed the queen's stiff heart.[82] Once again Gardiner, on 7 September, reported the king's 'most harty thankes for your laboures and paynes taken in that behaulf'.[83] Again Gardiner the next day wrote how the king 'liketh very wel your graces diuise for superseding the cause and desireth moch that the same be brought to effecte with al diligence possible if the quene canne be induced therunto wherin his highnes hath gret confidence in the high wisedom and dexterite of yor grace soo to worke with her counsail as nothing further thenne is alredy by yor grace diuised shalbe by the quene desired in that behaulf'. It would be better for the inhibition to be privately executed on Wolsey and Campeggio – as Wolsey seemed to have suggested – than to be publicly proclaimed in Flanders.[84] And a little later Gardiner again sent on Henry's most hearty thanks for Wolsey's 'dexteryte' in persuading the queen's council to be content with the exhibition of the brief directed to Wolsey, rather than the letters citatorial. The king trusted that Wolsey had arranged matters so that if Catherine wanted to go back on what she now seemed to be accepting, it would no longer be possible for her to do so.[85] Wolsey was thus performing important technical tasks for the king, for which his diplomatic skills and knowledge of canon law were very useful. But it is important to note the limits of Wolsey's role. He did not initiate policy. He was engaged in what was very much a matter of 'damage limitation', in which the English were trying to prevent, or to anticipate, actions taken by others, whether Catherine of Aragon and her advisers, or the pope; it was very unlikely that Wolsey would be able to achieve any significant advantages for the king. Wolsey's expertise and his position made his advice, for the time being, indispensable for the king. But it is hard to avoid concluding that he was being 'used' by Henry.

As well as the divorce, Wolsey was also needed by the king for matters of foreign policy. In these weeks Wolsey was asked for his opinion on a number of technical issues relating to the peace made between the French and the imperialists at Cambrai in early August. These demand attention since Ives has claimed that 'Wolsey ... continued to manage English diplomacy during the month of August' and that 'the king lost confidence in him ... as a result of the cardinal's miscalculation of the diplomatic priorities' that Henry's need for a divorce imposed.[86]

Wolsey was certainly consulted by the king, but that was not the same as managing English diplomacy. Much of what Wolsey was asked to comment on was highly specific. For example, Francis I had agreed, at Cambrai, to pay Charles V's debts to Henry VIII. Wolsey offered detailed suggestions on the timing and rate of such payments. In particular, where the English were being asked for the delivery of the obligation of indemnity, and acquittances, to the Emperor, Wolsey thought some sticking should be made at that: this would at least stop the French asking for any delays. Wolsey's advice, like the issue, was technical.[87]

Another complex issue on which Wolsey was asked by the king for his opinion was whether, if the Emperor did not ratify the peace with Francis, Henry should then demand the ratification of the peace he had concluded with the Emperor. Wolsey thought that Henry was bound to accept it, given that the peace between the king and the Emperor was a particular thing done and concluded apart. But Wolsey had no doubt that the Emperor would ratify the treaty agreed at Cambrai since it was so favourable to him: it was more to be feared that the Emperor would stick at ratifying the treaty with Henry.[88] The king asked Gardiner to give Wolsey 'his most herty thankes for your gret paynes and labours, taken in ansueryng, with such diligence, to the articles proponed by the french Oratours, wherin His Highnes thinketh Your Grace hath considred asmoch as coulde be excogitate and imagined'. But where Wolsey had voiced his doubts about the likelihood of the French keeping their promises, and had at first made the king rather uneasy, Henry, after examining the earlier Treaty of Madrid, had reassured himself that Wolsey's fears were exaggerated. As for that part of his instructions where Wolsey

> semethe to suspecte sumwhat of the French men, and impute unto them the not obseruation of their convenauntes agred upon at Amiens, touching the qualification of the treatie of Madryl; the Kinges Highnes, moch moved therwith, and adhering to Your Graces opinion in that behaulf, was moch kindled, and waxed warme, and thought himself not wel handled by them; in such sorte, as not spekyng with me, willed my Lorde Rocheforde to send for me, and to examine the treatie of Madryl with Your Graces instructions; which we dyd, and this mornyng, had moch reasonyng with His Highnes in that behaulf. Neuertheles, at the laste, it appered unto his Highnes, the treatie of Madyryl, without that qualification divised by Your Grace, not to be soo daungerous, as your Grace had noted it, in al poyntes.

Benet would elaborate further.[89] Later Gardiner reported to Wolsey that the king 'ensuyng partely such advise as Your Grace wrote unto him, and partely his owne opinion, and other of his Counsail, hath geven answer to Monsr de Langes' [the French negotiator]. Ives misreads these letters when he claims that it was Rochford and Gardiner who 'persuaded the king that the cardinal had misled him'. This misrepresents Henry's leading role, and the essentially technical nature of the matter under consideration; the claim that Rochford and Gardiner 'persuaded the king' is entirely speculative.[90]

Wolsey then was again being consulted on points of detail, and expressing opinions on more substantial issues, notably the trustworthiness of the French. His advice was not, however, in the end accepted by the king, as Gardiner's letter showed. It is striking that Wolsey's advice was sought by correspondence only: Wolsey's repeated offers of giving his opinions in person were not taken up. But it is also vital to note that, contrary to the impression given by Ives, there was no sudden breach between Henry and Wolsey as a result of the opinions expressed by the Cardinal. The king did not irrevocably break with Wolsey because Wolsey took a different view about the treaty of Cambrai and trusted the French less than Henry did. That was a disagreement about the interpretation of past treaties and a disagreement about the reliability of French promises. But it was not the sort of rift that could explain the dismissal of a minister. There was no violent argument. Henry's rejection of Wolsey's advice on this point did not stop the king seeking and approving Wolsey's advice on how the advocation of the divorce case should be handled. Henry did not cast Wolsey aside because of differences over foreign policy.[91] Indeed it was after that disagreement that Henry finally allowed the French ambassadors to see Wolsey;[92] would Henry have despatched the ambassadors to Wolsey if he was as displeased with Wolsey's line on the peace of Cambrai as Ives claims?[93] But however much he sought Wolsey's advice on the divorce and on the peace of Cambrai, Henry was no longer allowing Wolsey a directing role in government. Wolsey was becoming a simple spokesman, who could articulate and defend decisions that he had not been involved in taking: for example, he was given details of what had been said to the French ambassadors while they were with the king so that he 'might say to them conformably to that hath been spoken here, like as the Kinges Highnes desireth Your Grace to doo'.[94]

During August and September Wolsey was responding to requests from the king on particular issues but he was no longer in charge, as several observers noted, and as a close reading of correspondence has shown. In the immediately preceding weeks, Wolsey had warned that if the pope failed to grant Henry his divorce, and in particular if he advoked the case to Rome, then both he and the pope would lose their authority in England, warnings to which historians have not given sufficient weight in seeking to explain Wolsey's fall. In that light it may be suggested that, after months of increasing doubts, by August Henry had realised that the pope would not yield. It was time therefore to increase the pressure and to begin to put what had been threatened into action. Wolsey could still be useful to the king in dealing with Campeggio, in putting pressure on the queen, in supplying technical guidance on treaties. But Henry no longer trusted him, fearing, no doubt unfairly, that he suffered from divided loyalties. And above all the downfall of Wolsey could be immeasurably helpful to the king. The dismissal of a papal legate and cardinal for breaking the law of praemunire, simply because he was legate and cardinal, in an atmosphere of anti-clericalism, would signal clearly to the pope that Henry was serious in threatening to go it alone if the pope refused to assist him, and would contribute to the creation of a climate in England in which the king would eventually be able to neutralise opposition and secure what he wanted.[95] In that light it was Henry, not any faction, nor Anne Boleyn in any direct sense, that was responsible for the fall of Wolsey in 1529.

Notes

1. I should like to thank C.S.L. Davies, Peter Gwyn, the late Jennifer Loach, David Norris, T.B. Pugh, Mark Stoyle and two anonymous referees for their helpful comments on earlier drafts of this paper.
2. J.J. Scarisbrick, *Henry VIII* (1968), p. 229; D. Starkey, *The Reign of Henry VIII:*

Personalities and Politics (1985), p. 101; J.A. Guy, *The Public Career of Sir Thomas More* (Brighton, 1980), pp. 97, 106–7; C. Haigh, *English Reformations: Religion, Politics and Society under the Tudors* (Oxford, 1993), pp. 93–4, 111; J.S. Block, *Factional Politics and the English Reformation* (Woodbridge, 1993), pp. 13, 19. Cf. also H. Miller, *Henry VIII and the English Nobility* (Oxford, 1986), p. 111; V. Barrie-Curien, 'La reforme anglicane', in M. Venard (ed.), *Histoire du Christianisme des origines a nos jours. viii. Le Temps des Confessions (1530–1620/30)* (Paris, 1992), p. 188 n. 3. G.R. Elton, 'Thomas Cromwell's decline and fall', in *Studies in Tudor and Stuart Politics and Government* (Cambridge, 4 vols, 1974–92), i. 193 (Norfolk 'leading the assault' against Wolsey).

3. E.W. Ives, 'The fall of Wolsey', in S.J. Gunn and P.J. Lindley (eds), *Wolsey: Church, State and Art* (Cambridge, 1991), pp. 286–315 (cf. E.W. Ives, 'Henry VIII; the political perspective', in D. MacCulloch (ed.), *The Reign of Henry VIII: Politics, Policy and Piety* (1995), p. 19). Ives describes my earlier doubts about his interpretation as offered in his *Anne Boleyn* (Oxford, 1986), pp. 136–52 (G.W. Bernard, 'Politics and government in Tudor England', *Historical Journal*, xxxi (1988), pp. 159–82), as 'rhetorical questions and assertions' (Ives, 'Fall of Wolsey', p. 303 n. 74). This paper is a response to that implied invitation to offer a more substantial critique. It seeks to build on the perceptive and compelling arguments in P.J. Gwyn, *The King's Cardinal* (1990), pp. 504–98.

4. R. Rex, *Henry VIII and the English Reformation* (Basingstoke, 1993), p. 177.

5. S.J. Gunn, *Charles Brandon* (Oxford, 1988), pp. 109–10; S.J. Gunn and P.J. Lindley, 'Introduction', in Gunn and Lindley (eds), *Wolsey: Church, State and Art*, p. 25.

6. Gwyn, *King's Cardinal* (1990), esp. ch. 12; G.W. Bernard, 'The rise of Sir William Compton, early Tudor courtier', *English Historical Review*, xcvi (1981), pp. 754–7; idem, *War, Taxation and Rebellion in Early Tudor England* (Brighton, 1986), esp. pp. 40–45, 52, 60–66, 73; G. Walker, *John Skelton and the Politics of the 1520s* (Cambridge, 1988), esp. pp. 1, 5, 70–80, 84–8, 90, 97, 158–60, 168–85, 222; idem, 'The "expulsion of the minions" of 1519 reconsidered', *Historical Journal*, xxxii (1989), pp. 1–16 (reprinted in *Persuasive Fictions* (1996), pp. 35–53).

7. G. Cavendish, *The Life and Death of Cardinal Wolsey*, ed. R.S. Sylvester, Early English Text Society, ccxliii (1959), p. 104 (my italics).

8. Ives, 'Fall of Wolsey', p. 208. For discussion of Cavendish's account of the fall of Wolsey see Gwyn, *King's Cardinal*, pp. 584–5.

9. *Calendar of State Papers, Spanish*, III, ii. no. 621, pp. 886–7 (*LP*, IV iii 5255); cf. Ives, 'Fall of Wolsey', pp. 291, 302, 305.

10. V.L. Bourilly and P. de Vaissiere (eds), *Ambassades en Angleterre de Jean du Bellay* (Paris, 1905), p. 543 ('Wolsey is in great difficulty, for the affair has gone so far that if it do not take effect, the king will fall out with him': *LP*, IV iii 5210).

11. Ives, 'Fall of Wolsey', pp. 302, 294, 305.

12. Ibid., pp. 294–5, 297–8 n. 54; *LP*, IV iii 5749. Cf. Gwyn, *King's Cardinal*, pp. 613–14.

13. Ives, 'Fall of Wolsey', p. 295; E. Hall, *Chronicle* (1809 edn), pp. 758–9; cf. G. Walker, 'Wolsey and the satirists', in Gunn and Lindley, *Wolsey: Church, State, Art*, p. 247; G. Walker, *Plays of Persuasion: Drama and Politics at the Court of Henry VIII* (Cambridge, 1991), p. 112.

14. *LP*, IV iii 5750; e.g. Ives, *Anne Boleyn*, p. 141, and, most recently, W. Palmer, *The Problem of Ireland in Tudor Foreign Policy 1485–1603* (Woodbridge, 1994), p. 40.

15. P.L. Carver (ed.), *The Comedy of Acolastus, translated by John Palsgrave*, Early English Text Society, ccii (1937), pp. xxvii note 1; *LP*, III ii 2903–5, 3003; Hall, *Chronicle*, pp. 655–6.
16. Cavendish, *Life of Wolsey*, p. 90; Hall, *Chronicle*, p. 758; Vienna, Haus-Hof- und Staatsarchiv, England, Berichte, Karton 4, ff. 209v–210 (I am grateful to the British Academy for grants enabling study in Vienna); PRO PRO31/18/2/1 ff. 411–411v; *Cal. S.P., Spanish*, IV i no. 160, p. 236.
17. Vienna, Haus-Hof- und Staatsarchiv, England, Berichte, Karton 4, ff. 209v–210; PRO PRO31/18/2/1 ff. 411–411v; *Cal. S.P., Spanish*, IV i no. 160, p. 236. Cf. Gunn, *Charles Brandon*, p. 103 n. 162.
18. Gunn, *Brandon*, pp. 103–7, 113, 159–64, 199–201.
19. Cavendish, *Life of Wolsey*, p. 90; cf. Walker, 'Wolsey and the satirists', p. 247.
20. Hall, *Chronicle*, p. 758 (my italics).
21. Ives, 'Fall of Wolsey', p. 304; Gunn, *Charles Brandon*, p. 110.
22. *State Papers of Henry VIII* (11 vols, 1830–52), vii. no. ccl, p. 194 (*LP*, IV iii 5797) for Wolsey and the adjournment; cf. Gwyn, *King's Cardinal*, pp. 529–30. Henry's anger at the cardinals was specific and tactical. Before long he was urging the pope to make Jerome Ghinucci, bishop of Worcester, and one of the king's agents in Rome, a cardinal; and he was still pressing that suit as late as November 1532 (*LP*, IV iii 6292, 6387, 6705, 6757; V 28, 33, 1036, 1522). And Campeggio does not seem to have borne any grudges against the dukes: in June 1536 he counted Suffolk and Norfolk among his friends in England in whom he chiefly trusted (*LP*, X 1077).
23. Ives, 'Fall of Wolsey', p. 300; Ives, *Anne Boleyn*, pp. 142–3; *LP*, IV iii 5816.
24. 'Apart from the pillage of which he is accused, and the quarrels sowed by him between christian princes, so many other matters are brought against him that it has maddened him'; 'they regard it as lese-majeste that he held the [papal] legation for more than ten years against the laws of the land': R. Scheurer (ed.), *Correspondance du Cardinal Jean du Bellay* (Paris, 1969), p. 112 (*LP*, IV iii 6018–19); discussed by Ives, 'Fall of Wolsey', pp. 305–6; Hall, *Chronicle*, p. 760.
25. Ives, 'Fall of Wolsey', pp. 307–8; Hall, *Chronicle*, p. 724.
26. Ives, 'Fall of Wolsey', pp. 310–11; Hall, *Chronicle*, pp. 767–8.
27. Ives, 'Fall of Wolsey', pp. 311–12. E. Herbert of Cherbury, *The Life and Raigne of King Henry the Eighth* (1649), p. 274 (*LP*, IV iii 6075) for the signatories. The witnesses of the elevation of Wiltshire are in PRO C66/655 m. 19 (*LP*, IV iii 6085).
28. E.W. Ives, 'Henry the Great', *The Historian*, xliii (1994), p. 4.
29. Ibid., 'Fall of Wolsey', pp. 293, 304, 302.
30. E.g. *State Papers*, i. no. cix, pp. 194–5 (*LP*, IV ii 3217); cf. Gwyn, *King's Cardinal*, ch. 12.
31. *LP*, IV ii 4699.
32. *Cal. S.P., Spanish*, III ii. no. 614, p. 877.
33. Ibid., no. 621, pp. 885, 887.
34. *Ambassades de Jean du Bellay*, p. 543 (*LP*, IV iii 5210).
35. For a general review see Gwyn, *King's Cardinal*, pp. 587ff.
36. *State Papers*, vii. no. ccxxix, pp. 143–5 (*LP*, IV iii 5152).
37. *State Papers*, vii. no. ccxxxi, pp. 148–51 at 149 (*LP*, IV iii 5213).
38. *State Papers*, i. no. clxxi, p. 329 (*LP*, IV iii 5393).
39. *LP*, IV iii 5416.
40. PRO SP1/53 ff. 210–11 (*State Papers*, vii. no. ccxxxix, pp. 166–69 at 167; *LP*, IV iii 5481).

41. *State Papers*, vii. no. ccxxxix, p. 170 (*LP*, IV iii 5519). Ives, *Anne Boleyn*, p. 137 quotes but misses the significance.
42. PRO SP1/54 ff. 53–55 (*State Papers*, vii. no. 244, pp. 182–3 at 182; *LP*, IV iii. 5635). See Gwyn, *King's Cardinal*, pp. 587, 591.
43. *Correspondance de Jean du Bellay*, no. 22, pp. 63–4 (*LP*, IV iii 5862); cf. Gwyn, *King's Cardinal*, p. 590; cf. Walker, *Plays of Persuasion*, esp. pp. 231–4. For Wolsey's earlier suspicions about what was being said about him at the French court see *LP*, IV iii app. 193. The tone and contents of Suffolk's correspondence make it plain that he had been sent to France by the king. The suggestion by Jean du Bellay, the French ambassador, that it was Anne Boleyn who was responsible for the despatch of Suffolk to Francis I *(Correspondance de Jean du Bellay*, no. 17 p. 58 (*LP*, IV iii 5742, which, however, says it was the duke of Norfolk; Le Grand, *Histoire du divorce de Henry VIII* (3 vols, Paris, 1688); iii. 333, leaves blanks) (cf. Ives, *Anne Boleyn*, p. 140), contradicts what he wrote earlier about Suffolk going 'de la part de son maistre' (*Correspondance de Jean du Bellay*, no. 8, p. 25 (*LP*, IV iii 5601). The evidence of Henry's actions in 1529 so far discussed must also cast doubt on du Bellay's report on 22 May that 'les ducs de Soffort et Norfoch et les autres mectent le roy d'Angleterre en oppinion qu'il n'a tant avance le mariaige quil eust faict s'il eust voullu' (*Correspondance de Jean du Bellay*, no. 7 bis, p. 22 (*LP*, IV iii 5581)).
44. BL Cotton MS, Vitellius B xi. f. 169 (*LP*, IV iii 5703).
45. PRO SP1/54 ff. 96–7 at 96 v (*State Papers*, vii. no. ccxlvii, pp. 188–90 at 189; *LP*, IV iii 5711).
46. BL Cotton MS, Vitellius B xi. f. 166 (*State Papers*, vii. no. ccxlviii, pp. 190–91; *LP*, IV, iii 5715).
47. BL Cotton MS, Vitellius B xi. f. 194 (*LP*, IV iii 5762).
48. BL Cotton MS, Vitellius B xi. f. 192 (*LP*, IV iii 5761).
49. BL Cotton MS, Vitellius B xi. f. 203 (*LP*, IV iii 5780).
50. PRO SP1/55 ff. 5–8 (in cipher) (*State Papers*, vii. no. ccl, pp. 193–7 at 194 and 197; *LP*, IV iii 5897). Dating and authenticity discussed by Gwyn, *King's Cardinal*, pp. 527–8. Cf. Benet's later warning to the pope: *LP*, IV iii 5848.
51. *Cal. S.P., Spanish*, IV i. no. 83, pp. 132–3. Cf. also Wolsey's warning to the French ambassador in May that if Francis I did not help him over the king's divorce it would be his complete ruin: 'il pourroit estre seur d'avoir cause a mondict s^r le legat une totale ruyne' (*Correspondance de Jean du Bellay*, no. 7, p. 19 (*LP*, IV iii 5582)). For earlier threats that the king might be forced to break with the pope see *Ambassades de Jean du Bellay*, p. 543 (*LP*, IV iii 5210); *LP*, IV ii 3913, 4120, 4166, 4481, 4977.
52. Ives, 'Fall of Wolsey', pp. 304, 293, 302.
53. *State Papers*, vii. no. ccl, p. 193 (*LP*, IV iii 5797).
54. *LP*, IV iii 5801, 5881 (ii), 5883, 5884. I am grateful to David Norris for this suggestion.
55. *Correspondance de Jean du Bellay*, no. 20, p. 63 (*LP*, IV iii 5853); Gwyn, *King's Cardinal*, pp. 591–3.
56. *Correspondance de Jean du Bellay*, no. 5, p. 15 (*LP*, IV iii 5547); *Cal. S.P., Spanish*, IV i. no. 28, pp. 55–9.
57. PRO31/18/2/1 f. 390 (*Cal. S.P., Spanish*, IV, i. no. 132, pp. 189–90). Cf. Gwyn, *King's Cardinal*, p. 591.
58. *LP*, IV iii 5945; *Cal. S.P., Spanish*, IV, i. no. 31, p. 58.
59. Ives, 'Fall of Wolsey', pp. 293–4; N. Samman, 'The Henrician Court during Cardinal Wolsey's Ascendancy c. 1514–1529', University of Wales (Bangor)

PhD thesis (1988), pp. 218–20, 232, 386. (I am very grateful to Neil Samman for lending me a copy of his thesis.)
60. PRO SP1/55 f. 23 (*LP*, IV iii 5817: omitting the last words of the document).
61. PRO SP1/55 f. 29 (H. Ellis, *Original Letters Illustrative of British History* (11 vols in 3 series, 1824–46), 3rd series, i. 34–5; *LP*, IV iii 5825).
62. PRO SP1/55 f. 79–79v (*State Papers*, iv. no. ccx, p. 568; *LP*, IV iii 5886).
63. PRO SP49/2 f. 58 (*State Papers*, iv. no. xlv, pp. 79–80 (wrongly dated); *LP*, IV iii 5844).
64. *LP*, IV iii 5906 (16).
65. PRO E101/420/8, ff. 26v–27, cited by Samman, 'Henrician Court', p. 386, but the document records expenditure at Tittenhanger on 14 and 15 August only, not 16 August as well.
Apart from the sources discussed in the text, there are two letters from the duke of Norfolk to Wolsey, both of which refer to letters which the king had just received and asked Norfolk to forward to Wolsey. Norfolk's letters are dated Barnet, 15 and 16 August, but bear no year. The editors of *LP* calendared them under 1529 (PRO SP1/55 f. 46 and f. 47 (*LP*, IV iii 5850–1). If that is correct, they would suggest that Henry never left Barnet, but it is more likely that the letters in fact date from 1525 when other evidence (Samman, 'Henrician Court', p. 371) shows that the king was at Barnet on 13 and 16 August.
66. PRO SP49/2 f. 58 (*State Papers*, iv. no. xlv, pp. 79–80 (wrongly dated); *LP*, IV iii 5844).
67. BL Cotton MS, Vespasian F ix. ff. 144–6 at 144 (ink foliation) (*LP*, IV iii 5865).
68. BL Cotton MS, Vespasian C iv. ff. 337–8 at 338 (*LP*, IV iii 5893).
69. *State Papers*, i. no. clxxx, pp. 343–5 at 345 (*LP*, IV iii 5936). The *LP* version misleadingly says that Wolsey could explain his concerns 'further to the king when you arrive and relieve the king from this agitation', with its suggestion of an imminent meeting between king and cardinal. In fact the text here reads, referring to the matter about which Wolsey did not wish to write, 'or if it be any other matier in this realme, soo to towche in your said letters [some] parte therof, leaving the circumstances to be [explained] by Your graces mouth (at your cumming hither upon — next folowing, at which tyme Your Grace shal [do] your pleasour to repaire to His Highnes, as by mouth [I] have shewed vnto Your Graces servaunt Forest)'. This places the emphasis on Wolsey's dispelling the king's anxiety by writing at once, while a meeting between king and minister is pushed into a unspecified date in the future. (I am grateful to David Norris for drawing my attention to the *LP* reading).
70. BL Cotton MS, Vitellius B xii. 173 (H. Ellis, *Original Letters illustrative of British History* (11 vols in 3 series), 3rd series, i. 307; *LP*, IV iii 5953; cf. *LP*, IV iii 5995).
71. PRO PRO31/18/2/1 f. 394 (*Cal. S.P., Spanish*, IV, i. no. 152, pp. 213–15).
72. PRO SP1/55 ff. 77–8 at 77v (*State Papers*, i. no. clxxvii, pp. 338–9; *LP*, IV iii 5885).
73. BL Cotton MS, Titus B i. ff. 303–4 (*State Papers*, i. no. clxxviii, p. 342; *LP*, IV iii 5890); cf. Gwyn, *King's Cardinal*, p. 592.
74. *LP*, IV iii 5820 (cf. *Cal. S.P., Spanish*, IV, i. no. 182, p. 273); cf. Gwyn, *King's Cardinal*, p. 593.
75. BL Cotton MS, Vitellius B xii. ff. 169v–70 at 169v (*LP*, IV iii 5819).
76. PRO SP1/55 f. 59 (*LP*, IV iii 5867).
77. BL Cotton MS, Vitellius B f. 169 (*LP*, IV iii 5821).
78. BL Cotton MS, Vespasian F ix. f. 144 (*LP*, IV iii 5865).

79. BL Cotton MS, Vespasian F ix. ff. 144–6 (*LP*, IV iii 5865); Gwyn, *King's Cardinal*, pp. 592–3.
80. BL Cotton MS, Nero B vi. f. 28 (*LP*, IV iii 5868); Gwyn, *King's Cardinal*, pp. 592–3.
81. BL Cotton MS, Vitellius, B xii. 223–223v (*State Papers*, i. no. clxxv, p. 335; *LP*, IV iii 5864); Gwyn, *King's Cardinal*, pp. 592–3.
82. BL Cotton MS, Vitellius, B xii. 224–224v (*LP*, IV iii. 5923); Gwyn, *King's Cardinal*, pp. 592–3.
83. PRO SP1/55 f. 97 (*State Papers*, i. no. clxxxi, p. 345; *LP*, IV iii 5925); Gwyn, *King's Cardinal*, pp. 592–3.
84. BL Cotton MS, Vitellius B xii. f. 172v (*State Papers*, i. no. clxxxii, p. 347; *LP*, IV iii 5928); Gwyn, *King's Cardinal*, pp. 592–3.
85. BL Cotton MS, Vitellius B xii. ff. 171–2 (*State Papers*, i. no. clxxx, pp. 343–4; *LP*, IV iii 5936); Gwyn, *King's Cardinal*, pp. 592–3.
86. Ives, 'Fall of Wolsey', pp. 300, 302; Ives,'Henry VIII', pp. 17–18.
87. *LP*, IV iii 5891.
88. BL Cotton MS, Vespasian C iv. ff. 337–337v (*LP*, IV iii 5893).
89. *State Papers*, i. no. clxxix, pp. 342–3 (*LP*, IV iii 5894).
90. *State Papers*, i. no. clxxxi, p. 345 (*LP*, IV iii. 5925); Ives, 'Henry VIII', pp. 17–18.
91. Ives, 'Fall of Wolsey', pp. 300–301.
92. *State Papers*, i. no. clxxxi, pp. 345–6 (*LP*, IV iii 5925).
93. Ives, 'The fall of Wolsey', pp. 300–301.
94. *State Papers*, i. no. clxxxi, pp. 345 (*LP*, IV iii 5925).
95. Cf. G.W. Bernard, 'The pardon of the clergy reconsidered', *Journal of Ecclesiastical History*, xxxvii (1986), pp. 258–87; Gwyn, *King's Cardinal*, pp. 593–4.

4
The fall of Anne Boleyn[1]

In May 1536 Henry VIII's Queen, Anne Boleyn, her brother George, Viscount Rochford, Henry Norris, gentleman of the privy chamber and one of the king's closest servants, William Brereton and Sir Francis Weston, both gentlemen of the privy chamber, and Mark Smeaton, a groom of the privy chamber and a musician, were all arrested, tried and executed for an alleged series of adulteries. Anne, following her frail and carnal lust, had, according to the indictments, procured and incited her brother George to violate her, alluring him with her tongue in his mouth and his in hers; similar charges were made against the others. Such offences were held to be treason, Anne allegedly often saying she would marry one of them when the king died.[2]

How should we explain such extraordinary events? One popular explanation attributes the responsibility wholly to Henry VIII. Vexed by Anne Boleyn's failure to produce a male child, finding her pride and abrasive character increasingly intolerable,[3] Henry resolved to cast her aside, and accordingly invented a set of charges against her so that he could then marry his latest mistress, Jane Seymour. Such a picture of a monstrously selfish king able to implement every whim does not explain why Anne was accused of adultery, rather than some other treasonable, but less humiliatingly intimate, crime, and why, if she were falsely accused of adultery, she was accused of having had sexual relations with as many as five men. Above all, such an interpretation does not fit the evidence of Henry's relationship with Anne Boleyn.

Their marriage was undoubtedly not all sweetness and light. As early as August 1533 Eustace Chapuys, the imperial ambassador, wrote that the king's great affection to Anne had cooled and soon after he reported how Anne, full of jealousy, had (most probably) accused the king of flirting, to which he had responded by telling her that she must shut her eyes and bear it as more worthy persons did and that it was in his power to humble her even more than he had exalted her.[4] A year later Chapuys reported how Anne wanted to send away from court a very beautiful young damsel who had become the centre of the king's attentions; Henry again angrily told her to be content.[5] But if such reports should not be dismissed (even though the sources for them are indirect), for two reasons they must seen more as evidence of a tumultuous relationship of sunshine and storms than as precursors of the eventual disaster. First, Chapuys often cast doubt on the significance of the gossip he recorded. More than once he tempered his account of Anne's jealous words by adding that no doubt these were lovers' quarrels to which too great importance should not be attached.[6] Secondly, Chapuys's gossip must be set against the far greater weight of evidence that shows that Henry and Anne were often happily together and that despite occasional outbursts, their marriage seemed set to last. On many occasions the king and queen were reported as merry, notably in October 1535 when they went on progress together.[7] If then their relationship was at times frank, not to say quarrelsome, if something of the idyllic passions revealed in the love letters written in 1527–28 had passed, nonetheless Henry and Anne were still very much man and wife in autumn 1535.

Did Henry's feelings towards Anne change dramatically in early 1536? First, did Henry turn against Anne after she miscarried in January 1536, and what of a recent variant on that theme, that Anne allegedly gave birth to a deformed foetus making Henry think she was a witch? Secondly, did Henry fall increasingly in love with a new girl, Jane Seymour? In January 1536 Anne miscarried. The king showed great sadness. Possibly (if we accept a redating) it was then that he claimed that he had made this marriage seduced by witchcraft – 'seduict et contrainct de sortileges' – as was evident since God did not permit them to have any male issue: his marriage was therefore invalid and he could marry another.[8] How seriously should this outburst be taken? One recent writer has swallowed it completely and argued that Henry indeed suddenly claimed that Anne was a witch who had bewitched him into marrying her. What, according to this writer, prompted Henry was that the miscarriage was of a deformed foetus, and (we are told) it was well known that that was a sign of a witch.[9]

Unfortunately for connoisseurs of ingenious theories, there is not a shred of evidence that the foetus was deformed. The most that Warnicke can adduce is a remark of the Catholic historian Nicholas Sander, writing in 1585, that Anne gave birth to 'a shapeless mass of flesh', too vague a comment, even if it were well informed, to prove any deformity. Apart from that, Warnicke's case rests entirely on supposition. Moreover there is strong contemporary evidence that the foetus was not deformed. According to Chapuys, it looked like a male child which she had carried for only three and a half months.[10] Even, however, if it had been deformed, it is odd to see that giving birth to a deformed foetus would show that the mother was a witch. None of the demonologies cited by Warnicke support this claim.[11] Such a 'witch' would have shown herself surprisingly ineffective: a witch might more reasonably have been expected to use her craft to beget a healthy child. Moreover it is not clear how much credence should be placed on Henry's alleged reference to witchcraft. The report was brought to Chapuys on behalf of the marquess and marchioness of Exeter, notoriously unsympathetic to Anne, and Chapuys himself added, 'la chose mest bien dificille a croyre oyres quelle soit venue de bon lieu'. But supposing Henry did say it, surely his reference to Anne's bewitching him was simply a way in which he now, in moments of anger or regret or despair, referred back to his past infatuation; it in no way described her present behaviour. Chapuys did not mention witchcraft again.[12]

Despite the absence of evidence of any deformed foetus or any evidence that contemporaries thought that deformed foetuses proved the mother a witch, Warnicke goes on to offer a rather imprecise and circular account, both using Anne's fall to prove that she must have miscarried a deformed foetus, and also using Anne's deformed foetus to explain her fall. What is confusing is that she never offers a clear explanation of where the assault on Henry's honour, the ultimate spring of action, lay. Sometimes it seems to be the appalling discovery which Henry allegedly made, that his wife was a witch. Yet Anne was not explicitly charged with witchcraft. At times Warnicke seems to say that that is what she was in effect accused of: everyone would have known that the real charge was witchcraft.[13] At other times, however, she gives the impression that Henry's principal aim was to demonstrate to the world that he was not the father of the deformed foetus. Both the charges of incest and adultery brought against the queen and the others, and the efforts to present her as a witch, were intended to deny Henry's paternity. Yet Warnicke never explains just why a deformed foetus should in itself have been so shameful. It is difficult on her argument to see why the public revelation that his wife had committed incest and adulteries (or, if Warnicke's hints are accepted, was a witch) should be any less humiliating for the king than the report of a deformed foetus, which could always have been denied and which, if Anne were to conceive again, would soon be forgotten. Warnicke even claims that Henry wanted the evidence of his impotence entered into the public record so that he could not be seen as responsible for Anne's last pregnancy. This not only flies in the face of Chapuys's evidence (to which we shall return) that the government did not want it to become general knowledge but also most implausibly implies that impotence was seen as less humiliating than the paternity of a deformed foetus.[14]

Sometimes, however, Warnicke supports her theories with a very different argument, that 'illicit sexual acts were blamed for the birth of deformed children': therefore a deformed foetus was evidence that its mother had engaged in illicit sex.[15] It would have been reasonable to claim that Henry might have interpreted a deformed foetus as evidence that Anne had been unfaithful. But Warnicke does not go on to make the argument that the arrival of a deformed foetus made Henry suspicious of Anne's fidelity and led him and his ministers to seek out her lover or lovers. She rather claims that Henry's reaction was to seek to shift the responsibility for its paternity. 'The ministers were given the task of identifying several men among her acquaintances who could plausibly be accused of fathering her child, in order to establish that her gross sexual behaviour had caused its deformity'.[16] It is difficult to reconcile this claim, especially its implication that those who were condemned with Anne were innocent victims of a royal imperative, with Warnicke's conviction that 'Henry genuinely believed that Anne was guilty of the crimes for which she had died'.[17] Even if Warnicke's most extravagant speculations are allowed for the sake of argument, her elaborations of them fail to offer any coherent explanations of Anne's fall. Above all, of course, the lack of evidence of any deformed foetus remains an inescapable obstacle to acceptance of her claims. Moreover, those claims, as well as the more modest arguments that could be based on Henry's supposed rejection of Anne after her miscarriage, fail to explain why Henry did not act against her at once, and do not take account of Henry's continuing maintenance of the marriage.

Much more significant in assessing Henry's attitude than any speculations is evidence of what he did and said later. According to Chapuys, writing on 25 February, Henry had not been speaking much to Anne, and when she miscarried he scarcely said anything, except that he saw clearly that God did not want to give him male children. But when Anne attributed her misfortune in part to her love for the king so that her heart had broken when she saw that he loved others, Henry had been much grieved and had stayed with her (if only for a time).[18] Before we attach too much significance to Chapuys's report that Henry and Anne had not been seeing much of each other, it is worth noting that Henry and Anne both rejoiced at the news of the death of Catherine of Aragon in January: Henry had carried Princess Elizabeth, Anne's daughter, in triumph.[19] And Anne consoled her maids after the miscarriage by saying it was for the best: she would soon conceive again and then that baby son would be free from any taint since he would not have been conceived in the life of Queen Catherine.[20] What the evidence suggests is that the relationship between Henry and Anne was volatile, fluctuating between storms and calm. It may be that the merriment of October gave way to a period of coolness in early 1536, but this does not mean that Henry had finally tired of Anne or that her miscarriage had irrevocably damned her in his eyes.

Did the emergence of Jane Seymour threaten Anne? Our evidence comes wholly from Chapuys, whose despatches studied in full give a much more guarded impression of her importance than do quotations drawn out of context. In February, Henry, many said, was giving her great presents and, for a time, was unable to leave her for an hour.[21] On 1 April Chapuys reported how Jane had refused a purse full of sovereigns Henry had sent her, asserting that she was a gentlewoman of good and honourable parentage and would accept money from the king only when God sent her 'quelque bon party de mariage', thus marvellously increasing the king's love for her. In order to show that he only loved her honourably, Henry responded that in future he would not speak to her except in the presence of her kin.[22] How much should be made of all this? It seems vital to avoid the temptation of hindsight. Just because we know that Henry did indeed marry Jane Seymour, it should not be assumed that he was already set upon marriage with her in February and March.

On 19 May (after Anne Boleyn's downfall), Chapuys did report rumours circulating before Anne had been sent to the Tower that the king had spoken with Jane about their future marriage and the children they would have; but even if that was not just idle gossip, it most likely referred to a conversation in the days immediately preceding Anne's arrest, after she had been placed under suspicion. It cannot be taken as evidence that the king was intent on marrying Jane as early as February.[23] Indeed, given that Henry did take mistresses from time to time, it would seem far more likely that he was then seeking to make Jane his mistress rather than his wife. Moreover, read without hindsight, what is most striking about Chapuys's testimony is that Henry's courtship was somewhat crudely mercenary and that it was being rebuffed. The evidence that we have of Henry's interest in Jane Seymour up to the decision to investigate Anne Boleyn's activities points to two possible outcomes: that Jane might have become Henry's mistress for a while or, and this seems rather more likely, that she would have rejected his advances altogether. Besides, during these months Henry vigorously defended his divorce from Catherine of Aragon, his marriage to Anne Boleyn and his royal supremacy. Once Catherine was dead, Henry could have passed the divorce over in silence, the more so if he was thinking of discarding Anne: instead he continued, obsessively, to insist upon the exclusive validity of his interpretation of canon law, as the instructions sent to his ambassadors in France show.[24]

The strongest evidence of Henry's undiminished commitment to his marriage with Anne Boleyn appears in a most significant diplomatic development in April 1536. Ever since Henry had discarded Catherine, Chapuys, the imperial ambassador, had in his despatches always referred to Anne Boleyn as the concubine or the lady, and had never recognised or spoken to her. As recently as November 1535 he had described her as 'cette diablesse de concubine'.[25] But by a letter written on 26 March and received on 15 April, Chapuys was ordered by his master Charles V to negotiate seriously for an Anglo-Imperial alliance, and, in particular, not to break off negotiations on account of any demands over Anne Boleyn.[26] As part of those negotiations Chapuys was summoned to court to meet Henry on 18 April. He was cordially received by the councillors, including Anne's brother, George, Lord Rochford. Then Cromwell came to ask Chapuys to visit and to kiss Anne, which would especially please the king, though adding that if he had the least objection, he left it entirely to him. The ambassador replied that he was Henry's slave, but thought it better not to; Cromwell reported back to Henry, who took it in good part, and hoped that all would speedily be settled. Henry then came out greeting Chapuys warmly. The latter was then led to mass by Rochford. When the king and queen arrived during the offertory, a large number of people crowded round to see what faces – 'quelles mynes' – Chapuys and Anne would make at each other. Chapuys was standing to the side of the door through which Anne entered, so that she had to turn round to see him. He did not kiss or speak to her, but they did exchange the mutual reverence that politeness required. Later Chapuys again met Rochford. Then Henry came out and made a series of bold demands, asking, in effect, that Charles V should admit that he had wronged Henry over the break with Rome. What is of the utmost importance here is that Henry was clearly defending his marriage with Anne Boleyn. In asking and getting Chapuys to recognise Anne, he was seeking, and obtained, a significant diplomatic concession from the ambassador of Charles V who clearly believed that she was irremovable. And for our purposes this offers compelling evidence that at least up to 18 April Henry still regarded Anne as his wife and had not the slightest intention of discarding her.[27]

That conclusion is reinforced by the fact that Henry dissolved the Reformation Parliament on 14 April. Between 1529 and 1536 Henry had frequently prorogued it: the dissolution of parliament strongly suggests that he did not expect any urgent business that would require a parliament for some time, possibly for several years. If Henry had already been thinking of getting rid of Anne, he would very likely have kept parliament in being to deal with the problems of succession that a further divorce would cause; that he did not suggests that nothing was further from his mind. But then suddenly on 27 April Henry issued writs for a new parliament.[28] Did that mark a turning point? The first sign that something was amiss was the appointment of two almost identical special commissions of oyer and terminer on 24 April to investigate certain treasons. Letters that Henry sent on that day to his ambassadors in France and in Italy significantly do not mention the marriage. And on 27 April that the bishop of London was asked if the king could divorce Anne Boleyn. It is highly likely that something happened between 18 April and 24 April that called Henry's marriage with Anne into question.[29]

But before examining that we must deal with another interpretation of Anne's fall, one which has been very influential among recent historians, the notion that Henry VIII was essentially a weak king who was often the plaything of factions. Such a view was expressed crudely in 1536 by the vicar of Eastbourne, William Hoo: 'they that rule about the king make him great banquets and give him sweet wines and make him drunk, and then they bring him bills and he putteth his sign to them'.[30] Policies, on this view, were also determined by factions: as John Foxe, publishing in the 1560s, wrote of the fluctuations of religion, 'even as the king was ruled and gave ear sometimes to one, sometimes to another, so one while it went forward, at another season as much backward again, and sometimes clean altered and changed for a season, according as they could prevail, who were about the king'.[31] Foxe's general picture of a faction-dominated king has been absorbed by several recent writers, especially Ives, Starkey and Elton. They claim that many courtiers and noblemen had opposed the break with Rome, the divorce and the Boleyn marriage, but in vain. They always hoped that Henry would eventually discard Anne, and knowing his liking for mistresses, they tried to tempt him away from

Anne with another girl. Jane Seymour is seen as the tool of this conservative, 'Aragonese', faction. Ives, Elton and Starkey have developed this line further by suggesting a remarkable series of manoeuvres by Thomas Cromwell, who, realising (they say) that Anne Boleyn, his former ally, was falling, and that a conservative faction was about to come out ahead, joined the conservatives in bringing down Anne, added some rivals of his own, and then trumped the conservatives.[32]

Yet this supposed 'conservative faction' is elusive. There is very little even remotely plausible detail. Only once Chapuys did report a plot: its overall manager, he said, was Sir Nicholas Carew, together with the marquess of Exeter, Sir William Fitzwilliam, Lord Montagu, Geoffrey Pole, Sir Thomas Elyot and the dowager countess of Kildare. On 29 April he wrote that 'ne tiendra au dit escuies [Carew] que ladite concubine ne soit desarconnee et ne cesse de conseiler maistress Semel [Jane Seymour] ains autres conspirateurs pour lui faire vne venue'.[33] But none of this amounts to very much (Chapuys told Granvelle on the same day that he had nothing of importance to write)[34] and most importantly it appears to relate to a period when Anne Boleyn's conduct was already under investigation. It is suggestive that when Sir Francis Bryan was later examined whether he had heard anyone else talk about Princess Mary, he replied that *upon the disclosing of the matter of the late Queen*, he had heard Carew, Sir Anthony Browne, Sir Thomas Cheyney and the rest of the privy chamber talk generally about Mary. Once Anne was under suspicion, many wondered what the consequences might be; that does not prove that they had earlier conspired against her.[35] If some courtiers had indeed been critical of the break with Rome and the treatment of Catherine of Aragon and Princess Mary, it is hard to find any evidence that they acted as a coherent political group or that they manipulated the king. Nor is there any sign that such conservatives were becoming more influential in early 1536: the passage of the bill for the dissolution of the smaller monasteries, or the flight of Catherine of Aragon's confessor, George Athequa, bishop of Llandaff would rather suggest the contrary.[36]

A second serious difficulty in factional explanations lies in Cromwell's supposed motivation. Why should Cromwell have done all that he is alleged to have done? If the conservative threat to him has been exaggerated, and if it was unlikely that Jane Seymour would have become the king's new wife, then there was no need for Cromwell to have acted against Anne in order to win favour with them.[37] Ives incredibly suggests disagreements over foreign policy as another motive. Anne had been pro-French while Cromwell was much readier to consider a deal with the Emperor Charles V.[38] Yet Ives goes on to say that once Charles V, after Catherine of Aragon's death in January 1536, was prepared to negotiate with Henry VIII, Anne and her supporters saw advantages in just such an imperial deal.[39] At most, then, these differences between Cromwell and Anne were ones of timing; possibly Cromwell spotted the opportunity first. Moreover since Henry was himself quickly alive to the possibility of a deal with Charles as soon as Catherine of Aragon had died in early January, this evidently reduces the significance of any differences between Cromwell and Anne;[40] and by April 1536 there is no sign of any disagreement between Cromwell and Anne on this subject, as Ives appears to concede when he suggests a rather different reason why Cromwell should have come to think that the needs of foreign policy required Anne's destruction. Now he suggests that Anne's position as the queen was in itself an obstacle to the Anglo-Imperial agreement that Cromwell sought, and that it was when he saw how obstinately Henry was defending her to Chapuys on 18 April that Cromwell decided to destroy her. Yet here Ives seems to have been deceived by what he elsewhere sees as a visit to the court by Chapuys stage-managed by Cromwell. Was it not a standard negotiating technique for a minister to pretend to be speaking independently of his master, to pretend that there were serious differences between them? Were not Henry and Cromwell rather working together on 18 April in order to see just much the imperialists were prepared to offer for an alliance? And in any case, the notion that Cromwell as Henry's secretary would destroy the king's wife just to foster a foreign alliance that in the very fluid international relations of the 1530s was likely to be temporary seems to lack any sense of proportion.[41]

Another argument in support of faction is that, besides Anne, several members of the king's privy chamber were executed. Does this suggest that Cromwell wished to destroy a whole grouping, to bring down not just the queen but also his supposed enemies in the privy chamber?[42] There is, however, little evidence to suggest that those convicted with Anne formed a coherent group; indeed they might more reasonably be seen as competitors for Anne's favours. Were they rivals or enemies of Cromwell? Of those condemned, Lord Rochford, Anne's brother, was by far the most influential, though it would be hard to see him as a rival to Cromwell. Mark Smeaton, the musician, could hardly be spoken of in the same breath. Francis Weston was just a courtier. Henry Norris had been a close body servant of the king since 1527, remaining in great favour as the grant of the manor and advowson of Minster Lovell, Oxfordshire, on 14 March showed. Yet for all his proximity to the king it is hard to see much sign of any political activity directed against Cromwell. Both Norris and William Brereton have been seen as threats because of their local interests. Brereton, according to Ives, and Norris also according to Peter Roberts, could have been included in the indictments because of Cromwell's desire to reform the government of Wales.[43] But the claim is exaggerated. Neither Brereton nor Norris was an 'over-mighty' subject. Norris's power in Wales and the Marches was wholly dependent on that royal favour which had secured him the chamberlainship of North Wales in October 1531 and the constabulary of Beaumaris Castle.[44] Brereton, although he had family connections in the region, was influential not because of inheritance but again because of royal favour, combined with his own abilities and determination as an empire-builder. The offices he secured in the late 1520s and early 1530s – chamberlain of Chester from 1530, escheator of Chester from 1528, steward of the lordships of Chirk, Bromfield, Yale and the Holt, sheriff of Flint in 1532 – depended on continuing royal favour. He was 'a man wiche in the sayd countye of Chester hadd all the rewle and gouernaunce *under our souereigne lord the kynges grace*'.[45]

No doubt Brereton's methods were unscrupulous and partisan, but it is difficult to argue that his rule was so wicked and dangerous that he had to be removed. There is no sign of any attack on Brereton or Norris before the fall of Anne Boleyn. Had Brereton and Norris been seen as threats to good governance, they could simply have been dismissed. Norris, after all, had little personal involvement in Wales and the Marches. Brereton's position was more deeply rooted. But in 1525 Charles Brandon, duke of Suffolk, who had ruled (with his deputies) effectively if autocratically in those lordships of Chirk, Bromfield and Yale which Brereton now held, had been removed not because he was threateningly powerful but so that his offices could be better deployed in a reformed government of Wales. If Brereton was similarly thought to be providing a less efficient rule than might be possible by other means, why was he not similarly removed?[46] It hardly seems necessary to invent charges of adultery with the Queen to secure his dismissal. Moreover it is by no means clear that the reforms of Welsh government in 1534–36 were intended as a challenge to Brereton. The Acts of 1534 (which prohibited the suborning of juries and allowed certain cases to be tried by the council of the Marches) hardly affected him. In the Act of 1536 which introduced JPs into Wales it is significant that the chamberlain of Chester – Brereton – was to receive extretes of issues and fines from Chester and Flint. Similar arrangements were made for the chamberlain of North Wales, Norris. Moreover both posts survived their disgrace.[47] The local interests of Brereton and Norris do not then form an adequate motive for anyone to have sought to destroy them.

The factional argument, like all the explanations put forward so far, depends heavily on the assumption that Anne and those accused with her were innocent, and that the charges against them were preposterous. As John Foxe put it, 'such carnal desires of her body as to misuse herself with her own natural brother' and the others 'being so contrary to nature ... no natural man will believe it'.[48] 'Does any historian,' Professor Joel Hurstfield asked, 'seriously believe the charges, including incest with her brother, which were laid against Anne Boleyn?'[49] But let us not be intimidated by the martyrologist and the modern commentator and let us look more closely at contemporary accounts which suggest that Foxe may have been wrong.

The most plausible explanation may be derived from a source touched on, but never squarely tested, by historians. This is a poem written in French. The earliest surviving printed version is that published in Lyons in 1545.[50] The author was there given as Lancelot de Carles, then almoner to the dauphin, and later Bishop of Riez. But it had been written much earlier. In the text the date of composition is given as 2 June 1536, just weeks after the events it describes. A year later Henry VIII was sent 'the Frenche boke writen in forme of a tragedye', the author of which was 'oon Carle ... being attendant and neer about thambassador here'.[51] That the French were following matters closely emerges from the intercession (in vain, and for reasons that are obscure) on behalf of Sir Francis Weston made by the sieur de Tinteville, after he arrived to join the resident ambassador Antoine de Castlenau, bishop of Tarbes, on 17 May.[52] An account of Anne's fall written by someone with access to the court at the time of her trial deserves careful attention.[53]

The poem describes how one of the 'seigneurs du conseil plus etroit' noticed that his sister was giving much evidence 'd'aymer aucuns par amour deshonnete'. By good brotherly advice he admonished her: she was acquiring the shameful reputation of a loose-living woman. His sister agreed that she could not deny her actions. But she went on to claim that she was not the worst. 'Mais on veoit bien une petite faulte/ En moy, laissant une beaucoup plus haulte/ Qui porte effect de plus grand prejudice'. She then went on to accuse the queen. If her brother did not believe her, 'de Marc scaurez, dit elle, cette histoire'. And she proceeded to accuse the queen's brother: 'Me je ne veulx oubliera vous dire/ Ung poinct de tous qui me semble le pire,/ C'est que souvent son frere a avec elle/ Dedans ung lit acointance charnelle'. Mark would confirm her story. All this troubled the councillor. If he reported these charges, he would be speaking ill of the queen, and therefore risking conviction for treason. If he kept these charges to himself and they proved true, he would be guilty of treason for concealing the treason of the queen. So he told 'deux amys des plus favorisez du Roy' and they then told the king that the queen was sleeping with Mark, with her brother, and also with Henry Norris. Henry threatened them with punishment if what they said proved false. Meanwhile he treated the queen as if nothing was wrong. Mark Smeaton was interrogated and without any torture confessed. His confession persuaded Henry, who had Anne and the others arrested and tried.[54]

What makes this account so striking is that unlike all the other sources, it suggests how the stories of Anne's behaviour came to light and how the news of her behaviour first reached the king. Moreover, its testimony can be corroborated. It is not difficult to identify the loose-living lady at court who accused Anne Boleyn. Twice John Hussee, the London agent of Lord Lisle, deputy of Calais, in London, supplied her name. On 24 May, writing to Lady Lisle, Hussee identified 'the fyrst accuser, the lady Worserter, and Nan Cobham with one mayde mo[re] – but the lady Worseter was the fyrst grounde'. A day later he wrote: 'Tuching the Quenys accusers my lady Worsetter barythe name to be the pryncypall'.[55] The countess of Worcester was the wife of Henry Somerset (d. 1549), second earl of Worcester, whom she married before 1527.

She was the daughter of Sir Anthony Browne, standard bearer to Henry VII, and Lucy, daughter of John Nevill (d. 1471), marquess Montagu; the sister of Sir Anthony Browne (d. 1548); and the half-sister of Sir William Fitzwilliam (d. 1542), treasurer of the household, later earl of Southampton.[56] Was Sir Anthony Browne the brother who in the poem berated his sister for her loose living and did the countess of Worcester respond by attacking the queen? The countess certainly knew Anne Boleyn: Anne had lent her £100 in April.[57] And the countess was on Anne's mind when the queen was in the Tower. Sir William Kingston, the queen's gaoler, sent Cromwell reports of what Anne, obviously distressed, had been saying: she 'meche lamented my lady of Worcester for by cause her child dyd not store [stir] in hyr body, and my wyf sayd what shuld be the cause. She sayd for the sorow she toke for me'. In other words the countess was sorrowful that Anne had been arrested; and the countess could not feel her baby move, prompting Anne to fear that something might be going wrong with the pregnancy.[58]

That the countess of Worcester was pregnant is interesting. If the father was someone other than her husband, that would justify her brother's berating her 'qui maintz signes monstroit/ D'aymer aucuns par amour deshonneste',[59] and would explain why she reacted by making similar, but still more serious, charges against the queen. It is just possible that the countess was Thomas Cromwell's mistress. While we have no direct evidence of familiarity, there are none the less some letters which hint at a friendship unusual between a minister and a nobleman's wife. In March 1538 she thanked Cromwell for his kindness to her concerning the £100 she had borrowed from Anne Boleyn: she added that she did not want it to come to her husband's knowledge, since he did not know about her borrowing and using the money, and she did not know how he would take it.[60] At all events it would have been very serious if the countess had become pregnant by someone other than her husband. A double standard operated in the courts of early modern Europe and indeed beyond: men could marry, and then father illegitimate children with impunity, whereas a woman who became pregnant before marriage or outside the marriage bed was doomed.[61] Two years before Anne's downfall, her sister Mary was banished from court; it had been necessary to send her away because, as Chapuys put it, apart from the fact that she had been found guilty of misconduct it would not have been becoming to have seen her at court, that is, to have seen her pregnant at court. Mary, who secretly married Sir William Stafford, appealed to Cromwell for help: her sister, she wrote, was rigorous against them, her father, brother and uncle were all so cruel against them.[62]

It thus becomes possible to suggest what happened in spring 1536. The countess of Worcester became pregnant. Sir Anthony Browne, her brother, berated her on her misconduct. The countess defended her name by saying she was not the worst and accused the queen. Browne told two of the king's closest friends – might these have been his half-brother Sir William Fitzwilliam and

Thomas Cromwell? They in turn told the king. Interrogated, Mark Smeaton confessed: that convinced Henry of the truth of the charges. The ladies of the queen's privy chamber were questioned further and probably said more in detail. All this fits very well with the official line. Writing to Gardiner, ambassador to Francis I, on 14 May, Cromwell explained that the queen's incontinent living was so rank and common that the ladies of her privy chamber could not conceal it. It came to the ears of some of the council who told the king, although with great fear. Certain persons of the king's privy chamber and of the queen's were examined and the matter appeared so evident: there was even a conspiracy against the king's life. Hence the arrests.[63] When Gardiner pressed for more details, Cromwell explained that he had written as fully as he could unless he could have sent the very confessions 'whiche were so abhomynable that a greate part of them were neuer given in evidence but clerly kept secret'.[64] What happened, then, was no monstrous casting off of an unwanted wife by an utterly selfish king, no cynical and ingenious factional manipulation of a weak king by a conservative faction or a calculating minister, but a quarrel between one of the queen's ladies and her brother, provoked by a chance, but tragically, ineluctably, leading to accusations of conduct that no king could accept.

So was Anne Boleyn guilty of the charges? Unfortunately the records of the trials, including the depositions made by the ladies of the queen's privy chamber, do not survive, apart from the indictments and the verdicts. That might in itself seem suspicious. Could the evidence have been destroyed immediately after the trials or in the reign of Anne's daughter, Queen Elizabeth? Whatever the explanation, this means that we can approach only indirectly what the queen's ladies said. Yet the extravagant and factually inaccurate account of how an old woman in Anne's chamber hid Mark Smeaton in a closet in which sweetmeats were kept, and then brought him to the queen's bed at night when Anne called out for marmalade, shows how the evidence of the ladies of the queen's privy chamber could be significant. It also disposes of the argument that Anne's adulteries would have been impossible in an age when queens did not sleep apart from the ladies of their chamber: those ladies, or some of them, could readily connive at the secret affairs of their mistress.[65] According to the French poem, Anne, protected by the law that made it treason to speak against her, had the leisure, means and freedom to follow her desires.[66] After she was arrested and sent to the Tower, she did not remain silent, but talked and talked. Quite possibly Henry and Cromwell had deliberately sent ladies to provoke her into incriminating herself: but the accounts that her gaoler Sir William Kingston sent to Cromwell are too specific and deeply felt to suggest any fabrication. And these accounts, carefully read, seem, as we shall see, damning.[67]

What persuaded the king of Anne's guilt was Mark Smeaton's confession. Smeaton was the only one of those accused to admit his offences. How seriously should we take his evidence? And why should he have confessed?

What Mark confessed, according to the French poem and according to Chapuys, was that he had slept with the queen three times, and at the special sessions at which he was tried, he pleaded guilty to violation and carnal knowledge of the queen.[68] Was he tortured? The Spanish Chronicle suggests that he was threatened by a rope and cudgel around his head.[69] A few years later, George Constantine, who had been Norris's servant, said 'the sayeing was that he was fyrst grevously racked', but significantly he added, 'which I cowlde never know of a trewth' and he had begun by saying 'I can not tell how he was examined'.[70] The French poem explicitly states that Mark confessed 'sans tourment'.[71] What is most remarkable is that Mark maintained his confession to the end, saying at his execution that he deserved his death.[72] Why did Mark confess if what he said was untrue? A recent suggestion is that the queen's brother Lord Rochford was his lover and that as a young man of lower-class origins Mark was especially vulnerable to psychological blackmail about his sexual behaviour. The evidence for this is somewhat meagre. Rochford and Mark, we are told, 'had a common interest in music, for his lordship wrote poetry, which was often sung to old refrains'. And a music book which has been thought to be a gift from Mark to Anne was in fact a gift from Rochford to Mark.[73] But setting aside such extravagancies, there is a clue in the Spanish Chronicle's suggestion that Mark's success with Anne had made Norris and Brereton jealous. Anne decided to offer her favours on successive nights to Norris and Brereton, rather than Mark; the next night when Anne did call Mark, he told her what was in his heart; she laughed at him, but since he saw that she was deceiving him, he said no more; she gave him a purse full of gold sovereigns and told him to get ready for the May Day jousts.[74] The Chronicle continues by offering a rather different account of how Mark then came to be interrogated from that suggested above, but the vital clue that it offers is that Mark may well have confessed and maintained his confession out of jealousy and injured pride. After denying that he had been in her chamber except at Westminster where she had sent for him to play on the virginals, Anne admitted that when they had met on 29 April she had put him down haughtily.

> I fond hym standyng in the ronde wyndo in my chambr of presens, and I asked why he was so sad and he ansured and sayd it was now mater, and she sayd you may not loke to have me speke to you as I shuld do to anobull man by cause ye be aninferer persson. No no madam aloke sufficed me: and Thus fare you well.[75]

Evidently she knew him, and even on her own account she had been talking to him with remarkable familiarity. Had Mark been jilted after a brief affair that meant much more to him than it had to her?

What of the others accused of sleeping with Anne? Had Anne and her brother, George, Lord Rochford, committed incest? At their trial that is what they were accused of. Rochford denied it vehemently. He said that he had revered his sister and not abused her, answering his accusers with an eloquence greater than that of Thomas More.[76] According to Chapuys, Rochford defended himself so well that several of those present thought it was ten-to-one on that he would be acquitted; one account suggests that his judges were at first divided before they reached a unanimous verdict.[77] Chapuys also reported that 'contre luy ny aussy contre elle ne furent produictz nulz tesmoigns'.[78] According to the French poem Rochford appealed to the lords trying him, lamenting that 'par l'advis seulement d'une femme'[79] they should think him guilty of such a crime, implying that a woman had given evidence against him. Could that have been the countess of Worcester? In the French poem the councillor's sister who first accused Anne had claimed that she and her brother had slept together.[80] The Spanish Chronicle said that Rochford was arrested because the king was informed that he had been seen on several occasions going in and out of the queen's room dressed only his dressing gown. Rochford admitted that he had gone into her chamber, but said that all he had done was to speak with his sister when she was unwell. And this account again points to the role of the ladies of the queen's privy chamber in providing evidence against her.[81] Or was it Rochford's wife who testified against him? It was objected to Rochford that Anne had told his wife that the king was impotent – does that imply that it was his wife who had revealed it? Rochford was also accused of spreading stories that Princess Elizabeth was not the king's daughter, a charge he did not deny. Both Rochford and Anne were also accused of mocking the king and his clothes.[82] According to George Cavendish, Rochford was a womaniser: he has him admitting at his execution

> My lyfe not chaste, my lyvyng bestyall
> I forced wydowes, maydens I did deflower
> All was oon to me, I spared none at all,
> My appetite was all women to devoure.[83]

But accounts closer to the time suggest that after he had been convicted Rochford simply accepted that as a sinner (though without spelling out what those sins had been) he deserved to die, stoically accepting his fate.[84]

Suppose he had visited his sister in her chamber wearing his dressing gown; suppose that they had talked of the king's impotence; suppose that he had questioned the paternity of princess Elizabeth: that scarely amounts to a prima facie case, let alone proof, for a charge of incest. It might be concluded that the whole proceedings were a sham rigged by a monstrous king or a conspiring minister or a rising faction. Another possibility is that more damning evidence was presented than now survives. If the countess of Worcester or if Lady Rochford had indeed named him, if Mark Smeaton confirmed such charges, the case against him would look much stronger. It is possible that it was such evidence that convinced Henry of his guilt. However that may be, it is most likely that Rochford's behaviour at his trial gave the peers who convicted him sufficient reasons to believe the worst. It is always difficult to prove incest. But that difficulty of proof was a common feature of early modern criminal trials. Courts often faced the problem of determining the truth of charges that rested on circumstantial evidence, or on the word of one person against another. In such cases, the impression that the defendant made on those judging him was crucial: their estimation of his character, his sincerity, his trustworthiness could be more important than their judgment of 'the facts' available to them, indeed could rather guide their interpretation of what was often ambiguous, incomplete and circumstantial evidence.[85] Despite a clear request not to, Rochford read out in open court evidence that was presented to him not orally but in writing, relating to Henry's impotence.[86] Is that what damned him? George Constantine 'hearde say he had escaped had it not byn for a letter'.[87] By publicising the king's impotence, by defying the will of those organising the trial, Rochford was inviting his fellow peers to draw unfavourable conclusions about his character. Such effrontery lent credence to the evidence that he had gossipped mockingly about the king and that he had cast doubt on the paternity of Princess Elizabeth. In addition it might lead to the final conclusion that he was also indeed guilty of incest with his sister.

What of Anne and Henry Norris? He was examined by the king as they rode back to Westminster from Greenwich after the May Day jousts. George Constantine and the French poem said that the king offered him his pardon if he would tell the truth (again an instance of the double standard), but that Norris would confess nothing to the king. According to Constantine, Norris did then confess, only to say when he was arraigned that he had been tricked into doing so by Sir William Fitzwilliam; according to the French poem, Norris said he could prove the contrary.[88] Norris pleaded not guilty at his trial.[89] Chapuys was sceptical about the convictions, seeing them as 'par presumption et aucuns indices sans preue ne confession valide'.[90] Yet there might nonetheless be a case against Norris. One of the charges against Anne was that there was a promise between Norris and her to marry after the king's death, which was held to mean that they wished his death; another was that she had received and given him certain coins, which was interpreted as meaning that she had had Catherine of Aragon poisoned and was working out how to do the same to Princess Mary.[91] Significantly, it will be recalled, Rochford did not deny the charge that he had spread stories doubting that Princess Elizabeth was the king's daughter.[92] After the convictions, so Chapuys reported, Cranmer had declared that Princess Elizabeth was Anne's bastard daughter by Norris, not the king. That is not what was decided in the proceedings in which Henry's marriage with Anne was nullified. The evidence is confusing but the grounds for the annulment seem rather to have been either Anne's pre-contract with the later sixth earl of Northumberland or Henry's previous relationship with Anne's sister Mary. Chapuys nevertheless remained sceptical and still thought it might have been more honourably said that Elizabeth was Norris's daughter.[93] The French poem has Princess Mary implicitly doubting Elizabeth's paternity.[94] Once again the most telling evidence we have is what Anne said in the Tower, reported by Kingston. 'I can say no more but nay withyowt I shuld oppen my body and ther with opynd her gown adding O Norres hast thow accused me, thow ar in the towre with me, and thou and I shall dy together'. Weston had said that Norris 'came more unto her chamber for her than he did for Mage', the lady he was hesitating about marrying. Anne asked him why did not go through with his marriage and teased him, 'you loke for ded mens showys, for yf owth came to the king but good you wold loke to have me; and he sayd yf he should have any such thought he wold hys hed war of, and then she sayd she could undo him if she would and ther wyth thay fell yowt both.'[95] Such remarkably flirtatious talk, revealed by the queen, seems highly damaging to her cause: it cannot be conclusive, but it does allow the possibility that Anne and Norris were indeed lovers.

Was that also the case of Anne and Sir Francis Weston? His mother and his wife appealed to the king to spare him, as did the French ambassador, the bishop of Tarbes, and another Frenchman, the sieur de Tinteville. There was some gossip that Weston would escape death,[96] but the king did not yield. Once more the most telling evidence is that provided by Anne in the Tower. She feared Weston more than she feared Norris, she said. What did Anne fear? That Weston would confess and give evidence against her? Weston, she said, had said to her that Norris came more unto her chamber for her, than he did for Mage. Was Weston jealous of Norris's attention to Anne? Anne also said how she complained to him that he did not love her kinswoman Mrs Shelton: 'he sayd he loved not hys wyf' but that 'he loved won in hyr howse bettr then them both. And when the Quene saud who is this? He replied that it ys your self and then she defyed hym.'[97] Again this might signify more than light-hearted flirting. Weston drew up a list of debts which he asked his parents and wife to discharge, asking them to forgive him the offences he had done to them, and especially to his wife. Was his offence to his wife adultery, possibly with Mrs Shelton if not with Anne?[98] Finally what of Anne and William Brereton? 'By my troeth', said George Constantine some years later, 'yf any of them was innocent, it was he' because he had seemed to imply his innocence at his execution.[99] According to the Spanish Chronicle, he was named by Mark in his confession.[100] Did the countess of Worcester accuse him? Brereton had married the sister of the earl of Worcester. Anne did not mention him while in the Tower, except that when Kingston told her that Weston and Brereton were there too, 'she mayd very gud countenans'.[101] All one can say is that Anne knew Brereton.

Historians judging the guilt or innocence of Anne, her brother and her friends must, then, decide upon imperfect evidence. Much is incomplete and circumstantial. In the Tower Anne asserted to Kingston that 'I am as clere from the company of man, as for sin as I am clere from you and am the kynges trew wedded wyf'. According to the French poem Anne denied the charges; according to Wriothesley's Chronicle she 'made so wise and discreet aunsweres to all thinges layde against her, excusinge herselfe with her wordes so clearlie, as though she had never bene faultie to the same'.[102] Yet there may be more to be said for the verdicts of guilty than is usually allowed. There is certainly plenty of evidence of Anne's flirtatiousness. It is unconvincing to dismiss such flirting as merely an adherence to the conventions of courtly love. If flirting was always just a form of courtly love and never a hint of anything more, then it would have been impossible for it to serve as evidence against anyone. It was precisely because flirting was so ambiguous that guilt is hard to judge. We need to look at specific cases. The surviving evidence against Brereton is weak: the case against him rests largely on his knowing Anne. The case against Weston is far from strong: a flirtatious conversation with Anne, and hints that he had committed adultery (but with someone else). The case against Rochford was at best circumstantial, though given some credibility by his extraordinary behaviour at his trial. The case against Norris is rather stronger: Anne's remarks in the Tower, the talk of Norris as Elizabeth's father. Finally, Mark Smeaton's confession (whatever weight is placed upon unretracted confessions as evidence) must not be forgotten. Proof positive is never likely in such matters; yet it was not unreasonable for Henry VIII, for the juries that convicted the commoners, for the peers that convicted Anne and Rochford, to find against them. Perhaps the safest guess for a modern historian is that Anne had indeed committed adultery with Norris, and briefly with Mark Smeaton; and that there was enough circumstantial evidence to cast reasonable doubt on the denials of the others.

It must also be remembered that not everyone involved was tried and punished. That reinforces the suggestion that the accusations were not indiscriminate and that some attention was paid to the reliability of the evidence against those accused. The ladies of the queen's chamber, about whom we know only obliquely, do not seem to have suffered at all (the Spanish Chronicle's suggestion that the old woman was burnt can be dismissed).[103] Were they forgiven their roles as accessories because they gave testimony? According to the abbot of Woburn, giving evidence in 1538, Sir Francis Bryan was sent for by Cromwell in all haste at the fall of Queen Anne, 'as a worldly lucifer'. When he returned safely home, the abbot congratulated him that he had not been implicated. Bryan replied, 'sir in dede as you say I was suddenly sent fore marvellynge thereof and debated the matter in my mynd why thys shuld be'; but knowing his conscience clear he had gone to Cromwell, and then to the king, and there was 'no thing founde in me, nor never shalbe founde but juste and trewe to my master the kynges grace'.[104] Presumably a similar conclusion was reached in the case of Sir Richard Page, sent to the Tower in early May. Hussee reported on 12 May that his life was not in danger but that he would be banished from the king's court forever; and despite rumours a day later that he would also be tried, he evidently was not.[105]

That Henry and his ministers were genuinely examining the evidence is further suggested by the arrest and subsequent release of Sir Thomas Wyatt. Although he was put in the Tower, by 11 May Cromwell had assured his father that he would be spared, and so it proved.[106] Wyatt may, however, have had earlier dealings with Anne. According to a story told by his grandson, who was anxious to cleanse his reputation, Wyatt had fallen in love with Anne years before but Anne had rejected him because he had been married ten years. In a rather confused and unlikely episode, Wyatt is described as taking from Anne a jewel hanging from her pocket by a lace and refusing to return it. Later, when the king boasting of having won Anne's love tried to prove it by showing Wyatt Anne's ring, Wyatt countered by showing him Anne's jewel. But would a courtier so rashly compete with the king for the favours of a lady?[107] The tradition that George Wyatt was attempting to refute seems more plausible. According to the Spanish Chronicle, before Henry married Anne, he asked Wyatt what he thought of her: Wyatt had told the king not to marry her because she was a bad woman. The king had sent him away from court for two years as a result.[108] In May 1530 Chapuys reported that a gentleman of the court had again been dismissed after a report that he had been found 'au delict' with Anne: could that have been Wyatt?[109] According to the Spanish Chronicle, Wyatt, summoned by Cromwell and sent to the Tower once Anne had been arrested, wrote to Henry, reminding him of what he had said, and adding that he knew what Anne was like because she had been willing, many years ago, to kiss him, until they had been disturbed by the sound of stamping overhead.[110] Wyatt was a poet and his verse has often been interpreted as stimulated by his unrequited love for Anne. That is not impossible, but there is little that is definite in the texts. 'Whoso list to hunt: I know where is an hind/ But as for me, helas, I may no more', does appear to refer to a passion that is no longer permitted.[111]

> There is written her fair neck round about
> 'Noli me tangere', for Caesar's I am
> And wild for to hold, though I seem tame

might be describing the attitude of the newly elevated queen to her former suitor.[112] 'What word is that, that changeth not/ Though it be turned and made in twain', asks the poet, apparently intending the name 'Anna'.[113] 'Sometime I fled the fire that me brent', 'Alas, poor man, what hap have I/ That must forbear that I love best', and 'Pain of all pain, the most grievous pain/ Is to love heartily and cannot be loved again' all refer to unrequited love, but without any hint as to their object.[114] Quite possibly Anne and Wyatt had had a brief affair before the king took a fancy to her, but nothing in the poems or anywhere else suggests that Wyatt and Anne were lovers after she became queen, reinforcing the claim that it was because he was clearly innocent that Wyatt was freed.[115]

Wyatt's arrest does, however, raise the question of Anne Boleyn's past, and whether her character could affect the interpretation of the evidence against her in 1536. Of course as soon as Henry's divorce from Catherine of Aragon was known, Anne Boleyn was criticised: the difficulty is to know how far such denunciations were merely literary devices or political invective, and how far they truly reflected her character. The Prior of Whitby said that the king was ruled by one common stewed whore;[116] a priest called Rauf Wendon said that Anne was a whore and a harlot;[117] a priest called James Hamilton, called her a whore.[118] More elaborately Thomas Jackson, chantry priest, said the king lived in adultery before he married Anne and still did; he had previously kept her mother.[119] Mistress Amadas, wife of the king's goldsmith, said that Anne should be burnt because she was a harlot, that Norris was a bawd between the king and her; and that the king had kept both her mother and her sister, with her brother as bawd.[120] Sir Edward Bainton, the queen's chamberlain, sounding like Don Alfonso, told her brother in June 1533 that

> as for passe tyme in the quenes chamber, [there] was never more. Yf any of you that bee now departed have any ladies that ye thought favoured you, and somwhat wold moorne att parting of their servauntes, I can no whit perceyve the same by their daunsing and passetyme they do use here, but that other take place, as ever hath been the custome.[121]

Still more pointedly, the duke of Norfolk, Anne's uncle, called her 'grand putain', according to the earl of Northumberland reported by Chapuys, in late 1534; and evidently the duke went on speaking too freely of her the following year.[122] Does the fact that the treason laws had to be revised in 1534 to cover impugning the king's marriage also hint at Anne's poor name?[123] Evidently her controversial reputation could make charges of adultery and incest seem less implausible in her case than they would have been for another woman. The suggestion that Anne had talked about her husband's impotence may have seemed less surprising and more damning than if it had appeared totally out of character.

What we have then is the likelihood that Anne and at least some of her friends were guilty of the charges brought against them. But why should Anne have done it? One explanation might be, as Sir John Neale suggested long ago, that aware of Henry's at least intermittent impotence, Anne was trying to beget a child by other men, in order to produce Henry's much-wanted heir. Another might be that she was indeed a loose-living lady. Yet another, and perhaps the most plausible, might be her jealousy of Henry VIII's continuing affairs, a defiant resentment of the double standard which allowed that freedom to men but not to women. The French poem records her saying of the king: 'Et que souvent je n'aye prins fantasie/ Encontre luy de quelque jalousye'.[124] But this is to speculate. There can never be unambiguous evidence for human motivation, though there are many examples of men and women behaving foolishly, or taking extraordinary risks, in such matters. To the charge that the general interpretation advanced here is just the surmise of a man lacking in understanding of female psychology, just a 'wicked women' view of history that sees nymphomaniacs everywhere, it could be countered that Anne's behaviour has been presented as defiant rather than passive, and Jane Seymour's very differently interpreted. Above all, it has been an analysis of the evidence, not any prejudice, that has raised the possibility that Anne was unfaithful to her husband. That information came into the 'public domain' by chance, by the accident of a quarrel between one of the queen's ladies and her brother. In explaining what happened next, there is no need to portray Henry as a monster, no need to invent deformed foetuses, no need to elaborate 'factional' explanations: Anne's fall was surely inevitable once what she had been doing became known, once a prima facie case against her was accepted by the king.

The fall of Anne Boleyn is not just a salacious whodunnit: it has implications for our understanding of early Tudor politics. Perhaps Henry's reactions were harsh by our standards but they were not irrational. Nor should we assume in advance of a critical scrutiny of the evidence that people who did unusual things must have been manipulated. The explanation offered here thus casts considerable further doubt on the validity of the influential notion of faction as an explanation of political crisis in early Tudor England and raises the possibility that, on this and other occasions, Henry VIII was more in control and less the victim of factional manipulation than some recent accounts would claim.[125]

Notes

1. I should like to thank especially Mr T.B. Pugh for his generous encouragement. I am also grateful to Mr C.S.L. Davies, Mrs S.J. Loach, Dr P.H. Williams, Mr P.J. Gwyn, Dr J. Wormald, Dr S.J. Gunn, Dr G. Walker, Dr D.S. Katz, Professor A.G. Dickens and Mr W.R.B. Robinson for their comments. Earlier versions were given to the history societies of the Universities of Keele, Kent and Reading and to the Historical Association branches in Winchester, Richmond and Twickenham, and Hampstead. I am grateful to the British Academy and to the Advanced Studies Committee of the University of Southampton for grants enabling study in Vienna and Paris.
2. *LP*, X 793, 876 (7, 8), 848 (ix), 855, 865, 901, 919, 911; Vienna, Haus-, Hof- und Staatsarchiv, England, Karton 7, Korrespondenz, Berichten 1536, ff. 106v–107, 108v–110 (*LP*, X 908); G. Ascoli, *La Grande Bretagne devant l'opinion francaise depuis la guerre de cent ans jusqu'a la fin du XVIe siecle* (Paris, 1927), pp. 248–9, lines 522–47, pp. 257–60, lines 814–910, pp. 261–4, lines 928–1046, pp. 265–6, lines 1068–1114 (Rochford); pp. 267–71, lines 1125–1270; T. Aymot, 'A memorial from George Constantyne to Thomas, Lord Cromwell', *Archaeologia*, xiii (1831), 64, 66.
3. D. Starkey, *The Reign of Henry VIII: Personalities and Politics* (1985), p. 110, for this characterisation of Anne.
4. *LP*, VI 1018, 1069; cf. 975.
5. *LP*, VII 1193; and cf. VI 1054 (this is misplaced: it was written in 1534); VII 1297, 1554; VIII 263, 666.
6. *LP*, VI 975, 1018, 1069; VII 1193, 1554.

7. *LP*, VI 1293; VII 126, 682, 823, 888, 1581; IX 310, 525, 555, 571, 639, 663.
8. Vienna, Haus-, Hof- und Staatsarchiv, England, Karton 7, Korrespondenz, Berichten 1536, ff. 23–23v (Public Record Office, PRO31/18/2/2 f. 114v; *LP*, X 199; *Calendar of State Papers, Spanish* [13 vols in 20] v. part ii, no. 13, pp. 26–9); *LP*, X 282. Warnicke suggests that Henry must have known of the miscarriage when he made these remarks, even though Chapuys reports them without mentioning the miscarriage, when writing on 29 January, the day on which Chapuys later, and Wriothesley's Chronicle, said it happened: Warnicke thinks it may have happened earlier (R.M. Warnicke, 'Sexual heresy at the court of Henry VIII', *Historical Journal*, xxx (1987), 257–8; W.D. Hamilton (ed.), *Wriothesley's Chronicle*, Camden Society, 2nd series, xi (1875), p. 33; Ascoli, p. 242, lines 324–6.
9. Warnicke, 'Sexual heresy', pp. 247–68; R.M. Warnicke, *The Rise and Fall of Anne Boleyn* (Cambridge, 1989), pp. 191–234, 3–4. This argument has persuaded J. Guy, *Tudor England* (Oxford, 1988), p. 141 (Anne 'miscarried what by all accounts was a deformed foetus') and D.M. Loades, *Mary Tudor: a Life* (Oxford, 1989), p. 97.
10. Warnicke, 'Sexual heresy', p. 248 n. 4, Hamilton, *Wriothesley's Chronicle*, p. 33; Ascoli, p. 242, lines 324–6). For Anne's miscarriage or phantom pregnancy in 1534 see *LP*, VII 114, 556, 958, 1013, 1193; J. Dewhirst, 'The alleged miscarriages of Catherine of Aragon and Anne Boleyn', *Medical History*, xxviii (1984), 49–56; E.W. Ives, *Anne Boleyn* (Oxford, 1986), pp. 236–7.
11. One talks of witches using the aborted foetuses of other women and of witches ripping healthy foetuses from their mothers' wombs for evil purposes. It discusses what should be done with the normal children of convicted witches. (E.A. Ashwin, (trans.) and M. Summers (ed.), *Demonalatry by Nicholas Remy* (London, 1930), pp. 93–103, 94–5). Others write of witches who could kill infants in their mother's womb by a mere exterior touch, or who could induce impotence or sterility, (M. Summers (ed.), *Malleus Maleficarum of Heinrich Kramer* (London, 1927), pp. 55, 87–9); or discuss children, sometimes monstrous, but sometimes 'tall, very hardy and bloodily bold, arrogant beyond words and desperately wicked', that devils could beget – but by sexual congress with ordinary women, not witches (M. Summers (ed.), *L.M. Sinistrari, Demoniality* (London, 1927), p. 21; E. Fenton, *Certaine secrete wonders of nature* (1569), p. 17). Nowhere in the works cited by Warnicke, 'Sexual heresy', p. 249 n. 6, 99–103, 94–5, is there any suggestion that witches themselves gave birth to deformed foetuses.
12. Vienna, Haus-, Hof- und Staatsarchiv, England, Karton 7, Korrespondenz, Berichten 1536, ff. 23–23v (PRO PRO31/18/2/2 f. 114v (*Cal. S.P., Spanish*, v. (ii) no. 13, p. 28; *LP*, X 199). It was Chapuys not, as Warnicke implies (*Anne Boleyn*, p. 294 n. 2), Henry VIII, who had earlier said that Anne had enchanted and bewitched the king (*Cal. S.P., Spanish*, iv. (ii), no. 1161, pp. 884–5; *LP*, VI 1528). Warnicke's other evidence (*Anne Boleyn*, pp. 294–5, n. 2) refers to gossip in Louvain that the king must have been enchanted by potions (*LP*, V 1114).
13. Cf. Warnicke, *Anne Boleyn*, pp. 203, 214, 226, 231, 235, 241.
14. Ibid., p. 231. Cf. Vienna, Haus-, Hof- und Staatsarchiv, England, Karton 7, Korrespondenz, Berichten 1536, f. 107 (PRO PRO31/18/2/2 f. 144; *Cal. S.P., Spanish*, v. (ii) no. 55, p. 126; *LP*, X 908).
15. Warnicke, *Anne Boleyn*, p. 195; cf. G.R. Elton, *Thomas Cromwell* (Bangor, 1991), p. 37 n. 48.
16. Ibid., p. 202; Warnicke, 'Sexual heresy', p. 255, for wording quoted.

17. Warnicke, *Anne Boleyn*, p. 235.
18. Vienna, Haus-, Hof- und Staatsarchiv, England, Karton 7, Korrespondenz, Berichten 1536, f. 51 (PRO PRO31/18/2/2 ff. 124–124v; *Cal. S.P., Spanish*, v. (ii) no. 29, p. 59; *LP*, X 351).
19. *LP*, X 141, 199.
20. Vienna, Haus-, Hof- und Staatsarchiv, England, Karton 7, Korrespondenz, Berichten 1536, f. 53 (*LP*, X 352).
21. Vienna, Haus-, Hof- und Staatsarchiv, England, Karton 7, Korrespondenz, Berichten 1536, f. 31v (*Cal. S.P., Spanish*, v. (ii) no. 21, pp. 39–40; *LP*, X 282); Vienna, Haus-, Hof- und Staatsarchiv, England, Karton 7, Korrespondenz, Berichten 1536, f. 51 (PRO PRO31/18/2/2 ff. 124–124v; *Cal. S.P., Spanish*, v. (ii) no. 29, p. 59; *LP*, X 351).
22. Vienna, Haus-, Hof- und Staatsarchiv, England, Karton 7, Korrespondenz, Berichten 1536, f. 69 (*Cal. S.P., Spanish*, v. (ii) no. 43, pp. 84–5; *LP*, X 601).
23. *LP*, X 908.
24. *LP*, X 265–6, 584, 235, 308, 141.
25. *LP*, IX 777.
26. *LP*, X 575, 699.
27. Vienna, Haus-, Hof- und Staatsarchiv, England, Karton 7, Korrespondenz, Berichten 1536, ff. 80v–83 (PRO PRO31/18/2/2 ff. 131–139v; *Cal. S.P., Spanish*, v. (ii) no. 43a, pp. 91–4; *LP*, X 699); cf. Ives, *Anne Boleyn*, pp. 440, 352–3. Warnicke offers a bizarre reading of this report. She thinks that Chapuys refused to visit Anne in her apartments because he knew that she was falling from favour. If that were so, he would surely also have refused to recognise her, which he did here for the first time. His reluctance to go further was to avoid giving too great and too swift a diplomatic concession to the king. Warnicke then oddly supposes that by getting Chapuys to bow to Anne and to dine with her brother Rochester, Henry was inflicting a snub on Anne: yet surely Anne and her brother would have seen such recognition from the imperial ambassador as an encouraging endorsement of her status as Henry's lawful wife (Warnicke, *Anne Boleyn*, pp. 209–11, 224).
28. *LP*, X 736.
29. *LP*, X 848 (i, vi), 725–6; Vienna, Haus-, Hof- und Staatsarchiv, England, Karton 7, Korrespondenz, Berichten 1536, f. 95 (*Cal. S.P., Spanish*, v. (ii) no. 47, p. 106; *LP*, X 752). That on 23 April Nicholas Carew rather than Lord Rochford was elected to the Order of the Garter (*LP*, X 715) is not, as is often claimed, a clear sign that Henry VIII was now set against Anne and her brother (Starkey, *Henry VIII*, pp. 112–13; Warnicke, *Anne Boleyn*, p. 211). Each companion present at the chapter could nominate nine candidates, leaving the king to choose from those nominated. The king was not bound to choose the candidate with the highest number of votes, but in practice Henry VIII never chose anyone who did not have at least half the votes. In 1536 Carew had twice as many votes as Rochford: only once – in 1543, when choosing William Parr – did Henry ignore his knights' wishes to the extent that would have been needed to select Rochford. And it should not be presumed that the knights voted the way they did because they saw the way the supposed factional wind was blowing. (See S.J. Gunn, 'Chivalry and the politics of the early Tudor court', in S. Anglo (ed.), *Chivalry in the Renaissance* (Woodbridge, 1990), p. 115).
30. *LP*, XI 300 (ii).
31. J. Pratt (ed.), *The Acts and Monuments of John Foxe*, (8 vols, 1877), v. 135, 137. Foxe's specific explanation of Anne's fall, that she was the victim of 'some secret

102 *Power and politics in Tudor England*

practising of the papists', 'wily papists', especially Stephen Gardiner, bishop of Winchester, 'whispering in the king's ears what possibly they could to make that matrimony unlawful', seems wholly improbable, since Gardiner was Henry's ambassador in France in spring 1536 and far removed from immediate influence with the king.

32. Ives, *Anne Boleyn*, pp. 339, 346–8, 151; E.W. Ives, *Faction in Tudor England* (London, 2nd edn, 1986), pp. 16–18; Starkey, *Henry VIII*, pp. 108–12; G.R. Elton, *Reform and Reformation*, (London, 1977), p. 252. There are some differences of emphasis. Ives claims that Cromwell masterminded the coup after 18 April, while Starkey and Elton think that the conservatives initiated the attack on Anne when her miscarriage, the death of Catherine of Aragon and the rise of Jane Seymour played into their hands, Cromwell allegedly then taking over their plot.

33. Vienna, Haus-, Hof- und Staatsarchiv, England, Karton 7, Korrespondenz, Berichten 1536, f. 95 (*Cal. S.P., Spanish*, v. no. 47, p. 106; *LP*, X 752). R.M. Warnicke, 'The fall of Anne Boleyn: a reassessment', *History*, lxx (1985), 1–5, 13, makes the most outspoken claims for a conservative faction, yet most of them rest on supposition: 'After 29 January, many secret meetings amongst the conspirators must have taken place ... Although the evidence is slender, Sir Francis Bryan, long known as a boon companion of the king, was probably a key figure in the liaison between the Seymour faction and Mary's allies in their attempt to effect the disgrace of Queen Anne ... Bryan surely had ample opportunity to talk with Henry Courtenay, marquess of Exeter ... and Sir Edward Neville'. Warnicke is much more cautious in her book: *Anne Boleyn*, p. 207. There is a circularity in Ives's presentation: Jane Seymour's brother was using his new standing with the king to push Jane, yet his new standing depended on Jane's relationship with the king (Ives, *Anne Boleyn*, p. 347). Cf. T.F. Mayer, *Thomas Starkey and the Commonwealth: Humanist Politics and Religion in the Reign of Henry VIII* (Cambridge, 1989), pp. 4–5, 103, and 'A Diet for Henry VIII: the failure of Reginald Pole's 1537 Legation', *Journal of British Studies*, xxvi (1987), pp. 305–31, treating as axiomatic the existence of a 'Carew–Exeter faction'. For salutary scepticism (to be a faction 'they would have needed a political programme for action and not only coincidental similarities in their dislike for Henry's religious policies'), see C. Hollger, 'Reginald Pole and the legations of 1537 and 1539: diplomatic and polemical responses to the break with Rome', University of Oxford D.Phil. thesis, 1989, pp. 114, 84, 103–4, 122.

34. *LP*, X 753.
35. *LP*, X 1134 (4). My italics.
36. *LP*, X 429, 410, 282, 494, 308.
37. Ives, *Anne Boleyn*, pp. 353, 355–6. For more detailed criticism of Ives see G.W. Bernard, 'Politics and government in Tudor England', *Historical Journal*, xxxi (1988), pp. 160–62.
38. Ives, *Anne Boleyn*, pp. 340–41.
39. Ibid., p. 350.
40. *LP*, X 54, 141.
41. Ives, *Anne Boleyn*, pp. 353, 355, 358; Vienna, Haus-, Hof- und Staatsarchiv, England, Karton 7, Korrespondenz, Berichten 1536, ff. 82–84v, 85v, 87v–88v (PRO PRO31/18/2/2, ff. 131–139v; *Cal. S.P., Spanish*, v. (ii) no. 43a, pp. 91–102; *LP*, X 699); *LP*, X 373, 602. Ives's reliance on Cromwell's later claim to Chapuys that he decided to dream up and plan the destruction of Anne – 'a fantasier et conspirer le dict affaire – is unconvincing: Cromwell spoke these words after the event. Was he not trying to re-establish himself in Chapuys's eyes as a credible

interlocutor rather than admit that he had been taken by surprise by the events of the previous month? (*LP*, X 1069; Ives, *Anne Boleyn*, p. 358).
42. E.W. Ives, 'Faction at the court of Henry VIII: the fall of Anne Boleyn', *History*, lvii (1972), p. 174.
43. 'The Henrician courtiers Henry Norris and William Brereton between them held a nexus of offices under the crown in the three shires of the principality, the royal lordships of the northern marches and the county Palatine of Chester. They belonged to the Boleyn faction at court and in the country, and until Cromwell destroyed them in 1536, the way was not clear for the introduction of ambitious administrative and legal changes such as had been advanced by individual Welshmen and former members of the council in the marches'. (P. Roberts, review of G. Williams, *Recovery, Reorientation and Reformation. Wales c. 1415–1642* (Oxford, 1987) in *Times Literary Supplement*, 18 March 1988, p. 309). Ives has seen Brereton as 'a proconsul' who 'had little to learn from the text-book "over-mighty" subject', who 'personified all that was amiss' in Wales and the Marches and who was 'in himself a major obstacle to reform' creating a unitary sovereign state. 'The only solution to the dangerous isolation they [Brereton and men like him] embodied was the radical one actually under consideration in the last months of his life – the extinction of the politically separate palatinate and marcher lordships and their assimilation into the country at large'. (E.W. Ives (ed.), *Letters and Accounts of William Brereton of Malpas, Record Society of Lancashire and Cheshire*, cxvi (1976), pp. 34, 2, 36; 'Court and county palatine in the reign of Henry VIII: the career of William Brereton of Malpas', *Transactions of the Historic Society of Lancashire and Cheshire*, cxxiii (1972), p. 30.) Norris's appointment is *LP*, X 597 (27).
44. *LP*, V 506 (25); IX 1063 (11).
45. Ives, 'Court and county palatine', pp. 4–5, 28–9, 18–19. My italics.
46. S.J. Gunn, 'The regime of Charles, duke of Suffolk, in North Wales and the reform of Welsh government 1509–1525', *Welsh History Review*, xii (1985), pp. 461–94.
47. *Statutes of the Realm*, iii. 499, 502; 534–5; *LP*, XI 385 (16).
48. Foxe, *Acts and Monuments*, v. 136.
49. J. Hurstfield, review in *English Historical Review*, xcvi (1981), p. 614.
50. *Epistre contenant le proces criminel faict a l'encontre de la royne Anne Bovllant d'Angleterre* (Lyon, 1545); copy used: Paris, Bibliotheque Nationale, Res. Ye. 3668. I have also consulted MSS versions: Paris, Bibliotheque Nationale, Fonds francais, nos. 12795, 1742, 2370. I have here cited the text of the first edition, but have given references to the version printed in G. Ascoli, *La Grande Bretagne devant l'opinion francaise depuis la guerre de cent ans jusqu'la fin du XVIe siecle* (Paris, 1927), pp. 231–73; it is summarised in translation in *LP*, X 1036. I should wish to acknowledge my debt to Mr T.B. Pugh, to whom I owe my knowledge of this source: cf. T.B. Pugh, *Welsh History Review*, xiv (1989), 638–40.
51. BL, Add. MS, 25114 f. 267 (*LP*, XII (ii) 78).
52. *LP*, X 908.
53. Ives draws on the poem at several points: to support his claim that Queen Claude kept Anne in France after Mary Tudor was widowed (*Anne Boleyn*, p. 30), to reinforce his description of Anne as beautiful, elegant, with fine eyes, and as sophisticated in the French manner (pp. 51–2, 57), and to add to his description of Anne's coronation (pp. 227–8) and of her trial (pp. 387, 392). But he rejects de Carles's central account of Anne's fall, which he says 'must be fabricated' (p. 70). He does give a summary of de Carles's account, but by discussing it in the same paragraph as other, much more fanciful stories (including one in which Anne and

Rochford were planning to poison the king whom they suspected of intending to return to Catherine, a plot which was countered by two counsellors who accused Anne of adulteries), he discredits it by association and can conclude of all of them that 'though they may contain occasional vestiges of truth amongst the obvious error, they preserve what was essentially popular gossip and speculation' (p. 376). The French poem deserves closer attention than that. M. Dowling, 'William Latymer's Chronickille of Anne Bulleyne', *Camden Miscellany xxx*, Camden Society, 4th series, xxxix (1990), pp. 37–8, notes the poem but does not mention de Carles's account of Anne's downfall.

54. Ascoli, pp. 242–9, lines 339–560.
55. PRO SP3/12 ff. 37, 57 (*LP*, X 953, 964).
56. W.R.B. Robinson, 'Patronage and hospitality in early Tudor Wales: the role of Henry, earl of Worcester, 1526–49', *Bulletin of the Institute of Historical Research*, li (1978), pp. 20–36 at p. 30. Ives has twice described her as the daughter of Sir Anthony Browne of the privy chamber, who was in fact her brother (*Anne Boleyn*, p. 381; 'Faction at the court of Henry VIII', 176); he also has said that she was the niece of Sir William Fitzwilliam, who was in fact her half-brother (*Anne Boleyn*, p. 381); and speculated that she was the widow of the first Somerset earl of Worcester, when she was in fact then the wife of the second Somerset earl of Worcester ('Faction at the court of Henry VIII', p. 176 n. 46).
57. *LP*, X 912 (£10 is probably an error); XI 117 (6); XIII i 450.
58. BL Cotton MS, Otho C x. f. 229 (H. Ellis (ed.), *Original Letters Illustrative of English History* (11 vols in 3 series, 1824–26), 1st series, ii. 54–5; *LP*, X 793). Warnicke thinks that Anne was referring to the countess's sorrow at Anne's miscarriage, but this is against the sense of the document, and her argument that 'rumours identified the countess as a government witness', falls once the French poem is considered (*Anne Boleyn*, p. 202).

The countess of Worcester gave birth to a daughter called Anne (in memory of Anne Boleyn?) in the year ended Michaelmas 1536, according to the accounts of George ap Thomas, bailiff of the earl of Worcester's manor of Monmouth and Wischam: ap Thomas and his wife (who was to be wet-nurse) had incurred expenses in connection with the baptism and their lodging in London. (W.R.B. Robinson, 'The lands of Henry, earl of Worcester in the 1530s: part 3: central Monmouthshire and Herefordshire', *Bulletin of the Board of Celtic Studies*, xxv (iv) (1974), 460, 492. I am very grateful to Mr Robinson for this reference).

59. Ascoli, p. 242, lines 340–41.
60. *LP*, XIII i 450 (cited by M.St.C. Byrne (ed.), *Lisle Letters* (London, 6 vols, 1981), iii. 381; *LP*, VI 662 (not 1533), V 298, XI 117. I am grateful to Mr T.B. Pugh for drawing my attention to the correspondence between the countess of Worcester and Cromwell and for emphasising how unusual it is.
61. K.V. Thomas, 'The double standard', *Journal of the History of Ideas*, xx (1959), pp. 195–216.
62. *LP*, VII 1554, 1655.
63. BL Add. MS, 25114 f. 160 (*LP*, X 873). Ives noted that the account in the French poem 'is congruent' with Cromwell's letter (*Anne Boleyn*, p. 381), but offers no further comment or deductions. It is possible that the poet turned the official account into verse, but given the close involvement of the French in the fate of Weston (*LP*, X 908) it is unlikely that he would have set down what he did not believe. Perhaps it is the official account, rather than modern historians' speculations, that should be given the greater credence.
64. BL Add. MS, 25114 ff. 176–176v (*LP*, XI 29).

65. M.A.S. Hume (ed.), *Chronicle of King Henry VIII of England* (1889), pp. 66, 56–8.
66. Ascoli, p. 240, lines 263–74, p. 245, lines 420–25, 433–4.
67. Especially BL Cotton MS, Otho C x f. 229–229v (Ellis, *Original Letters*, I ii. 53–6; *LP*, X 93); BL Cotton MS, Otho C x f. 226 (Ellis, *Original Letters*, I ii. 58; *LP*, X 798).
68. Ascoli, pp. 246–7, lines 475–80; Vienna, Haus-, Hof- und Staatsarchiv, England, Karton 7, Korrespondenz, Berichten 1536, f. 106 (PRO PRO31/18/2/2 f. 143; *Cal. S.P., Spanish*, v. (ii) no. 55, p. 125; *LP*, X 908); *LP*, X 848 (ix).
69. Hume, *Spanish Chronicle*, p. 61.
70. Aymot, 'Constantyne', p. 64.
71. Ascoli, p. 246, line 478.
72. Ibid., p. 267, lines 1119–22; Aymot, 'Constantyne', p. 65.
73. Ives, *Anne Boleyn*, pp. 295–7, citing E.E. Lowinsky, 'A music book for Anne Boleyn', in J.G. Rowe and W.H. Stockdale (eds), *Florilegium Historiale* (Toronto, 1971), pp. 160–235, esp. pp. 169, 192, but questioned by Warnicke, 'Sexual heresy', p. 266 n. 57, and cf. 248, 265. The MS is BL, Royal MS 20 B xxi. 'Thys boke ys myn George Boleyn 1526' appears on f. 2; 'A moy m marc S' on f. 98.
74. Hume, *Spanish Chronicle*, p. 58.
75. BL Cotton MS, Otho C x f. 225v (Ellis, *Original Letters*, I ii. 58; *LP*, X, 798); *LP*, X 797.
76. Ascoli, pp. 258–60, lines 845–96.
77. Vienna, Haus-, Hof- und Staatsarchiv, England, Karton 7, Korrespondenz, Berichten 1536, f. 107 (PRO PRO31/18/2/2 f. 143v; *Cal. S.P., Spanish*, v. (ii) no. 55, p. 125; *LP*, X 908); cf. Ascoli, p. 260, line 901; *Wriothesley's Chronicle*, p. 39.
78. Vienna, Haus-, Hof- und Staatsarchiv, England, Karton 7, Korrespondenz, Berichten 1536, f. 107 (PRO PRO31/18/2/2 f. 143v; *Cal. S.P., Spanish*, v. (ii) no. 55, p. 126; *LP*, X 908).
79. Ascoli, p. 259, line 861 and note.
80. Ibid., p. 243, lines 369–72.
81. Hume, *Spanish Chronicle*, pp. 65–6.
82. Vienna, Haus-, Hof- und Staatsarchiv, England, Karton 7, Korrespondenz, Berichten 1536, ff. 106v–107 (PRO PRO31/18/2/2 ff. 143v–144v; *Cal. S.P., Spanish*, v. (ii) no. 55, p. 126; *LP*, X 908).
83. A.S.G. Edwards (ed.), *Metrical Visions by George Cavendish*, (Columbia, SC, 1980), p. 39.
84. Ascoli, pp. 265–6, lines 1068–114; Vienna, Haus-, Hof- und Staatsarchiv, England, Karton 7, Korrespondenz, Berichten 1536, ff. 107v, 109 (PRO PRO31/18/2/2 ff. 144, 145; *Cal. S.P., Spanish*, v. (ii) no. 55, pp. 127–9; *LP*, X 908); S. Bentley, *Excerpta historica* (1833), pp. 262–3; J.G. Nichols (ed.), *Chronicle of Calais*, Camden Society, 1st series, xxxv (1846), pp. 46–7; *Wriothesley's Chronicle*, pp. 39–40.
85. Cf. C.B. Herrup, *The Common Peace: Participation and the Criminal Law in Seventeenth-century England* (Cambridge, 1987), pp. 148–9, 158, 198; E. Powell, *Kingship, Law and Society: Criminal Justice in the Reign of Henry V* (Oxford, 1989), p. 80 ('the defendant, whose demeanour must greatly have influenced jurors').
86. Vienna, Haus-, Hof- und Staatsarchiv, England, Karton 7, Korrespondenz, Berichten 1536, f. 107 (PRO PRO31/18/2/2 f. 144v; *Cal. S.P., Spanish*, v. (ii) no. 55, p. 126; *LP*, X 908).

106 *Power and politics in Tudor England*

87. Aymot, 'Constantyne', p. 66.
88. Ibid, p. 64; Ascoli, pp. 248–9, lines 521–47.
89. *LP*, X 848 (ix).
90. Vienna, Haus-, Hof- und Staatsarchiv, England, Karton 7, Korrespondenz, Berichten 1536, f. 106 (PRO PROB31/18/2/2 ff. 143–143v; *Cal. S.P., Spanish*, v. (ii) no. 55, p. 125; *LP*, X 908).
91. Ibid., f. 106v (ff. 143v; pp. 125–6; *LP*, X 908).
92. Ibid., f. 107 (f. 144; p. 126; *LP*, X 908).
93. Vienna, Haus-, Hof- und Staatsarchiv, England, Karton 7, Korrespondenz, Berichten 1536, f. 112v (*Cal. S.P., Spanish*, v. (ii) no. 54, p. 121; *LP*, X 909); *LP*, X 896, 782, 864; BL Cotton MS, Otho C x f. 224 (*LP*, XI 41; *Wriothesley's Chronicle*, i. 40–41.
94. Ascoli, p. 250, lines 585–6.
95. BL Cotton MS, Otho C x ff. 229–229v (Ellis, *Original Letters*, I ii. 54–6; *LP*, X 793).
96. Ascoli, p. 257, lines 803–4; Vienna, Haus-, Hof- und Staatsarchiv, England, Karton 7, Korrespondenz, Berichten 1536, f. 108v (PRO PRO31/18/2/2 f. 145; *Cal. S.P., Spanish*, v. (ii) no. 55, p. 128; *LP*, X 908); *LP*, X 865.
97. BL Cotton MS, Otho C x f. 229v (Ellis, *Original Letters*, I ii. 55–6; *LP*, X 793).
98. Ibid.; *LP*, X 869.
99. Aymot, 'Constantyne', p. 65.
100. Hume, *Chronicle*, p. 61.
101. BL Cotton MS, Otho C x f. 225r (Ellis, *Original Letters*, I ii. 57; *LP*, X 798).
102. BL Cotton MS, Otho C x ff. 229–229v (Ellis, *Original Letters*, I ii. 54; *LP*, X 793); Ascoli, pp. 252, 262, lines 668, 958–61; *Wriothesley's Chronicle*, pp. 37–8. I do not think the letter (in an Elizabethan hand and rather florid style) purporting to be from Anne to Henry, protesting her innocence, is genuine (BL Cotton MS, Otho C x f. 228; *LP*, X 808). I have also disregarded the fanciful account by the Scottish reformer Alexander Ales (Alesius) presented to Queen Elizabeth on her accession (PRO SP70/7 ff. 1–11; *Calendar of State Papers, Foreign, 1559–1560*, no. 1303, pp. 524–34), a farrago of improbabilities and chronological impossibilities.
103. *Hume, Chronicle of Henry VIII*, p. 66.
104. BL Cotton MS, Cleopatra E ii f. 110 (*LP*, XIII i 981 (2)).
105. *LP*, X 798, 855, 865; Ascoli, p. 249, line 560.
106. *LP*, X 798, 840; XI 1492.
107. S.W. Singer (ed.), *The Life of Cardinal Wolsey* (2 vols, 1825), pp. 185–7.
108. Hume, *Chronicle of Henry VIII*, p. 68. Cf. Harpsfield's account of Wyatt's telling Henry that many had had carnal pleasure with Anne (N. Pocock (ed.), *N. Harpsfield, The Pretended Divorce of Henry VIII and Catherine of Aragon*, Camden Society, 2nd series, xxi (1878), p. 253).
109. *Cal. S.P., Spanish*, iv. (i), no. 302, p. 535.
110. Hume, *Chronicle of Henry VIII*, p. 69.
111. R.A. Rebholz (ed.), *Sir Thomas Wyatt: Complete Poems* (1978), p. 77, no. xi, lines 1–2.
112. Ibid., lines 12–14.
113. Ibid., p. 96, no. liv, lines 1–2; p. 374.
114. Ibid., p. 96, no. lv, line 1; p. 151, no. cxix, lines 1–2; p. 241, no. clxxxiii, lines 1–2 (possibly this poem is not by Wyatt).
115. K. Muir (ed.), *Life and Letters of Sir Thomas Wyatt* (Liverpool, 1963), p. 23. Cf. for even greater scepticism, R.M. Warnicke, 'The eternal triangle and court politics: Henry VIII, Anne Boleyn and Sir Thomas Wyatt', *Albion*, xviii (1986),

565–79, though in her book, Warnicke accepts the relevance of 'Who so list to hunt', and so seems to undermine her argument (*Anne Boleyn*, pp. 67–8). It is often supposed that 'Circa regna tonat' (*Wyatt: Complete Poems*, p. 155, no. cxxiii line 11) ('These bloody days have broken my heart') refers to the executions. 'In mourning wise since daily I increase' certainly does (ibid., p. 255, no. cxcvii). 'The axe is home, your heads be in the street/ The trickling tears doth fall so from my eyes,/ I scarce may write, my paper is so wet'. Wyatt explained that he 'must needs bewail the death of some be gone'. He lamented not Anne but those executed with her. Can his poem be used as evidence for their guilt? Wyatt lamented their deaths, not the injustice of their condemnations. He – and the world – did not mourn them equally. Of Mark Smeaton he wrote 'what moan should I for thee make more/ Since that thy death thou hast deserved best'; of Brereton he said that 'common voice doth not so sore thee rue/ As other twain that doth before appear'. But it seems that it was their past characters, rather than the charges against them, that swayed men's attitudes: if Rochford had not been so proud, more would have bemoaned him; Mark was criticised because he had tried to rise above his station. Only in the case of Norris did Wyatt allude to immediate actions: 'To think what hap did thee so lead or guide,/ Whereby thou has both thee and thine undone'. It would be unwise to press Wyatt's verse too hard as evidence here. It is unlikely that Cromwell protected Wyatt. It has been speculated that 'The pillar perished is whereto I lent' (Ibid., p. 86, no. xxix) refers to Cromwell, but there is no telling internal detail. Wyatt's father thanked Henry directly for his leniency (*LP*, XI 1492) while Wyatt himself later blamed the king for his arrest (*LP*, XIII ii 270 (5)). In relation to Wyatt Cromwell appears no more than an agent of the king (*LP*, X 840, 1131).
116. *LP*, V 907.
117. *LP*, VI 733.
118. *LP*, VI 964.
119. *LP*, VIII 862 (2); cf. William Peto's claim that Henry had slept with Anne's mother and sister: *LP*, XII ii 962.
120. *LP*, VI 923.
121. PRO SP1/76 f. 195 (*LP*, VI 613), cited by Dowling, 'William Latimer's Chronickille', pp. 33–4.
122. *LP*, VIII 1, 826.
123. *Statutes of the Realm*, iii. 473–4 (25 Henry VIII c.22 (5)).
124. Ascoli, p. 263, lines 1007–8.
125. For further discussion see E.W. Ives, 'The fall of Anne Boleyn reconsidered' and G.W. Bernard, 'The fall of Anne Boleyn: a rejoinder', *English Historical Review*, cvii (1992), pp. 651–74; R.M. Warnicke, 'The fall of Anne Boleyn revisited', *English Historical Review*, cviii (1993), pp. 653–65; T. Thornton, 'The integration of Cheshire into the Tudor nation state in the early sixteenth century', *Northern History*, xxix (1993), pp. 40–63 esp. pp. 47–52. Relevant also are discussions of Anne's religion. See M. Dowling, 'Anne Boleyn and reform', *Journal of Ecclesiastical History*, xxxv (1984), pp. 30–46; Ives, *Anne Boleyn*, esp. pp. 302–3, 313; G.W. Bernard, 'Anne Boleyn's religion', *Historical Journal*, xxxvi (1993), pp. 1–20; E.W. Ives, 'Anne Boleyn and the early Reformation in England: the contemporary evidence', *Historical Journal*, xxxvii (1994), pp. 389–400, esp p. 400 where Ives offers a new argument for faction; and T.S. Freeman, 'Research, rumour and propaganda: Anne Boleyn in Foxe's "Book of Martyrs"', *Historical Journal*, xxxviii (1995), pp. 797–819.

5
Elton's Cromwell[1]

For Sir Geoffrey Elton, Thomas Cromwell was 'one of the most remarkable English statesmen of the sixteenth century and one of the most remarkable in the country's history',[2] who 'instigated and in part accomplished a major and enduring transformation in virtually every aspect of the nation's public life'.[3] He was 'a statesman with real and even elevated purposes, a man of genuine understanding and affability, a tower of strength to those who sought his help',[4] Above all, he was the architect of the Tudor Revolution in Government, 'a revolution in the kingdom from which the nation emerged transformed and altered in every aspect of its life.[5] In his last book, Elton continued to assert essentially the same views of Cromwell's work: 'he instilled so novel a force and concentrated purpose into government that something like a major transformation took place in the relations between rulers and ruled'.[6] In contrast, Henry VIII, according to Elton, had 'an unoriginal and unproductive mind', one 'unable to penetrate independently to the heart of a problem'.[7] It was Cromwell who saw to the administration of the kingdom: 'the details of government, the day-to-day work of the executive, the control and reform of the administrative machine, these were in his hands'.[8] 'In Cromwell's years of power the king rarely interfered in administrative matters and ... Cromwell, not Henry, was really the government'.[9] By and large Elton's interpretation has commanded the field, owing not least to his tireless articulation of it over forty years. R.B. Wernham, who wrote a pungent review of *The Tudor Revolution in Government*, was unusual in questioning Elton's claims about the relationship of Henry VIII and Cromwell; but unlike Elton, he did not reiterate his views.[10] Later critics of *The Tudor Revolution in Government* concentrated, in what became a famous debate, on the issues of administration and government that Elton had raised, rather than on the specific question of king and minister. Meanwhile Elton received powerful support from A.G. Dickens:

> The eight years of Cromwell's ministry form a truly notable episode in the history of the English state. In that of the church they are equally revolutionary years, in part destructive, in part as highly constructive. And it cannot reasonably be questioned that Cromwell supplied their chief guiding force ... By contrast, outside these eight years, the reign of Henry VIII has scarcely a single creative or revolutionary achievement to its credit ... between the years 1532 and 1540 all is different.

Creation, destruction and change are visible on all sides; something like a planned revolution issues from the mind of a minister ... Cromwell had his own clear vision of the sovereign state.[11]

True, J.J. Scarisbrick's biography, *Henry VIII* (1968), is generally seen as modifying Elton in emphasising Henry's role – 'once again exalting Henry's personal responsibility for the reformation';[12] and Scarisbrick does indeed claim that 'as far as the central event of the 1530s is concerned, namely the establishment of the royal supremacy, he [Cromwell] was the executant of the king's designs ... he neither worked alone nor was the true initiator of these royal undertakings'. Yet those remarks followed a rather more Eltonian claim:

> That the 1530s were a decisive decade in English history was due largely to his [Cromwell's] energy and vision. He was immediately responsible for the vast legislative programme of the later sessions of the reformation parliament. He oversaw the breach with Rome and the establishment of the royal supremacy.

Later Scarisbrick described Cromwell as 'a genius, perhaps the most accomplished servant any English monarch had enjoyed, a royal minister who cut a deeper mark on the history of England than have many of her monarchs'.[13]

More recent studies of the reign of Henry VIII have emphasised faction as the key to the understanding of politics, building on a strand of Elton's arguments that were first elaborated in his discussion of the fall of Thomas Cromwell. 'No one has doubted that the machinations of Cromwell's enemies, with Norfolk and Gardiner at their head, were decisive in turning the king against his minister', Elton wrote, adding that it was 'not false polices or opposition to the king's religious desires really brought about his overthrow, but the personal enmity of the men whose power he had taken away'.[14] Yet such approaches have once again emphasised the dominant role of Cromwell until toppled, and, even when conceding an ultimate – though only occasional – role as arbiter to the king, correspondingly reduced that of Henry. E.W. Ives has summarised arguments he has been elaborating over two decades: 'government policy and initiative did not arise from the monarch's executive will; they emerged from the shifting political and individual context around him'.[15] J.A. Guy has on occasions adopted a strongly factional interpretation, for example, writing that Henry 'listened to his intimates far more than he supposed and was influenced and even manipulated by the prevailing balance at court'; and that 'Cromwell was ... the driving force behind the reformation in the 1530s'.[16] More recently, he has put forward a weaker version. But when he sees Cromwell executed in 1540 as 'a victim of faction politics', he is still endorsing Elton's assessment of the balance of power between Cromwell, his supposed opponents and the king.[17]

It is the contention of this paper, however, that Elton was wrong above all in minimising, as have so many of the historians who have followed him, the independent role of Henry VIII, so misrepresenting the relationship between king and minister. Given their long and continuing influence on a generation of Tudor historians, Elton's claims still demand close and critical attention. Cromwell, it will be argued here, was no more, and no less, than the king's loyal and hard-working servant. Much of Elton's case, when scrutinised, turns out, as we shall see, to rest on surmise and assertion. A typical instance is Elton's declaration that Cromwell chose for himself the most important of the offices to which he was appointed – principal secretary in *c*. April 1534, master of the rolls in October 1534 and lord privy seal in July 1536: 'Henry's share in the business was confined to allowing the minister to accumulate his collection of offices'.[18] But Elton offers no evidence whatsoever in support of this somewhat improbable claim.

* * *

Just what then was Cromwell's role? At the beginning of his University of London PhD thesis, 'Thomas Cromwell: aspects of his administrative work', (1948),[19] Elton, in a momentary hedging of his bets, suggested that 'it may be unprofitable to engage in a controversy which may for ever remain undecided. King and minister are so inextricably entangled with each other, and the evidence is so insufficient, that every answer will, in the last resort, remain a personal verdict'.[20] But within a page he had roundly declared that 'whatever of lasting value was done in England under Henry VIII was done while Cromwell was in power'.[21] He added:

> No one can now say with confidence exactly how much each man contributed to the work of the decade, but it is simply not possible to accept that the powerful revolutionary impulse of those years should have come from the king since there is no sign of it at all in the other parts of the reign. It came from the minister whose clear sight and willingness to take risks throughout contrasted with his master's habitual preference for caution and procrastination in face of all major issues.[22]

'Nothing', said Professor Elton, 'is further from the truth than the old prejudice which sees in him only a faithful instrument to his master'.[23] 'While it may be doubtful how far the policy of those years was his or Henry's, it is quite certain that the administration and detailed government of the country were in his hands alone. His correspondence testifies to that in ample manner'.[24]

The difficulty with Elton's argument is that he so often invokes the general to prove the particular: when this is done repeatedly it strains credulity. For example, when Elton discusses the court of augmentations, he comments:

> that it was Cromwell who designed the new organisation on the model of the duchy [of Lancaster] is a point which cannot be proved directly ... His outstanding position at this time, and his interest in administrative matters, cannot be in doubt, nor has it ever been suggested that he was not responsible for the policy of confiscating the monastic lands which made the court of augmentations necessary. The least that

must be said is that he is more likely than anyone else to have stood godfather to the new plan; if there is individual responsibility to be allotted, it must be to him.[25]

'If there was a single brain behind the administrative innovation embodied in the court of augmentations, it must have been his. A scheme so carefully worked out suggests one individual schemer; the plan requires a planner'.[26] It is a dangerously convenient style of argument.

Most vividly, Elton's Cromwell was the author of the break with Rome, devising both the practical policies that implemented it and the imperial ideology that justified it, and so saving a clueless and hesitant monarch from the embarrassment of failure. 'Henry turned to the man who intended to throw out the pope with the cast-off wife, to carry through the divorce in England, and to create the "empire" of England where no foreign potentate's writ should run'.[27] Elton reiterated this view some forty years later: 'Cromwell, the man who showed Henry the way out of the dilemma created by the pope's refusal to end that first marriage, brought to the task his vision of a strictly independent, unitary realm, organised entirely within its own borders and dedicated to reform in both the spiritual and the secular sphere'.[28] Such an interpretation now fails to convince since it is clear from materials for the king's cause compiled as early as 1527–29 and from diplomatic correspondence in the same years that Henry VIII was already deploying ideas and issuing threats that could lead to a break with Rome.[29] Moreover, when the bill of annates was attacked in parliament in March 1532, it was Henry who went to the house of commons in person on three occasions; in the end he forced the house to divide, with some members coming on to his side for fear of his indignation.[30] And a month later, when two MPs (according to the imperial ambassador) or one MP named Temse (according to Hall) dared to criticise the king's divorce, Henry sent for the speaker and twelve MPs, and made a long speech in denunciation of the oaths of allegiance that bishops swore to popes.[31] Such evidence of Henry's actions casts grave doubt on Elton's claims for Cromwell's role in the making of the break with Rome.

In making his case for Cromwell as the author of that policy, Elton relied heavily on his interpretation of parliamentary drafts. But here in many ways Elton became a prisoner of his sources. His early articles on Cromwell's work in preparing the parliamentary statutes that gave legal sanction to the break with Rome rested on a minute scrutiny of surviving drafts of the supplication against the ordinaries, the act of appeals and other statutes. But Elton assumed, rather than proved, that the ideas expressed in these acts were Cromwell's. Just because these drafts – or more often, corrections written on to those drafts – were in Cromwell's handwriting does not prove that the ideas which they expressed were themselves devised by Cromwell, as Elton tended to assume. That some (but not all) of the corrections in some of the drafts of the Supplication against the Ordinaries (A, B, C1, C2, but neither D, apart from what Elton sees as two small exceptions, nor E, to use Elton's notation) were in *Cromwell's hand* is less revealing of authorship and motivation than Elton claimed. If Cromwell had a master plan ready made in 1532, as Elton supposed – 'he ... supplied a new version [of the Commons supplication] based on the 1529 drafts'[32] – it is curious that he did not prepare a complete text wholly in his own writing. That all the surviving evidence of Cromwell's involvement lies in corrections to texts written by others does rather suggest that he was reacting to matters which others had raised. Others were also involved in the work of revision, notably Thomas Audley, whose revisions are found in draft D.[33] The complexity of the relationships between eight drafts and four fragments of the Act of Appeals – Elton offers a diagram – make the construction of an intellectual development a highly hazardous undertaking. In the end assertion backs up assertion. 'The man who appears again and again is Cromwell. His clerks drew up the drafts, or most of them. He supervised the drafting, himself added some of the more important clauses, and shaped the provisions one by one by constant correction. ... The act against appeals was his act. It embodied his political thought and marked the triumph of his policy in the counsels of the king'.[34]

Elton claims that in the course of the drafting of the Act of Appeals Henry added 'ill-considered' contributions which were then removed,[35] but the paper in which that claim is presented does not really validate it in detail. The most significant insertions by Henry – not included in the statute – were claims that temporal and spiritual authority 'ar deryved and dependeth frome and of the same imperiall crowne of this realme ... and in this manner of wise proceedeth the iurisdiccion spirituall and temporall of this realme of and from the said imperiall crowne and none otherwise'. If this brief addition and subsequent removal of such phrases has any special significance – and it need not have – it seems to point to Henry's, rather than Cromwell's, insistence on imperial ideology.[36] Elton himself briefly came close to conceding the criticism that the origin of the ideas in these bills is far from clear-cut when discussing the act 'concernyng the clerkes of the signet and privie seale' of 1536,[37] but only momentarily: 'on the other hand, it is of course possible that the first proposal came from someone else', he notes, before going on to conclude that 'however that may be, it is inconceivable ... that Cromwell should not have been squarely behind the act as passed; it ought to be considered as one of his administrative measures'.[38]

Similarly in a discussion of memoranda prepared for a council meeting on 2 December 1533, Elton asserts that the corrections in Cromwell's handwriting show that he was in charge. Cromwell made additions to what Elton sees as a second draft. 'Whoever prepared the first draft ... these and other corrections show who supervised the second. They demonstrate Cromwell's complete control of the council's agenda'. But why should Cromwell's handwriting prove any such thing? Why could he not simply be writing down what the king, or someone else, had said? Elton's failure to argue the point directly vitiates his approach. The matter under consideration was the households of Catherine, Mary and Elizabeth. Twice the minute states that 'the kynges highnez hath apoynted' who shall go there, and once that 'the kynges highnez hath apoynted' that Mary should be conveyed from her house to Hatfield. Elton remarks that 'the fact that this matter came up before the council only to be immediately taken out of its hands again suggests that Henry had little to do with the drawing up of the agenda'. A reading more attentive to what the record says would rather suggest that it was the king who was making the decisions and issuing orders on matters clearly of considerable personal concern.[39]

Elton also offered a convoluted argument concerning the Dispensations Act.[40] Cromwell drafted it; promoted it in the Commons before the king saw it; amended it at the king's instance by adding a clause delaying the coming into force of the act; and then overbore Henry a week later.

> The mess into which this very important bill got suggests strongly that Cromwell, in the Commons, was moving faster than the King found himself able to follow, an interpretation supported by the note for some very drastic anti-papal legislation planned on the eve of the session but of which nothing materialised.[41]

Here Elton is engaged in a doubtful attempt to reconcile conflicting and patchy evidence relating to three distinct bills or acts: (i) a bill or bills abolishing Peter's pence and papal dispensations, (ii) a bill abolishing the authority of the bishop of Rome, committed to Chancellor Audley, and (iii) the Dispensations Act as finally passed. Elton's elaboration rests on a series of guesses about origins and actions, which then produce a firm conclusion that leads to a re-reading of the whole story. All he says about the king being overborne is pure speculation. And what are Elton's grounds for claiming the Dispensations Act as Cromwell's work? 'Its whole tenor shows that it was'. What exactly was 'the mess' into which the bill fell? The bill was not to come into effect until the king confirmed it by letters patent – something Elton sees as 'that very belated afterthought', indicating 'discordant counsels within the government itself', namely 'Cromwell's singlemindedness and Henry's preference for procrastination': 'Cromwell, in the Commons, was moving faster than the king found himself able to follow'.[42] Yet that need not be so. Perhaps Henry 'was still eager to have some leverage in bargaining with the pope'.[43] Another explanation could be some opposition in parliament, which was contained by the offer of suspended implementation, not seriously intended, but a useful ploy. Whatever the reason, royal letters patent were issued a week after the end of the session.[44]

Elton also uses the evidence of parliamentary legislation to make a case for Cromwell as social reformer: 'Cromwell manifestly stands at the centre of whatever was being planned and done'.[45] Cromwell was involved in the sheep bill of 1536, writing a letter to the king that Elton characterised as 'quite uncommonly anxious, flamboyant and deferential.'[46] He corrected a petition about decayed towns.[47] He probably encouraged towns to seek acts to help rebuild ruinous houses (but no specific evidence is cited: this rests on Elton's hunch).[48] His memoranda contain notes for bills of parliament.[49] He introduced a bill for the establishment of a bourse in London, following Gresham, in 1539, a sumptuary bill in 1532, and a woodlands bill in 1540.[50] And there was of course what is usually seen as Cromwell's poor law.[51] Elton's evidence, and speculations, make a good case for the involvement of a minister in the preparation of parliamentary business, often in response to pressures, petitions, letters; and, no doubt, the hard facts of problems. What Elton does not squarely consider is whether he was unusual and how novel the measures of the 1530s were. How far did all this differ from Wolsey? Had not governments long attended to the problems of the common weal in this way? How clear is the supposedly unique position of Cromwell in all this activity?

Discussing a paper entitled 'A memoriall for the Kings Highnes, declaring the kynde of thingis wherein risith yerelye aswell his certein Reuenues as his Casuall Reuenues, and who be officers to his highnes in that behalf',[52] Elton claims that the facts that Cromwell (i) drafted the last paragraph – relating to the mint – and (ii) in places added some notes (none of them very striking) show that 'he was responsible for having it drawn up'.[53] That seems to run way ahead of the evidence. And Henry VIII may have been much more closely involved in the making of the poor law in 1536 than Elton allowed. A letter by Thomas Dorset to the mayor of Plymouth described how on Saturday [11 March] 'the kinges grace came in amonge the burgesis of the parliament, and delyvered theym a bille', asking them to examine it and weigh it in conscience, 'to see yf it be for a comyn wele to his subjectis'. He would come there again on the Wednesday to hear their minds. 'There shalbe a proviso made for poore people', Dorset continued, 'sturdye beggaris ... shalbe sett a worke at the kynges charge'. Henry was clearly taking a leading part in the parliamentary passage of what became the poor law. For Elton, Cromwell was in charge: 'he mobilized Henry VIII to help through a commonwealth measure'. But would it not be more convincing to see Henry's actions rather as strong evidence for his close involvement in the making of the policy?[54]

In Elton's early work, Cromwell was seen as an essentially secular figure. Later, most especially in *Reform and Renewal*, and in *Reform and Reformation*, Elton allowed Cromwell a religious dimension, seeing him as a proponent of evangelical reform, though still asserting that 'to Cromwell, the reformed church was to serve the purposes of the reformed commonwealth, whereas more definitely religious minds would have wished to reverse that order of priorities'.[55] Again Elton insisted on the primacy of Cromwell's role. 'Nearly always he [Cromwell] professed to be acting in the King's name, though twice at least he wrote in his own, but that the drive for this extremely vigorous activity (unknown before and much reduced thereafter) came from the minister both the documents and the probabilities make plain'. Cautiously, Elton noted that 'one can speak with less assurance of the mind behind the developing policies', before going on boldly to proclaim that

> there are general signs that in the four years or so from mid-1535 Cromwell applied himself to the building of a new commonwealth ... Changes in doctrine, changes in ceremonies, attacks on monasteries and purgatory and superstitions, the promotion of the English Bible, positive moves towards a better education for laity and clergy alike, the institution of parish registers – these and other manifestations of Cromwell's relentless reforming zeal brought real disturbance to the people at large.[56]

'The story of the English Bible in the 1530s provides very clear proof that, notwithstanding his careful professions of subservience, the vicegerent was quite capable of pushing on reforms not altogether pleasing to the supreme head and of doing this by disguising the truth of events from his master'.[57] Here Elton was linking his interpretation with that of A.G. Dickens,[58] and this emphasis on Cromwell as religious reformer has become fashionable.[59] The direct evidence for Cromwell's religion, however, is surprisingly thin, and claims for his evangelism tend to circularity: since he is supposed to be responsible for the policies pursued in the mid-1530s, then given their evangelical nature, he must have been an evangelical; since he was an evangelical, and given that the policies pursued in the 1530s were evangelical, he must have been in charge. Moreover, Elton himself did not elaborate these claims in anything like the detail which he had earlier deployed to make the case for Cromwell's part in the break with Rome, instead essentially endorsing the vision of Cromwell as reformer that Dickens had put forward. For that reason this will simply be noted here.[60] Despite Elton's confident claim that 'Cromwell ... in four years effortlessly swept some 800 monastic houses off the map of England',[61] and his remark (in a passage in which his main concern was to prove Cromwell's role in the setting up of the court of augmentations), '... nor has it ever been suggested that he [Cromwell] was not responsible for the policy of confiscating the monastic lands',[62] it is extraordinarily difficult to document Cromwell's supposed authorship of the dissolution of the monasteries. Elton offers a schematic picture of the evolution of Cromwell's policy from

> the erection of a principle (monastic seclusion is a false retreat from social duty, and the wealth thus locked up should be employed for social reform, especially education), through the collection of statistical data (the *Valor Ecclesiasticus*), to the first steps which tackled a manageable number of institutions, the carrying through of the vast programme in a mere four years, and the solution of the many administrative problems raised.[63]

But no references are cited in support of such claims, so leaving vexed questions unresolved. How far, for example, can the statute of 1536 dissolving the smaller monasteries be taken to reflect Cromwell's opinions? Does Cromwell's obvious involvement in the process of dissolution in the later 1530s prove that he was the author of the policy? Or might Henry himself have been instrumental? He was, after all, a king who, in orders to his ambassador Sir Ralph Sadler in 1543, could advise the earl of Arran, the governor of Scotland, to instruct commissioners 'most secretly and groundely to examyn all the religious of there conversacion and behavour ... wherby *if it be wel handeled* [my emphasis] he shal get knowleage of all there abhomynacions'. The knowingly cynical tone of that advice hints at the king's earlier role in achieving in England 'thextirpation of the state of monkes and fryers, thenterprise wherof requireth politique handelyng'.[64]

Elton, of course, made strong claims for Cromwell as author of a 'revolution in government', but those claims, always controversial, have not worn well, and even those of Elton's pupils who have written on aspects of the 1530s closest to their master's interest have increasingly dissented from them.[65] Much of what was done was simply obvious and necessary, such as the administrative arrangements to deal with the monastic lands acquired by the crown. It is hard, *pace* Elton, to see anything particularly creative or even especially distinctive about Cromwell's work (even Elton at one point concedes against the main thrust of his arguments that 'it is doubtful whether there was anything totally new about any of the ideas that became operative in the 1530s'[66]). Cromwell looks increasingly unconvincing as a supposed advocate of constitutional government as against royal despotism, despite Elton's insistence that 'in the sixteenth century the possibility of a despotism was deliberately and with care demolished, and this too was the work of Thomas Cromwell'.[67] Cromwell's supposed 'concept of a unitary state'[68] over-schematises what were neither particularly original nor radical approaches to the perennial challenges of ruling Wales and Ireland, heightened by obvious fear of potential opposition to the break with Rome. Moreover, such a formulation once again assumes that these measures must have been Cromwell's. Here it is interesting to note that while Peter Roberts, a pupil of Elton, endorses the general view of Cromwell as 'the architect of the legislative programme for the extension of the realm' in the 1530s, when he turns to his own special interest, Wales and the Act of Union, he offers a different assessment: 'though the problem of disorder in Wales appears regularly in Cromwell's own memoranda in these years, he was not responsible for devising the solution that was eventually adopted'.[69]

What is perhaps most remarkable is Cromwell's energy, his busy-ness – though the distinctiveness of even that may be an illusion created by the survival of more evidence relating to Cromwell than to other ministers. (It is worth remarking that one of the poet John Skelton's satires against Wolsey berated him precisely for being excessively, futilely busy: 'besy, besy, besy and besynes agayne',[70] and that Sir Thomas Wyatt's satire of Francis Bryan presented him as ever busy, 'to thee ... that trots still up and down/ And never rests, but running day and night/ From realm to realm, from city, street, and town', like a pig in royal service.[71]) It is best to see Cromwell as the king's hardworking secretary, writing his letters – 'why keep a secretary and write letters yourself', as Wernham wisely inquired many years ago in his review of *The Tudor Revolution in Government*[72] – sending out his instructions, dealing in a routine executive way with a mass of day-to-day concerns, contributing, no doubt, to the working out of details, but in the end much less influential than he has been presented, and probably less independent in action than Wolsey had been. As Elton himself momentarily recognized, 'it may be that Cromwell appears to dominate his age because his papers have survived', though he at once went on to say that 'the accident of preservation ought not to be ignored, but it must not be overstressed', and to claim that 'the record ... cannot really be suspected of serious distortion when it sets the stamp of Cromwell on nearly everything done in these ten years' [the 1530s].[73]

If Cromwell was not the author of the Reformation, no great social reformer, and not the architect of a revolution in government, was he none the less still the 'leader of a court faction', as Elton hinted in his early paper on the fall of Cromwell, and as his pupil David Starkey has extravagantly elaborated?[74] Such an interpretation once again asserts the dominance of Cromwell and minimizes the part played by Henry, seen more as puppet than puppeteer. In making such claims, both Elton and Starkey have tended to proceed by assuming the truth of their factional model of politics and then using it to rewrite the detailed narrative of events. What is largely missing, however, is any considered evaluation of the relationship between king and minister. Yet there is important and suggestive material on that question that Elton and Starkey have ignored or misinterpreted. And where much of what has been discussed so far has necessarily involved a sceptical assessment of Elton's claims, here it is possible to offer definite evidence in support of the proposition that Cromwell's role was in every sense that of a subordinate to the king.

* * *

Much may be gleaned from Cromwell's language. In his many surviving letters (confiscated when he fell), Cromwell always refers to the king's wishes and orders: 'the kinges highnes desireth you ...'; 'the kinges highnes pleasure and commandment is ...'; 'the kinges maieste whose graciouse pleasure is ...'; 'his magestye hathe willid me to sygnyfie vnto youe that his graciouse pleasur and commaundyment is ...'.[75] Was that mere form? Does this reflect just Cromwell's 'care to seem always to be executing only Henry's will'?[76] Was Cromwell actually acting wholly independently of the king, while referring to the king simply to cover himself? 'Even when writing on his own Cromwell would often pretend to be merely communicating orders received from king and council'.[77] But who would have been taken in? Is it conceivable that Cromwell should have acted in the form of a modern British government in which the prime minister and cabinet decide on bills which are first announced in the queen's speech written on their instructions, then passed by parliament and finally enacted as the queen's; or, more modestly, that Cromwell should have acted like a protector ruling during a royal minority? Are Cromwell's letters referring to the king's commands to be interpreted as really containing Cromwell's commands? Was Elton correct in suggesting that 'even when writing on his own Cromwell would often pretend to be merely communicating orders received from king and council',[78] or that 'everything was ostensibly by the king's pleasure, but in reality Henry's ministers had considerably [sic] latitude and discretion, provided they pretended to be authorized by his will'?[79] To prove that last assertion, Elton cites a letter from the council of the north to Cromwell in 1540 that seems to show the opposite of what Elton claims. The members of the council were anxious because Cromwell had informed them that the king's pleasure was that a property should go to a man he had named, even though Sir Richard Rich had at the same time written to them that it was the king's pleasure that it should go to someone else. They wanted to know what the king's pleasure really was. Clearly, they did not think that Cromwell – or Rich – could have the decisive say.[80] It is interesting that on receiving a letter from Cromwell in July 1537, the duke of Norfolk replied, 'my good Lord, to wright to you playnlie, as to myne especiall good Lord and frend, surely I thinke ye wolde not haue wryton to me concernyng this matier as ye did, but that His Majestie was pryvey therunto'.[81] In July 1536, when upbraiding Stephen Gardiner, bishop of Winchester, Cromwell declared that 'I will not wade in any priuate matier in the king my soueraign lordes name vnles I haue his commaundement soo to doo'.[82] Later, after 'suche contencyous matier' between them, Cromwell assured Gardiner that he had 'not writen more at any season vnto you in any matier thenne the kinges highnes hathe befor the sending of it furthe perused'.[83] Marillac, the French ambassador, wrote in April 1540 'ce roy commence a faire des ministres, en rappellant a credit et authorite ceux qu'il auoit rebutez, et en rabaissant ceux qu'il auoit eleuez': the stress is very much on the king here. It was rumoured that Tunstal would succeed Cromwell as vicar-general. But if Cromwell retained his credit and authority it would be 'a cause qu'il est fort assidu es affaires, bien qu'il soit grossier pour les manier, et qu'il ne fait chose qu'il ne communique premierment a son maistre': because Cromwell did nothing without first consulting the king his master.[84] When in April 1539 Cromwell wrote to Henry that 'this daye I have writen your graces advises to your seruauntes Christophor mount and Thomas Paynell to be declared vnto the duke and Landsgrave as your highnes prescribed vnto me', are we to suppose that Henry had in fact not given his minister any instructions and that Cromwell was simply pretending to the king to be following instructions that Henry had not actually given him?[85]

Scattered through his papers are notes that Cromwell regularly made of things to do. Typically, they begin in a secretary's hand and end with additions, often even greater in length, in Cromwell's own writing. Cromwell cannot have made these notes for any purpose other than to serve as reminders for himself; they were not meant for anyone else's eyes, apart from his own and his secretaries'. They may therefore be regarded as especially revealing. A good deal of business is simply listed. But, significantly, often Cromwell makes a note of the need to know what the king wants done. Cromwell frequently writes 'to know whether the king will ...' or 'to know the king's pleasure' or 'what the king will have done with ...'.[86] Often this involved dealings with foreign powers, whether Henry's ambassadors abroad, or foreign ambassadors in England. 'For knowleage of the kinges pleasur in the pointes to be treated of with thambassadors';[87] 'to speke with the kyng touching the duke of Bavyer's ambasyador for his dispache and what shalbe the effect of the kynges lettres that his highnes wyll wryte, and what gyftes he wyll gyue hym';[88] 'what answer the kyng wyll gyue to the duke of Lunnenborges messenger and Doctor Adam;[89] 'to remembre to knowe what reward the kynges highness will gyue the Lubek';[90] 'to knowe the kinges pleasure whenne the Lubikes shall repayre to his grace';[91] 'what the kyng myndyth for sendyng into Germanye';[92] 'to know whom the king will appoynt to go with Doctor Lee to Lubek';[93] 'to know his plesure whether he wyll wrytt any thing to Sir John Wallop'.[94] When Stephen Vaughan and Christopher Mont were negotiating with the duke of Saxony in autumn 1533 (not especially fruitfully since the duke was reluctant to add to his quarrel with Charles V by taking on Henry's cause as well), Cromwell noted: 'to know the kynges plesure whether Vaughan shall goo forward or return'. In the same set of remembrances he noted: 'To declare Cristopher [Mont's] and Stephyns Vaughans lettres and to know answer'.[95] That would appear to dispose of any claim that it was Cromwell who was masterminding a German alliance: Henry's attitude would appear to be crucial and Cromwell emerges as the executor of the king's wishes. Strategic decisions were the king's: 'what order the kinges highnes will take if the Scottes do not sue for peax after this treux and abstinence of warre and what promysions shalbe made in that behalf by cause the treux lakith but a yere'.[96]

State trials evidently required the king's decisions. Several remembrances refer to Elizabeth Barton, the nun of Kent. 'To know what the king will haue done with the None and her complyces';[97] 'what shalbe the kynges plesure for sendyng the Nun to Canterberye and whether she shall return';[98] 'what the kynges highnes wooll haue done with them that shall go to Canterburye to do penaunce';[99] 'to knowe whether the kyng wyll haue all the rest of the monkes and frers [involved with the nun of Kent] sent for', 'to know what way the kyng wyll take with all the sayd malefactors';[100] 'that all the other monkes of Cristes churche may be sent for also with conuenyent diligens and to knowe the kynges pleasure therein';[101] 'to know the kinges pleasure whether all they which haue bene prevey vnto the nonnes boke shalbe sent for or not'; 'whether the king will haue my lord of Rochestor send for not' [sic].[102]

In 1535 Cromwell's notes, in a set of 'remembrances at my next goyng to the courte', included the following: 'to aduertise the kyng of the orderyng of Maister Fissher'; 'to knowe his pleasure touchyng Maister More and to declare the opynyon of the judges'; 'whether Maister Fissher shall go to execucion, with also the other'; 'when shalbe done farther touching Maister More'.[103] Other remembrances also dealt with opposition: 'what the king wyll haue done at the Charterhouse of London and Rychmonde;[104] 'to knowe the kinges pleasure touching the Lord Mordant and suche other as Frere Forest named for his principal friendes';[105] 'for the dyettes of yong Courteney and Pole and also of the countes of Sarum and to know the kinges pleasur therin;[106] 'what the kyng wyll haye done with the lady of Sares [Margaret, countess of Salisbury];[107] 'what the kynges highnes will haue feder don with the late abbott of Westminster'.[108] The remembrances included religious matters: 'first touching the anabaptistes and what the king will do with them';[109] 'to know the kynges plesure for Tyndalle, and whether I shall wryt or not';[110] 'for the convocation of the clergy and what shalbe the kynges pleasure therin'.[111] More general policy questions and practical decisions also occur: 'to know the kinges pleasure for my lorde of Kyldare and my lorde of Osserooyde and for the determynation of the mattiers of Irelande';[112] 'to declare the matiers of Irland matters to the kinges highnes and to devise what shalbe done there';[113] 'to knowe the kinges pleasure touching a general pardon';[114] 'to know what the kingis pleasure shalbe for suche persons as be outlawed in all shires of this realme and what processe shalbe made agenst them';[115] 'to knowe the kinges pleasure when he will haue musters of his gonners and also to know whether he will have any of my men and when he will see them';[116] 'generall musters to be made thorow the realme yf so shall stand with the kynges plessure'.[117]

It is difficult to see why Cromwell should have made such essentially private notes for his own use in this form if he were in effect making decisions and ruling the country himself. There would have been no need to remind himself to learn the king's pleasure if he was not in actual fact doing so. These remembrances strongly suggest that the minister did not act without knowing what the king wanted. They show that the king was very much in command, that Cromwell referred constantly to him on any questions that needed judgment. Henry was asked to decide who should go abroad and when, to say at what moment ambassadors should be brought to see him, and to determine what answers should be made to letters, messages and requests from abroad. Henry was asked for instructions on how the principal opponents of the king's policies – the Nun of Kent, More, Fisher – should be dealt with. The strong impression is of a minister doing the daily executive work of government, drawing his master's attention to the need to fill vacant posts, but asking the king for guidance on how to act in all issues of importance. There is no sense whatsoever here of a minister acting on his own initiative, or manipulating his master, or making substantial suggestions to the king, or trying to temper the king's proposals.

Elton, of course, draws on these remembrances in places, but he does not consider what they might reveal when analysed together as a genre. And his detailed readings are open to challenge. He treats 'a long list of matters to be reported to the king' – including the despatch of money to Ireland, the delivery of £300 to Mr Gonson (clerk of the ships), the preparation of £1000 for building at Calais, the making ready of a similar sum for the making of the haven at Dover – as evidence that proves 'the closest personal attention to every detail involved in the office of a treasurer' such as Cromwell was. But that argument cuts both ways. If such lists are evidence of 'close personal attention to every detail', and if such lists are matters 'to be reported to the king', does not that suggest that the king – far from being 'a lazy king' – was maintaining a detailed oversight of the administration of his government? Was not Wernham correct in urging that Cromwell's 'submitting a whole string of quite minor details to the king ... powerfully suggest[s] that it was the minister and not Henry who did as he was told'?[118]

Other sources rather confirm the impression of the king in control. In a summary of council decisions taken on 2 December 1533, alongside item 14, which deals with a league and amity with German princes, is written the phrase, 'in the kynges arbytrement'; alongside item 15 – 'like practise to be made and practiced with the cytees of Lubeke, Danske, Hamburgh, Bromeswyke' and other Hanse towns – is written the instruction, 'to know when of the kyng'.[119] That would reinforce the claim that it was Henry who took the decisions. Sometimes Cromwell reveals a little more of how things happened. In August 1535 he received a packet of letters from Wallop, the king's ambassador in France,

> which indelayedlie I delyuered vnto the kinges highnes and conferred with his grace theffectes both of your lettres and all others within the saide packet being directed aswell to his highnes as to me. And after his highnes had with me pervsed the hole contentes thoroughlie of your saide lettres, ... ye shall vnderstonde that his highnes commaundid me to make you answer in this wise folowing ...

and there followed much detailed instruction.[120] It points to a close working relationship between king and minister, but one in which the king not only took a detailed interest in policy, especially in diplomacy, but told his minister what to say; Cromwell then set out his master's pleasure and instructions. In February 1539 Cromwell wrote to the king how Castillon, the French ambassador, who had just received letters from Francis I responding to proposals made by Henry, would not tell Cromwell what they said until he had first informed Henry: 'as touching the declaration of the special poinctes he shewed hymself so loth to declare them to me afore he had exposed them to your maieste that I could not conveniently with honeste presse hym of thesame'.[121] In 1540 Cromwell testified how Anne of Cleves often desired to speak with him – but he had not dared not, not until Henry allowed him to.[122]

Praising the king's presiding at the trial of the sacramentary John Lambert, Cromwell wished

> the princes and potentates of Christendom to have a meate place for them there to have seen it vndoubtedly they shuld have moch merveilled at his maiestes most highe wisedome and jugement and reputed hym non otherwise after thesame then in maner the Miroer and light of all other kinges and princes in christendom.

Should Cromwell's awed admiration be seen as disingenuous?[123] From Cromwell's supposed control of the signet, Elton argues that 'its use enabled Cromwell to control the king's correspondence, and this control was increased by the regular employment of signet clerks to draft Henry's letters which quite possibly he never saw until they were submitted ready for his signature'.[124] How can one be so sure that the contents of such letters were unknown to the king: is it not far more likely that they were written according to his instructions? In April 1540 Thomas Wyatt wrote to Cromwell from the emperor's court at Ghent. Cromwell passed on the letter – not just some summary of it, with obvious possibilities for doctoring – to the king. As Sadler informed Cromwell,

> the Kinges Majestie hathe seen these letters of Mr Wyates; the advertisements wherein His Grace liketh well. After the reding of the same, His Majestie commaunded me to remytte, and sende them agayn to your Lordeship; sayeng that, forasmoche as theye were directed to you, it is best that they be answered by you,

giving detailed instructions on what should answers should be made to Wyatt:

> these answers to be made to Mr Wyat by your Lordeshippes proper letters; prayeng you, nevertheless, after your Lordship hathe conceyved the same, to send the mynute thereof to His Highnes, before the post be depeched, to thintent that His Majeste (if it be not according to his mynde) may alter and refourme the same, as shall stonde with his gracious pleasure.[125]

Cromwell duly acknowledged these instructions, while offering some different suggestions on whether Wyatt should accompany Ferdinand de San Severino, Prince of Salerno, or return later – though it seems that they came together, contrary to Cromwell's preferences.[126] The impression Sadler leaves of a dominant king is unmistakable: the minister is ordered to draw up the letter, given detailed instructions on what to say, and required to show the draft to the king for final amendment. Occasionally there are further glimpses into the relationship between king and minister. When the French ambassador, Castillon, complained to the king about his treatment by Cromwell, who was so pro-imperial that Castillon thought he was at the court of the emperor, not that of the king of England, Henry 'a chante une chanson a mon milord Prive seel, disant qu'il estoit bon pour le mesnaige, mais non pour entremettre des affaires des roys; et n'en a pas fait moins a troys ou quatre dudict conseil'. Staged no doubt; yet revealing about the superiority of king to servant.[127] George Paulet, a commissioner in Ireland, brother of William, was alleged to have said of Cromwell how

> the king beknaveth him twice a weke, and sometyme knocke him well about the pate; and yet when he hathe bene well pomeld about the hedde, and shaken up, as it were a dogge, he will come out into the great chambre, shaking of the bushe with as mery a countenaunce as thoughe he mought rule all the roste.[128]

That makes Cromwell very much the king's slave. Under arrest in 1540, Cromwell wrote to Henry that 'if it were in my power to make you live for ever, God knows I would; or to make you so rich that you should enrich all men, or so powerful that all the world should obey you. For your majesty has been most bountiful to me, and more like a father than a master'.[129] The stricken Cromwell's appeal to Henry, 'I crye for mercye mercye mercye', is hard to read as anything other than the desperate and abject plea of a fallen servant to his tyrannical lord,[130] and would have been the more pointless if Cromwell thought the king to be a weak man now controlled by a rival faction. Cranmer's letter to Henry, on Cromwell's arrest, if it can be trusted (since what we have are extracts from a lost original quoted by Herbert of Cherbury), reinforces the sense of Cromwell as the servant of a tyrannical master, rather than the manipulator of a puppet. Cranmer was sorrowful and amazed that Cromwell should be a traitor:

> he that was so advanced by your majesty; he whose surety was only by your majesty; he who loved your majesty (as I ever thought) no less than God; he who studied always to set forwards whatsoever was your majesty's will and pleasure; he that cared for no man's displeasure to serve your majesty; he that was such a servant, in my judgment, in wisdom, diligence, faithfulness, and experience, as no prince in this realm ever had ... if the noble princes of memory, king John, Henry the Second, and Richard II had had such a councillor about them, I suppose that they should never have been so traitorously abandoned and overthrown as those good princes were ... I chiefly loved him for the love which I thought I saw him bear towards your grace, singularly above all other.[131]

For Elton, that merely shows that Cromwell 'was always careful to appear as the king's servant';[132] but it would be more convincing to conclude rather that Cranmer's description of Cromwell as studying always to set forwards whatsoever was Henry's pleasure was as shrewd as it was succinct.

Notes

1. I should like to thank those who have commented on drafts of this paper: C.S.L. Davies, T.B. Pugh, Mark Stoyle, Peter Gwyn, Greg Walker, Richard Hoyle, R.B. Wernham, Patrick Collinson and Penry Williams.
2. G.R. Elton, 'Thomas Cromwell Redivivus', *Archiv fur Reformationsgeschichte*, lxviii (1977), 192–208 at 192, reprinted in G.R. Elton, *Studies in Tudor and Stuart*

Government (4 vols, Cambridge, 1974–92) [hereafter, Elton, *Studies*], iii. 373–90, at 373.
3. Elton, 'Thomas Cromwell Redivivus', 192 (*Studies*, iii. 373).
4. Review in *London Review of Books*, 16 July 1981.
5. G.R. Elton, *Reform and Reformation* (1977), p. 295. The classic statement of these claims is G.R. Elton, *The Tudor Revolution in Government* (Cambridge, 1953).
6. G.R. Elton, *The English* (Oxford, 1992), p. 126.
7. G.R. Elton, 'King or Minister?: the man behind the Henrician Reformation', *History*, xxxix (1954), 216–32 at 218, reprinted in Elton, *Studies*, i. 173–88, 175.
8. G.R. Elton, 'Thomas Cromwell: aspects of his administrative work', University of London PhD thesis, 1948 [hereafter Elton, Thesis], p. 6.
9. Elton, *Tudor Revolution in Government*, p. 175; quoted by R.B. Wernham, *English Historical Review*, lxxi (1956), 95.
10. *English Historical Review*, lxxi (1956), 92–95, esp. 95.
11. A.G. Dickens, *The English Reformation* (2nd edn, 1989), p. 133. Cf. A.G. Dickens, *Thomas Cromwell and the English Reformation* (1959), pp. 174–6.
12. R. O'Day, *The Tudor Age* (1995), p. 293.
13. J.J. Scarisbrick, *Henry VIII* (1968), pp. 304, 303, 383.
14. G.R. Elton, 'Thomas Cromwell's decline and fall', *Historical Journal*, x (1951), 150–85, at 150, 185 (reprinted in Elton, *Studies*, i. 189–230, at 189, 229).
15. E.W. Ives, 'Henry VIII: the political perspective', in D. MacCulloch (ed.), *The Reign of Henry VIII* (1995), p. 33.
16. J.A. Guy, *Tudor England* (Oxford, 1988), pp. 83, 181.
17. J.A. Guy, 'Henry VIII and his ministers', *History Review*, xxiii (1995), 35–40 at 37–40. See above, pp. 5–6.
18. Elton, *Tudor Revolution in Government*, p. 123.
19. It is interesting to note that Elton's thesis, while advancing the bold claims for Cromwell's role and achievement that were to become so familiar, nowhere refers to any 'revolution in government'. Does that lend support to the anecdotal evidence (for which I am grateful to Dr Alastair Duke, Professor Patrick Collinson – cf. his obituary of Elton, *The Independent*, 9 December 1994, p. 16 – and Dr Peter Roberts) that the term was coined in the *viva* by one of his examiners, Professor C.H. Williams, who suggested to the candidate that 'you have stumbled upon – what shall I call it? – a "Tudor revolution in government"'? It is instructive here to note how profoundly influenced C.H. Williams, *English Historical Documents vol. v 1485–1558* (1967) was by Eltonian ideas, in marked contrast to his work in the 1930s. Unfortunately this may be no more than *ben trovato*. Professor R.B. Wernham, who was the external examiner at Elton's *viva* on 20 December 1948, does not recall any such remark. Instead, drawing attention to Elton's acknowledgement in the preface of *The Tudor Revolution in Government* of his 'very great' debt to Sir John Neale, in response to whose criticisms in particular Elton says that he had twice rewritten the book, Professor Wernham suggests that if that remark was made, then or later, 'it sounds to me more like Neale, who had a tendency to get hold of an idea (e.g. the "Puritan choir" in *Elizabeth and her Parliaments* and push it a bridge too far' (letter from Professor Wernham, 10 January 1997).
20. Elton, Thesis, pp. 3–4.
21. Ibid., p. 5.
22. Elton, 'Thomas Cromwell redivivus', p. 202.
23. Elton, *Reform and Reformation*, p. 172.

24. Elton, Thesis, p. 258.
25. Elton, *Tudor Revolution in Government*, p. 212.
26. Elton, Thesis, p. 258. It is interesting to note that earlier Elton did cite evidence as 'proof positive of Cromwell's hand in the establishment of the court of augmentations', namely a draft document drawn up by Thomas Wriothesley, Cromwell's chief clerk, and corrected by Cromwell (ibid., p. 261, from PRO E36 116 ff. 50–53 (*LP*, X 721 (4))). But such an interpretation is not the only possible reading and elsewhere Elton saw it rather as the commission for the commissioners for the dissolution, drafted by Wriothesley and corrected by Cromwell, and thus nothing to do with the court of augmentations (Elton, *Tudor Revolution in Government*, p. 212).
27. Elton, ibid., p. 95.
28. Elton, *The English*, p. 116.
29. G.W. Bernard, 'The pardon of the clergy reconsidered', *Journal of Ecclesiastical History*, xxxvii (1986), esp. 262–4; idem, 'The fall of Wolsey reconsidered', *Journal of British Studies*, xxxv (1996), 277–310; *The Divorce Tracts of Henry VIII* ed. E. Surtz and V. Murphy, (Angers, 1988), introduction; V. Murphy, 'The literature and propaganda of Henry VIII's first divorce', in D. MacCulloch (ed.), *The Reign of Henry VIII* (1995), pp. 135–58.
30. *LP*, V 879, 898.
31. *LP*, V 989; E. Hall, *Chronicle* (1809 edn), p. 788.
32. Elton, *Tudor Revolution in Government*, p. 95.
33. G.R. Elton, 'The Commons' Supplication of 1532: parliamentary manoeuvres in the reign of Henry VIII', *English Historical Review*, lxvi (1951), 507–34, at 507–9 (reprinted in Elton, *Studies*, ii. 107–36, at 107–111). J.P. Cooper, 'The supplication against the ordinaries reconsidered', *English Historical Review*, lxxii (1957), 616–41, stressed the independent role of the Commons in producing these drafts, and thus reduced Cromwell's role to assistance in the drafting of the Commons' ecclesiastical grievances.
34. G.R. Elton, 'The evolution of a reformation statute', *English Historical Review*, lxiv (1949) [hereafter Elton, 'Evolution of a reformation statute'], 174–97, at 196–7 (reprinted in Elton, *Studies*, ii. 82–106, at 105–6)).
35. Elton, 'Thomas Cromwell Redivivus', p. 201 (Elton, *Studies*, iii. 383), drawing on idem, 'The evolution of a reformation statute', pp. 196–7 (Elton, *Studies*, ii. 105–6).
36. Elton, 'Evolution of a reformation statute', p. 184 (Elton, *Studies*, ii. 91); B[ritish] L[ibrary], Cotton MS, Cleopatra E vi fos. 179–202 at fo. 185).
37. *Statutes of the Realm*, iii. 542–4 (27 Henry VIII c. 11).
38. Elton, *Tudor Revolution in Government*, p. 275.
39. *State Papers of Henry VIII*, i. no. xx pp. 411–5; (*LP*, VI 1486 (7–9)); Elton, Thesis, 399–404; idem, *Tudor Revolution in Government*, pp. 363–6;, endorsed by J.A. Guy, 'The Privy Council: Revolution or Evolution?', in *Revolution Reassessed* (Oxford,1986), ed. C. Coleman and D. Starkey, p. 71: 'by then Cromwell had achieved control of the Council's agenda and minutes'.
40. *Statutes of the Realm*, iii. 471–74 (25 Henry VIII c. 22).
41. G.R. Elton, *Reform and Renewal* (Cambridge, 1972), p. 89.
42. Ibid., pp. 89, 183.
43. S.E. Lehmberg, *The Reformation Parliament, 1529–1536* (Cambridge, 1970), p. 192; cf. the suggestion that the power of delaying the implementation of the bill may have been intended to provide 'bargaining-chips in some deal with the pope', D. MacCulloch, *Thomas Cranmer* (1996), pp. 116–17.

44. Elton, *Reform and Renewal*, pp. 87–9.
45. Ibid., p. 9.
46. Ibid., pp. 90–92, 102–6; R.B. Merriman (ed.), *Life and Letters of Thomas Cromwell* (Oxford, 2 vols, 1902), i. 373.
47. Elton, *Reform and Renewal*, p. 107.
48. Ibid., pp. 108–9.
49. Ibid., p. 115.
50. Ibid., pp. 120–21.
51. Ibid., pp. 122–6, for Elton's account.
52. PRO SP1/67 ff. 29–31 – and not 32–7 – (*LP*, V 397); cf. Elton, *Tudor Revolution in Government*, app. ii B.
53. Ibid., p. 160.
54. BL Cotton MS, Cleopatra E v. f. 110 (*LP*, X 462); Elton, *Reform and Renewal*, p. 123.
55. Elton, 'Thomas Cromwell Redivius', p. 378.
56. G.R. Elton, *Policy and Police* (Cambridge, 1972), p. 243; cf. idem, *Reform and Reformation*, pp. 171–2, 293; idem, *Reform and Renewal*, pp. 34–6; and idem, 'Thomas Cromwell Redivivus', pp. 196–7.
57. Elton, *Reform and Reformation*, p. 274.
58. Dickens, *English Reformation*, esp. pp. 134–5 and idem, *Thomas Cromwell*, esp. pp. 179–82.
59. Cf. 'Cromwell showed an increasingly "reformed" outlook after Wolsey's fall, and may have decided that England was best served by a form of protestantism after the Act of Appeals' (Guy, *Tudor England*, p. 178); 'Cromwell was an "evangelical": a proto-protestant' who gave 'covert support for protestantism' (Guy, 'Henry VIII and his ministers', 38–9).
60. I offer a very different view of Henry VIII and of Cromwell's religion in my paper 'The making of religious policy 1532–46: Henry VIII and the search for the middle way', *Historical Journal*, xli (1988), pp. 321–49, and I hope to deal further with the question of Cromwell's religion elsewhere.
61. Elton, *The English*, p. 116.
62. Elton, *Tudor Revolution in Government*, p. 212.
63. Elton, 'Thomas Cromwell Redivivus', 199.
64. *Hamilton Papers*, ed. J. Bain (2 vols, Edinburgh, 1890), i. no. 348 pp. 499–500 (*LP*, XVIII i 364); cf. J.J. Scarisbrick, *The Reformation and the English People* (Oxford, 1984), p. 79).
65. Cf. C. Coleman and D. Starkey (eds), *Revolution Reassessed* (Oxford, 1987).
66. Elton, 'Thomas Cromwell Redivivus', 200 (*Studies*, iii. 384).
67. G.R. Elton, *The English*, p. 131; contrast C.S.L. Davies, 'The Eltonian State', *Transactions of the Royal Historical Society*, 6th series, vii (1997), 177–95.
68. Elton, *The English*, p. 137; Elton, 'Thomas Cromwell Redivivus', 199–200 (*Studies*, iii. 384).
69. P. Roberts, 'The English Crown, the principality of Wales and the council in the marches, 1534–1641', in B. Bradshaw and J. Morrill (eds), *The British Problem c.1534–1707* (1996), pp. 118–47 at pp. 121–2, 124.
70. J. Scattergood (ed.), *The Complete English Poems of John Skelton* (1983), p. 232, line 57; cf. G. Walker, *John Skelton and the Politics of the 1520s* (Cambridge, 1988), p. 69.
71. R.A. Rebholz (ed.), *Sir Thomas Wyatt: the complete poems* (1977), no. cli, pp. 192–3.
72. Wernham, *English Historical Review*, lxxi (1956) pp. 92–5 at p. 95.

73. Elton, *Tudor Revolution in Government*, p. 5.
74. Elton, 'Decline and Fall', pp. 150, 185 (*Studies*, iii. 189, 229); *Reform and Reformation*, pp. 250–54, 289–92); D. Starkey, 'Court and Government' in Coleman and Starkey, *Revolution Reassesed*, p. 57; D. Starkey, *The reign of Henry VIII: personalities and politics* (1985), pp. 105–23, 171 (index entry).
75. R.B. Merriman (ed.) *Life and Letters of Thomas Cromwell* (Oxford, 1902, 2 vols, ii. 245–6, 68–9 (*LP*, XV 35, 90, 108; XII ii 457).
76. Elton, *Reform and Reformation*, p. 172.
77. Elton, *Tudor Revolution in Government*, p. 356.
78. Elton, Thesis, p. 388, incorrectly citing *LP*, VII 61 (8), 903, XIV i 1157.
79. Elton, *Tudor Revolution in Government*, p. 122.
80. PRO SP1/157 ff. 25 (*LP*, XV 36).
81. *State Papers of Henry VIII*, v. 91–3 no. cccxxii (*LP*, XII i 229).
82. *Life and Letters of Thomas Cromwell*, ii. 20 (*LP*, XI 29).
83. *Life and Letters of Thomas Cromwell*, ii. 136 (*LP*, XIII i 832).
84. G. Ribier, *Lettres et Memoires d'estat* (2 vols, Paris, 1666), i. 513 (*LP*, XV 486).
85. *Life and Letters of Thomas Cromwell*, ii. 212–13 (*LP*, XIV i 781).
86. *LP*, VI 1370, VI 1056, 1194, 1370, 1381, 1382; VII 48, 52, 143, 257, 263: VI 1194; VIII 527, 892; IX 498; XII i 1315; XII ii 192; XIII i 877; XIV ii 287, 427, 494, 548–9; XV 322, 438.
87. PRO SP1/122 f. 185 (*LP*, XII ii 192).
88. BL Cotton MS, Titus B I f. 448v (*LP*, VI 1370).
89. Ibid., f. 415v (*LP*, VIII 475).
90. Ibid., f. 459v (*LP*, VII 108).
91. Ibid., f. 413 (*LP*, VII 1436 (2)).
92. Ibid., f. 415v (*LP*, VIII 475).
93. Ibid., f. 420v (*LP*, VII 48 (2)).
94. Ibid., f. 460 (LP, VII 108).
95. Ibid., f. 449 (*LP*, VI 1370).
96. Ibid., ff. 446v and 478v.
97. Ibid., f. 422 (*LP*, VII 52).
98. Ibid., f. 462 (*LP*, VI 1382).
99. Ibid., f. 461v (*LP*, VI 1382).
100. Ibid., f. 448v (*LP*, VI 1370).
101. Ibid., ff. 446v and 478v.
102. Ibid., ff. 447 and 479.
103. Ibid., ff. 474–5 (*LP*, VIII 892).
104. Ibid., f. 415v (*LP*, VIII 475).
105. Ibid., f. 405 (*LP*, XIII i 877).
106. PRO SP1/153 f. 171 (*LP*, XIV ii 287).
107. BL Cotton MS, Titus B I, f. 439v.
108. Ibid., f. 427v (*LP*, XV 322).
109. Ibid., f. 415 (*LP*, VIII 475).
110. PRO E36/143 f. 69 (*LP*, IX 498).
111. BL Cotton MS, Titus B I, f, 429.
112. PRO SP1/82 f. 113 (*LP*, VII 107).
113. BL Cotton MS, Titus B I, f, 475 (*LP*, VIII 892).
114. Ibid., f. 450 (*LP*, XII, i 1315).
115. Ibid., ff. 446v and 478v.
116. Ibid., f, 476 (*LP*, XV 438).
117. Ibid., f. 464v (*LP*, VII 420).

118. Elton, *Tudor Revolution in Government*, p. 153, citing BL Cotton MS, Titus B i f. 433 (*LP*, VIII 527) (BL, Titus B i f. 425 is another copy, and there is also a second summary in *LP*, XIV ii 399); idem, *Tudor Revolution in Government*, p. 211 for 'lazy king'; Wernham, *English Historical Review*, lxxi (1956), 92–5; cf. S. Jack 'Henry VIII's attitude towards royal finance: penny wise and pound foolish', in C. Giry-Deloison (ed.) *Francois I et Henry VIII. Deux Princes de la Renaissance (1515–1547)* (Lille, 1996), pp. 145–63: 'Henry ... was in many ways his father's son with a shrewd appreciation of the value of money', attempting 'to keep personal, private control of his finances' (pp. 148, 163).
119. *State Papers*, i. no. xx, pp. 414–15 (*LP*, VI 1487).
120. *Life and Letters of Thomas Cromwell*, ii. 416ff (*LP*, IX 157).
121. Ibid., ii. 176 (*LP*, XIV i 227).
122. Ibid., ii. 266 (*LP*, XV 776).
123. Ibid., ii. 162 (*LP*, XIII ii 924).
124. Elton, Thesis, p. 315.
125. *State Papers of Henry VIII*, i no. cxxxiv, pp. 624–5 (*LP*, XV 468).
126. *State Papers*, no. cxxxv, pp. 625–7 (*LP*, XV 469); *LP*, XV 566.
127. J. Kaulek, (ed.), *Correspondance politique de MM de Castillon et de Marillac* (Paris, 1885), p. 50 (*LP*, XIII i 995).
128. *Life and Letters of Thomas Cromwell*, i. 153; *State Papers of Henry VIII*, iii. 551–2.
129. *LP*, XV 776.
130. *Life and Letters of Thomas Cromwell*, ii. 264–73, (*LP*, XV 776, 823).
131. J.E. Cox (ed.), *Writings and Letters of Thomas Cranmer* (*Parker Society*, 1846), p. 40 (*LP*, XV 770). It is worth remarking in passing that John, Henry II and Richard II were curious models of good kingship for Cranmer to choose and by implication to see Henry VIII as admiring. Perhaps Henry II is an error and Edward II was intended.
132. Elton, 'Thomas Cromwell', p. 315.

6
Court and government

'Is this a private fight or can anyone join in?'[1] In their heated argument in the pages of the *Historical Journal* over whether the Tudor Revolution in Government is disproved by recent writing on the Tudor court, both Professor Sir Geoffrey Elton and Dr David Starkey deliver shrewd blows, but neither finally convinces.[2] Although the debate is often very technical, it deals with issues of fundamental importance and therefore deserves clarification and further attention. Starkey is right to criticise Elton for exaggerating the difference between administration and politics.[3] For Elton the central administration under Thomas Cromwell in the 1530s became 'bureaucratic', 'national', 'modern', and functioned quite apart from the 'personal', 'informal', 'household' politics of the day, a distinction he presents as fundamental. Creative and hard-working administrators got on with things while courtiers were frivolously wasting everyone's time. Starkey has little difficulty in showing that so rigid a distinction between administration and politics, between administration and the court, cannot be sustained. But Starkey in turn fails to convince when he claims that politics and administration 'inescapably overlap and interact'.[4] The claim that all government is always 'political' is excessive. In such a world no one is doing anything for its own sake or for the general good but merely for personal advantage, which seems to be how Starkey defines 'politics'. What Elton and Starkey are offering is a choice between two oversimplified models: models which, it may be speculated, reflect the experience of living through in the one case, Clement Attlee's reforms (a revolution in government), (although Elton thinks such a suggestion preposterous), and in the other, Harold Wilson's style of ruling (paranoid fear of factional intrigues). Closer to the realities of early Tudor government would be an alternative that allowed degrees of interaction between administration and politics but also allowed some separation, while seeing neither interaction nor separation as inevitable. Both Elton and Starkey can write allusively, even contradictorily at times, and no doubt they could claim that they do not subscribe to the views attributed to them here and that they have always made qualifications or recognised exceptions to their principal lines of interpretation. But both do seem to me to return continually to the contrasting positions that I have outlined, especially in their efforts to clinch their respective cases. And the starkness of those fundamental beliefs leads them into misleading interpretations and bizarre deployments of the evidence as they try to squeeze every drop of polemical advantage.

Elton and Starkey battle vigorously over the location of the privy council. Elton says that the council continued to meet in the old Westminster palace after 1540, and that there was no council meeting in the adjacent new Whitehall palace until 1579.[5] Starkey counters by claiming that Elton has got this wrong.[6] But it seems to me that it is Starkey, not Elton, who has most seriously misunderstood the evidence. Starkey claims that references to 'Westminster' after 1536 refer to the new palace and that Elton is therefore wrong in claiming that the council did not meet in the new palace. Starkey's 'proof' is the text of the statute of 1536[7] which, he says, *transferred* the name of Westminster from the old to the new palace. But Starkey has misread the act, as he half acknowledges in his next sentence. That act did not transfer the name of Westminster, it *extended* it to cover the whole precinct, including both the old palace of Westminster and the new palace of Whitehall. References to Westminster after 1536 may thus be to all or any part of the precinct and palaces. They could refer to the new palace, but they need not. Starkey offers statement by a suitor describing his wait outside the council chamber, but that is inconclusive: he could have walked from one palace to the other. Starkey claims there are 'innumerable other references' but the one he offers mentioning the 'council chamber at Westminster' is inconclusive. Elton, I think, is nearer the truth in suggesting that the existence of the 'council chamber' in the new palace is conjectural. It appears on the map of the royal palace in *The History of the King's Works* but it is never mentioned in the text of that work. Starkey is mistaken to deny the existence of a council chamber in the old palace of Westminster, or to suggest that its existence was problematic, or that what had been the council chamber had now been taken over by the court of Star Chamber. Yet there is an account of 1535 for tilers engaged in 'ripping, lathing and new tithing not only the Star Chamber, *the Council Chamber of Examination*, the Duchy Chamber, the Dining Chamber, but also the gallery going to the said Duchy Chamber, and over the receipt', and another account of 1538 for the ceiling and wainscotting 'the court of augmentations at Westminster and the *council chamber* and evidence house there'.[8] These must refer to the old palace, since there is no dispute that that is where the courts of Star Chamber and Augmentations were housed. It is an extraordinary matter that we cannot be certain just where in the old and new palaces the privy council met, but the balance of probabilities suggests that Starkey's evidence that from 1536 it must have met in the new palace cannot bear the weight of interpretation that he would put upon it.

Whatever the intrinsic interest of the site of the privy council chamber, its determination has become a battleground of debate because both Elton and Starkey believe its location strengthens their respective general interpretations of Tudor politics and administration. Elton claims that because the council met in the old palace while the king and his courtiers lived and slept in the new palace, the council was therefore national, bureaucratic, impersonal, and not part of the court. The mere location of the council, however, seems insufficient to prove the point. After all, the old palace was barely 200 yards away from the new, so it would not be difficult for men to move from one to the other. Starkey by contrast claims that the council chamber was directly opposite the king's privy chamber and that therefore the council was part of the court, and politics and administration were inextricably intertwined. But that also seems insufficient. What the councillors did when they met could still in theory be national, bureaucratic, impersonal, even though they were sitting opposite the king's privy chamber. That a prime minister in the 1980s sleeps above the Cabinet Office does not make government personal, informal, medieval. Judging the character of government entails looking at what governments do, not at where they meet to do it.

Another area of debate is the financial role of the privy chamber. On the one hand, Elton seems concerned to restrict it, treating not just royal palace building but also the wars of the 1540s as 'the private concerns of the king'.[9] However much those wars may have been Henry VIII's personal initiative, they are more reasonably seen as national since they involved the mobilisation of men and the collection and expenditure of revenues on a vast scale. That some of the financing of those wars came from the privy chamber would seem to justify Starkey's claim that royal finance in the 1540s was still administered by 'informal', 'household' methods. On the other hand, Elton seems keen to claim that by the 1540s the privy chamber had been turned into a 'proper department' regulated by act of parliament along Cromwell's 'bureaucratic' principles.[10] Against that Starkey can readily stress the informality of its procedures during the war years. What, however, weakens Starkey's case is his failure to set the financial role of the privy chamber in the context of royal finance as a whole. The privy chamber raised no revenues of its own: it relied on windfalls from other financial departments, making its importance evanescent, utterly dependent on the personality of a monarch and the needs of the day. That the privy chamber served as a privy purse on a significant scale nevertheless clearly demonstrates the informality of early Tudor government: yet its precariousness and dependence suggest that it was a mixture of 'bureaucratic' and 'informal' mechanisms that characterised Tudor financial administration as a whole.

Elton and Starkey also debate the relationship of courtiers and counsellors. Elton seems unduly reluctant to allow that royal ministers, such as Thomas Cromwell, could be anything but bureaucrats. Cromwell could not be a courtier. On the other hand, courtiers such as men of the privy chamber did not play any formal secretarial role in government. Courtiers could not be administrators. Starkey once again can readily show that so sharp a division between politics and administration will not work. Cromwell may have been a honorific member of the privy chamber and he evidently had access to the king. Some members of the privy chamber did use their proximity to the king to secure grants for themselves and others. Yet the significance of this is not as Starkey wishes it. In an age of personal monarchy, all important counsellors were known to the king and many discussed policy with him. An effective king chose able advisers and they worked hard to serve him. To describe such men as courtiers as well as counsellors is usually a statement of the obvious. It was of course conceivable that a small group of intimates might dominate a king and his government, but whether that happened is a matter of enquiry, and it is clear that this was not so in the reign of Henry VIII. Starkey slides into excess when he makes such claims for the vital significance of men of the privy chamber, in, for example, securing the king's signature. It is far from evident that Henry VIII was ever manipulated by anyone in his privy chamber into signing anything he should not have signed. Starkey has in places qualified his earlier emphasis on the privy chamber but his detailed claims suggest that he has not changed his mind on what he sees as the essential role of the privy chamber. But if men in the privy chamber did well for themselves, it seems much less likely that they ever significantly influenced the making of policy or the making of important appointments in the reign of Henry VIII. Such judgements of course must rest on detailed investigation of the careers of men of the privy chamber and of councillors, and on detailed investigation of the politics of that reign. For all of Elton's and Starkey's ingenuity, it is hard to see that such conclusions can helpfully be drawn from an examination of lists allegedly naming councillors and courtiers.

What would make more sense of Tudor government and the Tudor court would be a recognition that politics and administration are not polarities but rather points along a spectrum. Some matters can be seen as purely politics, some as purely administrative, and others as combinations of politics and administration. Starkey, denying the existence of one end of the spectrum, fails to grasp that some matters, both in the court and in the council, could be purely administrative. The provision of bedding for the king was not an inherently political activity; nor was the execution of much agreed policy. A great deal of government simply involves real jobs-of-work that have to be done, and Tudor government was no exception. Elton, on the other hand, exaggerates the significance of the administrative end of the spectrum, and leaves out the mixed politics and administration in the middle. He too readily equates administration with government, he mistakes the assertion of royal power for a form of administrative reform and he is too quick to tidy developments into institutions. What does not fit is dismissed as merely political and personal. He is prone to take too high-minded a view of governments' motives, too coherent a view of their policies and too systematic a view of their methods. The interplay of personality and the role of chance characteristic of a personal monarchy escape him.

Notes

1. Borrowed from J.P.D. Dunbabin, *English Historical Review*, xcv (1980), p. 241.
2. G.R. Elton, 'Tudor government', *Historical Journal*, xxxi (1988), pp. 425–34; D.R. Starkey, 'Tudor government: the facts?', Ibid., pp. 921–31.
3. Starkey, 'Tudor government', p. 931.
4. Ibid.
5. Elton, 'Tudor government', p. 433.
6. Starkey, 'Tudor government', pp. 922–4.
7. 28 Henry VIII c.12.
8. H.M. Colvin (ed.), *History of the King's Works*, iv. 288–9; Bodleian Library, Rawlinson MS D 777 ff. 114–18; *LP*, XIII ii 457 (9).
9. Elton, 'Tudor government', p. 429.
10. Ibid., pp. 429–30.

7
The downfall of Sir Thomas Seymour[1]

If families had been political factions, then Sir Thomas Seymour, Lord Seymour of Sudeley, and his older brother Edward Seymour, earl of Hertford, who in a coup on the death of Henry VIII in January 1547 became duke of Somerset and Protector of the realm, might have been expected to work closely together. Like his elder brother, Sir Thomas Seymour had served in the king's privy chamber, in diplomacy and on the battlefield, though less prominently: he was ennobled and appointed Lord High Admiral at the same time as his brother became Protector. But far from co-operating, Seymour and his brother quarrelled bitterly, and in March 1549 Sir Thomas Seymour was executed for treason. A study of his activities between January 1547 and March 1549 makes an exciting story,[2] but it is much more than that. Seymour's career shows the possibilities open to ambitious noblemen; more broadly still, it shows where power lay, or was thought to lie, in mid-Tudor England.

What then did Seymour do? Marriage with a member of the royal family was an obvious source of power and advancement: the Seymours had of course greatly benefited from their sister Jane's marriage to Henry VIII. Seymour followed her example. In June 1547 the French ambassador reported rumours that Seymour had considered making suits to Princess Mary or Anne of Cleves;[3] a later French account suggested that he had tried for Princess Elizabeth.[4] What Seymour in fact did was to marry Henry VIII's widow, Catherine Parr. Catherine had apparently been interested in Seymour before Henry had taken a fancy to her. She told Seymour that she would not have him think that her honest goodwill towards him proceeded from 'any sodayne motyon or passyon', because 'as truely as god ys god my mynd was fully bent the other tyme I was at lybertye, to marye you before any man'.[5] According to the possibly extravagant Leti, she had been very unhappy in her marriage with Henry – he had, she felt, done her great wrong to marry so young a woman – and she was not displeased to marry someone young and vigorous. Leti added that Seymour made overtures to her the day after she was widowed, that they were soon kissing shamefully, and that they were married thirty-four days after Henry's death.[6] Vertot suggested that Catherine had not been a widow for a month when Seymour declared his love for her.[7] Such speed is not implausible. One of the charges against Seymour was that he had married the queen so abruptly after Henry had died that if a child had come soon it would have been doubtful whether it was his or the king's.[8] Another charge accused Seymour of having first married the queen secretly and of then concealing the marriage.[9] Undated letters between Catherine and Seymour, presumably from early 1547, suggest that Seymour was putting pressure on Catherine to mourn the king for two months, not two years.[10] But Catherine was clearly very much in love. She asked Seymour not to be offended that she sent sooner to him than she had said: 'for my promys was but ones in a fortened howbeyt the tyme ys well abrueyated by what meanes I knowe not excepte the weakes be schorter at Chelsey than in other places'.[11] Seymour noted that 'it hath pleased your highnes to the be the furst breker of yor a poynttement'.[12] Soon he was visiting Catherine at her suggestion early in the morning and leaving by seven o'clock, 'so I suppose ye may come without suspect'. Evidently they discussed how best to win Somerset's acceptance of their marriage. 'Your Brother hathe thys Afternoone a lytell made me warme', wrote Catherine. 'Yt was fortunate we war so muche dystant, for I suppose els I schulde have bytten hym. What cause have they to feare havyng suche a Wyff?'[13] She thought Seymour was 'in sum fere how to frame my lord your brother to speke in your fauour' and felt he should not 'importune for hys good wyll, yf yt cum nott frankely at the fyrst, yt schalbe suffycyent ones to haue requyre yt, and after to cesse'. She suggested getting letters from the young king in their favour and also seeking 'the ayde and furtherance of the most notable of the counsell'.[14] Seymour appealed unsuccessfully to Mary for her support. Mary reacted to the 'strange newes concernyng a sewte you haue in hande to the quene for maryage': if Catherine was keen, Mary could do but small pleasure; if Catherine was not keen, 'if the remembrance of the Kynge mayestye my father (whose soule God pardon) wyll not suffre her to grawnt your sewte, I ame nothyng able to perswade her to forget the losse of hyme, who is as yet very rype in myn owne remembrance'. But she excused herself for advising on 'woweng matters ... wherin I being a mayde am nothyng connyng'.[15] According to Leti, Mary was horrified, but thought Catherine more to blame than Seymour. She appealed to Elizabeth, but her half-sister told her they lacked credit at court and so they should suffer what they could not prevent.[16]

Seymour did make efforts to win over the king. He took up Catherine's idea and got Edward to write her a letter, the contents of which he evidently dictated. Dated 25 June, this letter made the marriage appear as Edward's request to Catherine. 'We thank you hartely, not onlie for your gentle acceptatione of our sute moved unto you, but also for your loyinge accomplishinge of the same', it read. It added an assurance that Somerset would not trouble her about the marriage: 'Wherfore ye shal not nede to feare anie grefe to come, or to suspecte lake of ayde in nede; seing that he, being mine uncle, is so goode an nature that he will not be troblesome'.[17] But Seymour had run into difficulties in trying to obtain this letter. Earlier he had asked John Fowler of the king's privy chamber to ask the king what he thought about his marriage plans: unhelpfully Edward had suggested Seymour marry Anne of Cleves or Mary. Possibly an earlier letter from Edward to Catherine shows that Edward had been put off writing to Catherine and that Somerset was taking great care that no interview between Edward and Catherine took place. Seymour at some point did manage to see Edward in person: possibly that is when he got Edward to write.[18] The king's journal leaves no doubt that Somerset was angry at the marriage: 'the lorde Seimor of Sudley maried the quene, whos nam was Katarine, with wich mariage the lord Protectour was much offended'.[19] Did he unwittingly further it? One of the charges against Seymour was that he had deceived his brother, persuading him to ask Catherine to bear her favour towards Seymour, to suggest that she made a marriage that had already been consummated.[20] If Somerset did for a while then accept the *fait accompli*, the marriage led to friction between the brothers and their wives. Seymour tried to secure certain jewels previously given to Catherine by Henry VIII and now held by Somerset. He took legal advice and was very agitated about this matter throughout 1547 and 1548. He asked his servant Wightman to find out whether the jewels and household stuff which Henry had had delivered to the queen were 'by waye of Gift or lone', and to ask divers gentlemen 'as neare they coulde' to tell him 'the verye Woords his Majestye spake at the sending of such Jewells or Household Stuffe unto her'. He wrote to nine or ten lawyers asking what judgement they would give.

Even after Catherine's death in September 1548, Seymour carried on his campaign. Catherine's will, significantly because unnecessarily, bequeathed to Seymour all her manors and goods that she had, or, a notable addition, 'of right ought to haue had'.[21] He appealed to Princess Mary for her support and her testimony 'howe and after what sorte the Kinges maiestie vsed to departe with thinges vnto her, and namely those iewelles whiche his hieghnes delivered her against the Frenche Admiralles cooming in': were they gifts or just temporarily lent?[22] There were difficulties as well over Catherine's lands.[23] Just how strongly Seymour felt about these injustices can be seen in his trust that the baby that Catherine was carrying 'wyll revenge such wroonges as nether you nor I can at this prisent'.[24] Most seriously, Seymour's marriage provoked the bitter jealousy of Somerset's wife, Anne Stanhope. Who had precedence – Anne as the Protector's wife or Catherine as Dowager Queen? A later writer thought that Seymour responded by trying to disinherit her children in favour of Somerset's children by his first marriage.[25] Seymour's marriage did immediately raise his status, but it also created problems.

Seymour's interest in the royal family also included Princess Elizabeth. But if Seymour was flirting with Elizabeth, it does not follow that his marriage with Catherine had broken down. By early 1548 she was pregnant and gave birth in September 1548; a few days later she died. It is most unlikely that Seymour had poisoned her.[26] Later he spoke of his shock and confusion 'in a tyme when partelye with the Quenes Highnes deathe, I was so amased that I had smale regard eyther to my self or to my doinges'.[27] And it is worth recalling the obvious pride and affection with which Seymour had written about 'my lettell man' when Catherine was pregnant.[28] Nevertheless there is much evidence of the familiarity between Seymour and Elizabeth while she was living with Catherine and him. Seymour sometimes came to her chamber alone.[29] For a while he used 'to com up every mornyng in his nyghtgown, barelegged in his slippers, where he found commonly the Lady Elizabeth vp at hir Boke. And then he wold loke in at the galery dore, and bid my Lady Elizabeth god morow, and so go his way'.[30]

> He wold com many mornyngs into the said Lady Elizabeths chamber, before she were redy, and sometyme before she did rise. And if she were up, he wold bid her good Morrow, and ax how she did, and strike hir vpon the bak, or on the buttocks familiarly and so go forth through his lodginge ... And if she were in hir bed he wold put open the curteyns, and bid hir good morrow, and make as though he wold come at hir: And she wold go further in the bed, so that he could not com at hir; And one mornyng he strove to have kissed hir in hir Bed.[31]

On another occasion, when Elizabeth (with Catherine) was walking in the garden, Seymour 'wrastled with hir and cut hir gown in c [a hundred] peces': 'sche was so tremed', said her servant Kate Ashley who remonstrated with her; Elizabeth claimed that Catherine had held her while Seymour cut her gown.[32] Ashley thought that Seymour 'loved her but to well, and hadd so done a good while' and that 'the Quene was jelowse ouer hir and him, in somoche that, one tyme the Quene, suspecting the often accesse of the Admirall to the Lady Elizabeth's Grace, cam sodenly vpon them, wher they were all alone, (he having her in his Armes)'.[33] Was it Catherine's jealousy, or wish to prevent a scandal, that explains why Elizabeth was sent away in June or July 1548? Or was it Catherine's pregnancy?[34] Seymour allegedly told John Seymour, who was bringing Elizabeth to Hatfield, to ask her 'whither her great Buttocks were grown eny les or no?' And Elizabeth wrote in veiled terms to Seymour, possibly at this time, that he did not need to send an excuse to her 'for I coulde not mistruste the not fulfillinge of your promes to prosede for want of good wyl, but only oportunite serveth not': 'I am frende not wonne with trifels, nor lost with the like'.[35] Much of the evidence of Seymour's relationship with Elizabeth comes from statements made by Kate Ashley, Elizabeth's servant, when Seymour was under investigation in early 1549 and may have been secured through psychological torture. Yet it difficult to see why it should have been invented. Elizabeth was certainly sent away.[36] And, if Ashley's testimony is believed, Elizabeth was certainly pondering the chances of a marriage with Seymour after the death of Queen Catherine. 'You may haue hym yf you will', Ashley told Elizabeth, adding that Elizabeth would not refuse him if Somerset and the council agreed to it. But Elizabeth kept denying it. On another occasion when Elizabeth was playing cards, she drew Seymour 'and chast hym a way': Ashley toldd her she would not refuse him if Somerset and the council did bid her, 'and she sayd yes by her troth'.[37] If at another time Elizabeth said she would not have him 'because that she, that he had before, ded so Myskary', that shows rather just how seriously Elizabeth was thinking about it all. Is it significant that after Seymour's execution his close servant John Harrington gave Elizabeth his portrait with a pretty verse written on it, a picture which in the 1580s was hung in the gallery at Somerset House?[38]

After Catherine's death, Seymour was clearly interested in proposing to Elizabeth: that is the impression from a complex series of letters and messages between Elizabeth, Seymour, Ashley and Thomas Parry, the Queen's cofferer. Seymour was very interested in Elizabeth's lands, boasting to Lord Russell how much they were worth, and inquiring about their location, values and conditions, and making suggestions for exchanges.[39] He asked Thomas Parry 'of the state of her graces howse, and how many persons she kept'; 'what howses she hadd and what landes'; 'if it were good landes or no'; 'what state she had in the lands, for terme of lief, or how'; 'whether she hadd out her letters patentes or no'.[40] Elizabeth, anxious to have somewhere to stay in London, asked Seymour to be a suitor to Somerset on her behalf for Durham Place; Parry wrote and delivered the letter; Seymour replied that Durham Place was going to be turned into a mint but offered Elizabeth his own household. Or was this just a ploy? Parry suspected 'they used me but for an Instrument, to serve their purposes to be brought to passe, and to have entered farther, under the pretence of the Sute for a House, and such like affayres'.[41] Vertot and Leti both suggest that Seymour quickly proposed to Elizabeth.[42] 'Men did thynk that my Lord Admirall kepes the Quenes maydens together to wait vpon the lady Elizabeth, whom he entended to mary shortly, as the bruyt went'.[43] There are hints that Somerset or the council banned Seymour from marrying Elizabeth and there were fears of another secret marriage. Lord Russell warned Seymour 'if ye go abowte any soche thinge, ye seke the meanes to vndo your selfe', adding, 'yt is cleane agayne the kinges wille'.[44] Seymour told the marquess of Northampton 'he was credibly informed, that my Lorde Protector had said he wold clappe him in the Tower if he went to my ladie Elizabeth'.[45] A later French account suggested that Somerset got parliament to pass a bill declaring anyone who without telling the Protector and without the approval of the council tried to marry the princesses was guilty of lese-majesty.[46] Possibly Seymour took note: when Ashley asked him if he wanted to marry Elizabeth, he replied that 'I loke not to lose my life for a wife. It has been spoken of, but it cannot be'.[47] Or possibly, as we shall see, Seymour had wider intentions.

Seymour was from the start highly dissatisfied with his standing in the regime. A would-be contemporary historian of these years wrote that 'the cause of the falling owte of the Protector and the Admyrall was the ambytion of the Admirall and the envy he hadd that his brother should be more advaunced then he'.[48] He was incensed that his brother should be both Protector of the realm and Governor of the king; those functions should, he claimed, be divided and he should have one. According to Sir William Sharrington, 'he thought yt was not the Kinges will that dead ys, that eny oon man sholde haue bothe the gouernement of the King that now ys, and also the Realme. And that in tyme past, yf ther were two Unkills, being of the mothers syde, thoon sholde haue thoon, thother thother'.[49] Seymour confessed that he had searched through chronicles for precedents and discovered 'that there was in England at one tyme one Protectour and an other Regent of Fraunce and the Duke of Exeter and the Busshopp of Winchester, Governours of the Kinges persones'.[50] Two sources suggest that it was John Dudley, earl of Warwick, who put Seymour up to this, promising him his support if he raised the matter in council; when Seymour did so, Somerset rose without saying a word and the council meeting ended.[51] Other sources suggest that Seymour was dissuaded from pressing the point after it was pointed out to him that he had signed the instrument making Somerset governor of the king's person with his own hand.[52] Somerset explained his reluctance to accept his brother's demand by pointing to the dangers of repeating the discord between Humphrey, duke of Gloucester, and Cardinal Beaufort.[53]

Certain sources hint that Seymour was not satisfied and began intriguing. During the Scottish military campaign in summer 1547, Seymour, despite his office of Admiral, stayed in London while his brother went north to fight: 'howe being admirall he would not goe in person in the iorney againste Scotland'.[54] (A year later he again failed to serve, staying at Sudeley and just sending out orders.)[55] Somerset won a smashing victory at Pinkie but then left the borders very hastily without pursuing his military advantage. Almost certainly that was in order to counter his brother's plotting. Somerset rushed back because 'il apprit, par un courier qu'on lui depecha expres, que l'amiral son frere formait a la cour un puissant parti contre lui, et qu'il avait pris des mesures secretes avee le roi meme; pour lui enlever la charge de gouverneur de ce jeune prince'. In Somerset's absence Seymour had won over men in the privy chamber.[56] In 1549 it was claimed against him that 'by corrupting with gieftes and faier promises diverse of the privie chamber he went about to allure his highnes to condescend and agree to the same his most heynous and perillous purposes'.[57] Some of the privy chamber, a later source suggested, had become Seymour's 'pensioners'.[58] Seymour confessed that 'he gave money to ii or iii of them which were about the King' and also to the grooms of the chamber.[59] Seymour's chief man in the privy chamber was John Fowler. They chatted together repeatedly, with Seymour frequently asking Fowler to remember him to Edward. 'Many and sundrie tymes', testified Fowler, Seymour 'wolde com into the privie Buttrie and drinke there alone and aske me whether the kyng wold say any thing of him'.[60] Fowler got the king to write to Seymour when his uncle was away in the country and often told him to be grateful for Seymour's gifts. It was probably at this time in Somerset's absence that Seymour was able to see the king, play with him and spoil him; it was at this time that he got the king to write a letter in support of his marriage. He tried to persuade Edward that the responsibilities of Protector and Governor were incompatible – when the protector was away with the army, there was no Governor for the king – and possibly prepared a letter which he hoped Edward would sign stating that Seymour should be Governor.

Seymour was also helped by John Cheke and Thomas Wroth. Fowler, Cheke and Wroth were blamed after the plot of summer 1547, though Fowler and Cheke at least soon recovered their standing.[61] Seymour's contacts with them show his awareness of the importance of gaining influence, if not control, over Edward: even a king who was a minor was potentially influential and could sign letters and grants. If Somerset's return was enough to halt Seymour's immediate hopes, he nonetheless continued to try to persuade Edward to agree to his plan to secure the governorship. He urged Edward to take upon himself the ruling of his kingdom. He told him that within four years he would be sixteen, and 'Rewler of his own thynges'; that he trusted that by that time the king would himself help his men with such things as fell within his gift. Edward testified how Seymour said 'I was to bashfull in myne owne matters, and asked me, why I dyd not speak to beare rule as well asother kyngs do. I sayd, I neded not, for I was well enough'.[62] Undaunted by Edward's reticence, Seymour asked Fowler 'to put the kinges majeste ... in mynde' if Somerset criticised him to the king, and to inform Cheke and Wroth.[63] He attempted to get him to sign a letter on his behalf for the parliament that was meeting in autumn 1547. He sent John Cheke to take it to the king. It read 'Mi Lordes I prai yow fauor my Lord Admiral mine vncles sute which he wil make vnto yow'. But on Cheke's advice, Edward refused to sign it. Edward said that during the parliament Seymour had come to him asking him to write a thing for him, claiming it was nothing ill but for the queen. Edward responded with precocious discretion that if Seymour's suit were good, the lords would allow it; if it were ill, then he would not write.[64] That all this related to Seymour's ambitions is suggested by his later confession that just before he drew up that bill, he 'cawsed the King to be moved by Mr Fowler whether he coulde be contented that he shulde have the governance of him as Mr Stanope had'.[65] Sir Michael Stanhope, Somerset's brother-in-law, was loyally guarding the king. But Somerset was sufficiently worried by all this intriguing to have the letters patent declaring him Protector and Governor confirmed in parliament. Perhaps that is also why Somerset chose to have special precedence in the House of Lords, sitting alone 'upon the myddes of the bench or stole stondyng nexte on the right hand of our siege reall'. It is not surprising in turn that Seymour said 'he mislyked that he was not placed in the parlament howse as woon of the king his vnkylls'.[66] He continued to discuss the possibility that he might become Governor. He talked of advancing Edward's age of majority. He boasted to the marquess of Dorset and the earl of Rutland that within a year (or two years, or three years) the king should rule his own affairs. But Seymour did not have that much contact with the king. Fowler saw him far more often than Seymour: that is why he was so important for Seymour. Seymour saw Edward in summer 1547, just before and during Somerset's absence on the Scottish borders, and again during parliament later that year. The various conversations that Seymour had with the king may well all date to those periods: but even if they took place at other times as well, nonetheless the impression is that they were scattered and intermittent. Somerset evidently largely succeeded in keeping his brother away from the king. Seymour continued to exploit his contacts with Fowler and Cheke to send money to Edward, although it cannot be established exactly when. On several occasions, sums of £5 and £10, and as high as £40, were given by Seymour to Fowler and Cheke for giving to the king. Seymour encouraged Edward to write to him for money which he did, for example, on 26 June 1548: 'My lord send me for Latimer as much as ye think good and deliver it to Fowler'.[67] Seymour had told the king 'ye are a beggarly king ye haue no monie to play or to geue'.[68] He described how Edward moaned 'my Unkel off Sumerset deylyth very hardly with me and kepyth me so strayt that I cane not have mony at my wylle but my lord Admyral both sendes me mony and gyves me mony'.[69] Whether that was true or not, Seymour was clearly trying to use Edward's understandable desire for more spending money to insinuate himself into his favour. If Seymour and Edward had lived longer, such a relationship might have seen significant developments.

As we have already noted, Seymour believed that he could use parliaments to further his purposes. He tried to recruit several noblemen to support his various causes, often speaking with them on their way to or from parliament, the marquesses of Dorset and Northampton, the earls of Rutland and Southampton, Lords Russell and Clinton. For example, Seymour told Clinton that he intended to put a bill into parliament. 'He ment to get som auctoryte that waye whyche he thought otherwise he could not attayne'. After he had been in the parliament chamber for an hour 'he callyd me owte and after he had talkyd with some of the lordes ther he requyred me agen to gyue my consent to the byll and make hym as many frendes as I cold'.[70] Was Seymour the keener to lobby because he was 'an il speker' himself?[71] He also attempted to assemble a group of associates and servants in the Commons.[72] In autumn 1547 he threatened to disrupt the parliament. He was accused of saying: 'I haue herd spekyng of a black parlament and they vsse me as they doo begyn by goddes preshios soule I wyll make the blakiste parleament that euer was in England'.[73] Somerset's letters patent of 12 March 1547 had confirmed Henry VIII's alleged oral appointment of Somerset as Governor and Protector. Now Seymour made a great fuss over the bill confirming those letters patent in the light of the noble victory that God had given Somerset over the Scots, presumably disguising his real reasons for opposing it by 'surmysing that he [Somerset] would therby geve away Callies'; our source went on to note 'what sturre was in the parliament by that meanes'.[74] There are hints that such a bill ran into difficulties. Read three times in the Lords between 1 and 9 November, it was replaced by another bill which was read in the Lords on 19 November, and sent to the Commons 'cum provisions eidem connectenda'. There it was read four times between 22 November and 12 December. Seymour and the marquess of Dorset dissented when it returned to the Lords on 14 December.[75] Very likely it was to block this bill that Seymour tried to get a letter from the king.[76] According to the charges in 1549 Seymour 'wrote a lettre with his own hande, whiche lettre the kinges majestie shuld haue subscribed or writen again after that Copie to the parliament howse'; then he had resolved to take that letter into the Commons himself, 'and there with his fauvorers and adherentes before prepared to haue made a broile or tumulte and vprore'.[77] He seems also to have been angry at the repealing of an act for speaking of words – presumably the Treason Act – 'wherin my lord admirall wold a had a promyse that men shold not haue had lyberty to a spokyn any thing ayenst the quene'.[78]

Seymour was very much aware of the need to build local support. The advice he gave those noblemen that he hoped to recruit to his cause is an eloquent account of the operation of landed power. Northampton said how in early 1548 Seymour had advised him 'to go and set vpp howse in the Northe countrey where as my landes laye thinkyng it to be muche for my commodite'.[79] Dorset told how in the late summer of that year 'thadmyrall diuising with me to make me stronge in my countrey, aduised me to kepe a good house'.[80] Seymour himself allegedly boasted 'it is good abiding at home, and to make mery with our neighbors in the contry', telling Northampton 'he liked well' country life.[81] To Dorset he gave more detailed advice. He should not trust the gentlemen of the county too much 'for they have sumwhat to loose'. Instead

> I wold rather aduise you to make muche of the head yeomen and frankelyns of the cuntreye, specially those that be the ringleaders, for they be the men that be best hable to perswade the multitude and may best bring the number and therefore I wold wishe you to make muche of them, and to goo to their houses, nowe to oon and nowe to an other, caryeng with you a flagon or two of wyne, and a pasty of veneson, and to use a familiaritie with them, for so shall you cause them to love you, and be assured to haue them at your commaundemente.

'This maner (I may tel you)', Seymour continued, 'I entende to vse miself'.[82] He said much the same to Rutland, advising him

> to make moche of the gentilmen in my countrey, but more of suche honeste and welthy yemen as wer ringleaders in good townes ... as for the gentilmen ther is no gret trust to be had to them, but for the other making moche of them and somtymes dyning lyke a good fellow in one of their houses I shuld by that gentill enterteynment allure all their good willes to go with me wither I woolde leade them.[83]

Seymour's conception of local power was competitive. He advised Dorset 'to kepe my house in Warwikeshire ... because yt war a cuntrey full of men, but chiefly to match with my lorde of Warwike, so as he should not be hable to matche with me there'.[84] Rutland said Seymour 'thought me to be so frended in my country as I was hable inough to matche with my lorde of Shrewesbury'.[85] One of the charges against Seymour was that 'he hath parted as yt were in his imagination and entent the Realme, to set noble men to contervale suche other noble men as he thought wolde let his devilishe purposes and so labored and travelid to be strong at al his devises'.[86] Sir William Sharington testified how Seymour

> wold divers tymes loke vpon a charte of England which he hath and declare vnto this Examinate how strong he was and how far his lands and dominions did stretche; and how it lay all to gither betwene his house and the Holt and what shire and places wer for hym; and that this way he was emong his frends; so notyng the places and when he cam to Bristow, he wold say; this is my Lord Protectors; and of other, that is my Lord of Warwikes; to the which two, this Examinate knoweth he had no great affection.

Riding from the marquess of Dorset, Seymour 'vsed sondry tymes to shewe me as we rodde togithers the cowntrees rounde about sayeng all these which dwell in thes parties be my frendes'. 'And so he did vaunt ... that he had as great a nombre of gentlemen that loved hym, as eny noble man in England'. 'And further said that he thought that he had more gentlemen that louved hym than the Lord Protector had and vpon that he said he was happye that hath freends in this world what so ever shuld chaunce'.[87] Such evidence was echoed in the charges against him: 'he hath parted as yt were in his imagination and entente the Realme, to set noble men to contervale suche other noble men as he thought wolde let his devilishe purposes'; 'he ment to have matched and sett one Noble man against such an other Noble man, as he thought he cowlde never compasse and wynne to assent to his factyon and false conspiracye'.[88] Talking about his office of Lord Admiral he boasted that 'nowe I shall haue the rule of a good sort of shippes and men'. 'And I tell yow it is a good thing to haue the rule of men'.[89] Discussing his lands in the Marches with Parry, Seymour boasted how they were 'of goodly manredde'.[90] In the light of such boasts, it is not surprising that he was accused of retaining. It was alleged that 'he hath reteynid yonge gentlemen and hed yemen to a great multitude and farre above suche number as is permitted by the lawes and statutes of the realm or were otherwise necessarie or convenient for yor service, place, or estate to the fortifyeng yor towardes all yor evill ententes and purposes'.[91] Moreover 'he hath not onely studied and imagined how to haue rule of a nombre of men his handes, but he hath attempted and gotten diverse stuardshipps of noble mens landes, and the manredes to make his partie stronge for his purposes'.[92] And he 'especially moved the noble men and who he thought not to be contented to departe into ther contreys and make them selfes strong'.[93] All this offers remarkably vivid insights into a world of lordship often thought to have disappeared by the mid-sixteenth century. But how far were Seymour's boasts matched in reality?

Seymour undoubtedly tried to create a following among other noblemen; as one of the charges put it, 'he hath labored and gone about to combyne and confederate him self with som persones to haue a parte and faction in a redynes'.[94] Henry Grey (executed 1554), marquess of Dorset, was won over by Seymour's promise to marry his daughter, Jane, to the king. Harington, Seymour's servant, came to him immediately after Henry VIII's death, and told him how Seymour was likely to hold great authority and that being the king's uncle 'and placed as he was', he might 'doo me much pleasure', urging him to go to him and 'entre a more frendeship and familiaritie with him'. If he agreed to put his daughter Jane in Seymour's household, he would secure her marriage to the young king, was the gist of Harington's message, but it was conveyed by hints. He described Jane 'as handsom a lady as eny in England, and that she might be Wife to eny prince in christen, and that, if the kinges Majestie, when he came to Age wold mary within the realme, it was as likely he wold be there, as in eny other Place'; he continued that if she were in Seymour's household 'she were as like ... to haue a gretter and better turn, then he wold thynk; and that he durst not tel what it was; and that beyng kept in my lord's hows, who was vncle to the Kyng, yt were never the wors for hyr; and that my Lord wold be right glad, if the king's majestie could like eny in his howse'. So Dorset went to Seymour within seven days and heard similar arguments from him. Harington did not deny having seen Dorset or having urged him to be friendly with Seymour, but claimed he did it without any instruction from Seymour.[95] Jane was duly sent to Seymour's household. At the same time Seymour lent Dorset money, sending £500 as soon as he despatched Jane, and taking no bond – except Jane herself.[96] Seymour may have fancied her himself: he told Thomas Parry 'ther hath bene a talke of late (no Force) they say now shall mary my lady Jane'; adding, 'I tel you this but meryly, I tell you this but meryly'.[97] Immediately after Queen Catherine's death Seymour, distraught and fearing he would have to dissolve his whole household, sent Jane back to Dorset but very soon was anxious to have her back. Dorset testified how shortly afterwards Seymour 'came to my house himself and was soo ernestly in hand with me and my wief that in the end because he wold haue no naye, we were contented she shoulde againe returne to his house'. Sir William Sharington 'travailed as ernestly with my wief' as Seymour had with him. On that occasion, said Dorset, Seymour 'renued his promise vnto me for the mariage of my doughter to the kinges majeste'.[98]

Later in autumn 1548 Jane became another cause of contention between Seymour and his brother. Seymour told Harington that there would be 'muche ado' for her since Somerset and his wife would do what they could to persuade the marquess to give her to them.[99] Looking back, Dorset said that he 'was so seduced and aveugled by the said Lord Admirall, that he promised him that except the kinges Majesties Person only, he wold spend his lief and bloode in his the said Lorde Admiralles parte against all men'.[100] But Harington said that when asked whose part he would take if Somerset and Seymour fell out, Dorset had replied that 'he wold take his Part that toke the kinges Parte'.[101]

Earlier, Dorset had joined Seymour in dissenting from the bill confirming Somerset's letters patent as Protector in November–December 1547.[102] Dorset remained close to Seymour until Seymour's arrest, riding with him from parliament on the day of his committal.[103] Seymour also tried to recruit the earl of Rutland, the marquess of Northampton and the earl of Southampton. Wiliam Parr (d. 1571), marquess of Northampton, brother of Seymour's wife Catherine Parr, testified how in early 1548 Seymour, supposing that he was not content (possibly because of the way his wish to remarry while his wife, who had left him, was alive was being handled), 'vsing me also very freendly ... aswell in dedes as also in wordes, saying I shuld lacke nether money nor any other thing that he had', gave him 'a certaign specialtie of good valewe' and 'shewed me muche freendshipp and gentleness'.[104] Just before his arrest Seymour confided his fears in Northampton and wanted him to take a message to Somerset in which Seymour set out his terms for answering the council's questions.[105] Thomas Wriothesley (d. 1550), earl of Southampton, testified how on their way to dinner during parliament, 'after a litle comen talk' Seymour said to him, 'ha my lord of Southampton, you were well handeled touching yor office. Why shuld you not haue it again?'[106] That must have referred to his surrender of the Lord Chancellorship and unsuccessful resistance to Somerset's seizure of the protectorate in January–March 1547; and Southampton would again be prominent when Somerset fell in autumn 1549.[107] Seymour clearly attempted to win over noblemen. In his defence, however, Harington declared that while Seymour might 'peradventure' say to him that he or he was his friend, 'but to say, that eny Man were his assurid, or that I have this, or this Man assurid, or eny Thyng foundyng to makyng a Party, he never hard hym speke such Thyngs in his lief'. And according to Robert Tyrwhit, Seymour recognised his dependence on the crown, asking 'ame not I mayd by the Kyng? Hav not I all that I hav by the Kynge?'[108]

What of Seymour's country living? Since 1536 he had been steward of Holt, Chirk, Bromfield and Yale in the Welsh Marches, and in 1547 he had received further grants of land there and in adjacent counties, including the lordship of Sudeley, Gloucestershire, and the manor of Bewdley, Shropshire. He also received ex-Howard lands in Bramber and other parts of Sussex.[109] (Is it significant that these grants were made on 19 August, just before Somerset left for the Scottish borders? Was Strype right to suggest that Somerset was trying to bridle his brother with liberality?[110]) The patent rolls for 1547–48 suggest vigorous buying, selling and leasing of lands. Soon he was building at Sudeley Castle, Gloucestershire, and at Bromham. More significantly still, Seymour was fortifying Holt Castle, Denbighshire, 'a goodly castel', at a key crossing point on the Dee and astride 'the gateway from north Wales to the south'. In a survey most probably made during the reign of Henry VIII, it was described as 'beyng more strongly builded with stone and tymber then stately lodgeing or convenyant', with a 'towre very strongly builte upon a rocke' and surrounded by a moat 150 feet broad connected to the river. Within the castle there were 'all howses of office mete for a prynce to kepe his house yn'. It could serve as a focus for the prosperous gentry of Flint and Denbighshire and for tenants holding their lands by semi-military tenures, in an area rich in men.[111] Here Richard Fitzalan (d. 1397), earl of Arundel, had held out for six weeks against Robert de Vere in 1387 and defied John of Gaunt in 1393; here Sir William Stanley (executed in 1495) and William Brereton (executed in 1536) had both made their base.[112] The potential was significant. But did Seymour succeed in creating an affinity? John Harington remained loyal to Seymour even after Seymour's arrest: 'He labors to haue byn in the towre with the Lord Admyrall', dryly noted Petre under his answers.[113] In 1582 for the benefit of his son he

> wrote with his owne hand the names of those who were then living of the old Admiraltie (so he called them that had bene my lords men and there were then xxxiiii of them living) of which many were knights and men of more reverence than himselfe, and some were but meane men, as armorers, artificers, keepers, and farmers, and yet the memorie of his service was such a band among them all of kindnesse as the best of them disdained not the poorest and the meaner had recourse to the greatest for their countenance and ayd in their honest causes.[114]

And his son then saluted Seymour's memory in verse: 'Temp'rate at home, yet kept great state with staie/ And noble house that fed more mouthes with meet,/ Than some advanced on higher steppes to stande'.[115] Yet one must suspect the exaggerations of nostalgia here. Elsewhere various of Seymour's neighbours complained to Somerset about Seymour's activities.[116] And there is virtually no detailed evidence that Seymour seriously attempted to create a following in North Wales or the Marches, whatever his dreams, whatever his boasts that he could raise ten thousand men.[117]

Did he try to turn those dreams into reality in late 1548 and early 1549? On 24 November 1548 he ordered his steward Edward Rous to make preparations for beer taken to Bewdley where he was intending to keep his house from the following May into summer: Rous was to prepare 'all the housys ther sayinge for the tyme of his contynewance ther he wolde kepe as great a house and of large expences as he did in the quynes lyffe tyme'.[118] Was he exloiting his office as Admiral to get money? He was accused of maintaining pirates and taking a share of their spoil.

> Diverse of the hed pirates being brought vnto yow, yow have let the said pirates go agayn free vnto the seas, taking away from the takers of them not onely all their commoditie and profit, but from the true owners of the shipps and goodes al suche as ever cam into the pirates handes, as though yow were authorised to be the chief pirate, and to have all thadvauntage thei could bring vnto yow.

Goods taken by pirates were daily seen in Seymour's household where they were distributed amongst his servants and friends.[119] He asked Sir William Sharington, under-treasurer of the mint at Bristol, who had been manufacturing testoons for his own pocket, and was possibly hoping to be protected from the consequences by high-placed friends (Seymour had described him as 'my frend' in 1547 and Sharington had sat in parliament for Bramber later that year, probably as a result of Seymour's influence),[120] whether he could coin money for him. He asked him 'how muche money will find ten thousand men a moneth, and vppon that accompting a whill with himself, he dyd cast that after the rate of vi^d a daye for a man, x$^{m\,li}$ or thereaboutes wold serve'.[121] According to a charge in the draft list of accusations but not retained in the final list, Seymour 'removed also his howse to the Holt at Christmas last past'.[122] In the act of attainder it was claimed that Seymour had put the king's castle of Holt 'wherof he had the keping even nowe a late in a redynes, and there cawsed to be prepared a great furniture of wheat malte bestes'.[123] Some light on what Seymour was planning appears in the part of this charge that was retained. Seymour's deputy, steward and other officers at Holt had

> against Christmas last past at the saide Holte made suche provision of wheate, malt, beefes and other thinges as be necessarie for the sustenance of a great nomber of men, making also by all the meanes possible a greate masse of money, in so much that all the countray dothe greatly marvaile at yt, and the more becausse your servantes have spred rumours abrode that the Kinges Majeste was ded; wheruppon the countrey is in a great m ... dowbte and expectation loking for some broile, and wolde have bene more if at this present by your apprehension it had not bene staied.[124]

What this shows are suspicions that Seymour was planning to use Holt Castle in Denbighshire as a strongpoint from which he could defy his brother. Perhaps he also had in mind the Isles of Scilly and Lundy as a final refuge.[125] What was Seymour hoping to do? A later French account offers an answer. He 'resolut de tout hasarder pour se rendre maitre de la princesse et du gouvernement'. Secretly he assembled his friends: 'on convint qu'il falloit enlever le roi et la princesse; que l'amiral l'epouseroit aussitot aux yeux du prince, dont la presence tiendroit lieu de consentement et qu'il se serviroit ensuite de son autorite pour detruire celle du duc et pour lui enlever la regence'. It was to Holt Castle that he hoped to take Edward and Elizabeth.[126] Significantly when in custody Seymour denied 'that euer I went about to take the kyng from my lord my brother by force; I never ment it, nor thought it'.[127] If he had hoped to have custody of the king it was only with the consent of the realm.[128] Yet Fowler testified how Seymour had once come to St James's at 9 a.m. and voiced his surprise that there were so few people there: 'a man might stele away the king now for there cam more with me than is in all the howse besides'.[129] And Seymour himself admitted that about Easter 1548 he had said to Fowler 'that if he might have the King in his custodie ... he wolde be glad, and that he thought that a man might bring him through the Galery to his chamber, and so to his howse', but this, Seymour insisted, 'he spoke merely meaning no hurte'.[130] Interestingly, when Seymour was persuading Dorset to send back his daughter to his household, he told Dorset that 'he durst warraunt me' that Edward would marry Jane, 'if he might ones get the kinge at libertye'.[131]

If Seymour was indeed plotting to kidnap Edward and Elizabeth, marry Elizabeth and have himself made Protector in place of his brother, it is not surprising that he was arrested and tried once his plans were discovered. How was he found out? One letter offers a clue. This was written by John Burcher in Strasbourg to Henry Bullinger on 15 February 1549. Burcher had most horrible intelligence to pass on. Seymour 'has attempted, by an unheard of treachery and cruelty, to destroy with his own impious hands, in the deep silence of the night, our innocent king'. Burcher went on to describe how Seymour obtained from one of the king's chamberlains who knew his plans a key which opened into the royal bedchamber. Seymour went there at dead of together with some servants. But then things went wrong. In the space between the door through which he entered and the king's chamber was a little dog, 'the most faithful guardian of the youth', who had that night been accidentally shut out of the chamber. When the dog saw Seymour moving towards the door of the king's chamber, 'he betrayed the murderer by his barking'. Seymour killed the dog and was on the point of killing Edward when one of the king's guards, roused by the noise, came out after waking the other bodyguards. When he saw Seymour he asked him what he was doing: Seymour said he was checking that the prince was securely guarded. But that excuse was unavailing and the next day Seymour was in the Tower.[132] Was Burcher's intelligence in part inaccurate? Was not Seymour trying to kidnap rather than to murder the king, for which he could have no motive? Or is this fanciful evidence? Wightman, Seymour's servant, testified that a week before his arrest, Seymour 'vsed ... diuers nightes to repayre frome his house to the courte after nyne of the clocke at night', leaving Dorset and Huntingdon behind at his house. Was he preparing a kidnap?[133]

From Dorset's and Northampton's depositions, it appears that Seymour was committed to the Tower after Henry (1526–63), second earl of Rutland, had first been examined by Somerset and then made a declaration against Seymour to council. What Rutland said and why remains obscure. Seymour had talked to him the previous summer about advancing the declaration of the king's majority and denounced Somerset's bill confirming his letters patent, hoping that he would in due course have Rutland's voice in the parliament.[134] And Seymour told Dorset about 'such comunicacion' that there had between Rutland and himself, 'where of he made a longe discourse'. What they talked about is unknowable. Had Rutland been so shocked by Seymour's schemes that he had gone to the council? Did he give evidence that Seymour was planning to kidnap the king and did this reinforce that interpretation of Seymour's night-time visits to court? However that may be, Seymour seems to have got wind of Rutland's statement from one of his servants whose brother was a servant of Rutland. Just before he was committed to the Tower, he told Northampton that he would be called before the council that day to answer articles that Rutland had declared against him. Seymour said he was willing to answer all things if he was left at liberty and if the Lord Privy Seal (John (d. 1555), Lord

Russell) and Mr Comptroller (Sir William Paget (d. 1563)) were sent to him, but would not answer if shut up, presumably if he were imprisoned. He struck Dorset, who visited him at his house after dinner, as 'muche afrayed' of going to the council and appears to have thought of securing Mr Comptroller as a pledge, claiming defiantly that otherwise he would not go to the council. It was left to Dorset's brother Thomas to advise Seymour to trust Somerset, since he was 'a man of muche mercy' and, in any case, 'if he list to have you, it is not this house that canne kepe you, though you had x tymes so many men as you haue'.[135] Possibly he refused to come to the council when summoned: one of the charges against him was how 'being sent for by thauthoritie to answere to suche thinges as were thought to be refourmed in him, he refused to com, to a verie evill example of disobedience'.[136] That day Seymour also called Sharington to him, thinking that the council were going to see if they could get anything out of him. Had Sharington's arrest for coining led to the discovery of any agreements between the two men and particularly of Seymour's grand plans for manufacturing testoons to pay a private army? Was that what had led to conciliar inquiries?[137]

Seymour was arrested on 17 January 1549.[138] Examined on 25 January, he wrote an abject submission to Somerset on 27 January. Many were interrogated: several noblemen, of whom the earl of Rutland had been one of the first (he was examined by Somerset and then declared certain articles against Seymour to the council); Elizabeth's servants, Thomas Parry and Katherine Ashley. The Lord Great Master (William Paulet (d. 1572), Lord St John, later marquess of Winchester) and Mr Denny (one of the chief gentlemen of the king's privy chamber) came to interrogate Parry, who was terrified.[139] Both Parry and Ashley were put in the Tower.[140] Elizabeth was interrogated by Paget, Denny and Tyrwhit.[141] Tyrwhit was convinced that 'ther hayth beyne some secrett Promys, betwyne my lady, Mestrys Aschley, and the Cofferer, never to confesse to deythe': only the king or Somerset would extract it from her.[142] Meanwhile Parry confessed in the Tower,[143] prompting Elizabeth to condemn him as a 'false wretche, and sayd he had promyssed he wold never confesse yt to Deyth'.[144] Ashley also confessed in part.[145] 'They all synge onne Songe, and so I thynke they could not do, vnles they had sett the nott be for'.[146] But Elizabeth would not confess and claimed forgetfulness, protested against the unpleasant things said against her and asked for a proclamation against such rumours.[147] But what was admitted then by Ashley, Parry, and by several noblemen and servants of Seymour largely provides the evidence for Seymour's activities over the previous two years. Some members of the council were clearly turning this information into articles against him. Seymour was examined on 18 February; the council discussed the matter on 22 February; Seymour was examined again on 23 February, but refused to answer unless his accusers stood before him, and would not even subscribe the answers he had earlier begun to make. On 24 February the councillors reported to the king, Somerset 'declaring how sorowfull a case this was unto hym', but regarding his duty to the king greater than that to his brother. The councillors sent once again to Seymour who would answer no more than three of the articles. On 25 February a bill was introduced into parliament, unopposed in the Lords (Somerset was allowed for natural pity's sake to be absent), but 'very much debated and argued' in the Commons, in which lawyers declared that Seymour's offences 'were in the compasse of High Treason'. On 5 March the bill was passed, the Commons 'being marvailous full almost to the number of iiii^c persons, not x or xii at the most giving their nays tharunto'. On 19 March Seymour was executed.[148] To the end Seymour continued his plotting. A later writer noted 'howe yt was saied he hadd writen with cyfre of an oriege in paper, and saved hytt in his shooe and being on scaffold willed his men to remember what he saied, to him, whoe dysclosed yt'.[149] Latimer denounced Seymour in a sermon.

> The man beyng in the tower wrote certayne papers whyche I saw miselfe. They were two lyttle ones, one to my Ladye Maryes grace, and an other to my Lady Elizabeths grace, tendynge to thys ende, that they shoulde conspyre agaynst my lord Protectours grace ... [these two papers] ... were founde a showe of hys. They were sowen betwene the solles of a veluet showe. He made his ynke so craftely and with suche workemanshyp as the lyke hath not sene ... He made his pen of the aglet of a poynte that he plucked from his hosse, and thus wrought these letters so seditiouslye.

Latimer accused Seymour of religious indifference. When Queen Catherine had ordained twice-daily prayers in her household, Seymour 'gets him out of the way like a mole digging in the earth'. He continued by casting doubt on Seymour's subsequent fate.

> And as touching the kind of his death, whether he be saved or no, I refer that to God only. What God can do, I cannot tell. I will not deny, but that he may in the twinkling of an eye save a man, and turn his heart. What he did, I cannot tell. And when a man hath two strokes with an axe, who can tel but that between two strokes he doth repent? It is very hard to judge. Well, I wil not go so nigh to work: but this I will say if they ask me, what I think of his death, that he died very dangerously, irksomely, horribly ... He was a man the farthest from the fear of God that I knew or heard of in England.[150]

How far should the conventionally pious verses supposedly written by Seymour before his death mitigate Latimer's harsh judgement?

> Forgetting God to love a kynge
> Hath been my rod, or else nothynge
> In this frail lyfe, being a blaste
> Of care and stryfe till yt be paste
> Yet God did call me in my pryde
> Leste I shulde fall and from hym slyde
> For whom he loves he muste correct
> That they may be of his electe.
> Then, Death, haste thee, thou shalt me gaine,
> Immortally with Hym to raigne

> Lord! sende the kinge in years as Noye
> In governinge this realme in joye
> And after thys frayl lyfe such grace
> That in thy bliss he may find place.[151]

Was Seymour brought down by his brother? Was their relationship marked by discord, then suspicion and finally extreme hatred?[152] Was Somerset pushed into reluctant hostility by his wife or by 'makebates' or some 'crafty merchant'?[153] Elizabeth later thought on these lines. 'I have harde in my time of many cast away, for want of comminge to the presence of thir Prince'. She had heard Somerset say that 'if his brother had been suffered to speak with him, he had never suffered; but the persuasions were made to him so great, that he was brought in belief that he could not live safely if the Admiral lived, and that made him give his consent to his death'.[154] But Elizabeth may not have been an impartial witness. More is known about Seymour's feelings than Somerset's. Seymour claimed just before his arrest that Somerset was very jealous of him and increasingly frightened, recently going 'better furnisshed with men aboute him then he was wont'.[155] Seymour seems, however, to have feared the council more than Somerset – 'I am suer I can have no hurt, if thei do me right; thei can not kyll me, except thei do me wrong' – and appeared confident Somerset would never commit him to the Tower.[156] On the day before Seymour's arrest the council had 'great secret conferences … in the garden'; and it is striking how full a part the council took in the examinations, discussions and decisions of mid to late February. Just how large a part was Somerset playing in all this?[157] Leti's account, in which Somerset is seen as merely reacting to teach Seymour a lesson, but being pushed into harsher courses by other councillors and by the sheer weight of information emerging against Seymour, seems worth pondering. Was the earl of Warwick behind Seymour's fall? Had he been jealous of Seymour since he had relinquished the Admiralty to him in early 1547? Seymour boasted how 'he was as glad of that office as of any office within the realm and that no man shuld take that office from him but that he shuld take his lif also'. Had Warwick felt his loss as strongly?[158] Had he provoked the quarrels between the two brothers by encouraging Seymour's ambitions to become Governor? Seymour confessed how 'he *harde*, and uppon that sought out certain precedentes'.[159] There is evidence that there was no love lost between them: Seymour wanted Dorset to keep house in Warwickshire to match with Warwick; there were rumours that they were not friends; they quarrelled over Stratford-upon-Avon; a later would-be historian noted 'howe Warewick was lodged with Somersett in his howse for feare of his brother the Admerall'. Some lines written after discussions between Seymour and Rutland were delivered to Warwick, and perhaps Warwick urged that Seymour be struck down hard in 1549.[160] Clearly there was strong pressure on the judges to deal with Seymour firmly. According to a would-be historian's notes, when the examination of Seymour's treason was committed to Montagu, the king's serjeant and attorney, and Gooderick and Gosnall, the latter two doubted whether Seymour's offences involving Sharington were treason. Montagu told them not to stick on that point; Gooderick retorted that he should then be tried by the common law; Montagu thought it better done by parliament lest if Seymour were condemned by common law they should be blamed when the king came of age; if it was done by parliament they would be discharged.[161] What that suggests is a sense that Seymour's behaviour had been treasonous even if it would be difficult technically to convict him of treason in particular points: it was his plans and boasts, more than his actions, that condemned him. More telling still than any fratricidal bitterness or any factional stirring seems to be quite simply what was found out about Seymour's activities and ambitions during the investigations in January and February 1549. He had done and said quite enough to have provoked not only his brother but all his fellow councillors. 'After divers examinacions of those whiche for suspicion and maters laied against them in the lorde Admiralles case were committed to the Tower', it appeared to Somerset and 'all the council that the divers and sundry articles of high treason sorely charged against him 'semid so manifestly proved against him by diverse wais that it appearid not able to be avoided but he shulde be giltie of them'.[162] If in addition he had been caught in the act of kidnapping the young king, it becomes even less necessary to seek out 'factional' motives for his downfall.

What then is the significance of Seymour's behaviour? What his actions and boastings vividly show is where power lay, or was thought to lie, in mid-Tudor England. At one level that remains true even if Seymour was in fact innocent. He married a dowager-queen and perhaps hoped to marry a royal princess. He sought a position close to the king and exploited his friendship with several members of the privy chamber. He tried to abuse the youthful goodwill of the king by giving him money and getting him to write letters in his favour. He used parliaments to stir up opposition against his brother and to recruit noblemen to his cause. He was keen to acquire lands and jewels and money. He fortified his castle at Holt. He spoke vividly of retaining and leading men. Finally he attempted, in a gambler's last throw, to seize Edward and Elizabeth. Seymour in the event failed. He tried to do too much too quickly and there was as much rhetoric as action. He won insufficient support among his fellow counsellors: even if Dorset, Northampton, Rutland and Southampton were keener than they allowed themselves to appear in their interrogations, Seymour never won any wholehearted commitment. He hardly had any coherent political programme, even if he agreed with his wife's criticism of the distribution of crown lands,[163] or attacked Somserset's Scottish invasion of 1547 for risking the loss of a great number of men and for costing 'a great summ of Money in vayn',[164] or suggested that Somerset would give up Calais to the French,[165] or declared generally that 'he mislyked the procedinges of the lord Protector and counsayle' and sought 'the alteracion of the state and ordre of the Realme'.[166]

Yet suppose he had delayed his plots until the autumn of 1549, he might have gathered more support after the continuing military difficulties and the serious popular rebellions of the summer. Seymour moved too soon. And his failure was as much a matter of temperament. It was very difficult, and it had always been very dangerous, for a nobleman to risk launching a rebellion. Dissident nobles might talk of joining in, but just like the gentry they could not be greatly relied upon because 'they have sumwhat to loose'.[167] A successful politician in the mid-sixteenth century needed a more subtle approach: Seymour should have been more patient. Wightman, his servant, testified how 'if he had oones conceyved opynion by his owne perswasions, neyther Lawyer nor other could tourne him'.[168] His fiery nature and his soaring ambition told against him. 'This day', said Elizabeth on hearing of his execution, 'died a man with much wit, and very litle judgment'.[169]

Notes

1. I should like to thank Dr S.L. Adams, Mr C.S.L. Davies, Mr P.J. Gwyn, Dr R.A. Houlbrooke, Mr H. James and the late Mrs J. Loach for their comments.
2. Earlier accounts include L.B. Smith, *Treason in Tudor England: Politics and Paranoia* (1986), pp. 20–35; R.L. Davids and A.D.K. Hawkyard, *sub* Seymour in S.T. Bindoff (ed.), *The History of Parliament: The House of Commons 1509–1558* (3 vols, 1982), iii. 297–301; B.N. de Luna, *The Queen Declined: an Interpretation of Willobie his Avisa* (Oxford, 1970), pp. 47–54, 137–52 (though the relationship of the text to Seymour is speculative) (I owe this reference to Mr H. James); W.K. Jordan, *Edward VI: the Young King* (1968), pp. 368–82 (Jordan's chronology is often inaccurate); J.E. Neale, *Queen Elizabeth* (1960 edn), pp. 25–33; J. Strype, *Ecclesiastical Memorials* (3 vols in 6 parts, 1822–24), II ii. 191–209; G. Burnet, *The History of the Reformation of the Church of England* (ed. N. Pocock) (Oxford, 6 vols, 1865), ii. 1146, 181–6.
3. G. Lefvre-Pontalis (ed.), *Correspondance politique de Odet de Selve* (Paris, 1888), no. 176 pp. 152–5.
4. Abbe de Vertot (ed.), *Ambassades de Messieurs de Noailles en Angleterre* (Leiden, 5 vols, 1763), i. 102–3. (The first volume of this edition of ambassadors' correspondence includes an anonymous account of politics in the reign of Edward VI: I am very grateful to Miss P. Tudor for showing me the significance of this account).
5. E. Dent, *Annals of Winchcombe and Sudeley* (1877), pp. 162–3.
6. G. Leti, *Historia Overo Vita di Elisabetta regina d'Inghilterra* (Amsterdam, 2 vols, 1693), i. 180 (also accessible in a French translation, *La vie d'Elizabeth reine d'Angleterre* (Amsterdam, 2 vols, 1694), i. 165–6). Gregorio Leti, born a catholic in Milan in 1630, died in Amsterdam in 1701 as a calvinist. He wrote many works of history as well as treatises against the Catholic church, several of which were placed on the Index. In his preface, Leti tells how for thirty years he had thought of writing the life of Elizabeth. He had talked to many English lords, including some knowledgeable in history, but found that opinions were too polarised, the Protestants seeing Elizabeth as an angel, the Catholics as a devil. But when business again took him to England, he met Lord Anglesey who

encouraged him to write his lives of Elizabeth and Cromwell. The French translator commented in his preface that Leti 'a trouve en Angleterre par le moyen d'un seigneur considerable de ce pais-la, des memoires particuliers que Camden, le plus exact de tous les auteurs qui ont parle de cette reine, n'avoit jamais vus'. The seigneur in question might have been Arthur Annesley (1614–86), first Earl of Anglesey, whom the *Dictionary of National Biography* describes as 'perhaps the first peer who devoted time and money to the formation of a great library', which was, however, sold on his death. The difficulty with Leti's text is that he does not give references for some remarkable letters which he prints in full or for several unusual stories. It is possible that these are inventions – and Leti published a whole volume of letters supposedly by Paolo Sarpi which is regarded as largely spurious (*ex inf.* Professor J.I. Israel) – but usually they seem sufficiently plausible to be worth adding to the body of evidence on which an account of Seymour must rest. (I am very grateful indeed to Dr P.J. Holmes for his help in pursuing Leti).

7. Leti, *Historia Elisabetta*, i. 178 (164); Vertot, i. 101–3.
8. BL Harleian MS, 249 f. 38v (19b).
9. BL Harleian MS, 249 f. 38v (19C).
10. Bodleian Library, Ashmole MS, 1729 f. 5; PRO SP10/1/43.
11. Dent, *Annals*, between pp. 162–3.
12. PRO SP46/1 f. 14.
13. S. Haynes, *A Collection of State Papers at Hatfield* (1740), pp. 61–2.
14. Bodleian Library, Ashmole MS 1729, f. 5.
15. BL Lansdowne MS, 1236 f. 26.
16. Leti, *Historia Elisabetta*, i. 182–6 (167–70).
17. J.G. Nichols, *Literary Remains of Edward the Sixth* (Roxburghe Club, 2 vols, 1857), i. no. xlvi, p. 45; Jordan, Edward VI, p. 370, citing Strype, *Ecclesiastical Memorials*, II i. 208–9, takes Edward's congratulations at face value.
18. PRO SP10/6/10.
19. Nichols, *Literary Remains*, ii. 215.
20. BL Harleian MS, 249 f. 38 (19C); Vertot, *Ambassades*, i. 101–3; Leti, *Historia Elisabetta*, i. 186–7 (169–71).
21. PRO PROB11/32/19.
22. BL Hatfield Microfilms, M485/39, vol. 150 f. 126 (Haynes, *State Papers*, p. 73). I am grateful to the Marquess of Salisbury for permission to consult and to cite passages from the Cecil Papers.
23. Ibid., pp. 84, 71–2.
24. PRO SP10/4/14.
25. J. Hayward, *The Life and Raigne of King Edward the Sixth* (1630), p. 82; Vertot, *Ambassades*, i. 132; J.A. de Thou, *Histoire universelle* (11 vols, 1740), i. 497 n. 4; BL Add. MS, 48023 f. 350v; Odet de Selve, no. 304, p. 287.
26. Burnet, *History of the Reformation*, ii. 181. Cf. S.E. James, 'Queen Kateryn Parr (1512–1548)', *Transactions of the Cumberland and Westmorland Antiquarian and Archaeological Society*, lxxxvii (1988), pp. 115–18.
27. BL Hatfield Microfilms, M485/39, vol. 150 f. 119 (Haynes, *State Papers*, p. 77).
28. PRO SP10/4/14.
29. BL Hatfield Microfilms, M485/39, vol. 150 f. 74 (Haynes, *State Papers*, p. 93).
30. BL Hatfield Microfilms, M485/39, vol. 150 f. 86 (Haynes, *State Papers*, p. 100).
31. BL Hatfield Microfilms, M485/39, vol. 150 f. 85 (Haynes, *State Papers*, p. 100).
32. PRO SP10/6/21; BL Hatfield Microfilms, M485/39, vol. 150 f. 85v (Haynes, *State Papers*, pp. 99–100).

33. BL Hatfield Microfilms, M485/39, vol. 150 f. 80v (Haynes, *State Papers*, p. 96).
34. T. Hearne, *Titi-Livii Foro-Juliensis viat Henrici Quinti, regis angliae, accedit sylloge Epistolarum, a variis angliae principibus scriptarum* (Oxford, 1716), pp. 165–6; PRO SP10/2/25.
35. Hearne, *Titi-Livii*, pp. 211–12.
36. BL Hatfield Microfilms, M485/39, vol. 150 ff. 85–88 (Haynes, *State Papers*, pp. 96, 100; Hearne, *Titi-Livii*, pp. 165–6).
37. PRO SP10/6/19, 10/6/22.
38. R. McNulty (ed.), *Ludovico Ariosto's 'Orlando Furioso' translated by Sir John Harington, 1591* (Oxford, 1972), p. 217; R. Hughey, *John Harington of Stepney: Tudor Gentleman: his life and works* (Ohio, 1972), pp. viii, 52 (I owe this reference to Dr S.L. Adams).
39. PRO SP10/6/16; BL Hatfield Microfilms, M485/39, vol. 150 f. 81v (Haynes, *State Papers*, p. 97).
40. BL Hatfield Microfilms, M485/39, vol. 150 f. 81v, cf. f. 84 (Haynes, *State Papers*, p. 97; cf. pp. 98–9).
41. BL Hatfield Microfilms, M485/39, vol. 150 ff. 79–84, esp. 83–84v (Ibid., pp. 95–8).
42. Vertot, *Ambassades*, i. 137; Leti, Historia Elisabetta, i. 190–91 (173–5).
43. BL Hatfield Microfilms, M485/39, vol. 150 f. 87v (Haynes, *State Papers*, p. 101, cf. p. 72).
44. PRO SP10/6/16; cf. BL Hatfield Microfilms, M485/39, vol. 150 f. 44v (Haynes, p. 69).
45. PRO SP10/6/14.
46. Vertot, *Ambassades*, i. 138.
47. H. James, 'The fall of Thomas, Lord Seymour, Lord Admiral, and North East Wales', citing J.A. Froude, *History of England from the Fall of Wolsey to the Death of Elizabeth* (12 vols, 1893 edn), iv. 369. (I am grateful to Mr H. James for showing me this unpublished paper.)
48. BL Add. MS, 48023 f. 350v. Ff. 350–369v in the bound volume BL Add. MS 48023, part of the Yelverton Manuscripts, are in the same hand. Ff. 350–351v deal with Edward VI's reign; ff. 352–369v with the years 1559 to 1562, interrupted by interludes treating the siege of Exeter in 1549 and the loss of Calais in 1558. The later folios are quite full, and from f. 359v are set out in the form of a diary under monthly headings. The folios dealing with the reign of Edward VI are often brief jottings, sometimes memoranda for further work, rather like the working notes of a would-be historian. Unfortunately the author has not been identified, but on his own account he knew several royal officials, took a considerable interest in foreign and economic affairs, and was keen to report gossip. He writes in similar vein as the anonymous eye-witness of BL Add. MS 48026 ff. 6–16 about the quarrels between Somerset and Warwick.
49. BL Hatfield Microfilms, M485/39, vol. 150 f. 71 (Haynes, *State Papers*, p. 90).
50. J.R. Dasent, *Acts of the Privy Council* [hereafter *APC*] (32 vols, 1890–1907) ii. 259. Seymour's allusion is to the minority of Henry VI. John, duke of Bedford, one of Henry VI's uncles, became regent of France (on the refusal of the duke of Burgundy). Another, Humphrey, duke of Gloucester, was appointed 'Protector and Defender of the realm and church in England and principal councillor of the king' for the duration of Bedford's absence overseas by the Lords in parliament on 5 December 1422. But he had also wanted to be regent or have the governance of the realm. He supported that claim not just by his birth but on the grounds that when, in the codicil of his will, the dying Henry V had granted him the principal

tutorship and defence ('tutelam et defensionem ... principales') of the baby king, he had meant by that phrase to confer on Duke Humphrey the government of the kingdom itself. But the Lords, after searching the 'precydentes of the governaill of the land in tyme and cas semblable', found Duke Humphrey's desire 'not accordyng with the lawes of this land'. A king, they claimed, could not devise such powers by will without the assent of parliament. They accordingly refused to call him Tutor, Lieutenant, Governor or Regent, but settled, 'to appese you', for the description of Protector and Defender 'which emporteth a personell duetee of entendance to the actuell defense of the land' against enemies abroad and rebels at home. Gloucester did not then demur. (In the light of the Lords' reasoning, which we know from the Lords' reply to Gloucester's later request in 1428, it seems unlikely that Henry V had meant by the phrase 'tutellam et defensionem ... principales' simply the responsibility for the personal property of the king.) In 1426, as part of his broader complaints against Henry Beaufort, cardinal bishop of Winchester, the most influential councillor in the mid-1420s, Gloucester put forward a further claim: he was the one 'to whom, off alle persones or that shulde be in the londe, by the wey off nature and birthe yt belongeth to se unto the governaunce of the kynges persone'. It is not entirely clear who had had the day-to-day keeping of the young Henry VI. Henry V's codicil had distinguished between the 'tutelam et defensionem ... principales' of the king, granted to Gloucester, and the 'persone sue regimen et gubernationem' which Henry entrusted to Thomas Beaufort, duke of Exeter. Most likely it was indeed Exeter who had undertaken that task, but possibly he shared the responsibility with his brother Henry Beaufort. Gloucester's bid for the governorship evidently failed. Next, on 3 March 1428 he asked the Lords in parliament for a definition – presumably he meant an enlargement – of the scope of his power and authority as Protector, but the Lords simply reminded him of his agreement to their decisions in 1422. Seymour was thus justified in arguing that responsibilities had been divided in the minority of Henry VI and that no one had held so great a combination of powers as Somerset did in the minority of Edward VI: the repeated rejection of Gloucester's claims, even though Gloucester's title of Protector conferred far less on him than the same title did on Somerset, would have further encouraged him. (For this complex episode see J.S. Roskell, 'The origins of the office and dignity of protector of England, with special reference to its origins', *English Historical Review*, lxviii (1953), esp. pp. 194, 198, 200, 203–7, 210, 216, 218, 220, 228; P. and F. Strong, 'The last will and codicils of Henry V', *English Historical Review*, xcvi (1981), p. 85; R.A. Griffiths, *The Reign of Henry VI: the Exercise of Royal Authority 1422–1461* (1981), pp. 17–22, 51, 70–81; G.L. Harriss, *Cardinal Beaufort: a Study of Lancastrian Ascendancy and Decline* (Oxford, 1988), pp. 115–17, but note crucial criticism by R.G. Davies, *English Historical Review*, cv (1990), p. 399; T.B. Pugh, *Henry V and the Southampton Plot* (Southampton, 1988), pp. 144–5; *Rotuli Parliamentorum*, iv. 175, 326; C.L. Kingsford (ed.), *Chronicles of London* (Oxford, 1905), p. 77. (I am grateful to Dr R.G. Davies and Mr T.B. Pugh for advice.)

51. BL Add. MS, 48023 f. 350; BL Add. MS 48126 ff. 6–7; and cf. Paris, Bibliotheque Nationale, MS Ancien Saint-Germain, Fonds Francais, 15888 f. 186v.
52. *APC*, ii. 259.
53. BL Add. MS, 48126 f. 6; Griffiths, *Henry VI*, pp. 31, 70–81; Harriss, *Beaufort*, pp. 136–44, 150–52.
54. BL Add. MS, 48023 f. 350v.

The downfall of Sir Thomas Seymour   157

55. Vertot, *Ambassades*, i. 104. Does the charge that Seymour 'did withdraw yourself from the Kinges Majestes service, and being moved and spoken unto for your owne honour and for thabilitie that was in yow to serve and aide the Kinges Majestes affaires and the Lord Protectour, yow wolde alwais draw back and feyn excuses, and declare plain that yow wolde not do yt' refer to Seymour's failure to fulfil his military duties? (*APC*, ii. 252 (22)).
56. Vertot, *Ambassades*, i. 129–31; cf. Burnet, *History of the Reformation*, ii. 84, 114–16; BL Add. MS, 48023 f. 350v.
57. *APC*, iii. 260.
58. Vertot, *Ambassades*, i. 129–31.
59. *APC*, iii. 259; cf. PRO SP10/6/27.
60. PRO SP10/6/10 (5).
61. PRO SP10/6/10 (7).
62. BL Hatfield Microfilms, M485/39, vol. 150 ff. 64v, 51 (Haynes, *State Papers*, pp. 79, 87–8, 74).
63. BL Harleian MS, 249 ff. 29–29v.
64. PRO SP10/6/26; BL, Hatfield Microfilms, M485/39, vol. 150 f. 51 (Haynes, *State Papers*, p. 74).
65. *APC*, iii. 260.
66. Nichols, *Literary Remains* i. cxx; R.H. Brodie (ed.), *Calendar of Patent Rolls: Edward VI* (6 vols, 1924–29), i. 217; BL Hatfield Microfilms, M485/39, vol. 150 f. 71v (Haynes, *State Papers*, p. 91).
67. PRO SP10/4/31; SP10/6/10 (10).
68. Bodleian Library, Ashmole MS, 1729 f. 9.
69. BL Hatfield Microfilms, M485/39, vol. 150 f. 112 (Haynes, *State Papers*, p. 75).
70. PRO SP10/6/11.
71. PRO SP10/6/26.
72. R.J.W. Swales, 'The Howard interest in Sussex elections, 1529–1558', *Sussex Archaeological Collections*, cxiv (1976), pp. 49–60; Bindoff, *House of Commons*, iii. 299–300 (somewhat speculative); J. Loach, *Parliament under the Tudors* (Oxford, 1991), pp. 90–91.
73. PRO SP10/6/7 (10, 11); BL Hatfield Microfilms, M485/39, vol. 150 f. 61 (Haynes, *State Papers*, p. 85); BL Harleian MS, 249 f. 34 (5).
74. *Cal. Pat. Rolls, Edward VI* ii. 96–7; BL Add. MS, 48023 f. 350v.
75. *Lords' Journals*, pp. 295–9, 307, 313; *Commons' Journals*, p. 2.
76. BL Hatfield Microfilms, M485/39, vol. 150 f. 51 (Haynes, *State Papers*, p. 74).
77. BL Harleian MS, 249 f. 34 (4).
78. PRO SP10/6/11; BL Hatfield Microfilms, M485/39, vol. 150 f. 113 (Haynes, *State Papers*, p. 76).
79. PRO SP10/6/14 (1).
80. PRO SP10/6/7 (6).
81. PRO SP10/6/13 (16); SP10/6/14 (2).
82. PRO SP10/6/7 (6); cf. SP10/6/12.
83. PRO SP10/6/12; cf. BL Harleian MS, 249 f. 35v (14).
84. PRO SP10/6/7 (7).
85. PRO SP10/6/12.
86. BL Harleian MS, 249 f. 35 (13).
87. BL Hatfield Microfilms, M485/39, vol. 150 f. 93v (Haynes, *State Papers*, p. 105); PRO SP10/6/13 (5, 6, 7).
88. BL Harleian MS, 249 f. 35 (13); *Statutes of the Realm*, iii. 63.
89. PRO SP10/6/13.

90. BL Hatfield Microfilms, M485/39, vol. 150 f. 84 (Haynes, *State Papers*, pp. 97, 99).
91. BL Harleian MS, 249, f. 35v.
92. Ibid., f. 35v (15).
93. Ibid., f. 35 (12).
94. Ibid.; cf. *Statutes of the Realm*, iv. 62; Vertot, *Ambassades*, i. 132; Leti, *Historia Elisabetta*, i. 193 (176–7).
95. PRO SP10/6/7 (1–3); BL Hatfield Microfilms, M485/39, vol. 150 ff. 53–53v (Haynes, *State Papers*, p. 83).
96. BL Hatfield Microfilms, M485/39, vol. 150 f. 115 (Haynes, *State Papers*, p. 76).
97. BL Hatfield Microfilms, M485/39, vol. 150 f. 84v (Haynes, *State Papers*, p. 98).
98. BL Hatfield Microfilms, M485/39, vol. 150 ff. 119–20 (Haynes, *State Papers*, pp. 77–9); PRO SP10/6/7.
99. PRO SP10/6/14 (3).
100. BL Hatfield Microfilms, M485/39, vol. 150 f. 115 (Haynes, *State Papers*, p. 77).
101. BL Hatfield Microfilms, M485/39, vol. 150 f. 54v (Haynes, *State Papers*, p. 83).
102. *Lords' Journals*, p. 307.
103. BL Hatfield Microfilms, M485/39, vol. 150 f. 43v (Haynes, *State Papers*, p. 68); PRO SP10/6/7 (11).
104. M.A.R. Graves, *The House of Lords in the Parliaments of Edward VI and Mary* (Cambridge, 1981), pp. 115–16; PRO SP10/6/14 (2).
105. PRO SP10/6/14.
106. PRO SP10/6/15.
107. R. Grafton, *Chronicle; or History of England* (1809 edn), pp. 499–500; Strype, *Ecclesiastical Memorials*, ii. app. HH, p. 109; BL Add. MS, 48126 ff. 6–16; BL Add. MS, 48023, ff. 350–51v; BL Harleian MS, 249 ff. 16–18; D.E. Hoak, *The King's Council in the reign of Edward VI* (Cambridge, 1976), pp. 43–5, 231–9; A.J. Slavin, 'The fall of Lord Chancellor Wriothesley: a study in the politics of conspiracy', *Albion*, vii (1975), pp. 265–86.
108. Haynes, *State Papers* pp. 82–3; BL Hatfield Microfilms, M485/39, vol. 150 f. 103v (Haynes, *State Papers*, p. 104).
109. *Cal. Pat. Rolls, Edward VI*, i. 25–33; cf. H. Miller, 'Henry VIII's unwritten will: grants of lands and honours in 1547', in E.W. Ives, R.J. Knecht and J.J. Scarisbrick (eds), *Wealth and Power in Tudor England: essays presented to S.T. Bindoff* (1978), pp. 102, 104.
110. Strype, *Ecclesiastical Memorials*, II ii. pp. 194–5.
111. James, 'Seymour and North East Wales', citing Leland, *Itinerary*, iii. 69; A. Palmer, 'The town of Holt, Denbighshire', *Archaeologia Cambriensis* lxvi (1907), pp. 313–14.
112. James, 'Seymour and North East Wales', citing R.R. Davies, *Lordship and Society in the Marches of Wales 1282–1400* (Oxford, 1978), pp. 56–8, 72; and I.D. Thornley and A.H. Thomas (eds), *The Great Chronicle of London* (1938), p. 258. Cf. also R.R. Davies, 'Richard II and the principality of Chester 1397–9', in F.R. du Boulay and C.M. Barron (eds), *The Reign of Richard II* (1971), pp. 256–79; J.L. Gillespie, 'Richard II's Cheshire archers', *Transactions of the Historic Society of Lancashire and Cheshire*, cxxv (1974), pp. 8, 12; M.K. Jones, 'Sir William Stanley of Holt: politics and family allegiance in the late fifteenth century', *Welsh History Review*, xiv (1988), pp. 1, 10.
113. BL Hatfield Microfilms, M485/39, vol. 150 f. 57 (Haynes, *State Papers*, p. 85).
114. McNulty, *Harington*, p. 217.
115. H. Harington (ed.), *Nugae Antiquae* (2 vols, 1804), ii. 330.

116. PRO SP10/5/1. F.E. Warneford (ed.), *Star Chamber Suits of John and Thomas Warneford, Wiltshire Record Society*, xlviii (1993 for 1992), pp. 30, 37–8, xc–xvi, includes a dispute between John Warneford, for nine years in Sir Thomas Seymour's service as steward and surveyor of his lands in Wiltshire and Gloucestershire, and Sir John Bridges, deputy-governor of Boulogne from 1544. After Seymour's fall, Bridges accused Warneford of cruel exactions on Seymour's tenants, claiming that Seymour had angrily dismissed Warneford once he realised what he was doing. More plausibly, Bridges also claimed that Warneford was encouraging Seymour to extend his local influence at Bridges' expense during his absence in Boulogne. No doubt, now that Seymour had fallen, Bridges was trying to recover the local influence he had earlier lost.
117. PRO SP10/6/13 (5,6,7); cf. BL Harleian MS, 249 f. 35v; *Statutes of the Realm*, iv. 62.
118. PRO SP10/6/8.
119. BL Harleian MS, 249 ff. 37–37v (24–26) and cf. 37v–38 (27–28); BL Add. MS, 48023 f. 350v; Leti, *Historia Elisabetta*, i. 196 (178).
120. PRO SP10/1/43; BL Harleian MS, 249 f. 36v (21, 22); Swales, 'Sussex elections', pp. 54–6 (though the impressive-looking evidence is in fact rather tentative: three connections seem certain); C.E. Challis, *The Tudor Coinage* (Manchester, 1978), pp. 100–103.
121. PRO SP10/6/13 (9).
122. BL Harleian MS, 249 f. 39v (I am grateful to Mr H. James for drawing my attention to this point).
123. *Statutes of the Realm*, iv. 63.
124. *APC*, ii. 255–6 (I am grateful to Mr H. James for this reference).
125. *APC*, ii. 247–56 (23). Seymour visited the Scilly Islands in 1547 and may have taken the initiative in fortifying them the following year (H.M. Colvin (ed.), *The History of the King's Works, 1485–1600 (part ii)*, iv. (1982), p. 588).
126. Vertot, *Ambassades*, i. 139–40.
127. BL Hatfield Microfilms, M485/39, vol. 150 f. 99v (Haynes, *State Papers*, p. 106).
128. BL Hatfield Microfilms, M485/39, vol. 150 f. 101v (Haynes, *State Papers*, p. 108).
129. PRO SP10/6/10 (6).
130. *APC*, ii. 258–9; PRO SP10/6/27.
131. PRO SP10/6/7.
132. H. Robinson (ed.), *Original Letters relative to the English Reformation, Parker Society* (2 vols, 1846–47), ii. no. ccci p. 648 (I owe this reference to Dr A.D.M. Pettegree).
133. BL Hatfield Microfilms, M485/39, vol. 150 f. 43v (Haynes, *State Papers*, p. 68).
134. PRO SP10/6/12 (5); BL Hatfield Microfilms, M485/39, vol. 150 f. 64 (Haynes, *State Papers*, p. 87); PRO SP10/6/14 (6), 10/6/7 (11).
135. PRO SP10/6/7 (11); cf. Haynes, *State Papers*, pp. 107, 84–6; PRO SP10/6/14 (5, 6).
136. BL Harleian MS, 249, f. 34 (6).
137. Jordan, *Edward VI*, pp. 373–4.
138. Dorset testified that Seymour and he rode from parliament together on the day that Seymour was committed (PRO, SP10/6/7 (11)): the last day that Seymour was marked as present in the House of Lords was 17 January (*Lords' Journals*, p. 332). Instructions to search Seymour's house are dated 18 January (PRO, SP10/6/2).
139. Haynes, *State Papers*, pp. 70–71.

140. Ibid.
141. Ibid.
142. BL Hatfield Microfilms, M485/39, vol. 150 f. 70 (Haynes, *State Papers*, pp. 88–9.
143. BL Hatfield Microfilms, M485/39, vol. 150 ff. 79–84 (Haynes, *State Papers* pp. 94–5).
144. BL Hatfield Microfilms, M485/39, vol. 150 f. 78 (Haynes, *State Papers*, p. 95).
145. PRO SP10/6/19; BL Hatfield Microfilms, M485/39, vol. 150 ff. 85–88 (Haynes, *State Papers*, pp. 99–100); PRO SP10/6/20.
146. BL Hatfield Microfilms, M485/39, vol. 150 f. 91 (Haynes, *State Papers*, p. 102.)
147. Bodleian Library, Ashmole MS, 1729 f. 11 Arch F. c. 39; BL Lansdowne MS, 1236 ff. 33–33v (Ellis, *Original Letters*, 1st series, ii. 155–8), f. 35 (*Original Letters*, 1st series, ii. 153–5).
148. *APC*, ii. 246–7, 256–8, 260.
149. BL Add. MS, 48023 f. 351.
150. *Latimer's Sermons, temp. Edward VI* (1549), sig. M ii[v]–iii; Nichols, *Literary Remains*, i. cxxiii–iv; G.E. Corrie (ed.), *Sermons and Remains of Hugh Latimer*, Parker Society, xvi, xx 1844–45, pp. 161–5; cf. Hayward, *Edward VI*, pp. 83–4.
151. Harington, *Nugae Antiquae*, ii. 328–9.
152. J. Pratt (ed.), *The Acts and Monuments of John Foxe* (8 vols, 1877), vi. 283.
153. Hayward, *Edward VI*, p. 82; Foxe, *Acts and Monuments*, vi. 283; Latimer, *Sermons*, sig. M ii[v]–iii.
154. Dent, p. 193, citing Ellis, *Original Letters*, 2nd series, ii. 256.
155. PRO SP10/6/14 (5).
156. BL Hatfield Microfilms, M485/39, vol. 150 f. 56v (Haynes, *State Papers*, p. 84).
157. PRO SP10/6/14 (5); *APC*, ii. 246–7, 256–8, 260.
158. PRO SP10/6/13.
159. *APC*, ii. 259; cf. PRO SP10/6/27.
160. PRO SP10/6/7 (7); Vertot, *Ambassades*, i. 140; Haynes, *State Papers*, pp. 83–4, 107; PRO SP10/6/13 (4); BL Add. MS, 48023 f. 351v (cf. BL Add. MS, 48126 f. 7).
161. BL Add. MS, 48023 f. 351.
162. *APC*, ii. 246–7.
163. Haynes, *State Papers*, p. 104.
164. Bodleian Library, Ashmole MS 1729 f. 9.
165. BL Add. MS, 48023 f. 350v.
166. BL Hatfield Microfilms, M485/39, vol. 150 f. 60v (Haynes, *State Papers*, p. 85); BL Harleian MS 249 f. 34 (4)).
167. PRO SP10/6/7 (6).
168. BL Hatfield Microfilms, M485/39, vol. 150 f. 45 (Haynes, *State Papers*, p. 70).
169. Dent, p. 193; Leti, *Historia Elisabetta*, i. 201 (182).

8
Amy Robsart[1]

Born in about 1532, Amy Robsart was the daughter of Sir John Robsart of Syderstone, Norfolk, a prominent county gentleman who served as knight of the shire and (twice) as sheriff of Norfolk. Robert Dudley, also born about 1532, later earl of Leicester, came from a more remarkable family.[2] His grandfather was Edmund Dudley, Henry VII's grasping minister who was executed for alleged treason in 1509. His father was John Dudley, who rose in Henry VIII's service, especially in the 1540s, to become earl of Warwick, and then the effective ruler of England in the latter part of the minority of Edward VI, between 1549 and 1553, taking the title of duke of Northumberland in 1551. Northumberland attempted on Edward VI's death in 1553 to divert the succession away from Mary to Lady Jane Grey, an attempt that failed and led to his ultimate execution for treason in 1554. In more prosperous times Northumberland had been trying to establish himself as an influential regional magnate, acquiring lands in Norfolk held by the Howards dukes of Norfolk. As part of this policy, no doubt, he married Robert, one of his younger sons, to Amy Robsart, a marriage that brought a potential inheritance of several north-west Norfolk manors. It is also possible (though speculative) that Northumberland was also paying off some political debts to the Robsart family, if one supposes that the rebellion in East Anglia led by Robert Ket may in part have been instigated or at least furthered by Northumberland to embarrass Protector Somerset. A prosperous yeoman-farmer-cum-tanner, Robert Ket married Alice Appleyard, brother of Robert Appleyard whose widow married Sir John Robsart, whose daughter Amy married Robert Dudley in 1550. How significant was that real but indirect link between Ket and Northumberland? Northumberland held the manor of Wymondham and leased it to Ket: Ket was his tenant. In late 1549 Robert Ket was hanged for his part in the rebellion. In June 1551 Northumberland gave Ket's son William a new lease of the manor of Wymondham, a striking gesture given that William's father had been executed. This raises the possibility – the faint possibility – that Warwick, anxious to topple Protector Somerset, may have sought to demonstrate the disastrous consequences of his rule by getting his tenant Ket to exploit agrarian discontent, to stir up or to further riots. What actually happened might on such an interpretation have been much more than was originally intended and it may have gone way beyond anything that Warwick would have envisaged. All

161

162   *Power and politics in Tudor England*

this is fascinating, but in the last resort, I think, unpersuasive: after all it was Warwick who ultimately bloodily defeated the Norfolk rebels.[3]

However that may be, there is no reason to imagine that the marriage between Robert and Amy was a love match. It was celebrated in style on 4 June 1550 with the young king present at the royal palace at Sheen. We know very little about relations between the young couple thereafter. Robert became a gentleman of the king's privy chamber in August 1551 and so presumably served a good while at court but also evidently attempted to establish himself in Norfolk, for which he was returned a knight of the shire in 1553. In July 1553 his father sent him to seize Mary after Edward VI had died; Robert failed in that task but did succeed in having Lady Jane Grey proclaimed queen at King's Lynn. After the failure of the coup Robert was imprisoned in the Tower until released in October 1554. Some vague hints that he served abroad are not confirmed by legal records for 1555 and 1556, but in early 1557 he did accompany Queen Mary's husband Philip of Spain, most probably on a sea crossing from Calais, and later that year he served under him in the French wars (in which Calais was later lost) as master of the ordnance. As a result he was restored in blood in March 1558. On Mary's death he was immediately prominent as adviser and companion of Queen Elizabeth. He became master of the horse in January 1559, knight of the garter in April and a member of the privy council. Of Amy's activities in all these years we know very little. What is striking, and unusual, is that Robert Dudley seems to have had no family home of his own. In the summer of 1558 he was considering the purchase of a manor in Norfolk but nothing came of it. Dudley therefore lodged his wife with various of his servants – Mr Hyde (whose father had bought land from Dudley) at Denchworth, Mr Foster at Cumnor, and possibly others. Amy may also have stayed at Camberwell, just south of the city of London. From his steward's accounts we know that Robert visited Amy at Denchworth five times at least in 1559. A letter Amy wrote to Mr Flowerdew, her steward in Norfolk, concerning sheep on the manor of Syderstone, mentioned the sudden departing of her husband.[4] Accounts also show Amy's buying clothes and gowns at this time. Was it a happy marriage? It does not seem very successful. It is interesting, if not conclusive, that there were no recorded children and it is puzzling that Amy apparently did not join Robert at court, to participate at least occasionally in court ceremonial. A later account, to which we shall return, says that 'when the Lorde Rob went to his wief he went all in blacke, and howe he was commaunded to saye that he did nothing with her, when he cam to her, as seldome he did'.[5]

There is a marked contrast between what we know of Robert's relationship with Amy and his relationship with Elizabeth. Later Robert said he had known Elizabeth since she was eight (that is, since 1541); they may have met as prisoners in the Tower of London in the years 1553 and 1555.[6] According to a very doubtful source he may have vowed her his eternal devotion and offered to lend her £200 in 1557–58.[7] On Elizabeth's accession, Dudley was one of her closest attendants. He was with her when she arrived at London on 23 November, rode immediately behind her on 28 November; and was prominent in the coronation procession in January 1559. On 18 April 1559 the Spanish ambassador, de Feria, reported that during the last few days Lord Robert had come so much into favour that he did whatever he liked with affairs and it was even said that her Majesty visited him in his chamber day and night. People talked of this so freely that they went so far as to say that his wife had a disease in one of her breasts and that the queen was only waiting for her to die to marry Lord Robert.[8] In November 1559 de Feria's successor, Bishop Quadra, noted Robert's favour, or intimacy, with the queen.[9] One Mother Dowe appeared before the magistrates in Essex and confessed to having spread stories that Elizabeth was pregnant by Robert.[10] Just before Amy's death in September 1560, William Cecil told Quadra that he foresaw the ruin of the realm through Robert's intimacy with the queen who surrendered all affairs to him and meant to marry him.[11] Of the closeness of Robert's relations with Elizabeth there is little doubt. From the number of letters to Dudley asking him to use his influence on behalf of the supplicants, it is clear that he was thought to have very considerable influence with the queen.[12] Moreover Dudley was also recreating a following including many men and families previously associated with his father the duke of Northumberland in the early 1550s.[13] In the early years of Elizabeth's reign, Dudley was obviously a rising man. If he had been unmarried, he might well have become Elizabeth's husband, which would further have increased his power.

On 8 September 1560 Amy Robsart died at Cumnor Lodge. Before considering the circumstances of her death, it is important to review the kinds of evidence we have. There are several letters written by the Spanish ambassador to his master in Spain. There are a few letters written to or from the English representative at the French court. Five letters sent between Dudley and one of his servants, Thomas Blount, whom Dudley despatched to Cumnor immediately after Amy's death, survive in copies in the Pepys Library.[14] There are details of Amy's funeral in Oxford on 22 September 1560. Seven years later Amy's half-brother, John Appleyard, made certain accusations against Dudley and these and the consequent investigations survive.[15] In 1584 a vitriolic tract, *Leycester's Commonwealth*, was published, accusing Dudley of leading a debauched life and of being a poisoner.[16] New evidence has been found in a remarkable document in the Yelverton papers in the British Library. Add. MS 48023 ff. 350–369v is a manuscript of some forty pages, part the working notes of a would-be historian of Edward VI's reign, and part a diary of events month by month between 1559 and 1562. It is anonymous and it is often critical of Dudley: but, unlike *Leycester's Commonwealth*, it is not a polemic, for its author was interested in a range of matters, from the rebuilding of St Paul's to reports of monstrous births.

Did Amy commit suicide? There are hints of this in the letter that Thomas Blount wrote to Dudley from Cumnor on 11 September. He described what he had heard about Amy's angry insistence that her servants should go to Abingdon fair, and then continued, 'Certainly, my lord, as little while as I have been here, I have heard divers tales of her that maketh me to judge her a strange woman of mind'. Picto [Amy's maid] had told him that 'she was a good virtuous gentlewoman, and daily would pray upon her knees; and divers times she saith that she hath heard her pray to God to deliver her from desperation. Then, said I [wrote Blount], she might have an evil toy in her mind. No, good Mr Blount, said Picto, do not judge so of my words; if you should go there, I am sorry I said so much ...'. Blount concluded 'but truly the tales I do hear of her maketh me to think she had a strange mind in her; as I will tell you at my coming'.[17] Why should Amy have committed suicide? She may have been distressed by her faltering marriage: on 7 August 155(?9) she wrote to Mr Flowerdew [her agent in Norfolk] of her husband, 'I not beyng all to gether in quyet for his soden departyng'.[18] If Amy was ill, if she was dying of cancer of the breast, then this might have made her desperately unhappy. Yet that rests very heavily on the claim that she was indeed ill. Moreover throwing one self down a flight of stairs is by no means the most certain way of committing suicide. And it is worth emphasising that Blount's remarks are not very strong evidence: after all, Picto, Amy's servant, did deny it when Blount pressed her. 'No, good Mr Blount, ... do not judge so much of my words; if you should go there [i.e. believe that Amy killed herself], I am sorry I said so much ...'.[19]

Amy's death could have been a genuine accident, the result of sheer carelessness in walking downstairs. Dudley told Thomas Blount on 9 September that he had learned that 'my wife is dead ... by a fall from a pair of stairs'; Blount then wrote to Dudley, 'too true it is that my lady is dead, and, as it seemeth, with a fall'.[20] Similarly the innkeeper at Abingdon had heard that Amy died 'by a misfortune', 'by a fall from a paier of stares'.[21] On 13 September Blount wrote 'the circumstances and as many things as I can learn doth persuade me that only misfortune hath done it, and nothing else'.[22] Queen Elizabeth told the Spanish ambassador, 'she broke her neck, she must have fallen down a staircase'.[23] Henry Killegrew informed Throckmorton at the French court on 10 October that 'she brake her neck down a pair of stairs, which I protest unto you was done only by the hand of God to my knowledge'.[24] The coroner's jury which inquired into Amy's death apparently concluded that it was misadventure. Dudley told Blount that he had heard from the foreman of the jury that 'it doth plainly appear ... a very misfortune'.[25] In 1567 John Appleyard, Amy's half-brother, was shown a copy of the jury's verdict 'in which verdict I do find, not only such proofs testified under the oaths of fifteen persons, how my late sister by misfortune happened of death, but also such manifest and plain demonstration thereof, as hath fully and clearly satisfied and persuaded me'.[26] Another account says the same but also shows why this explanation has seemed less than convincing: 'it was found by this enqueste, that she was cause of her owne death, faling downe a paier of stayers, which by reporte was but eight steppes ...'.[27] It was a rather unlikely kind of accident.

Could such an accident be less accidental than it seemed, could it be the consequence of some illness? That is the explanation that carries most opinions today. It was put forward in 1956 by Ian Aird, professor of surgery at University College London;[28] it was also worked out, though never published by Norman Fourdrinier, vicar of Syderstone, Norfolk, at the same time.[29] Theories that Amy was ill rest on just one comment by Count de Feria, the Spanish ambassador, on 18 April 1559. People went so far in talking of the queen's relationship with Lord Robert 'as to say that his wife has a malady in one of her breasts and the Queen is only waiting for her to die to marry Lord Robert'.[30] Is this sufficient evidence to bear the weight of the theory that Amy was dying of cancer of the breast? Was she a sick woman for a long time, was it the state of her health that compelled her to live in the country away from court? Professor Aird argued that Amy's suffering from cancer of the breast accounted for her irritability and anxiety revealed in Blount's letters: Picto 'hath heard her pray to God to deliver her from desperation'.[31] Then, according to Professor Aird, as the cancer progressed, diseased and aged bones in Amy's spine deteriorated under its pressure, and suddenly and spontaneously her spine fractured as she was walking downstairs. She would have collapsed gently, giving the impression of having fallen and broken her neck. If this happened on the last flight of steps, or as she was leaving the staircase, it could even be that (as *Leycester's Commonwealth* put it) she fell 'without hurting of her hood that stood upon her head'.[32] Unfortunately attempts in 1946 to exhume Amy's remains and test them for traces of cancer proved inconclusive. Fourdrinier, on the suggestions of a medical friend, argued that Amy was suffering from aortic aneurism, a morbid enlargement of the great artery issuing out of the left ventricle of the heart. Pains in the chest and an insufficient supply of blood to the brain would lead to irritability; a slight jerk, an accidental fall, would burst the membrane enclosing the aneurism, causing instant death. Suppose Amy experienced an attack of giddiness, collapsed, fell, broke her neck, at the same time as the membrane burst ... On learning of Professor Aird's argument, Fourdrinier withdrew his own, as his hypothesis did not explain why Amy's neck should break (unless she fell from a height that would not have left her head dress intact) and would have entailed Amy's being an invalid far more than he allowed. Both these medical theories, however, rest on very little firm evidence. Possibly, further support for the view that Amy was ill may be read into the Spanish ambassador's report in March 1560: 'I have understood Lord Robert has told somebody, who has not kept silence, that if he live another year, he will be in a very different position from now ... They say that he thinks of divorcing his wife'.[33] Could this mean that Amy was dying? Or is that straining the evidence? Against that there is the ambassador's report in September 1560 of his conversation with William Cecil. According to Bishop Quadra, Cecil said that Amy was publicly announced to be ill, although she was quite well. How should we understand that 'quite'.[34] All in all, the evidence for Amy's illness is not conclusive. She was just 28 years old in 1560. And any medical explanation, in the absence of detailed investigations, does rest on some astonishing coincidences.

These explanations, which obviously absolve Dudley, are often accompanied by various general presumptions about Dudley's innocence. Unhappily these are not as clear-cut as they may at first sight seem. To say, for example, that Dudley was innocent because the coroner's jury found no evidence of injuries suggesting foul play is to accept that the jury was impartial and independent. To claim that Dudley's relationship with the queen was not in itself evidence of an intention to murder his wife is obviously true but it does not in itself dispose of that intention. To say that because Anthony Foster was of honest character, well versed in the classics and later became an MP, therefore he could have had no part in murder, is not conclusive. To assert that because Dudley was later raised to the earldom of Leicester, therefore he could not have been a murderer, does not adequately counter suspicions. To say that because Dudley sent for John Appleyard, Amy's half-brother, at the time of the inquest, therefore Dudley must have been innocent, is, as we shall see, not conclusive. Of course, it is fair to object that much of the criticism of Dudley comes from hostile witnesses, from Dudley's political enemies who used whatever they could find against him, especially to block a marriage with the queen that they feared would harm them. But that means not that we should simply dismiss such evidence but that we should examine it very closely and critically; and it makes any details that we have about Dudley from sources not hostile to him particularly important.

Let us now look at arguments that Dudley was innocent based on those letters between Dudley and Blount in the days immediately after Amy's death. Do they show, as has been suggested, that Dudley was in no way implicated in it, that he made no attempt to stifle any inquiry, that on the contrary he was very anxious that the whole truth should come out? Dudley wrote to Blount on 9 September that he had no way to purge himself of the wicked world's malicious talk

> but one – which is the very plain truth to be knowen, I do pray you, as you have loved me, and do tender me and my quietness, and as now my special trust is in you, that [you] will use all the devices and meanes you can possible for the learning of the truth; wherein have no respect to any living person. And, as by your own travaill and diligence, so likewise by order of law, I mean by calling of the Coroner, and charging him to thuttermost from me to have good regard to make choice of no lyght or slight persons, but the discreetest and [most] substantial men, for the juries, such as for their knowledge may be able to search thoroughly and duly, by all manner of examinations, the bottom of the matter, and for their uprightness will earnestly and

sincerely deal therein without respect; and that the body be viewed and searched accordingly by them; and in every respect to proceed by order and law.

Dudley also wrote that he had sent for Appleyard and other of Amy's friends to be there. On 12 September Dudley acknowledged Blount's reassuring reply:

> yo do well to satisfy me with the discreet jury you say are chosen already; unto whom I pray you say from me, that I require them, as ever I shall think good of them, that they will, according to their duties, earnestly, carefully, and truly deal in this matter, and find it as they shall see it fall out; and, if it fall out a chance or misfortune, then so to say; and if it appear a villany (as God forbid so mischievous or wicked a body should live) then find it so.... I seek chiefly troth in this case ... without any favour to be showed either one way or other.

In another letter Dudley again desired that the jury should continue in their enquiry and examination to the uttermost, and when they had given their verdict 'assuredly I do wish that another substantial company of honest men might try again for the knowledge of truth'.[35] Do these letters, then, show that Dudley was as anxious as anyone to find out the cause of his wife's death, do they offer evidence that he was in no way guilty of murder?

What evidence is there to support a charge of murder? There are two letters written by the Spanish ambassador which suggest that the possibility of a murder was talked of *before* Amy's death. On 13 November 1559 Bishop Quadra wrote, 'I heard from a certain person who is accustomed to giving me veracious news that Lord Robert has sent to poison his wife. Certainly all the queen has done with us and with the Swede [the Swedish prince who was briefley Elizabeth's suitor], and will do with the rest of us in the matter of her marriage, is only keeping Lord Robert's enemies and the country engaged with words until this wicked deed of killing his wife is consummated'. On 11 September 1560 Bishop Quadra, reporting a conversation he had had a few days earlier with William Cecil, said that Cecil had told him that Robert was thinking of killing his wife, who would take very good care they did not poison her. The next day, continued the ambassador, the queen told him as she returned from hunting that Robert's wife was dead or nearly so.[36] It is pretty clear that there was a good deal of gossip after Amy's death was known that she had been murdered. The Dudley–Blount letters show how Dudley feared 'the malicious talk that I knowe the wicked world will use'. The Abingdon innkeeper whom Blount asked the common opinion of Amy's death said 'some were disposed to say well, and some evil ... By my troth ... I judge it a misfortune because it chanced in that honest gentleman's house; his great honesty ... doth much curb the evil thoughts of the people'.[37] On 17 September Thomas Lever, a senior clergyman, wrote to Sir Francis Knollys and Sir William Cecil from Coventry that 'in these parts seemeth vnto me to be a grievous and dangerous suspicion and muttering of the death of her which was the wife of my lord Robert Dudley'.[38] On 10 October Henry Killegrew wrote from London, 'strange rumours were here of the death of my lady Dudley ... who can let men to speak and think in such cases?'[39] Throckmorton's letters in October make it plain that at the French court 'it is openly bruited ... that her neck was broken; some say what religion is this that a subject shall kill his wife'.[40] On 22 January 1561 Bishop Quadra reported a conversation with Henry Sidney, Dudley's brother-in-law. As to Amy's death, Sidney had examined the circumstances carefully, and was satisfied that it had been accidental, although he admitted that others thought differently. Bishop Quadra retorted that Lord Robert would find it difficult to persuade the world of his innocence. And Sidney agreed that there was hardly a person who did not believe that there had been foul play, adding that the preachers in the pulpits spoke of it, not sparing even the honour of the Queen.[41] In September 1561 Bishop Quadra reported a quarrel between Lord Robert and the earl of Arundel: Arundel had gone home and, with others, was drawing up copies of the testimony given in the inquiry about the death of Amy. Robert was reportedly doing his best to repair matters as it appeared that more was being discovered in that affair than he wished.[42]

All these references amount to no more than gossip, though they do make it fairly certain that at the least many people thought that Amy's death was suspicious. In 1566 Cecil noted of Dudley, 'he is infamed by the death of his wife'.[43] More explicit charges were made by John Appleyard in 1567 and in the diatribe against Dudley known as *Leycesters Commonwealth* published in 1584.

In 1567 John Appleyard, Amy's half-brother, questioned the circumstances of his sister's death. Apparently he had been approached by someone who suggested that 'if he were content to stir some matter against him [Dudley] for the death of his wife, he should find good maintenance therein and should not [lack] £4000 to relieve him'. One Tryndell gave evidence that when he brought Leicester's reply – that he could not help him in his requests as he desired – 'Appleyard used words of anger, and said among other things that he had for the earl's sake covered the murder of his sister'. Appleyard himself, when before the council, at one point referred to the 'murder of his sister', though immediately saying he took Dudley to be innocent.[44] Appleyard had been brought before the council on 8 May, abjectly submitted by 31 May, and then spent some days at least in the Fleet prison. He asked to see the verdict of the coroner's jury; this was shown to him; and on 4 June Appleyard declared himself fully satisfied and persuaded.[45] But how seriously can we take either the accusations against Dudley by a man whose career shows him something of an adventurer if not waster or his new-found convictions which he developed while in the Fleet?

In 1584 a stinging polemic against Dudley appeared, known as *Leycesters Commonwealth*. Its author, or at least co-ordinating editor, was most probably the Jesuit Robert Parsons (though a less plausible case has been made for Charles Arundell, a Catholic gentleman who fled to France in 1583).[46] Its Catholic provenance of course immediately raises doubts about the charges it brought against Dudley, who was supposed to have been involved in a series of murders, especially poisonings. Let us examine what it tells us about Dudley and Amy.

> His Lordship hath a speciall fortune, that when hee desireth any womans favour, then what person so ever standeth in his way, hath the luck to die quickly for the finishing of his desire. As for example, when his Lordship was in full hope to marry her Majesty, and his owne wife stood in his light, as hee supposed: hee did but send her aside to the house of his servant Forster of Cumner by Oxford, where shortly after shee had the chance to fall from a paier of staires, and so to breake her necke, but yet without hurting of her hood that stood upon her head. But Sir Richard Varney who by commandement remained with her that day alone, with one man onely, and had sent away perforce all her servants from her, to a market two miles of, hee (I say) with his man can tell how shee died, which man being taken afterward for a fellony in the marches of Wales and offering to publish the manner of the said murder, was made away privily in the prison. And Sir Richard himselfe dying about the same time in London, cried pitiously, and blasphemed God, and said to a Gentleman of worship of mine acquaintance, not long before his death: that all the Divels in Hell did teare him in peeces. The wife also of Bald Butler, kinsman to my lord, gave out the whole fact a little before her death.[47]

Later, in a discussion of why Lord Robert acted as he did, the author suggested that 'it is not also unlikely that hee prescribed unto Sir Richard Varney at his going thither, that he should first attempt to kill her by poison, and if that tooke not place then by any other way to dispatch her, howsoever'.[48] He then cited the report of Dr Bayly, professor of physick at Oxford:

> This learned grave man reported for most certaine, that there was a practize in Cumner among the conspiratours, to have poisoned the poore Lady a little before shee was killed, which was attempted in this order. They seeing the good Lady sad and heavy (as one that well knew by her other handling that her death was not farre of) began to perswade her, that her disease was aboundance of Melancholly and other humours, and therefore would needs consaile her to take some potion, which she absolutely refusing to doe, as suspecting still the worst: they sent one day, (unawares to her) for Doctor Bayly, and desired him to persuade her to take some litle potion at his hands, and they would send to fetch the same at Oxford upon his prescription, meaning to have added somewhat of their owne for her comfort as the Doctor upon just causes suspected, seeing their great importunity, and the small need which the good Lady had of Physick, and therefore hee flatly denied their request, misdoubting (as hee after reported) least if they had poisoned her under the name of his Potion: hee might after have beene hanged for a cover of their sinne. Marry the said Doctor remained well assured that this way taking no place, shee should not long escape as after ensued. And the thing was so beaten unto the heads of the principall men of the Vniversity of Oxford, by these and other meanes: as for that shee was found murdered (as all men said) by the Crowners inquest; and for that shee being hastely and obscurely burned at Cumner (which was condemned above as not advisedly done), my good Lord, to make plaine to the World the great love hee bare to her in her life, and what a grief the losse of so vertuous a lady was to his tender heart, would needs have hir taken vp again and reburied in the Vniversity Church at Oxford, with great Pomp and solemnity: that Doctor Babington my Lordes Chaplaine, making the publique funerall sermon at her second buriall, tript once

or twice in his speech, by recommending to there memories that vertuous lady so pittifully murdered, instead of so pittifully slaine.[49]

All that is suggestive but hard to corroborate: Verney's sending away Amy's servants; the murder of Verney's man when he later offered to talk; Verney's remorse on his deathbed; the suspicion of Dr Bayly that efforts were being made to poison Amy by adultering her medicine; Dudley's chaplain's reference to murder when she was reburied at Oxford.

The new evidence which I have discovered offers some suggestions that take the case against Dudley a little further. First, there is more evidence about Verney. According to *Leycesters Commonwealth*, as we have seen, Verney and his man can tell how she died, Verney himself died with piteous cries (presumably from guilt); moreover Verney carried out the murder on Dudley's orders.[50] Of Verney we know little more than that he was a Warwickshire gentleman once sheriff of that county. In a letter with no year Verney wrote to Dudley, 'I and anything else mine are and always shall be to my best power advanced in your affairs or commandment when opportunity offreth'.[51] This suggests that Verney was a dependent of Dudley's but its language is not much more lavish than was unusual in the mid sixteenth century. BL Add. MS 48023 adds some interesting detail which must make us consider *Leycesters Commonwealth* more seriously. We are told that Lord Robert left Amy 'firste at Hydes house in Hertforshere, where she saied she was poysoned, and for that cause he desired, she might no longer tarry in his house, from thence she was removed to Varney's house in Warwickshere, and so at leingth to Fosters howse'. That is the only evidence that Amy spent some time with Verney. 'This Varney', we are told, 'vsed before her death, to wyshe her death, which made the people to suspecte the warse'. Add. MS 48023 then offers an account of Amy's death:

> Howe the Lorde Robertes wief brake her necke at Fosters Howse in Oxfordshere in die natiuitatis Marie Ao 1560 her gentellwomen being gon forthe to a fier. Howebeyt yt was thought she was slayne for Sir Varnye was there that daie, and whyleste the deade was doing was goinge over the fier, and tarried there for his man, who at leingthe cam, and he saied thowe knave whye tarieste thowe? he answered shoulde I com before I had don. haste thowe don q Verney. Yea q the man I haue made hytt sure, so Verney cam to the courte.[52]

The precision of the detail is remarkable: it is sufficient evidence, or mere hearsay?

Secondly, there is more evidence about the coroner's inquest. We know already for fairly sure that the jury concluded that it was death by mischance. We also know from a letter that Dudley wrote to Blount that one of the jury, who seemed to Dudley to be the foreman, was called Smith. An interesting connection between Dudley and Smith has been noted: Anthony Foster's accounts for 10 May 1566 include an entry about a gown, 'whyche gowne my lord [Dudley] doth gyve to Mr Smythe the quenes man' [that is, one of the servants in the queen's household]. But Smith is of course a common name, and perhaps the connection is only coincidental. Here the evidence of Add. MS 48023 is significant. 'This woman was viewed by the Coroners queste, wherof one Smyth was foreman, whoe was the Quenes man being Lady Eliz. and was putt owte of the howse for his lewd behavior. It was found by this enqueste, that she was cause of her owne death, falling downe a paier of stayers, which by reporte was but eight steppes'.[53] The connection is remarkable. Was the foreman of the jury a man known to the queen, previously, and perhaps again later, in her service at court? How useful could a man capable of 'lewd behaviour' be? Was the coroner's jury in any way rigged?

Let us return to the letters between Dudley and Blount, which have usually have been read, as I have shown above, as evidence of Dudley's innocence. 'How any one who has read this correspondence can suspect that the jury was a packed one I must own surprises me'.[54] Yet they can surely nonetheless be seen as evidence of an attempt by Dudley to suborn the jury. Why should he have been so anxious if Amy had died of disease or in an accident? On hearing the news of his wife's death, Dudley instructed Blount to charge the coroner 'to thuttermost from me to have good regard to make no choice of light or slight persons, but the discreetest and [most] substantial men, for their juries'. Should we read this as an attempt to pack the jury?[55] When Dudley instructed Blount three days later about the jurors 'unto whom I pray you say from me, that I require them, as ever I shall think good of them, that they will, according to their duties, earnestly, carefully, and truly deal in this matter, and find it as they shall see it fall out',[56] was he in effect making his interest very clear to the jurors? Blount was clearly meeting the jurors: he told Dudley he had done his message to them and that he was arranging to meet with one or two of them at Abingdon. But perhaps the most important details here appear in an undated letter from Dudley to Blount. Here Dudley reveals 'I have received a letter from one Smith, one that seemeth to be the foreman of the jury', and later adds, 'touching Smith and the rest, I mean no more to deal with them, but let them proceed in the name of God accordingly; and I am right glad they be all strangers to me'.[57] How much should one make of Dudley's obvious and admitted dealing with the foreman of the jury? This reading cannot be conclusive but given the above references to Smith, it seems at least arguable that pressures (to say no more) were being brought to bear on the coroner's jury.

If Amy were murdered, one must still raise some questions. The most likely scenario would be this. Dudley ordered Verney and Forster to do the deed. He then sent Blount to find out just what had been done, to find out what people had been saying (which explains his discussion with the Abingdon innkeeper), to fix the jury and to look for various possible covers (for example, suicide). He would also make sure Appleyard, Amy's half-brother, was persuaded to accept the jury's verdict. It is likely that Elizabeth knew what was going on: that would explain her cryptic remarks to the Spanish ambassador, Cecil's nervousness, and the involvement of Smith. But there are a few more variants. It is possible that one or more of Dudley's zealous servants – Verney, Forster – may have acted independently, hoping later to benefit when Dudley married the queen. If Dudley knew nothing of the plots of his servants, that would make his letters to Blount understandable. It is also possible that Dudley did order the murder, but that Blount knew nothing of his master's designs. Another possibility – if this is not super-subtle and having it both ways – is that (1) there was indeed a plot, in which both Dudley and Elizabeth were involved, to murder Amy, but that (2) Amy was not murdered. She might, on this view, have died spontaneously, from illness or from an accident, as suggested above, just when preparations for her murder were going ahead. Alternatively she may indeed have committed suicide, because she was terrified by the pressures that Dudley and his servants were putting on her. Such induced suicide would of course count as murder. 'They seeing the good Lady sad and heavy (as one that well knew by her other handling, that her death was not farre of), began to perswade her, that her disease was abundance of Melancholy, and other humours ...'.[58] The account in Add. MS 48023 hints at such pressures: Amy said she was being poisoned at Hyde's house in Hertfordshire; 'many times before, yt was bruted by the L[ord] Rob[ert] his men, that she was ded. And P used to saie that when the lorde Rob[ert] went to his wief he wentt all in black, and how he was commaunded to saye that he did nothing with her, when he cam to her, as seldome as he did'. 'This Varney and divers others his servanutes vsed before her death to wyshe her death'.[59] If Dudley suddenly discovered that his wife had died accidentally or had killed herself out of fear just before plots to murder her could take effect, that could make sense of his letters to Blount. It is an engaging theory, one which makes it possible to accept many features of the various explanations canvassed. Unfortunately much of the evidence is tantalisingly vague and ambiguous. It would be difficult to convict Dudley in a court of law. But a good case can be made for saying that he intended to murder his wife and very likely did.

Notes

1. This paper was first written at the invitation of Professor R.J.W. Evans and presented at a meeting of the Cumnor Local History Society. It is published here for the first time.
2. The following paragraph is largely drawn from D. Wilson, *Sweet Robin: a Biography of Robert Dudley, Earl of Leicester 1533–1588* (1981), N. Fourdrinier, 'Amy Robsart', typescript, Norfolk Country Record Office, MC 5/33 (387 x 1 and 2).
3. These suggestions were first raised, speculatively, by C.S.L. Davies in a paper at St John's College, Oxford, Hilary Term 1973. Dr S.J. Payling has recently discovered an indenture relating to Amy's marriage (PRO E328/101) which

suggests that it was a hurried matter, since only matters of immediate concern were addressed. Amy was the heir apparent but was not to have anything until both parents had died. I am very grateful to Dr Payling for this reference.

4. J.E. Jackson, 'Amye Robsart', *Wiltshire Archaeological and Natural History Magazine*, xvii (1853), p. 61.
5. BL Add. MS, 48023 f. 353.
6. Fourdrinier, 'Amy Robsart', p. 126.
7. Leti: see above, p. 153 note 6.
8. *Calendar of State Papers, Spanish: Elizabeth, i 1558–67*, ed. M.A.S. Hume (1982), no. 27, p. 57.
9. Ibid., no. 74, pp. 112–13.
10. Fourdrinier, *Amy Robsart*, p. 158.
11. *Cal. S.P., Spanish*, i. no. 119, pp. 174–5.
12. W. MacCaffrey, *Elizabeth I* (1993), pp. 71–2.
13. S.L. Adams, 'The Dudley clientele, 1553–1563', in G.W. Bernard (ed.), *The Tudor Nobility* (Manchester, 1992), pp. 241–65.
14. These are available in print in G. Adlard, *Amy Robsart* (1870), pp. 32–41.
15. *Historical Manuscripts Commission, Hatfield*, i nos. 1131, 1136, 1137, 1150–55.
16. D.C. Peck (ed.), *Leicester's Commonwealth* (Athens, Ohio, 1985). See n. 48 below.
17. Adlard, *Amy Robsart*, pp. 36–7.
18. BL Harleian MS, 4712.
19. Adlard, *Amy Robsart*, p. 36.
20. Ibid., pp. 32, 35.
21. Ibid., p. 35.
22. Ibid., p. 40.
23. *Cal. S.P., Spanish*, i. no. 119, p. 176.
24. *Calendar of State Papers, Foreign 1560–61*, ed. J. Stevenson (1865), no. 627.
25. Adlard, *Amy Robsart*, p. 41; cf. Blount's whisperings that they can find no presumptions of evil': ibid., p. 40.
26. J. Gairdner, 'The death of Amy Robsart', *English Historical Review*, i (1886), p. 257.
27. BL Add. MS, 48023 f. 353.
28. I. Aird, 'The death of Amy Robsart', *English Historical Review*, lxxi (1956), pp. 69–79.
29. N. Fourdrinier, 'Amy Robsart', typescript, Norfolk Country Record Office, MC 5/33 (387 x 1 and 2).
30. *Cal. S.P., Spanish*, i. no. 27, p. 58.
31. Adlard, *Amy Robsart*, p. 36.
32. See below, note 48.
33. *Cal. S.P., Spanish*, i. no. 95.
34. *Cal. S.P., Spanish*, i. no. 95, p. 141; no. 119, pp. 174–5; Gairdner, 'Amy Robsart', pp. 239–40.
35. Adlard, *Amy Robsart*, pp. 32–3, 38–9, 41.
36. *Cal. S.P., Spanish*, i. nos. 74, 119, pp. 112, 174–5.
37. Adlard, *Amy Robsart*, pp. 32, 34–5.
38. Ibid., pp. 42–3.
39. *Cal. S.P., Foreign*, no. 627, p. 3.
40. *Cal. S.P., Foreign*, nos. 621, 623, 625, 685, 690.
41. *Cal. S.P., Spanish*, i. no. 122, p. 179.
42. *Cal. S.P., Spanish*, i. no. 139, p. 213.

43. Gairdner, 'Amy Robsart', p. 247.
44. Ibid., pp. 249, 251, 250.
45. *Historical Manuscripts Commission, Hatfield*, i. 1150–51.
46. F.J. Burgoyne (ed.), *Leycester's Commonwealth* (1904); D.C. Peck (ed.), *Leicester's Commonwealth* (Athens, Ohio, 1984); P. Holmes, 'The authorship of "Leicester's Commonwealth"', *Journal of Ecclesiastical History*, xxxiii (1982), pp. 424–30.
47. Burgoyne (ed.), *Leycester's Commonwealth*, p. 37; Peck (ed.), *Leicester's Commonwealth*, pp. 81–2.
48. Burgoyne (ed.), *Leycester's Commonwealth*, p. 53 (Peck (ed.), *Leicester's Commonwealth*, pp. 90–91).
49. Burgoyne (ed.), *Leycester's Commonwealth*, pp. 53–5 (Peck (ed.), *Leicester's Commonwealth*, p. 91).
50. Burgoyne (ed.), *Leycester's Commonwealth*, pp. 37, 53 (Peck (ed.), *Leicester's Commonwealth*, p. 81).
51. E. d'Oyley, 'The death of Amy Robsart', *History Today*, vi (1956), p. 260.
52. BL Add. MS, 48023 f. 353.
53. Ibid.
54. Gairdner, 'Amy Robsart', p. 244.
55. Adlard, *Amy Robsart*, p. 32.
56. Ibid., p. 38.
57. Ibid., p. 41.
58. Burgoyne (ed.), *Leycester's Commonwealth*, p. 54; Peck (ed.), *Leicester's Commonwealth*, p. 91.
59. BL Add. MS, 48023 f. 353.

9
Architecture and politics in Tudor England[1]

The best-known buildings of Tudor England are among 'the most magnificent, romantic or ingenious houses in England'.[2] Hampton Court or Longleat or Hardwick have scarcely lost their power to impress today. But what can such buildings tell us about royal and noble power? Do styles of building hint at political values? What problems are raised by attempts to give studies in power a visual dimension by a consideration of architecture?

The most striking claims for the political significance of Tudor architecture have been claims that these houses were 'power houses', built by men who possessed or who were making a bid for power.[3] And, similarly, building by kings is presented as 'the evocation of power, magnificence and abundance to bolster the image of the monarch'; 'the Tudor royal palace was a theatre of kingship'.[4] Architecture, in short, was an instrument of power.

Undoubtedly, newly risen men, especially courtiers and politicians, built great houses to impress. For a new man, such a house announced his arrival among the political and social elite. It would assert or reinforce claims to power over neighbouring gentry or tenantry. It is not then surprising that Henry VIII's groom of the stool Sir William Compton should have built a picture book country-house at Compton Wynyates, Warwickshire,[5] that Sir Henry Marney should have begun an astonishing tower house at Layer Marney, in Essex,[6] that Charles Brandon, newly raised as duke of Suffolk, should have built at Westhorpe.[7] At Ightham Mote, near Sevenoaks, Sir Richard Clement, a courtier, transformed the existing house by building a new chapel, crenellating the gatehouse, refronting the private apartments and reglazing the windows.[8] Sir William Sandys, later Lord Sandys, built The Vyne, near Basingstoke, with a notable long gallery.[9] What such courtiers and administrators were doing was converting the wealth that they were acquiring from their position and from royal favour into something more permanent, establishing their families as large landowners. They were buying lands, often greatly extending existing family holdings, and then building, or substantially improving, a residence that would reflect their rising status. Often they built in the village from which their family sprang, sometimes combining the building or rebuilding of their house with that of the parish church, as Sir Henry Marney did at Layer Marney. This was a society in which power was based on the ownership of land. It is striking that while such men may have also possessed urban residences in London, their principal interests were centred on country estates, usually in more or less coherent concentrations of land, of which an imposing country house would be the centre. From the 1540s such men often acquired and remodelled monasteries, for example Sir Thomas Wriothesley at Titchfield, Sir William Sharington at Lacock, Sir Anthony Browne at Battle. Such builders often used their buildings to demonstrate their family connections and their political allegiance. When Sir Richard Clement remodelled Ightham Mote he plastered badges of the Tudor kings all over the houses: badges of Henry VIII, Catherine of Aragon were on the bargeboards, in the glass in the new windows of the hall, on the painted waggon-roof of the chapel.[10] At The Vyne Lord Sandys installed magnificent oak panels along the Long Gallery – panels of the badges of Henry VIII, Catherine of Aragon, his own family, families with whom his children were linked by marriage, and various bishops and some noblemen.[11] At Haddon Hall the Vernons, kings of the Peak, proclaimed their attachment to the Tudor dynasty and their marriage connections to the Talbots earls of Shrewsbury by the Tudor roses and Talbot hounds painted on the ceiling of their solar. At Hardwick Hall in the later sixteenth century Bess of Hardwick, married to the sixth earl of Shrewsbury, would build a long gallery in which portraits of her family and connections would hang. In some cases the royal connection was more direct still. Queen Elizabeth often stayed with noblemen and courtiers, which encouraged them to rebuild their houses so that they were fit to welcome royalty. In 1572 Elizabeth came to Lord Keeper Bacon's house at Redgrave (Gorhambury) and said, 'my Lord, what a little house have you gotten?', to which Bacon replied 'Madam, my house is well, but it is you that have made me too great for my house' – and promptly began rebuilding.[12] William Cecil, Lord Burghley, Elizabeth's leading minister, built three houses: one in London, 'for necessity', another at Burghley, 'of computency, for the mansion of his barony', and a third, Theobalds, for his younger son, which 'at the first, he ment but for a litle pile ... but after he came to enterteyne the quene so often there, he was inforced to enlarge it, rather for the quene and her greate train, and to sett [the] poore on worke, then for pompe or glory.'[13]

If courtiers and counsellors built to impress, that would seem true of kings as well. Monarchs could be builders on a grand scale. Henry VII built Richmond Palace. Henry VIII was 'one of the greatest builders in English history',[14] 'certainly the most prolific, talented and innovative builder to sit on the English throne',[15] improving, developing or building some fifty houses.[16] There is no doubting his personal interest and involvement: there are many plans and drawings, references in accounts to such 'plats' being drawn on his orders or shown to him; he visited building work in progress.[17] Half a dozen were large enough to accommodate the entire court; the rest served as hunting lodges or places for a short stay while on progress. He took over Hampton Court from

Cardinal Wolsey and rebuilt the great hall, spending some £46,000 between 1529 and 1538 on the palace.[18] He also added to Wolsey's palace at Whitehall, since destroyed.[19] He built a gatehouse and chapel at St James's Palace between 1532 and 1540.[20] There were significant works at Bridewell, New Hall, Oatlands and Greenwich.[21] At Nonsuch he built a completely new palace modelled on Francis I's Chambord.[22] Many more temporary buildings, often fantastically lavish, were built for tournaments and for diplomatic and ceremonial occasions such as the Field of Cloth of Gold in 1520.[23] Henry's daughter Elizabeth did not build at all. The Stuart kings would revive the practice of royal building, though not matching the scale of Henry's activity.

On the face of it, then, kings and counsellors built to increase their power. But it must be noted that unfortunately there is very little evidence that directly throws light on builders' motivations. Written or printed comments about architecture in this period are rare and laconic. What contemporaries intended or thought about buildings must therefore usually be deduced from the evidence of the buildings themselves, which risks circularity of argument. Only a small number of drawings and plans survive, mostly for the buildings of Robert Smythson and John Thorpe. Few books on architecture were published in Tudor England, John Shute's *Grounds of Architecture* (1563) being an isolated if notable exception. There was no English architectural (or artistic) literature, unlike in Italy, though works, especially pattern books, by foreign architectural writers such as Serlio did circulate. In the late 1530s and 1540s John Leland went on a series of tours of England and then wrote his *Itinerary*, but his brisk judgements of a building's worth are frustratingly uninformative on details and on builders' motives. Often it is impossible precisely to date a Tudor building: building accounts rarely survive, and even passing references in correspondence are not common. That adds to the hazards of using buildings to illustrate political or social trends. And the surviving buildings themselves, while potentially of value as sources in themselves, nonetheless have rarely remained unaltered over time, thus reinforcing the problems of dating.[24] It may well be the very lack of compelling contemporary evidence for the motives and purposes of their builders that has made possible the imposition on the study of Tudor houses of such grand theories linking building and power.

Yet perhaps the claim that these houses always had political purposes, that buildings were fundamentally assertions of power, can be overdone. Colvin has commented sceptically on 'the way in which it has been assumed that because power meant wealth and wealth usually resulted in architectural display, the converse was necessarily the case'.[25] That relates to more general suggestions that early modern rulers exploited the arts and created representations and images of their authority in order to increase it: art seen as propaganda, as an instrument of 'absolutism', as part of the rise of the monarchical nation-state, with monarchs and their advisers as comparable to modern spin-doctors. But the broad claims that Tudor country houses were power houses built to assert the power of their owners, that 'Henry [VIII] became during the 1530s and 1540s an experienced, exacting, and innovative domestic architect for the image of monarchy that had emerged during his reign',[26] prompt the subversive reflection, which I owe to Cliff Davies, 'who was taken in?' If you do not fall for your own propaganda, why should anyone else? How do you come to be uniquely both beyond influence and yet capable of influencing others? Did anyone obey or respect a builder of such houses simply because he had built them? Could a king create and project an image of monarchy through his building that would provoke respect even from those who were uneasy about his policies? It was, it has been suggested, 'the overall opulence' of Henry VIII's great hall at Hampton Court that was meant to impress: 'the power which was able to command a structure of such size and to decorate it without regard to the enormous cost was what separated the king from his subjects',[27] and the building itself visibly demonstrated that power and wealth. But was 'the most blatant display of this power'[28] really going to surprise, or to intimidate? But how many, apart from a tiny number of intimates, courtiers, and perhaps ambassadors, would see, and how many of them could understand the abstruse meanings of, works of art often executed in a complex symbolic and allegorical style of astruse meanings? Nonsuch, the most remarkable of Henry's buildings, was also among the most private, not intended for the whole court. Did 'anyone at all, even their creators, regard ... these iconographic programmes as more than shows of learning, homages to antiquity, or jeux d'esprit', as Rabb has asked?[29] And, lower down the hierarchy, could new men build their way into social respectability? William Turner would acidly remark in 1555, 'as for buyldyng of costlye houses and trimmynge of them wyth costly hangynges and fayre waynscot, manye marchauntes use to do those thynges, better then many gentlemen do, and yet so, for all that, are no gentlemen'.[30] Or was it more that there were expectations that people in authority, kings above all, would live in a certain style – with the risk that if your house was small, your furniture shabby, you would lose respect? You could lose face – but you could not seize status. Rather than being assertive, were new men simply seeking to fit in; was Henry VIII, in building Nonsuch, very largely just trying to keep up with the architectural achievements of Francis I?

Moreover, every large landowner needed some sort of administrative headquarters at which tenants could pay their rents and negotiate leases; and since distances were considerable, it might be necessary to offer them hospitality. Gentlemen often invited their tenants to a grand Christmas feast. Country houses were in this respect then not vehicles for the assertion of of some new power: they were very practical centres of the business of estate administration. Moreover they were also places where their owners relaxed and enjoyed their wealth, hunting, gambling, entertaining neighbouring gentry, in surroundings of opulence and beauty.[31] That was even more true of kings, who obviously needed to accommodate the officials who adiministered the realm as well as their many servants, and also sought some privacy in which to enjoy themselves. An act of parliament declaring the limits of the king's palace of Westminster said how the king had recently 'most sumptuously and curiously hath buylded and edified many and distincte beautifull costely and pleasaunt lodgynges buyldynges and mansions for his gracis singuler pleasure comforte and commodite, to the great honour of his highnes and of his realme; and therunto adjoynyng hath made a parke walled and envyrined with brick and stone, and therin hath dyvised and ordeyned many and singuler comodyous thynges pleasures and other necessaries, most apte and convenyent to apperteigne oonly to so noble a prynce for his singuler comforte pastyme and solace'.[32]

That concern for privacy can be read at face value but it has also been treated as an argument in terms of power politics. A distinction between public and private rooms in royal residences was, it has been claimed, 'adopted as much for reasons of power as privacy; access to the private rooms was limited, and determining who[m] to allow into them, and how far, gave the king a valuable weapon in the power game. There was constant pressure to gain access to these rooms, so that the outermost room tended to become less private with the passing of time, and new private rooms had to be created in compensation'.[33] Other historians have turned this into an argument in support of factional intepretations of politics, emphasising the opportunities for restricting access to those not in favour.[34]

But what such arguments overlook is that for some builders, both kings and their leading subjects, building became something of an obsession, done not because it was necessary to assert their power or to meet some practical need, but simply because they were fascinated by buildings. Henry VIII, builder, designer, decorator, Protector Somerset, and Bess of Hardwick fall into that category. Of Henry VIII Pevsner wrote 'what had earlier been a proper artistic pride had become something very like megalomania'.[35] In 1532 du Bellay, the French ambassador, wrote that whenever he visited any of the king's houses, Henry 'shows it to me and tells me what he has done, and what he is going to do'.[36] If they wished to impress others, it was those who were as obsessed by building as they were, who could thus appreciate the finer points of their new creations.

But how far did styles of building have a broader significance – is there a link between style and politics? Here the intriguing questions are those posed by the adoption of classical styles of architecture by a number of mid-sixteenth-century builders. Medieval houses had evolved from very basic arrangements of rooms – a great hall, with a kitchen and a buttery on one side, and a raised platform or dais, where the lord would sit and eat, on the other; a spiral staircase might lead from the dais to an upper room, a solar or a parlour or a chamber, a more intimate room in which the lord would live and sleep, as at Stokesay, Shropshire, a fortified house of *c*. 1270–80, built by a rich Ludlow clothier – to the complex pattern of the greater late medieval houses. These, with their suites of rooms – in royal palaces a great chamber, a presence chamber, a privy chamber and a bedchamber – became sprawling and haphazard collections of towers and rooms, as at Haddon Hall, replaced, altered and extended as need arose. In the early sixteenth century, some builders came increasingly to value symmetry in outward appearance, as at Sutton Place, Surrey, built 1521–33, by Sir Richard Weston (whose son was executed on a charge of adultery with Anne Boleyn in 1536) with a perfectly symmetrical hall range, with windows of identical height and detail that do not correspond with the internal arrangements of the house.[37] That concern for symmetry was perhaps the first manifestation in England of an interest in Renaissance ideals (although there were also medieval examples of symmetrical buildings, particularly castles such as Harlech (c. 1300), Bodiam (late fourteenth century), and archbishops' palaces such as Knole, Kent, or Oxburgh, Norfolk, which have a show front with a great gatehouse in the middle). Renaissance architecture was more than just symmetry. 'A classical building', to borrow Sir John Summerson's definition, 'is one whose decorative elements derive directly or indirectly from the architectural vocabulary of the ancient world': that 'vocabulary' included in particular standard types of columns, doors and windows. But a classical building was more than just a building using columns and particular sorts of windows, doors and mouldings. Classical buildings reflect a theory of how buildings should be designed: 'the aim of classical architecture has always been to achieve a demonstrable harmony of parts' … 'by ensuring that the ratios in a building are simple arithmetical functions and that the ratios of all parts of the building are either those same ratios or related to them in a direct way'.[38] Renaissance architecture flourished in fifteenth-century Italy and by the early sixteenth century French palaces were being designed in such a style. But the impact of the renaissance in England was slow, piecemeal and limited. At first it was confined to particular detailed features produced by foreign, usually Italian, craftsmen – 'ornamental devices, not yet any understanding of classical architecture':[39] the terracotta roundels of classical emperors at Wolsey's Hampton Court,[40] Pietro Torrigiano's tomb of Henry VII at Westminster Abbey,[41] the ornamental motifs of the temporary buildings erected for the Field of Cloth of Gold in 1520,[42] the Italianate terracotta ornamentation, especially of panels of naked cupids at Sutton Place, the capitals of the columns of Chelsea parish church, rebuilt in 1528, Lord Marney's tomb at Layer Marney, Essex, and the terracotta motifs in the windows of his gatehouse, the screen of King's College Chapel, Cambridge 1533–35, the pendants of the roof of the hall at Hampton Court with scrolls, balusters and putti, the ceiling of the chapel at St James's Palace. What did the adoption of such features reflect? Henry VIII's Nonsuch (begun 1538, incomplete but habitable by 1547) had painted classical orders on the exterior and a remarkable series of classical panels of Roman emperors on the inward-facing walls of the inner court and the outer faces on three sides. Colin Platt has suggested that 'these repeated classical reminders were, of course, political. By obliterating the Middle Ages, they helped diminish some of the pain of Henry's policies'.[43] That may be so, but roundels of classical emperors had recently been used by the perfectly orthodox and quintessentially late medieval Lord Chancellor, Thomas Wolsey, cardinal and papal legate, at Hampton Court. And if here, as in tapestries or cups, Henry drew on 'Renaissance' style, his funeral was entirely traditional, with an absence of classical reference.[44] Moreover if, like many new buildings in the 1520s and 1530s, Nonsuch was regular and symmetrical in shape, if it made use of classical decorative features, especially panels of plaster-stucco (the design of which has been plausibly attributed to an Italian artificer, Nicholas Bellin of Modena, who had previously worked for Francis I at Fontainebleau, as painter, sculptor and stucco-worker), it still looked in plan and in structure more like a late medieval than a Renaissance palace, with the standard arrangement of outer and inner courts, with a great gatehouse leading into the outer court and a smaller gatehouse leading into the inner court, following the pattern of Richmond and Hampton Court. And the extraordinary upper storey of timber-framed construction was not at all classical in spirit. Pevsner sees the king as employing a variety of artists and heaping their products on to the pile; 'the inside was presumably a kind of museum collection of the works of whatever artists Henry could get together. Coherence and integrity were the last things to be expected: this was the bullfrog puffing and blowing'.[45] 'The symmetry of the plan did not lead to a visually integrated building, but an uneasy juxtaposition of old-fashioned Tudor Gothic and up-to-date Franco-Flemish mannerism'.[46] Similarly while much was done by the king at Whitehall in the 1530s and beyond, including a great hall, several gatehouses, and a tennis court (a large building), this was not done on a concerted plan: Whitehall was 'a rambling assemblage of buildings, large and small, high and low'.[47]

For all the scale and intensity of Henry VIII's architectural enthusiasm, he did not inspire his immediate successors: his death was apparently followed by a sharp break in practice. In the middle of the sixteenth century several builders built in a fully classical Renaissance style, showing 'a much stricter adherence to the proprieties of classical architecture than seen previously in England'.[48] These were many of the political leaders of England in the minority of Edward VI, often at odds amongst themselves, but building obsessively and in the same new, revolutionary, style. Protector Somerset had the greatest opportunity, and his Somerset House 1547–52, which does not survive, marked a significant change in English architectural style. It is a true classical design, owing nothing to the late medieval past. It is a world away from Haddon Hall. Its use of classical proportions and classical orders is correct. It has a flat skyline, balustrades, two-storey window-units (that is, arranged one above another) without inner arches to the lights, with a classical pediment on top, all equally spaced along the walls, the frontispiece with superimposed orders, including columns and pilasters. The showcase front to the Strand was in fine ashlar masonry rather than brick.[49] Somerset's brother Sir Thomas Seymour, who quarrelled so bitterly with him, built in the same style at Sudeley, Gloucestershire. Sir William Sharrington, Seymour's fellow-conspirator, built in this style at Lacock, Wiltshire, especially the tower there.[50] John Dudley, earl of Warwick, later duke of Northumberland, built an exquisite Renaissance loggia of five bays with Ionic columns, now partly in ruins, at Dudley Castle, Staffordshire.[51] An earlier version of Sir John Thynne's Longleat building from 1554 was more classical than the present façades. Thynne had supervised construction of Somerset House.[52] When mid-sixteenth-century paintings or engravings show architectural details, these are often now classical: especially columns and bases. The famous woodcut in the 1563 edition of Foxe's *Acts and Monuments* shows Hugh Latimer preaching before the young Edward VI from a severely classical pulpit in a courtyard at the back of which was a classical loggia.

Where had these builders acquired the taste for classical architecture and what was the significance of it? Was it simply a rejection, on stylistic grounds, of excessively ornamented buildings of the previous generation in favour of a simpler, purer style? Was it seen as more pointedly a rejection of a now tainted late medieval English way of building in the aftermath of the break with Rome and the introduction of Protestantism? Was it 'politically inspired' and 'the architectural equivalent of the vernacular text of the Bible or the simpler liturgical music required in protestant worship'? All in all, it is hard to see the mid-century classical moment as 'Protestant', or as 'reflecting a sense of nationhood', or 'the idea of commonwealth'.[53] What is Protestant, what is English, what reveals any concern with the plight of the poor, in the costly building of great houses (financed by not a little corruption) in a classical style ultimately derived from pagan Rome through the mediation of Catholic Renaissance Italy and France, in bold defiance of late medieval English traditions? What does it say about these builders' commitment to Protestantism, with its rejection of the visual and its fear of idolatry? Intriguingly, the same pure classical style was shortly, after the change of regime in 1553, to be used in the chantry of Bishop Stephen Gardiner, one of the leading advocates of religious persecution in Queen Mary's reign, though also one of the rare critics within Mary's government of her proposed marriage to Philip of Spain. The Ionic reredos in his chantry chapel in Winchester Cathedral (almost certainly built soon after his death in 1555) is as pure an example of Renaissance classical architecture and as definite a departure from the English late medieval perpendicular style used in the corresponding chantry by Bishop Richard Foxe (d. 1528) on the opposite side of the presbytery as one can imagine.[54] That remains true even if the classicism of Gardiner's chantry is seen as more free-flowing and French than the strict Roman correctness of Somerset's classicism,[55] and, of course, even allowing for the more conventional Gothic style of the outer structure of Gardiner's chantry. Gardiner's reredos makes it very strained to see classical style as exclusively or as especially protestant.[56]

Whatever the difficulties in associating the classical style with religious beliefs, national sentiment or social thought, there is, however, no doubt of these builders' immense personal interest in architecture. Northumberland was a patron of John Shute, the future author of *Grounds of Architecture*, whom he sent to Italy in 1550 'to confer with the doinges of the skilful maisters in architecture and also to view such auncient monumentes hereof as are yet extant' – a journey that suggests little previous acquaintance with Italian work, though an awareness of its possible importance, not least surviving buildings from ancient Rome as models.[57] Some correspondence reveals their obsession. Where did it come from? Can it be linked back to Cardinal Wolsey's interest in classical decoration, just when Seymour and Dudley were first rising men?[58] Could it have been stimulated by the temporary triumphal arch – 'fatto a l'anticha' in the words of the Venetian observer Gasparo Spinelli, with a large central arch and minor arches on either side, and thus 'a true classical triumphal arch' – designed by Giovanni da Maiano and erected at Greenwich in 1527 to receive a French delegation?[59] Could it reflect the example of Renaissance buildings erected in the Low Countries in the 1540s, notably Utrecht Town Hall, completed by 1547, 'the first grand renaissance town hall in the Netherlands'?[60] Can it be linked to Henry VIII's Nonsuch? Nonsuch in its entirety is so aggressively unclassical in spirit that any direct connection seems unlikely. But some of its decorative details are in many respects more purely classical, and it is possible that foreigners employed on it, notably Nicholas Bellin, though not responsible for its overall ground plan and buildings, but rather for its remarkable decorative scheme, nonetheless shared their supposed wider knowledge of Italian classical architecture with the king and his courtiers and counsellors, as Biddle has surmised.[61] It is just possible that Henry VIII himself commissioned, or at the least approved, that classical pulpit and loggia in the preaching place at Whitehall. It was the first of several 'pieces of worke' that Robert Trunckey, an artificer, would list in a petition to Queen Elizabeth in order to illustrate his 'good seruice' to Henry: 'with whiche peces of workes your saide father beinge well pleased', Trunckey continued, 'of his bounteous liberalitie graunted to your saide orator a yerely pencion of twentie powndes by worde of mouth before his right honorable counsaillors', a pension that had never been paid but which Trunckey was now seeking to receive. Trunckey went on to describe Nicholas Modeno – Nicholas Bellin – as 'his master', a relationship which has prompted Biddle to deduce that Trunckey would have made the preaching place to Bellin's designs.[62] If the preaching place was indeed designed while Henry VIII was alive, and even more so if it was done to the king's pleasure, then any explanation of the 'classical moment' in mid-sixteenth-century English architecture could not confine itself to Edward VI's reign alone. But Trunckey's petition, while intriguing, is perhaps not conclusive. After all, he had on his own admission never received the pension that he claimed that Henry had orally granted him, and it had been Nicholas Bellin's death that apparently prompted him to to make his petition when he did, long afterwards. Elizabeth very much saw herself as her father's heir, and claims early in her reign based on grants her father had allegedly made might well have been seen as more likely to win favourable attention than any references to Protector Somerset or the duke of Northumberland, England's rulers in the reign of Edward VI. The other 'peces of work' that Trunckey cites as his are not easily datable. The 'makinge of barbes for houses and targettes for tharmye to serue at Bulloyne' could refer to any year between 1545 and 1550;[63] and 'the Banquetinge howse at Hampton Courte' is hard to identify, let alone date.[64] Another of the 'peces of work' cited by Trunckey, 'the Banquetinge howse in Hide Parke agenst the commynge of the Frenche Ambassadors', most probably refers not to the French admiral's visit in 1546 (for which there is no evidence that anything was done in Hyde Park), but to the visit in April 1551 of Marshal St Andre and several noblemen to hand over the French order of St Michel to which Edward VI had been elected, a visit marked by 'spectacular celebrations', including the erection of a banqueting house in Hyde Park, independently evidenced by a surviving statement of account which gives details of the building's dimensions. That would mean that (if he was involved) Trunckey was in official employment in the reign of Edward VI.[65] So it is just possible that Trunckey's petition is less than conclusive as evidence for the dating of the preaching place at Whitehall: it may be wise to allow that it may have been built after Henry's death. Interestingly, Edmund Howes, continuator of John Stow's *Annales*, states under 1548 that 'The 17 of March, being Wednesday, was a pulpit set vp in the Kings priuie Garden at Westminster, and therin Doctor Latimer preached before the King, where he might be heard of more then foure times so many people as could haue stoode in the Kings Chappell: and this was the first Sermon preached there'. That either the day of the week or the date must be wrong – 17 March was a Saturday in 1548 – does not invalidate this testimony, which further casts doubt on the Henrician origins of the preaching place.[66]

But just what this remarkable moment in English architecture signifies, especially in terms of its political meaning, remains tantalisingly obscure. Possibly not everyone was affected by it. William Paget, Protector Somerset's close confidant, acquired the manor of West Drayton in 1546 and built what must have been a spectacular manor house – only walls and the shortened gatehouse survive – but it is in the style of Richmond and Hampton Court, not that of Somerset House. If it is just possible that the house was in fact built earlier, it would still be interesting that Paget did not remodel it in the style favoured by his colleagues. But the history of the manor makes an earlier building date implausible. It was a manor of St Paul's Cathedral and either held by a canon residentiary or leased to a layman. Building on any grand scale was thus unlikely. William Paget secured the lease in 1537; in 1546 he contrived the acquisition of the manor by Henry VIII who then granted it to him in fee. A act of parliament of 1549 allowed Paget and his heirs to have and enjoy forever the churchyard of the parish church of West Drayton 'adioyning to the mansion house of the said lorde Paget'. While that suggests that the house was already standing by then and might conceivably support a much earlier date of building, it is much more likely that it was the recent erection of the house that prompted Paget to seek to incorporate the churchyard into its grounds.[67] Sir Thomas Smith, in Protector Somerset's service during the protectorate 1547–49, built extensively at Hill Hall, Essex, but the first phase to include classical decorative features has been dated to 1568–69: the earliest reconstruction, dated to 1557–58, has on the evidence of fragments of moulded bricks been suggested to be Tudor Gothic.[68] The mid-century classical moment was thus no more than a brief moment; and the numbers of builders and houses involved small. In Elizabethan England those who built the great 'prodigy houses' (including in some cases the same men who had built in a pure classical style in the mid-century) employed a remarkably eclectic style that rejected the pure Italianate Renaissance of Somerset House and instead combined the basic shape of English late medieval country houses with the liberal, not to say extravagant, use of classical forms of decoration. It was a curious hybrid, not to be found anywhere else in Europe. Columns and pilasters appear next to bay-windows with transoms and mullions that strongly emphasise the vertical and the horizontal. If it had an ancestor, it was in Henry VIII's Nonsuch, seen as a whole, with its traditional late medieval forms receiving the weight of a heavy application of classical panels. The most striking examples are Burghley, outside Stamford, Lord Burgley's house, late 1570s–1580s, with its large mullioned and transomed windows, its countless tall chimneyshafts, but also its balustrade, spiky obelisks, open arcading;[69] Kirby Hall, Northamptonshire, 1570–75, with its amazing mixture of very up-to-date classical motifs, especially the giant order of pilasters, fluted, with exaggerated Ionic capitals, on the porch and arched gateways, but also very traditional features, notably the grid of transomed and mullioned windows;[70] Longleat, Wiltshire, the work of Sir John Thynne, a maniacal builder, especially the pilastered bay windows.[71] The most extraordinary house of all is Wollaton, Nottinghamshire, built by Sir Francis Willoughby from the profits of the coal mines on his estates, designed by Robert Smythson. There are huge grids of transomed and mullioned windows, the hall rises in the middle above the main roof. Everywhere classical decoration is employed – but nothing like it could be imagined in Italy, no Wollaton rises from the plain of the Veneto or adorns the banks of the Tiber. One scheme of decoration is stacked on top of another, all correct in detail, but making for an astonishing hybrid in overall effect, 'something of a monster ... something of the quality of nightmare'; 'stylistic indigestion is exemplified at every turn'.[72] It is a long way from the purity and restraint of Somerset House.

What does all this mean? Buildings like Kirby and Wollaton characterise the reign of Elizabeth just as Somerset House and the loggia at Dudley Castle characterise the mid-Tudor period. These buildings seem to be trying to tell us something about their builders and their values, and about the society that produced them. But what, exactly, they are saying remains for me uncertain, indeed has become increasingly uncertain. It is easy to assert that 'one of the reasons why the exterior design of some buildings changed so dramatically in mid-sixteenth century England was because powerful figures in society needed to respond to the political and social changes which shaped their lives'.[73] But what exactly do such claims mean and how are they proved? Was Henry VIII's attachment to traditional forms, as been suggested, a reflection of 'the insecurity of the early Tudors' hold on the crown and Henry VIII's continued concern about the succession', seeing those traditional forms 'as an appropriate symbol of established monarchy'?[74] Does that not exaggerate Henry VIII's insecurity and take at face value the concern about the succession which often seems more a useful justification for his divorce and remarriage? It is very tempting for historians to construct links between social history, particularly social change, and changes in architectural styles. But the danger is that such links will 'assume [as fact] socio-economic changes whose nature, timing and significance are very much open to question'.[75] It is tempting for historians to suppose that what they are increasingly calling 'cultural' history – 'that network of languages, customs, practices and rituals through and by which contemporaries discerned and constructed meaning and the values of their society'[76] – contains the answers to the questions they ask about the nature of power and politics. But there is a great danger of circularity, of building in one's answers into the terms of one's questions, and, in such writing, awkward gaps yawn between the claims made and the evidence cited in support, to the point even – on occasion – of raising doubts about what kind of evidence could ever support such claims. The buildings discussed here were built by men (sometimes by women) of power. But which was cause and which effect? What were the consequences, if any? Why did Henry VIII build so much and Elizabeth build so little? Many of these buildings were built by new men – courtiers, administrators, leading servants of the crown. Fewer great houses were built or rebuilt by the older nobility, though they were not wholly inactive. Is that evidence that the old nobility was in decline – or did noblemen of ancient lineage possess sufficient inherited castles and fortified manor houses not to need to indulge in a mania for building? Most of the politician-builders of Edward VI's reign built in the same pure classical style. What then does one make of their often bitter personal rivalries? Did it provoke competition in surpassing each other's achievements? But imagine what historians would be saying if, for example, Somerset and Northumberland had built in different, rather than similar, styles! How far were changes in building styles simply the arbitrary and unpredictable expression of changes in fashion, just as fashions in clothing mysteriously evolve? (Fashion is a change an historian cannot explain.) Did the remarkably eclectic style of Elizabethan architecture simply reflect diminished opportunities for the spread of cultural influences in a period of civil wars in France? It appears to us as a distinctively English style, with no parallels abroad, and yet its decoration was heavily dependent on French, Italian and Low Countries examples, disseminated through pattern books that owners and designers pored over and used as models.[77] How much building was in fact pursued for its own sake, for the satisfaction it gave the owners, rather than for purposes of power? Was in the end architecture not simply more about architecture, reflecting private architectural passions and obsessions that only the great and wealthy were able to realise, pursued for their own sake, than it was about power or politics or anything else?

Notes

1. I should like to thank especially Ken Fincham for his encouraging criticism and also Greg Walker, Mark Stoyle and Peter Gwyn for their comments.
2. M. Girouard, *Robert Smythson and the Elizabethan Country House* (1983), p. 2.
3. M. Girouard, *Life in the English Country House* (1978).
4. M. Girouard, 'Henry VIII, king of builders: how Tudor palace architecture became a weapon in the power game', *Times Literary Supplement*, 14 January 1994, pp. 16–17; D. Howarth, *Images of Rule: art and politics in the English Renaissance, 1485–1649* (1997), p. 12.
5. G.W. Bernard, 'The rise of Sir William Compton, early Tudor courtier', *English Historical Review*, xcvi (1981), pp. 754–77, esp. pp. 773–4.
6. N. Pevsner and E. Radcliffe, *The Buildings of England: Essex* (2nd edn, 1965), pp. 261–5.
7. S.J. Gunn and P. Lindley, 'Charles Brandon's Westhorpe: an early Tudor courtyardhouse in Suffolk', *Archaeological Journal*, cxlv (1988), pp. 272–89.
8. D. Starkey, 'Ightham Mote: the house and its buildings', *History Today*, xxx (January 1980), pp. 58–60; 'Ightham Mote: politics and architecture in early Tudor England', *Archaeologia*, cvii (1982), pp. 153–63.
9. N. Pevsner and D. Lloyd, *The Buildings of England: Hampshire* (1967), pp. 634–8. The Vyne will be treated in a forthcoming study by Maurice Howard.
10. Starkey, 'Ightham Mote', pp. 154–8 (though more recent research suggests that the chapel ceiling panels were painted *in situ* and not, as Starkey hypothesised, brought to Ightham from the royal revels store).
11. W.R.D. Harrison and A. Chandos, *Illustrated Catalogue of Carvings, Oak Gallery, The Vyne* (Basingstoke, 1979).
12. J. Spedding (ed.), *The Letters and the Life of Francis Bacon* (1872), vii. 144.
13. F. Peck, *Desiderata Curiosa* (1779), p. 25, cited M. Airs, *The Making of the English Country House 1500–1640* (1975), p. 12.
14. Colvin, *History of the King's Works*, iv. 7.
15. S. Thurley, *The Royal Palaces of Tudor England* (1993), p. 39.
16. Colvin, *History of the King's Works*, iv. 1–7, and passim for descriptions of individual buildings.

188   *Power and politics in Tudor England*

17. Colvin, *History of the King's Works*, iv. 5; Girouard, 'Henry VIII, king of builders', *TLS*, 14 January 1994, p. 16.
18. Colvin, *History of the King's Works*, iv. 128–40 esp. 129; S. Thurley, 'Henry VIII and the building of Hampton Court: a reconstruction of the Tudor Palace', *Architectural History*, xxxi (1988), pp. 1–57, reprinted as *Henry VIII's Hampton Court* (n.d.).
19. Colvin, *History of the King's Works*, iv. 307–15.
20. Ibid., iv. 241–2.
21. Ibid., iv. 53–8, 99–106, 172–5, 205–9; S. Thurley, 'Greenwich Palace', in D. Starkey (ed.), *Henry VIII: a European Court in England* (1991), pp. 20–25.
22. Colvin, *History of the King's Works*, iv. 179–202.
23. S. Anglo, *Spectacle, Pageantry and early Tudor Policy* (Oxford, 2nd edn, 1997), pp. 140–44.
24. For an instructive example of the difficulties of dating, see Barrington Court, Somerset, redated to the 1560s and to the initiative of William Clifton, who bought the 'lordship, manor and park', in 1552, rather than being seen as built in the 1510s by Henry Daubeney (d. 1548) (*Victoria County History, Somerset*, iv. 115).
25. Personal communication 7 July 1996.
26. Thurley, *Royal Palaces*, pp. 48–9.
27. M. Airs, 'Architecture', in B. Ford (ed.), *16th Century Britain: the Cambridge Cultural History* (Cambridge, 1992), p. 59.
28. Ibid.
29. T.K. Rabb, 'Play, not politics, who really understood the symbolism of renaissance art', *TLS*, 10 November 1995, cited by D. Howarth, *Images of Rule: Art and Politics in the English Renaissance, 1485–1649* (1997), p. 6; cf. scepticism in S. Anglo, *Images of Tudor Kingship* (1992), esp. p. 130: 'There is little evidence to support the view that the English monarchy employed a propaganda machine other than sporadically, and the notion that there was a carefully-thought-out systematic sales promotion of recondite imagery to the nation at large is a wholly modern, academic invention'.
30. Cited, without comment, by M. Howard, 'Self-fashioning and the classical moment in mid-sixteenth-century English architecture', in L. Gent and N. Llewellyn (eds), *Renaissance Bodies: the Human Figure in English Culture c.1540–1660* (1990), p. 213.
31. Girouard, *Life in the English Country House*.
32. *Statutes of the Realm*, iii. 668 (28 Henry VIII c. 12). Cf. later act stating how Henry VIII had of late been pleased 'to erecte buylde and make a goodlie sumptuous beautifull and princelie mannor, decent and convenient for a kinge', provided 'withe manyfolde thinges of pleasure for the disportte pastyme comforte and consolacion of his highnes his heires and successors' (*Statutes of the Realm*, iii. 721 (31 Henry VIII c. 5).
33. Girouard, 'Henry VIII, king of builders', *TLS*, 14 January 1994.
34. H.M. Baillie, 'Etiquette and the planning of the state apartments in Baroque palaces', *Archaeologia*, ci (1967), pp. 169–99. Baillie's approach was applied to late medieval and Tudor architecture by D. Starkey, 'Houses and History', *Times Educational Supplement*, 27 February 1981, pp. 32–33.
35. N. Pevsner and I. Nairn, *The Buildings of England: Surrey* (2nd edn p. 37).
36. Colvin, *History of the King's Works*, iv. 5, citing *LP*, V 1187.
37. It is possible that that symmetry is a later rearrangement: N. Cooper, 'Sutton Place, East Barsham and some related houses: some problems arising', in

38. M. Airs (ed.), *The Tudor and Stuart Jacobean Great House* (Oxford, 1994), pp. 35–6.
38. J. Summerson, *The Classical Language of Architecture* (1980 edn), p. 8.
39. N. Pevsner and B. Cherry, *The Buildings of England: London 2: South* (1983), pp. 486–7.
40. P.G. Lindley, 'Playing check-mate with royal majesty? Wolsey's patronage of Italian renaissance sculpture', in P.G. Lindley and S.J. Gunn (eds), *Cardinal Wolsey: Church, State and Art* (Cambridge, 1991), pp. 279–81.
41. Colvin, *History of the King's Works*, iii. 220–22; P. Lindley, 'Collaboration and competition: Torrigiano and royal tomb commissions', in P. Lindley, *Gothic to Renaissance: Essays on Sculpture in England* (Stamford, 1995), pp. 47–72.
42. Anglo, *Spectacle, Pageantry and Early Tudor Policy*, pp. 140–44.
43. C. Platt, *The Great Rebuildings of Tudor and Stuart England* (1994), pp. 100–101.
44. J. Loach, 'The function of ceremonial in the reign of Henry VIII', *Past and Present*, cxlii (1994), pp. 56–66.
45. N. Pevsner and I. Nairn, *The Buildings of England: Surrey* (2nd edn, 1971), p. 37.
46. Girouard, 'Henry VIII, king of builders', p. 17. It is fair to note that Martin Biddle, who directed the excavations at Nonsuch a generation ago, saw more merit and unity in Bellin's designs (M. Biddle, 'Nicholas Bellin of Modena: an Italian artificer at the courts of Francis I and Henry VIII', *Journal of the Archaeological Association*, 3rd series, xxix (1966), pp. 106–21).
47. N. Pevsner, *The Buildings of England: the Cities of London and Westminster* (1957), p. 467.
48. Howard, 'Self-fashioning and the classical moment', p. 201.
49. Summerson, *Architecture in Britain*, pp. 45–6.
50. Ibid., pp. 42–3.
51. N. Pevsner, *The Buildings of England: Staffordshire* (1974), p. 119.
52. Summerson, *Architecture in Britain*, pp. 62–7.
53. Howard has suggested that 'the "meanings" which particular architectural patrons understood and contested in relation to their political self-identity can be grouped under three headings: protestantism, a sense of nationhood and the idea of "commonwealth"': Howard, 'Self-fashioning and the classical moment', pp. 208–17, esp. p. 208.
54. For the best description see M. Biddle, 'Early Renaissance at Winchester', in J. Crook (ed.), *Winchester cathedral: Nine Hundred Years* (Chichester, 1993), pp. 281–7. For Foxe's chantry see A. Smith, 'The chantry chapel of Bishop Fox', *Winchester Cathedral Record*, lvii (1988), pp. 27–32, P. Lindley, 'The sculptural programme of Bishop Fox's chantry chapel', *Winchester Cathedral Record*, lvii (1988), pp. 33–7, reprinted in Lindley, *Gothic to Renaissance*, pp. 207–12.
55. I owe this suggestion to C.S.L. Davies. Gardiner's chantry chapel and Somerset House are, however, included in a group of buildings and monuments reflecting French influence by A. Wells-Cole, *Art and Decoration in Elizabethan and Jacobean England* (1997), p. 33.
56. See K. Thomas, 'English Protestantism and Classical Art', in L. Gent (ed.), *Albion's Classicism: the Visual Arts in Britain 1550–1660* (1995), pp. 221–38 for the ambivalence of the attitudes of Elizabethan and early Stuart Protestants towards classicism.
57. Cited by Airs, *The Making of the English Country House*, p. 21. I owe this suggestion to Dr Kenneth Fincham.
58. I owe this suggestion to Edward Chaney.

59. H.M. Colvin, 'Pompous entries and English architecture', in H.M. Colvin (ed.), *Essays in English Architectural History* (1999), p. 70 (I am grateful to Sir Howard Colvin for this reference); Anglo, *Spectacle, Pageantry and Policy*, p. 214. Cf. W. Kuyper,*The Triumphant Entry of Renaissance Architecture in theNetherlands* (Alphen, 2 vols, 1994), for an exploration of this theme in the Low Countries.
60. Kuyper, *Triumphant Entry of Renaissance Architecture*, pp.114–5.
61. Biddle, 'Nicholas Bellin', pp. 115–16.
62. BL Add. Charter, 1262*; Biddle, 'Nicholas Bellin', pp. 115–16 esp. p. 116 n. 9; Colvin, *History of the King's Works*, iv. 313.
63. Colvin, *History of the King's Works*, iii. 383–93.
64. Ibid., iv. 138.
65. Ibid., iv. 157, pace iv. 30: *Historic Manuscripts Commission, Salisbury*, i. 92–3; Loach, *Edward VI*, p. 143.
66. J. Stowe, *Annales* (1631 edn), p. 595. I owe this reference to P.E. McCullough, *Sermons at Court: Politics and Religion in Elizabethan and Jacobean Preaching* (Cambridge, 1998), pp. 42–4, though McCullough questions its value. D. MacCulloch, *Tudor Church Militant: Edward VI and the Protestant Reformation* (1999), p. 225 n. 31, accepts the testimony but redates it to 1540, in which year 17 March was a Wednesday. It would, however, seem much more plausible that Howes mixed up his day and date than his year.
67. House of Lords Record Office, 3 Edward VI, no. 25; *Victoria County History, Middlesex*, iii. 192–3.
68. P.J. Drury, '"A fayre House, buylt by Sir Thomas Smith": the development of Hill Hall, Essex, 1557–81', *Journal of the British Archaeological Association*, cxxxvi (1983), pp. 98–123, esp. 118–19.
69. N. Pevsner, *The Buildings of England: Bedfordshire* (1968), pp. 218–20.
70. Summerson, *Architecture in Britain*, pp. 47–8.
71. Girouard, *Robert Smythson*, pp. 39–65.
72. Girouard, *Robert Smythson*, pp. 88–108, esp. p. 108; T. Mowl, *Elizabethan Jacobean Style* (1993), p. 100; P. Marshall, 'The archaeological survey of Wollaton Hall: some revelations', in Airs (ed.), *The Tudor and Jacobean Great House*, pp. 73–90.
73. Howard, 'Self-fashioning and the classical moment', p. 198.
74. Airs, 'Architecture', p. 60.
75. A formulation owed to J. Miller, review in *English Historical Review*, xcii (1977), p. 134.
76. The phrasing is that of Kevin Sharpe.
77. A. Wells-Cole, *Art and Decoration in Elizabethan and Jacobean England: the Influence of Continental Prints 1558–1625* (1997).

10
The Church of England *c*. 1529–*c*. 1642[1]

One of the historical issues that has been most heatedly debated in recent years is the nature of the Church of England in the century between the break with Rome and the civil wars of the 1640s. At the centre of this controversy have been the arguments of Nicholas Tyacke, especially because of the way they have been developed by Conrad Russell. What Tyacke claimed, first in an Oxford D.Phil. thesis submitted in 1968, then in an influential article published in 1973 and most recently in the book of his D.Phil. thesis, *The Anti-Calvinists*, published in 1987, was that the dominant doctrine in the early seventeenth-century Church of England was predestination, the belief that God had chosen some men to be saved but that most would be damned. Tyacke went on to claim that that belief was vigorously challenged by a group of Arminians, notably William Laud, Archbishop of Canterbury from 1633, who allegedly followed the teaching of the Dutch theologian Arminius (d. 1609) that Christ had died for all men and that men could in practice use their free will to seek salvation. The Arminians' attack, supported by King Charles I, bitterly divided the Church of England, both clergy and laymen, and has been seen as the key to understanding the civil wars of the 1640s, which John Morrill has called England's 'wars of religion'.[2]

How persuasive is Tyacke's claim? A weakness of his argument is that he begins briefly with the 1590s and then writes in detail on the period from 1600: does he start too much in medias res? If the Church of England is to be understood, all early seventeenth-century developments must be firmly set in the context of the principal landmarks of the sixteenth century. Tyacke's argument does implicitly rest on a particular view of the English Reformation, a view that owes most to the martyrologist John Foxe. Henry VIII's break with Rome in the 1530s is seen as to a significant extent theologically inspired. His dissolution of the monasteries, his authorisation of the translation of the Bible into English, his adoption, at times, of religious formulations owing much to the striking ideas then being developed in Lutheran Germany and Zwinglian Switzerland have also been seen as important, if sometimes intermittent, steps towards protestantism. Protestant reform was, on this view, pushed much further by the governments of Edward VI's reign, only to meet with a temporary setback when catholicism was restored. Then Elizabeth came to the throne as the heir to a continuing protestant tradition and a lasting protestant religious settlement was brought about.[3]

Matters were not, however, so simple. Henry VIII did indeed cast off papal jurisdiction and assert his authority over the church, but he did so because he failed to secure an annulment of his marriage to Catherine of Aragon through the usual channels of papal diplomacy and canon law, not because of any theological dispute. He had destroyed the monasteries at least in part because he saw them as centres, actual in the case of the Carthusians, potential elsewhere, of opposition to the break with Rome, not least because of their continuing links with their orders overseas. In order to contain opposition and in order to see such a programme safely implemented, Henry was driven to rely on men like Cromwell and Cranmer, who agreed with him, though for rather different reasons, that the pope's authority should be abolished and that Henry should be supreme head of the English church. They were in touch with the European religious ferment of the day, and they hoped that Henry's break with Rome would be a stage in the further reformation of the king's realm. Henry would be a godly prince who would banish superstition, destroy idolatry and favour God's word. In so far as this meant the reform of abuses, Henry went along with it, just as he had worked with Cardinal Wolsey to reform the church in the 1520s. But confronted by the need to define true doctrine and worship if the unquestioned horror of diversity of religious opinions was to be avoided, Henry's definitions were largely conservative. If at times he did accept some of the teachings and emphases of continental reformers, he remained opposed to any fundamental change of doctrine, notably refusing to accept any traces of Luther's justification-by-faith alone. His great achievement was to harness the rhetoric of the continental Reformation to the defence of the royal supremacy.[4]

At first glance Henry's policies seem confused and uncertain; on closer examination they are better described as deliberately ambiguous. For Henry knew what he wanted well enough and was sufficient of a politician to know how and when to compromise. He realised that there were practical limits to his powers of compelling belief. He grasped that among churchmen and, increasingly, among the educated laity, religious convictions were polarising. If he were to win acceptance for the break with Rome and the royal supremacy, the pope would have to be denounced, but if radical religious changes were to be enforced, or even if they were simply to be advocated from the pulpits, he risked provoking serious rebellions like the Pilgrimage of Grace. For all the extravagant claims of the Act of Six Articles that it would abolish diversity of opinions, Henry more realistically aimed at steering a path between the extremes. A proclamation in April 1539 criticised some who 'minding craftily by their preaching and teaching to restore into this realm the old devotion to the usurped power of the Bishop of Rome, the hypocrite religion, superstitious pilgrimages, idolatry and other evil and naughty ceremonies and dreams justly and lawfully abolished and taken away by authority of God's word' and 'some other, taking and gathering divers Holy Scriptures to contrary senses and understanding, do wrest and interpret and so untruly allege the same to subvert and overturn as well the sacraments of Holy Church as the power and authority of princes and magistrates, and in effect all laws and common justice, and the good and laudable ordinances and ceremonies necessary and convenient to be used and continued in this realm'. Addressing parliament in December 1545, Henry lamented that 'charity and concord is not among you, but discord and dissension beareth rule in every place ... What love and charity is amongst you, when the one calleth the other heretic, and anabaptist; and he calleth him again papist, hypocrite, and pharisee'. The clergy preached daily against each other, 'some be too stiff in their old "mumpsimus", others be too busy and curious in their new "sumpsimus". Once again he was urging a middle way.[5]

Nor was the Elizabethan religious settlement unequivocally protestant. Elizabeth would have preferred something closer to her father's catholicism without the pope and without egregious superstition. That, in the absence of clinching evidence, seems the most plausible interpretation of one of the most teasing of historical conundrums. There is no evidence that any committee of divines met to prepare that theologically up-to-date statement of doctrine that might have been expected if the government had embarked on a clearly protestant course. But Elizabeth's preference, for royal supremacy, for English litanies, for communion in both kinds, but little more, proved unobtainable. The Marian bishops, and, probably, though the evidence is less clear, catholics in the commons, refused to acquiesce in it, forcing Elizabeth to go further.[6] Yet the limits to her protestantism must be emphasised. She chose as her principal advisers William Cecil and, as Archbishop of Canterbury, Matthew Parker, both committed protestants, but significantly neither of them so committed that they had felt unable to compromise with Mary's catholic regime, and neither of them radicalised by the experience of religious exile. In her own religious practice, in her concern for ceremonies, proper clerical dress, crucifixes and images, she was remarkably 'catholic'. A book of prayers probably in her hand is wholly conventional, revealing little more than that she was a Christian: 'the theological and devotional expressions taken as a whole would have been appropriate within any of the christian communities of Europe'.[7] Yet that is in itself significant. In what she said here and elsewhere about religion there was no sign of the 'cant' (used here as a technical term in the sense of language used by a sect) that some might see as the mark of the truly evangelical protestant. She never saw the much more radical Scottish Reformation as a model; she disliked excessive preaching. Later, she was not prepared to accept Grindal's so-called moderate puritanism, seeing it as loosening royal control over the church and over foreign policy: to have regarded the pope as Antichrist would have increased the weight of ideological considerations in English diplomacy and made any diplomacy, let alone marriage negotiations, with France or Spain impossible. Above all, Elizabeth saw the settlement as final: she never sympathised with demands for further reformation.[8] Yet she grasped that if many of her subjects were still essentially catholic, others wanted that further reformation; and so Elizabeth agreed to a profoundly, perhaps deliberately, ambiguous settlement. Just where was the communion table to stand – at the east end of the church or in the middle of it, or was it to be moved for services? Were wafers to be offered at communion or might common bread be used? Were both the unaccompanied congregational singing of psalms and the chanting of anthems allowed? Was there a gap between the statutes making the settlement, the Acts of Supremacy and Uniformity, together with the Book of Common Prayer on the one hand, and, on the other, the possibly more radically protestant views of those men who were appointed to bishoprics and deaneries by Elizabeth in the early years of her reign (not least because she had little choice) and who produced the doctrinal formulations known as the Thirty Nine Articles in 1563? But were those Articles themselves ambiguous in places? Was there a difference between what was legally required and what was in practice allowed or ignored? And was this indeed a final settlement, or a stage on the road to a fuller reformation?[9]

Thus in grasping the nature of the Church of England after the break with Rome and after the Elizabethan settlement, an important place must be found for the preferences, intentions and compromises of Henry VIII and of Elizabeth. They saw the monarch as in control of the church, appointing bishops, determining doctrine and liturgy, and capable even of suspending an archbishop from exercising his powers, a view perhaps symbolised by the placing of royal arms inside parish churches. At the heart of this monarchical view of the church lay a desire that was essentially political, but which could be expressed without insincerity in more idealised language (and would be in the poetry of John Donne and George Herbert), a desire for comprehensiveness, for a church which would embrace all their subjects. Religious uniformity was natural in itself; religious dissension wrecked social harmony and political peace. Continental experiences – from the peasants' wars of 1525 through the French wars of religion to the Thirty Years' War – reinforced English rulers' fears of the disastrous consequences of religious divisions, and their success, until 1642, in sparing their realm from such horrors further strengthened their conviction of the efficacy of the policy. Elizabeth could thank God (in the French prayer in her book of devotions) for 'the good things I have enjoyed until now to the honor and the relief of thy church, while my nearest neighbours have felt the evils of bloody warfare'.[10]

This is not to claim that monarchs could do as they pleased, nor that they were all agreed on every particular. My argument is that they placed secular and political considerations of order above purely ecclesiastical and theological considerations (though, as we shall see, that did have religious implications), and that from the start, from the 1530s, rulers faced limitations because some of their subjects were papists and some of their subjects wanted further reformation. Given the fact of religious difference, given that rulers knew that their subjects, especially the more educated, were divided, sometimes in response to theological debates European rather than just national in scope, a measure of compromise and ambiguity, particularly on points of doctrine or of local liturgical practice, was deliberately fostered. The virtues of the mean were forcefully asserted – by Henry VIII, by Lord Keeper Bacon in his speech to the Lords in 1559.[11]

As part of a policy of maintaining such a mean, whenever the temperature of religious quarrels rose, efforts were made to cool the passions. Sometimes drastically repressive measures were taken against public unorthodoxy: Thomas Norton, the parliamentarian and 'man of business', was sent to the Tower in 1581, Peter Smart, prebendary of Durham cathedral, was imprisoned after an inflammatory sermon in 1628. From the start of Elizabeth's reign it was made clear that foreigners resident in London were not allowed to have churches free from royal and episcopal control that might become centres of radical Protestantism offering an alternative model to the Church of England. Their churches were for the use of foreigners and immigrants who were officially welcomed or tolerated for the economic advantages they were seen as bringing. The stranger churches were placed firmly under the bishop of London, and not allowed to be ruled by foreign superintendents. In 1571 the Dutch church in London was not permitted to send representatives to a general synod in Emden since that would have conceded the existence of a higher authority abroad. In 1573 and 1577 the stranger churches were warned not to allow Englishmen to attend their services. No doubt the government never saw them as more than a temporary expedient. More generally in the church of England, a large place was left for the notion of adiaphora, the belief that there were unknowable mysteries and matters indifferent whose resolution was not essential to salvation and should not therefore be allowed to jeopardise political society. Discussion of knotty theological problems was to be limited to the universities and to the learned: public preaching of such controversies was frequently prohibited. Intense enthusiasm was considered dangerous unless it suited the government's immediate political purposes. Henry VIII's social restrictions on the reading of the Bible in 1543, Elizabeth's ban on preaching in 1559, Archbishop Parker's actions against all provocative writers and preachers are instances. When Samuel Harsnett, then a young Cambridge academic, preached a controversial sermon at Paul's Cross in 1584, he was reprimanded and the sermon was not published. When disputes over predestination and free will raged in the University of Cambridge in the 1590s, Elizabeth thought the subject 'a matter tender and dangerous to weak ignorant minds'.[12]

In the early seventeenth century these attitudes were maintained. James I continued such monarchical containment of religious passions. In 1603 he informed Archbishop Whitgift that he would not 'suffer any disordered persons in this church' and did not want any unlicensed preachers.[13] On his orders canons for the discipline and government of the church were issued in 1604: all candidates for holy orders and all university graduates were required to subscribe to them.[14] 'There have never been hitherto,' James said in 1610, 'any particular church in the world (for aught that we have read or heard) that hath allowed such ministers to preach in it as have refused to subscribe to the doctrine and discipline settled in it and maintained by it'.[15] It was in accordance with this approach that James authorised a standard translation of the Bible and issued a Declaration of Sports in 1618 which dealt with the increasing debate over what was permissible on the sabbath. Notes made by John Bois, one of the panel preparing the revised translation of the Bible, show 'again and again ... how concerned the translators were to achieve as open a rendering as possible'. By a heavy use of co-ordinating clauses, by imposing only a relatively weak impression of sequentiality, by 'merely placing one thing after another, and leaving us to interpret for ourselves the degree to which the things described are sequential or simultaneous', the translators left the Authorised Version open to a range of meanings. 'It seems to have been an important principle that its renderings be capable of embracing differing, even apparently incompatible, interpretations – partly one assumes because there were many puritan and catholic critics only too ready to accuse it of partiality. A translation which could admit ambiguity was nearly always to be preferred to a narrowly interpretative one.' Such a Bible was a fitting work for a monarchical church.[16] He rebuked Lancelot Andrewes, bishop of Winchester, for preaching a controversial sermon at court in 1618. When Robert Abbot, Regius Professor of Divinity at Oxford, complained against John Howson, then a prebend of Oxford cathedral, and William Laud, then president of St John's College, James 'did not give his unequivocal backing to either party', acquitting Howson of heterodoxy, but rebuking him for his contentious preaching.[17] In May 1613 James, writing to the Dutch about theological controversies, advised the states-general that 'experience has taught us that such differences are rarely to be decided by the conference of divines, but that it is much more proper to put an end to them by public authority, forbidding your clergy to touch upon such subjects in the pulpit or among the common people, and strictly requiring them to preserve peace by a mutual toleration of the differing opinions which each side has embraced concerning those points'.[18] In 1618 he instructed the divines he sent to the Synod of Dort to advise the Dutch churches 'that the ministers do not deliver in pulpit to the people those things for ordinary doctrines, which are the highest points of schools, and not fit for vulgar capacity, but disputable on both sides'.[19] Bishop Overall had written the previous year how James thought it 'a very bold attempt for men to dispute so nicely about such questions of God's predestination and so peremptorily to decide matters as if they had been in heaven and had assisted at the divine council board'.[20] In 1622 (referring back to measures taken by Henry VIII) James issued directions to preachers, amplified by Archbishop Abbot: no preachers other than bishops or deans were to 'presume to preach in any popular auditory the deep points of predestination, election, reprobation, or of the universality, efficacy, resistability of God's grace; but leave those themes rather to be handled by the learned men, and that moderately and modestly by way of use and application, rather than by way of positive doctrines, being fitter for the schools than for simple auditories'.[21] When Charles I and Laud issued further prohibitions in 1626 and 1628 they were continuing a well-established and very understandable rulers' attitude to the disruptive social and political consequences of religious controversy. Men with strong views (like Richard Montagu, author of *Appello Caesarem*, the suppression of which was ordered in a royal proclamation in January 1629) felt less certain than some modern historians do that this was doing them a favour or that it represented the confident reticence of victors who no longer needed to project their ideas.[22]

Richard Hooker's *Laws of Ecclesiastical Polity*, written in the 1590s, is the boldest statement of the character of this monarchical church. But Hooker did not, as Peter Lake and Conrad Russell claim, *invent* 'anglicanism'. Lake's claim for Hooker's novelty rests in large part on his analysis of what Archbishop Whiftgift wrote in an earlier controversy with the Cambridge divine Thomas Cartwright. Yet in assessing Whitgift, Lake consistently minimises the Hookerian implications of Whitgift's arguments: in regarding ceremonies as aids to order and uniformity, Whitgift came close to arguing that they edified; in insisting on the importance of membership of the visible church, Whitgift was pointing to the value of the parish church and to a style of piety which gave the sacraments a central place. In latching on to Whitgift's claim that his presbyterian opponents were essentially in agreement with him as proof of a common protestant world view, Lake takes as an accurate description what was rather a debating device. Nor do similarities in the scholarly and exegetical techniques and arguments used by Whitgift and Cartwright prove the existence of an Elizabethan protestant consensus. Lake concedes that over predestination Whitgift drew different conclusions, and admits that 'beneath the surface of the debate two very different views of the nature of true religion, the Christian community and its relations with the cause of social and political order, can be seen in conflict'.[23] Conrad Russell has suggested that Hooker may have written in response to a request from the Scottish divine Patrick Adamson to Whitgift for a study of how the church should be ordered: that would further strengthen the links between Whitgift and Hooker.[24] Moreover in presenting Hooker as outside the 'mainstream of English protestantism', Lake seems in danger of implying that the Elizabethan church was also outside the 'mainstream of English protestantism', which would be absurd.[25] Far from inventing 'anglicanism', Hooker rather articulated Elizabeth's policy, showing how the mean was the aim of the founding fathers of the Elizabethan church, and providing as Lake perhaps inadvertently admits 'an entirely unembarrassed defence of the ecclesiastical status quo and the unpreaching ministry that went with it'.[26]

Any view of the Church of England that fails to give due weight to its 'monarchical' element is thus misleading, and especially when special attention is paid to just those theological controversies which rulers were so intent on muffling. Before any theology can be claimed as a norm, as dominant, as establishment orthodoxy,[27] it has to be set in the context of this 'monarchical' church, that is in the context of a church controlled to the limits of their power by rulers with an obvious and consistent interest in promoting comprehensive, eirenic, politique policies in order to hold together a religiously divided society and church. This Tyacke has failed to do.

In claiming that the Church of England was essentially calvinist at the turn of the century, Tyacke relies largely on two sources, printed sermons, especially those preached at Paul's Cross, and theses submitted at Oxford and Cambridge. There are difficulties, which several historians, notably Peter White, have pointed out in Tyacke's handling of his theological evidence: he isolates one element, predestination, in men's views, making that the key issue of difference, without showing that that doctrine was at the heart of late Elizabethan and Jacobean theology; he treats belief in predestination as if it were homogeneous, failing to distinguish differences in types of predestinarian belief.[28] In one sense all Christians must believe in predestination, since if God is omniscient, he must know whether a man will be saved or damned. But what is at issue here is whether the doctrine known as double predestination – that God had not only predestined some to salvation but had reprobated others to damnation – was the doctrine of the Church of England. That latter question of reprobation was not dealt with explicitly in the characteristically ambiguous Article XVII of the Thirty Nine Articles. Moreover, Tyacke disregards the importance of the consequences that men drew from a belief in predestination, that is, its relative place in a man's belief and practices, the enthusiasm with which some sought precisely to elaborate its implications while others shunned analysis of great mysteries that were simply to be wondered at, and especially the conclusions that might, but need not, be drawn from a belief in predestination on how the church should be organised, on whether the true church was not the Church of England but rather a smaller group of those predestined to be saved. Such difficulties weaken Tyacke's case.[29]

But, allowing his definitions for the sake of argument, his own evidence suggests that, in the period in which he claims that calvinists were dominant, there was a nonetheless vigorous minority at Oxford and Cambridge holding different views, that there was 'a debate, not an unchallenged calvinist oration'. Some of the most important academic posts were held by men with very different views, including Peter Baro, Lady Margaret Professor of Divinity from 1574 to 1596, John Overall, Regius Professor of Divinity from 1595 to 1607, and John Richardson, Regius Professor of Divinity from 1607 to 1617.[30]

Here, interestingly, Russell significantly dissents from Tyacke, seeing a bitter struggle within the church of England between different theological viewpoints.[31] Tyacke's playing down of anti-predestinarian views in the 1590s makes it easier for him to claim that 'Arminianism' was a novel movement in the 1620s.

But the most telling difficulty with Tyacke's characterisation of the Church of England lies in his failure to set his view in the context of the monarchical character of the Elizabethan and Jacobean church. He does not grasp the implications for his argument of the actions and attitudes of Elizabeth, the younger Cecil and Archbishop Whitgift. When an attempt was made to enshrine the doctrine of double predestination in the Lambeth Articles of 1595, Elizabeth blocked the publication of that statement.[32] Whitgift's attitudes are in part a matter of controversy but the boldest claims made for him seem excessive. Undoubtedly the Lambeth Articles defined and amplified the doctrine of predestination and they were later seen as a touchstone of calvinist orthodoxy. On the other hand, it is quite possible that Whitgift saw them as a compromise in which he had managed to remove or to qualify some of the starkest claims and he did not intend that they should serve more than to quieten the heated debates in Cambridge. He may have been surprised by the force of Elizabeth's reaction but his general position on the inadvisability of public controversy on such matters was far closer to the attitude of the queen than to the advocates of the articles in Cambridge.[33]

Tyacke is also forced to claim James I as a predestinarian calvinist.[34] This is possible only because of the looseness of Tyacke's categories. For at the Hampton Court Conference in 1604 James refused to allow any expansion of those parts of the Thirty Nine articles dealing with predestination, free will and grace,[35] and later he refused to adopt the Lambeth Articles or the Irish Articles or the decrees of the synod of Dort, all of which elaborated the doctrine of double predestination.[36] In 1610 he opposed the appointment of Conrad Vorstius to a chair at Leiden, but not because that Dutch theologian 'was a rigid calvinist with a dogmatic attachment to one particular version of the doctrine of predestination but because he saw Vorstius' outspokenness as leading to angry debate tending to the destruction of the state'.[37] His intervention in the synod of Dort was intended not to support any particular theological position but to not press for moderation and for a middle way: as John Davenant, Master of Queens' College, Cambridge, one of the king's delegation, wrote, 'we had a special charge in our instructions to endeavour that positions be moderately laid down which may tend to the mitigation of heat on both sides'.[38] In 1619 he denounced 'the extremitie of some Puritans, who by consequent make God the author of sin'.[39] In 1622, as we have seen, he issued a proclamation banning preaching about predestination.[40] Significant here are James's episcopal appointments. He appointed Richard Bancroft as Archbishop of Canterbury, Richard Neile successively to Lichfield in 1610, Lincoln in 1613 and Durham in 1617, John Overall successively to Lichfield in 1613 and Norwich in 1618, George Montaigne successively to Lincoln in 1617 and London in 1621, Anthony Buckeridge to Rochester in 1610, Lancelot Andrewes to Winchester in 1618, John Howson to Oxford in 1618, Samuel Harsnett to Norwich in 1619, Valentine Carey to Exeter in 1621 and William Laud to St David's in 1621, none of whom were thoroughgoing predestinarians, to say the least. Of course 'particular promotions are affected by particular circumstances',[41] but no partisan calvinist would have been so careless of the doctrinal beliefs of men he was raising to the episcopate. James's appointments were rather a deliberate balancing, as the appointments of George Carleton to Chichester in 1619 and John Davenant to Salisbury in 1621.[42] All this shows that James maintained an erastian, monarchical view of the church and refused to espouse predestinarian dogma. His policy 'was often conceived and presented as a via media' between the extremes of papists and presbyterians and he was keen to incorporate moderates from both sides within the national church.[43] He saw persistent nonconformity as open defiance of his authority as supreme governor of the church. He was sympathetic to catholics, releasing them from the political proscription of Elizabeth's reign, but his views hardened for a time after the assassination of Henri IV of France in 1610, a climate in which Abbot (rather than Andrewes) was appointed Archbishop of Canterbury in 1611.[44] He did not believe in 'further reformation'. He believed passionately in ecumenism: he hoped that the divisions of Christendom could be healed. That was how de Dominis, sometime roman catholic archbishop, could, once he had denounced papal primacy, be welcomed in England and made dean of Windsor for a brief period until he renounced the church of England in turn and returned to Rome, to die in a papal prison.[45] His foreign policies were not shaped by religion: indeed his domestic religious policies were rather shaped by his diplomatic perceptions. In the face of the outbreak of confessional war in the Holy Roman Empire, James avoided English and Scottish involvement and pressed for a Spanish, catholic, bride for his son Charles in 1621, circumstances from which those 'Arminian' churchmen listed above benefited in the early 1620s, as the trend of royal foreign policy diminished the influence of those 'calvinist' bishops who continued to advocate active support of the protestant cause in Germany.[46] The 'rise of Arminianism', if by that is meant the promotions of churchmen, such as Neile and Laud, who were to be prominent in Charles I's reign, thus occurred before the accession of Charles in 1625.

Moreover Tyacke's view is limited to the world of the universities and sermon writers. Yet predestinarian views had little practical relevance for bishops and JPs and muster masters and councillors and diplomats. There was an immense gulf between the high points of theology and the day-to-day business of running church and state. And it misleads to imply that theological debate was of greater importance or all-pervasive. Moreover it is hard to accept that the *moderate* calvinist position that Patrick Collinson and Peter Lake have seen as characteristic of several Cambridge professors and heads of houses[47] was a tenable position in the long run outside, or even inside, the university. To see religion as a straight choice between popery and reformed purity, to denounce the pope as Antichrist, to adhere rigidly to a closely defined body of doctrine, was perhaps feasible in the study, but such an exclusive view of religion was at odds with pastoral and diocesan realities, royal preferences, the Book of Common Prayer and the needs of foreign policy, and furthermore it was troubled by its internal contradictions.

Tyacke also neglects the realities of religious life in the parishes, underestimating the cumulative effects of the Elizabethan religious settlement, essentially untouched over Elizabeth's long reign. The inherited and largely unreformed episcopal and parish structure, the Book of Common Prayer, the provision of the sacraments had a powerful influence.[48] As Diarmaid MacCulloch has observed, 'perhaps inevitably, the catholic structure of the church began to exert its own emotional pull'; the inherited church buildings, despite their whitewashed walls and new emptiness, spoke of the catholic past and offered 'a constant background threat of architectural seduction'.[49] If much that passed for religion was social habit, rustic semi-pelagianism, salvation-by-good-works, crypto-catholicism, nonetheless there was an increasing vitality, as shown by the increasing frequency of communion and astonishingly high participation in Easter communion, and by the large numbers of catechisms from which many surely learned the basic points of Christianity.[50] All that was part of the Church of England too, as much as academic tracts on predestination. Indeed 'for many of the parish clergy, the crucial decisions may have concerned the day-to-day matters of pastoral work among a largely illiterate population rather than the resolution of controversies being debated miles away'.[51] When some parish clergy preached double predestination they met with resistance: moreover it is difficult to imagine how they could have conducted burial services while preaching such doctrines. Scholastic predestinarian calvinism was quite alien to parish life.[52] There under the influence of 'innumerable processes of custom and habit',' the church was becoming more catholic in the later sixteenth century': 'parish anglicanism', with renewed attention given to the physical fabric of the church, was a significant force.[53]

* * *

Did the Church of England change its nature after the accession of Charles I? Did, as Tyacke suggests, a group of 'Arminian' divines capture the commanding heights of a previously generally calvinist church? Or was the struggle between competing groups that Russell and Lake see now won by the 'Arminians'? Did Charles and Laud deliberately move away from a period of 'eirenic compromise' and support one 'faction' within the church? Was there a change? If not, how should the hostility towards Arminianism and the role of religion in the English Civil War be explained?

Was Laud an 'Arminian'? Kevin Sharpe has denied it. Laud eschewed controversy, prevented the public discussion of thorny matters, and so fitted into a long tradition of monarchical religion. He framed no new doctrinal articles, wrote no new catechism, published little. On royal orders he wrote against the roman catholics, answering the thrust of counter-reformation propaganda. He never wrote theologically against predestinarians or puritans; as Chancellor of Oxford or as Archbishop of Canterbury he never tried to create an Arminian clergy, indeed he censored and restrained extreme forms of Arminianism; and in his personal life, he was stern, sombre, ascetic.[54]

A key document is a letter that three bishops, Buckeridge, Howson and Laud wrote to the duke of Buckingham, Charles's favourite, on 2 August 1625 in defence of Richard Montagu, then a country rector, who had just published a controversial work, *A New Gagg for an Old Goose*? The bishops assimilated the Lambeth Articles to the 'fatal opinions' of Dort and in so doing they implicitly rejected an emphasis on predestination. Significantly they did so not for theological reasons but because they saw it as incompatible with civil government and external ministry. They implicitly approved Montagu's views, but thought only some – not all – of them as the resolved doctrine of the Church of England: some of his views were fit only for the schools, that is to say they should be argued over in the universities by learned theologians, and nowhere else. Once again what the bishops were expressing was a monarchical view of the church. Whether Montagu himself was an 'Arminian' in the strict sense of someone influenced by Arminius is a further complication.[55]

Further 'evidence' that has been cited to show that Laud was an 'Arminian' is at best technical and rests on inference. He generally approved of William Chillingworth's *Religion of Protestants*, not a book admired by calvinists. Responding to William Prynne in the 1640s, Laud critised the implications of his bitterest critic's predestinarian views: did Prynne, he asked, believe that 'the true saints of God may commit horrible and crying sins, die without repentance, and yet be sure of salvation'? In December 1624 Laud drew up a tract for Buckingham (now lost) about doctrinal puritanism in which (according to Heylyn, writing much later, and perhaps misleadingly) calvinist teaching on predestination was defined as puritan. At Oxford his chaplains allegedly would only license Arminian sermons – yet that claim has been effectively challenged.[56]

Was there then no Arminian plot, no Arminian conspiracy to capture the church from the late 1620s? The evidence given for such a plot is slight. The proclamations of 1626 and 1629 were not intended to proscribe calvinism but to suppress controversy: 'if ... by reading, preaching, or by making books, either pro or contra, concerning these differences, men begin anew to dispute, we shall take such order with them, and those books, that they shall wish they had never thought upon these needless controversies'.[57] Royal attitudes to the pulpit and to the printing press were like those Blair Worden has found characterising royal attitudes to the theatre: 'the government's principal concern in the exercise of censorship – an understandable one in view of the traditional and common association of the theatre with public disturbance – was evidently to forestall not criticism but disorder'.[58] Nor were such prohibitions all that effective. New editions of works by calvinist theologians were published in the 1630s. Catechisms such as that by the Elizabethan divine William Perkins continued to be reprinted (though perhaps its calvinist doctrine was diluted by simplification).[59] The appointments of 'Arminians' to bishoprics and deaneries reflected not a conspiracy (and of course many such 'Arminians' had been appointed in the 1610s) but the chance incidence of vacancies – it may be significant here that there were so many appointments made in 1628–29 – and the changing theological fashions in the universities as the shocking implications of the Synod of Dort were vigorously debated. In Oxford and Cambridge predestination remained an issue, as it had long been, with a survey of Cambridge in 1640 uncovering 'an enormous range of opinions on grace and free will, faith and works', but as theologians struggled to sort out the internal contradictions and the implications of a belief in predestination, fewer of them and especially fewer of the younger generations accepted a calvinist view of it, particularly that rigid scholastic version of Calvin's teachings that had developed in the later sixteenth century. John Hales, chaplain of Dudley Carleton, the English ambassador in the United Provinces, attended the Synod of Dort and was so shocked that 'there I bid John Calvin good night'. Barnaby Potter, bishop of Carlisle, admitted that in his youth he had taught against the Arminians but now believed that the ancient fathers agreed more with the Arminians. Indeed in the 1640s and 1650s an Arminian critique of pre-destinarian Calvinism was to emerge from within the heart of nonconformity. Meanwhile how many high calvinists were denied preferment by Charles and Laud? Joseph Hall was appointed to Exeter in 1627, Thomas Morton to Durham in 1632.[60]

What then went wrong? Why did 'Arminianism' become so universally unpopular by 1640 if it was not because Arminians had captured a previously calvinist or a previously more accommodating church? Perhaps Arminianism – or the monarchical Church of England – was not so universally unpopular as the events of 1640–41 might superficially suggest. Perhaps it was *not* true that 'Charles had put himself at the head of a faction in the church whose aims jarred significantly with the preferences and beliefs of the greater part of his subjects'.[61] What at first sight looks like good evidence of religious alienation may be less telling than it first seems: migration to the New World, for example, might be economic in motivation, as that of under-employed clothworkers, or, when involving liberty of conscience, that of religious extremists whose views few high calvinists would have tolerated, and who left not because of any new 'crisis' in England in the 1620s and 1630s but because of the much deeper dilemma of living among the 'prophane'.[62] A study of the Laudian church in Buckinghamshire found very little sign of particular pressures on parishioners over 'Laudian' issues: far more people were presented for working on Sundays than for failing to kneel at the appropriate moment in services.[63] There is very little sign that bitter doctrinal or liturgical disputes were at all widespread in the parishes. The degree of enforcement of altar policies in the 1630s, for example, was higher than compulsion or grudging compliance can explain. Some unpublished studies suggest that 80 to 90 per cent of parishes in areas studied had railed their communion tables at the east end. The iconoclasm of 1640–41 was intermittent and the work of minorities and of soldiers, and in any case, the erection of rails is a better test of general commitment than their destruction.[64] There was no significant decline in the framework of the Church of England as measured by the rates of baptism, churching and communion in Southwark before 1640.[65] Much of the evidence of the allegedly provocative enforcement of Arminianism cited by Anthony Fletcher is based on complaints made and evidence collected in 1640–42: the earlier evidence for disputes in cathedral closes is more telling, but such jurisdictional disputes were endemic and had little to do with doctrine.[66] The petitions in defence of episcopacy and the prayer book in 1641 betray little sign that petitioners thought themselves to be defending any church other than that of the 1630s. In referring to the tradition and longevity of episcopacy, and to its apostolic origins, in noting the anarchic implications of religious sects, in praising (as in Rutland) bishops for 'their performance of miracles, their building of churches and colleges, and their example by public acts of piety', they show, as Fletcher notes, 'a strong sense of the corporate nature of the church', reflecting 'Laud's concept of worship as solemn, dignified, uncontentious and evocative', and making it plain 'that the notion of the Ecclesia Anglicana, which embodied a middle way and was equally resistant to Romish superstition and Genevan innovation, had struck deep roots'. The petitioners were defending the monarchical church of England.[67] The defence of episcopacy in the Long Parliament itself in 1641, the evidence of continuing loyalty to the Prayer Book in the 1640s and beyond, and the rallying to the church of England in 1660–62 are also striking.[68] But clearly many did in the 1640s oppose it. Why?

Hugh Trevor-Roper would answer that it was because Arminianism, which he sees as an intellectual movement within the established church of England (and indeed Europe), gradually but accidentally became in its English form part of a political and religious synthesis rightly judged a frontal challenge to the political elite. Opposition to Arminianism was thus just the self-interested and self-fulfilling manipulation of popular sentiment by a political class constitutionally alienated from a king whom it supposed to be introducing what we would now label 'absolutism'. The king and his bishops were denounced as Arminian and papist because this was a way of rooting aristocratic constitutionalism in popular feeling. We call the royalists and bishops papists to make them odious though we know it is not true, admitted the jurist and scholar John Selden. The war was fought not for bishops or for a service book, the parliamentary peer Saye and Sele claimed, but to destroy the parliament, that is the government, of England. But Selden was unusual in his rationalism while Saye and Sele was making his claim in the context of opposition to Scottish religious demands, in which it served his political purpose to deny that religion had been the issue of the wars. And this general view of aristocratic manipulation of their inferiors fails to persuade in the light of Robin Clifton's studies of the fear of catholics, which suggest that most anti-catholic acts between 1640 and 1642 were spontaneous, provoked by genuine anxieties especially of Charles I's motives in negotiating with the Scots, the Irish and foreign powers, and of his involvement in army plots, and, more broadly, in the light of many studies of popular rebellions in the sixteenth and seventeenth centuries that show the sheer practical difficulty of mobilising the Commons and that stress the autonomy of popular political action.[69]

Another explanation of hostility to 'Arminianism' has been found simply in what Laud and his colleagues allegedly did in the 1630s. Life in the 1630s may have become, or may have seemed, less comfortable for those of high calvinist views of predestination, such as Robert Woodford,[70] or whose antipathy to catholics made them as violently critical of what they saw as 'unconscious' popery as of outright recusancy.[71] Can the work of Laud and the bishops be described as a campaign? Was it driven by their 'Arminian' theology? Was it so novel?

It is likely that religious policies, like other policies, were more confidently and effectively enforced in the early and mid-1630s by a king now free from the distractions of war and by a number of committed and energetic bishops who set themselves and expected from others the highest standards. There was less winking at occasional conformity than there had been in London under Bishop King (1611–21) or Bishop Montaigne (1622–28): discipline was tightened up.[72] Should this be described as a campaign? It would be misleading to deny it by claiming that there were just different actions by bishops in their respective dioceses, or by looking in turn at various religious policies – the altar policy, the book of sports and so on – and concluding that each was in itself modest, largely uncontroversial, and that no one was punished for offences against any single policy alone.[73] A more strictly chronological study of the cumulative impact of Charles's and Laud's policies might well give a greater impression of a campaign than do such attempts to atomise those policies. It would be more convincing to accept that undoubtedly some were discontented by what they saw, fairly or not, as a campaign in the 1630s.

Was it doctrinally driven? Was it the implementation of 'Arminian' policies? If none of the evidence offered gives any very telling support for the proposition that Laud was an 'Arminian', or that he was driven by deeply held and closely elaborated theological views, then that might seem to dispose of the question. But to leave it there, and simply to deny that Laud was an 'Arminian', is perverse. In very many ways Charles and Laud were simply continuing the Henrician-Elizabethan-Jacobean monarchical view of the church. Charles and Laud believed in order, in external obedience to the established church, in a Church of England which was seen as a part of the universal catholic church. Disputes were to be settled by king and bishops, private reservations were possible, but there should be no public contention about insoluble controversies. Following Henry VIII, Elizabeth, Parker, Whitgift and Bancroft, both Charles and Laud wanted a uniform and decent order of worship in church. Churches should be repaired and properly furnished. The church and its clergy should be adequately financed. None of that amounts in itself to doctrinal Arminianism. But if one can distinguish between an active, informed and proselytising Arminianism on one hand, and a passive, implicit Arminianism not defined in theological writings and pronouncements but rather reflected in actions on the other, then surely the monarchical religion that very largely characterised government policy from Henry VIII, throughout Elizabeth's reign, during James's reign and now under Charles I and Laud was in this sense deeply and ineradicably 'Arminian'. Such a redefinition of 'arminianism' rests on the conviction that theological views are not found exclusively in works of theology but can be implicit both in writings not explicitly dealing with such questions and, above all, in actions. To emphasise external observance, to dismiss controverted matters as adiaphora and to deplore public disputes on difficult matters, to see the maintenance of civil order as the primary goal of government, to stress the importance of churches as buildings, to assert the value of ceremonies and sacraments, to emphasise the importance of corporate worship, to dwell on the beauty of holiness (or the holiness of beauty), to serve as a bishop administering a diocese or as a parish parson ministering to his flock, all this implies an Arminian view of predestination that allows full scope for grace, merit, free will, human involvement in the process of salvation, an Arminian view of the church as inclusive. Such attitudes did not spring from a study of Arminian doctrines or from a cruder desire to destroy predestinarian views; they came from an independent tradition of monarchical views of the church, but in practice these attitudes were imbued with Arminian attitudes. Such attitudes predated Arminius: if their theological roots are to be sought, it might be more fruitful to search in the practice of the churches established in Germany under Luther's guidance, and much further back into the medieval past, into (for example) the spiritual world of late fourteenth-century Yorkshire.[74]

In such a monarchical church, those holding high calvinist views would always, and not just in the 1630s, feel some tension between their beliefs and the actions required of them. They would in this sense be correct to criticise the church as 'Arminian' and they might be more or less embarrassed by having to take part in ceremonies with 'Arminian' implications. But what is at issue here is whether they were more entitled to criticise in the early and mid-1630s than at other times. In a society in which there had by now long been different religious views but in which governments continued to stress the importance of outward uniformity, some would always feel uncomfortable, whatever the exact policies or degrees of implementation: the point at issue here is whether the 1630s were exceptional. That seems doubtful. Bishops had attempted to enforced discipline before, not just during Laud's archiepiscopate: most Jacobean bishops, for instance, had been conscientious rather than lax.[75] Royal and episcopal policy was above all concerned to secure outward conformity and did not disturb everyone. In some places, for example Warwickshire, a small group of godly were able to continue their practice of sermon-gadding in the 1630s: there only a minority of the scholar Thomas Dugard's friends among the clergy had any trouble with the ecclesiastical authorities.[76] Charles I and Laud, anxious to lower the political temperature after the feverish years of war taxation in the late 1620s, may well have raised suspicions or allowed misunderstandings to arise by failing to make their intentions sufficiently clearly understood: Laud, Clarendon wrote, 'did court persons too little; nor cared to make his designs and purposes appear as candid as they were by showing them in any other dress than their natural beauty and roughness'. He was the first post-Reformation bishop with no reputation for generous hospitality.[77] An variant of that argument is the claim that Laud's religious policies prompted an outburst of lay anticlericalism. But that had more to do with the overzealousness of individual bishops and clergy and with the complexities of jurisdictions and property rights, especially in cathedral cities, and in a few *causes célèbres*, than with theology, and there is otherwise little evidence of exceptional tension, and much for an opposite view of lay–clergy relations, most notably in continuing lay resort to church courts.[78] Some anti-clericalism, such as that of Lord Falkland and his circle, did indeed arise from a latitudinarian resistance to clerical pretensions, but such attitudes were very rare.[79]

Nor do arguments over liturgical matters in the early and mid-1630s appear sufficient to warrant harsher criticisms of the policies of Charles and Laud than of those of Elizabeth or James. Much that was allegedly novel then can be found earlier. Maintenance of parish churches had been a concern long before Laud: Whitgift ordered a thorough survey of churches in 1602.[80] Ceremonies had been justified by John Jewel early in Elizabeth's reign on grounds of propriety. 'We do reteine and reuerently exercyse not onely suche as we know were commended vnto vs by the Apostles, but also certen others, suche as semed vnto vs mighte be borne without any hurte in the church, bicause we wold have all thinges done in the holy assembly ... comly and in order'.[81] When James I visited Holyrood in 1617, he wanted the chapel decorated with gilded figures of apostles and patriarchs for 'comeliness': he commended Bishop Harsnet for the practice of introducing religious pictures in his diocese. As a recent writer has noted, 'the "beauty of holiness" didn't begin with Charles and Laud.'[82]

The position of the communion table in parish churches came to be a preoccupation in the mid-1630s but again one must guard against exaggeration. Laud's metropolitical visitation articles of 1635 did indeed ask whether the communion table was used 'as is not agreeable to the holy use of it', by sitting on it, and throwing hats on it, writing on it: but far from introducing a new concern, in this he was following Archbishop Abbot's visitation articles of 1616 word for word.[83] It might be noted (in the absence of any published full studies) that some communion tables had been moved to the east end well before Laud: we should need to know much more of 'typical' practice both in cathedrals and in parish churches before concluding that the Laudians were radically altering chancels and modes of communion. Of course the position of the communion table could be seen as having theological implications, but there was also a strong practical argument on grounds of decency for railing it in, just as objections to this could be based on the practical problems of the cost or the audibility of clergy at the east end of a long chancel. To a large extent it was a matter of chance, a matter of the fluctuations of liturgical fashions, that it was the highly visible position of the communion table in parish churches that came to be a such an issue in the mid-1630s.[84] Moreover while liturgy has theological implications, it also has its own logic: what John Cosin, master of Peterhouse, pursued in Cambridge was the extreme of one fashion, and naturally provoked discussion, but it should not be taken as typical.[85] It is by no means obvious that the religious and ecclesiastical controversies of the early/mid-1630s were more bitter than, for example, those of the 1560s over clerical vestments or those of the mid-1600s in which some 80 to 90 clergy were deprived of their livings.[86] In the light of the continuities of monarchical policies from Henry VIII to Charles I, as well of the continuing fact of religious divisions, it is hard to see the early/mid-1630s as unique.

It is then the obviously disastrous Scottish policy of Charles I and in particular the military defeats that he suffered at Scottish hands in 1639-40 that offer the best explanation of criticisms made of royal religious policies in 1640-42. For Charles's Scottish policy had been the tactless extension of the monarchical Church of England to Scotland, where the Reformation had produced a very different, Presbyterian, church. That Scottish policy at once deepened the sense of alienation of those in England already uneasy at Charles's and Laud's religious policies, although if the Scots had not rebelled, or if the rebellion had been quickly crushed, such alienation would not have been very significant. But the disastrous military failure seemed to vindicate their criticisms. It gave credence to wilder conspiracy theories – to popish plots in which Charles was a secret papist or was the puppet of papist schemers. Such conspiracy theories were not in themselves new. But they were thought credible and they shaped action only in moments of great tension when they offered immediate explanations, consolation or remedies. Overt anti-Catholic feeling was very slight in the three years before the Short Parliament, and the beginnings of fear and persecution, Robin Clifton has shown, date from the days after its dissolution. But then in such an atmosphere, bishops would be damned as agents of popery, Arminianism as a betrayal of true religion.[87] It became much harder to defend and to explain the proper nature of the monarchical Church of England, and attempts to do so, such as the canons of 1640, seemed simply provocative. Moreover in the political storm resulting from military failure, Charles's policies in the early/mid-1630s were reinterpreted in the light of recent disasters, and methods of ruling that were arbitrary, but by the standards of rulers in the previous century by no means exceptionally arbitrary, were condemned as tyrannical. Sir Edward Dering briefly emerged as a leading critic of episcopacy but this was not directly provoked by his dealings with the church in the 1630s (his disputes with local clergy did not arise from any alleged 'Laudian' initiatives). Moreover his actions during the 1630s suggest that he could resolve local tensions within the existing political and ecclesiastical framework. What the Scots war (in which he was loyally involved as late as May 1640) did was to prompt him to re-examine the past decade and to draw more radical, crisis-inspired, conclusions.[88] Since the Scots' revolt involved religion, it was inescapable that Charles's religious policies would be seen as part of that alleged tyranny. Worse, the Scots' religious demands were insoluble in the context of a monarchical national church. A church based on comprehension, on ambiguities and compromises, was now confronted by demands for a presbyterian system of church government. Fears that the church was at the mercy of popish plots intensified opposite fears that it was threatened by a calvinist international.[89]

Such a clash not only brought out into the open differences of opinion previously accommodated within the church of England, but made those religious divisions much more important in relation to other issues, especially those discussed in parliament, than they had been. Just as there is a good deal of ruin in a country, there is a good deal of ruin in a national church. Larger cracks can be papered over than one might suppose. But in extraordinary circumstances, if contradictions with which men have long deliberately or unconsciously lived can no longer be accommodated or overlooked, if a monarchical church is faced by urgent demands for unambiguous, uncompromising decisions on divisive questions, then the ensuing collapse can be violent. When Englishmen ultimately turned to war in 1642, those differences of religion which the monarchical church had striven to contain but to which it was always vulnerable proved to be the most embittering determinant of men's allegiance.[90]

Notes

1. I wish to acknowledge the inspiration of Hugh Trevor-Roper and thank Kevin Sharpe and Peter Gwyn (especially), and Cliff Davies, Jennifer Loach, Peter White, Steve Gunn, Ken Fincham, David Katz, Ralph Houlbrooke, T.B. Pugh and Christopher Haigh for their comments on drafts.
2. N.R.N. Tyacke, *The Anti-Calvinists: the rise of English Arminans* (1987); 'Puritanism, Arminianism and Counter-Revolution', in C.S.R. Russell (ed.), *Origins of the English Civil War* (1973), pp. 119–43; 'Arminianism and English culture', in A.C. Duke and C.A. Tamse (eds), *Britain and the Netherlands*, vii (1981), pp. 94–105; C.S.R. Russell, *The Causes of the English Civil War* (Oxford, 1990; 'Introduction', in *Origins*, pp. 1–31; 'Religion and the English Civil War', paper read at the Institute of Historical Research, University of London, 23 November 1987; *Parliaments and English Politics 1621–1629* (1979), pp. 29–32 (where Russell enters a caveat that predestination 'was the normal, though not quite the official, doctrine of the church of England', though a few lines later he refers to 'the official predestinarian view' (p.29)); P. Collinson, *The Religion of Protestants* (Oxford, 1982); 'England and international Calvinism, 1558–1640', in M. Prestwich (ed.), *International Calvinism 1541–1715* (Oxford, 1985), pp. 197–223, esp. pp. 213–14, 220–23; J.S. Morrill, 'The religious context of the English Civil War', *Transactions of the Royal Historical Society*, 5th series, xxxiv (1984), pp. 155–78; 'The attack on the church of England in the Long Parliament, 1640–42', in D. Beales and G. Best (eds), *History, Society and the Churches* (Cambridge, 1985), pp. 105–6; P. Lake, 'The impact of early modern protestantism', *Journal of British Studies*, xxviii (1989), p. 300. See also the use to which Tyacke's arguments have been put: R. Ashton, *The English Civil War: Conservatives and Revolution 1603–1649* (2nd edn, 1988), pp. 109–14 ('if there is one person to whose actions and policies the fall of the Stuart monarchy can be attributed'); *Reformation and Revolution 1558–1660* (1984), pp. 279–83; A.G.R. Smith, *The Emergence of a Nation State: the Commonwealth of England 1529–1660* (1984), pp. 282–3; L. Stone, *The Causes of the English Revolution 1529–1642* (1972), pp. 128–9; J.P. Kenyon, *Stuart England* (2nd edn, 1985), pp. 106–8, 120–23 (but contrast his *Stuart Constitution* (Cambridge, 2nd edn, 1986), pp. 130–34); B. Coward, *The Stuart Age* (1980), pp. 148–9; C. Cross, *Church and People, 1450–1660* (1976), ch. 8, esp. pp. 174–5; 'Churchmen and the royal supremacy', in F. Heal and R. O'Day (eds), *Church and Society in England: Henry VIII to James I* (1977), pp. 32–4; A. Fletcher, *The outbreak of the English Civil War* (1981), pp. xx–xxiv, xxix, 94; W. Hunt, *The Puritan Moment: the Coming of Revolution in an English County* (Cambridge, Mass., 1983), pp. 125, 312; M. Finlayson, *Puritanism and the English Revolution: the Religious Factor in English Politics before and after the Interregnum* (Toronto, 1983), pp. 73, 97, 183 n. 42, 98–102; J.P. Somerville, *Politics and Ideology in England 1603–1640* (1986), pp. 44–5, 220 (but contrast with pp. 193–4, 222–3 where doctrine is played down); E.S. Cope, *Politics without Parliaments 1629–1640* (1987), pp. 48–9; D.D. Wallace, *Puritans and Predestination: Grace in English Protestant Theology* (North Carolina, 1982), pp. 29, 79, ch. 3, esp. pp. 102–4, 220 n. 2; J.M. Atkins, 'Calvinist bishops, church unity and the rise of arminianism', *Albion*, xviii (1986), pp. 424–7; K. Fincham, 'Pastoral roles of the English episcopate in Canterbury province 1603–1625', University of London PhD thesis, 1985, p. 223.
3. J. Foxe, *Acts and Monuments* (ed. J. Pratt, 8 vols, 1877), esp. p. 45ff.
4. On Henry VIII see J.J. Scarisbrick, *Henry VIII* (1968); on Wolsey see P.J. Gwyn,

The King's Cardinal (1990). [Since this paragraph was written, my views have evolved, and I should now see Henry's commitment to reform of the church, especially the rooting out of abuses, idolatry and superstition, as sincere rather than opportunistic. I hope to develop and substantiate these claims in a forthcoming study of the Henrician Reformation. See my papers 'The making of religious policy, 1533–1456: Henry VIII and the search for the middle way', *Historical Journal*, xli (1998), pp. 321–49, and 'The piety of Henry VIII', in N.S. Amos, A. Pettegree and H. van Nierop (eds), *The Education of a Christian Society* (Aldershot, 1999), pp. 62–88.]

5. P.L. Hughes and J.F. Larkin (eds), *Tudor Royal Proclamations* (3 vols, 1964–69), i. no. 191, pp. 284–6.
6. G.W. Bernard, review of N.L. Jones, *Faith by Statute: Parliament and the Settlement of Religion* (1982), and W.S. Hudson, *The Cambridge Connection and the Elizabethan Settlement of 1559* (Durham, North Carolina, 1980), in *The Heythrop Journal*, xxv (1984), pp. 228–32. Cf. J. Loach, 'Conservatism and consent in parliament, 1547–59', in J. Loach and R. Tittler (eds), *The Mid-Tudor Polity c. 1540–1560* (1980), pp. 21–2; T.E. Hartley (ed.), *Proceedings of the Parliaments of Elizabeth I* i. 1558–81 (Leicester, 1981), pp. 4–32.
7. W.P. Haugaard, 'Elizabeth Tudor's "Book of Devotions": a neglected clue to the Queen's life and character', *Sixteenth Century Journal*, xii (1981), pp. 79–105, esp. p. 92.
8. See for a recent discussion M. Aston, *England's Iconoclasts: vol. i Laws against Images* (Oxford, 1988), pp. 294–325. Cf. P. Collinson, 'The Church: religion and its manifestations' in J.F. Andrews (ed), *William Shakespeare: His World, His Works, His Influence* (New York, 1985), pp. 21–40. In making a case for Elizabeth's Protestantism, C. Haigh, *Elizabeth I* (1988), relies largely on evidence from 1559–60 and may not draw out the significance of Elizabeth's reluctance to go further.
9. Russell, *Causes of the English Civil War*, ch. iv. 'The Church of England 1559–1642: a church designed by a committee'; 'Religion and the English civil war', paper read at the Institute of Historical Research, University of London, 23 November 1987; N. Temperley, *The Music of the English Parish Church* (Cambridge, 2 vols, 1979), i. 39–41.
10. Haugaard, '"Book of Devotions"', p. 101.
11. Hartley, *Parliaments of Elizabeth I*, p. 51.
12. P. Collinson, 'Puritans, men of business and Elizabethan parliaments', *Parliamentary History*, vii (1988), pp. 187–211; Tyacke, *Anti-Calvinists*, pp. 164, 214; A. Pettegree, *Foreign Protestant Communities in Sixteenth-Century* (Oxford, 1986), pp. 134–9, 262, 269, 274–5; Jones, *Faith by Statute*, pp. 38–9; P.G. Lake, 'Calvinism and the English Church 1570–1635', *Past and Present*, cxiv (1987), p. 35; H.C. Porter, *Reformation and Reaction in Tudor Cambridge* (Cambridge, 1958), pp. 373–4.
13. F. Shriver, 'Hampton Court revisited: James I and the puritans', *Journal of Ecclesiastical History*, xxxiii (1982), p. 54.
14. J.P. Kenyon, *The Stuart Constitution* (2nd edn, Cambridge, 1986), p. 113.
15. Ibid., p. 114.
16. G. Hammond, 'English translations of the Bible', in R. Alter and F. Kermode, *The Literary Guide to the Bible* (1987), pp. 660–61, 663; *The Making of the English Bible* (Manchester, 1982); W. Allen, *Translating for King James* (Vanderbilt, 1969).
17. Tyacke, *Anti-Calvinists*, p. 45; N. Cranfield and K. Fincham, 'John Howson's

answers to Archbishop Abbot's accusations at his "trial" before James I at Greenwich, 10 June 1615', *Camden Miscellany*, xxix, *Camden Society*, 4th series, xxxiv (1987), p. 325.

18. J. Platt, 'Eirenical anglicans at the Synod of Dort', *Studies in Church History, Subsidia 2: Reform and Reformation: England and the Continent c.1500–c.1750* (Oxford, 1979), p. 224.
19. D. Wilkins, *Concilia Magnae Britanniae et Hiberniae* (4 vols, 1737), iv. 460.
20. Platt, 'Eirenical anglicans', p. 224.
21. Wilkins, *Concilia*, iv. 465–6.
22. As suggested by H.R. Trevor-Roper, *Catholics, Anglicans and Puritans* (1987), p. 69; contrast S. Lambert, 'Richard Montagu, Arminianism and censorship', *Past and Present*, cxxiv (1989), pp. 56, 62.
23. P. Lake, *Anglicans and Puritans? Presbyterianism and English Conformist Thought from Whitgift to Hooker* (1988), pp. 13–66, esp. pp. 24, 28. In *Moderate Puritans and the Elizabethan Church* (1982), Lake argued for an Elizabethan Protestant consensus of which Whitgift and William Whitaker, Regius Professor of Divinity at Cambridge, were both part, but his admission that in significant points, such as whether the pope was antichrist, undermines his claims for a consensus (pp. 210–11, 220–21). Cf. P. Lake, 'The significance of the Elizabethan identification of the Pope as Antichrist', *Journal of Ecclesiastical History*, xxxi (1980), p. 176; F. Heal, *Historical Journal*, xxiv (1981), pp. 201–10; P. Collinson, 'England and international Calvinism', pp. 213–14. On Hooker's debt to Whitgift, see W.D.J. Cargill-Thompson, *Studies in the Reformation: Luther to Hooker* (1980), pp. 143–7. My argument does not assume that Elizabeth I had read Hooker, or that Hooker wrote at her command or that Hooker's works were influential in Elizabeth's reign.
24. Russell, *Causes of the English Civil War*, pp. 36–7.
25. Lake, *Anglicans and Puritans?*, pp. 145–229, esp. p. 171.
26. Ibid., p. 183.
27. Tyacke has never used the term 'calvinist consensus'. It was apparently coined by Peter Lake ('Dr Tyacke's "calvinist consensus"', *Journal of Ecclesiastical History*, xxxi (1980), pp. 177–8; 'the "calvinist consensus" of the English church'; 'termed by Dr Tyacke the "calvinist consensus" of the early Jacobean church'; *Moderate Puritans*, pp. 227, 239.
28. P. White, 'The rise of Arminianism reconsidered', *Past and Present*, ci (1983), pp. 34–54.
29. Lake, 'Calvinism and the English Church', pp. 32–76, esp. pp. 39–45; *Anglicans and Puritans?*, pp. 37–40; O. O'Donovan, *On the Thirty Nine Articles: a Conversation with Tudor Christianity* (Exeter, 1986), pp. 84–6.
30. Porter, *Reformation and Reaction*, pp. 287.
31. *TLS*, 21 August 1987, p. 899.
32. Porter, *Reformation and Reaction*, pp. 373–4.
33. Cf. P. White, 'A rejoinder', *Past and Present*, cxv (1987), pp. 221–2; Lake, *Moderate Puritans*, pp. 202–5, 210–11, 216–17, 220–21, 229; Porter, *Reformation and Reaction*, pp. 354–5, 360, 367–74.
34. Tyacke, 'Puritanism, Arminianism and Counter-Revolution', pp. 123–4. Contrast Lake, 'Calvinism and the English Church', pp. 48–51; White, 'Rise of Arminianism reconsidered', pp. 37–45; 'Rejoinder', pp. 223–5.
35. F.J. Shriver, 'Hampton Court revisited: James I and the puritans', *Journal of Ecclesiastical History*, xxxiii (1982), pp. 48–71, esp. p. 59.
36. White, 'Rise of Arminianism reconsidered', pp. 38–9, 41–5.

37. F.J. Shriver, 'Orthodoxy and diplomacy: James I and the Vorstius affair', *English Historical Review*, lxxxv (1970), pp. 449–74, esp. p. 455.
38. Platt, 'Eirenical anglicans', esp. p. 240.
39. Tyacke, *Anti-Calvinists*, p. 102.
40. Wilkins, *Concilia*, iv. 465–6.
41. Trevor-Roper, *Catholics, Anglicans and Puritans*, p. 51n.
42. E.B. Fryde, D.E. Greenway, S. Porter and I. Roy (eds), *Handbook of British Chronology* (3rd edn, 1986), pp. 225–84, 289–99; Lambert, 'Richard Montagu', pp. 36–68 (the apparent shift away from 'Arminian' appointments after 1621 (p. 43), seems as much a function of the paucity of episcopal vacancies in the last years of James's reign).
43. P. Lake and K. Fincham, 'The ecclesiastical policy of King James I', *Journal of British Studies*, xxiv (1985), pp. 169–207, esp. p. 170. Cf. J.P. Somerville, 'The royal supremacy and episcopacy "jure divino"', *Journal of Ecclesiastical History*, xxxi (1983), p. 558.
44. K. Fincham, 'Prelacy and Politics: Archbishop Abbot's defence of protestant orthodoxy', (*Bulletin of the Institute of) Historical Research*, lxi (1988), pp. 36–64, esp. pp. 40–41.
45. W.B. Patterson, 'The peregrinations of Marco Antonio de Dominis 1616–24', *Studies in Church History*, xv (1978), pp. 241–57; cf. H.R. Trevor-Roper, 'The Church of England and the Greek Church in the time of Charles I', ibid., p. 218. For an account of de Dominis's career, see N. Malcolm, *De Dominis (1560–1624): Venetian, Anglican, Ecumenist and Relapsed Heretic* (1984), which, however, tends to minimise the constraints limiting James's freedom to pursue his ecumenical ideas in practice, and to take de Dominis's varying characterisations of the church in England too readily at face value (see esp. pp. 38–9, 44, 56, 61–74).
46. This point emerges against the thrust of his own argument in N. Tyacke, 'The rise of Arminianism reconsidered', *Past and Present*, cxv (1987), p. 211.
47. Collinson, *Religion of Protestants*; Lake, *Moderate Puritans*, esp. p. 208.
48. C. Haigh, 'The church of England, the Catholics and the people' in C. Haigh (ed.), *The Reign of Elizabeth I* (1985), pp. 169–220; 'The church of England and its people, 1604–42', paper read at the University of Southampton, 25 May 1983; White, 'Rejoinder', p. 219.
49. D. MacCulloch, *History Today*, xxxviii (May 1988), p. 61; *Groundwork of Christian History* (1987), p. 205. Cf. G.W.O. Addleshaw and F. Etchells, *The Architectural Setting of Anglican Worship* (1948), pp. 30–31, 40–41 on chancels.
50. Haigh, 'The church of England and its people'; J. Boulton, *Neighbourhood and Society: a London suburb in the seventeenth century* (Cambridge, 1987), p. 282 and cf. p. 286; I. Green, '"For children in yeeres and children in understanding": the emergence of the English catechism under Elizabeth and the early Stuarts', *Journal of Ecclesiastical History*, xxxvii (1986), pp. 397–425, esp. p. 413.
51. I. Green, 'Career prospects and clerical conformity in the early Stuart church', *Past and Present*, lc (1981), p. 111.
52. Haigh, 'The church of England and its people'; I. Green, 'Changing form and content of religious instruction in early modern England', paper read at Corpus Christi College, Oxford, 20 January 1987.
53. Collinson, *Religion of Protestants*, esp. ch. v; A.L. Rowse, *The England of Elizabeth: the Structure of Society* (1950), pp. 472, 513.
54. K. Sharpe, 'Archbishop Laud', *History Today*, xxxiii (August 1983), pp. 26–31. Cf. W.M. Lamont, *Godly Rule: Politics and Religion 1603–1660* (1969), pp. 66–9

(though cf. p. 165); J.S. McGee, 'William Laud and the outward face of religion', in R.L. DeMolen (ed.), *Leaders of the Reformation* (1984), esp. pp. 318, 323–7.
55. Tyacke, *Anti-Calvinists*, pp. 266–8; cf. Lambert, 'Richard Montagu'.
56. Tyacke, *Anti-Calvinists*, pp. 269–70, 84–5, 166–7, 81–2; cf. K. Sharpe, 'Archbishop Laud and the university of Oxford', in H. Lloyd-Jones, V. Pearl and B. Worden (eds), *History and Imagination: Essays in Honour of Hugh Trevor-Roper* (1981), pp. 146–64.
57. J.F. Larkin (ed.), *Stuart Royal Proclamations vol. ii. Royal Proclamations of King Charles I 1625–1646* (Oxford, 1983), p. 219. (I owe this reference to Mr. P. White.)
58. B. Worden, 'Literature and political censorship in early modern England', in A.C. Duke and C.A. Tamse (eds), *Britain and the Netherlands*, ix (1987), p. 48; S. Lambert, 'The printers and the government, 1604–37', in R. Myers and M. Harris (eds), *Aspects of Printing from 1600* (Oxford, 1987), p. 1.
59. Haigh, 'The church of England and its people'; Green, 'English catechisms', esp. pp. 411–12 and n. 65; 'Religious instruction'.
60. Fryde et al., *Handbook of British Chronology*, pp. 225–84, 289–99; Lambert, 'Richard Montagu', pp. 36–68; D. Hoyle, 'A Commons investigation of Arminianism and popery in Cambridge on the eve of the Civil War', *Historical Journal*, xxix (1986), pp. 424–5; Platt, 'Eirenical anglicans', p. 237; D.D. Wallace, *Puritans and Predestination: Grace in English Protestant Theology 1525–1695* (North Carolina, 1982), p. 94; E. More, 'John Godwin and the origins of the new Arminianism', *Journal of British Studies*, xxii (1983), esp. p. 50; and above all P. White, 'Archbishop Laud and Arminianism', paper read at the University of Southampton, 8 May 1985, and subsequent discussion.
61. Pace J.S. Morrill, 'The attack on the church of England in the Long Parliament 1640–42', in D.E. Beales and G. Best (eds), *History, Society and the Churches* (Cambridge, 1985), p. 105. Cf. G.E. Aylmer, *Rebellion or Revolution? England from Civil War to Restoration* (Oxford, 1986), p. 4.
62. D. Cressy, *Coming Over: Migration and Communication between England and New England in the Seventeenth Century* (Cambridge, 1987); A. Zakai, 'The gospel of reformation: origins of the great puritan migration', *Journal of Ecclesiastical History*, xxxvii (1986), pp. 584–602.
63. E.R.C. Brinkworth, 'The Laudian church in Buckinghamshire', *University of Birmingham Historical Journal*, v (1955–56), pp. 50–51.
64. Haigh, 'The church of England and its people'; White, 'Archbishop Laud and Arminianism'.
65. Boulton, *Neighbourhood and Society*, p. 285.
66. A. Fletcher, 'Factionalism in town and countryside: the significance of Puritanism and Arminianism', *Studies in Church History*, xvi (1979), pp. 291–300; K. Fincham, 'The Jacobean episcopate in provincial society', paper read at the Institute of Historical Research, University of London, 22 June 1987.
67. A. Fletcher, *The Outbreak of the English Civil War* (1981), pp. 284, 286–9.
68. J.S. Morrill, 'The church of England 1642–9', in J.S. Morrill (ed.), *Reactions to the English Civil War* (1982), pp. 89–114. Morrill's distinction between 'the healthy stem' of the church of England and 'the cuttings recently grafted on' by Laud (p. 113), seems to me to fly in the face of his own evidence.
69. Trevor-Roper, *Catholics, Anglicans and Puritans* (1987), pp. 40–119, esp. pp. 103, 113; J.S.A. Adamson, 'The Vindiciae Veritatis 1654 and the political creed of Viscount Saye and Sele', *Historical Research*, lx (1987), pp. 45–63; R. Clifton, 'The fear of Catholics in England from 1637 to 1645, principally from central

sources', University of Oxford D.Phil. thesis, 1967, ch. 7, esp. pp. 301–4, 322, 328. On the mobilisation of the Commons see C.S.L. Davies, 'Popular religion and the Pilgrimage of Grace', in A. Fletcher and J. Stevenson, *Order and Disorder in Early Modern England* (Cambridge, 1985), pp. 58–91.
70. J. Fielding, 'Opposition to the personal rule of Charles I: the diary of Robert Woodford, 1637–1647', *Historical Journal*, xxxi (1988), pp. 778–80.
71. Russell, *Causes of the English Civil War*'; Foster, 'Church policies of the 1630s', pp. 193–223.
72. O.U. Kalu, 'Continuity in change: bishops of London and religious dissent in early Stuart England', *Journal of British Studies*, xviii (1978), pp. 28–45.
73. J. Davies, 'The perception of Arminianism in the early seventeenth century', paper read at St John's College, Oxford, 1 May 1984; 'The genesis of the Laudian altar policy', paper read at the Institute of Historical Research, University of London, 11 March 1985; 'The book of sports (1633) reconsidered', paper read at the History Faculty Library, Oxford, 17 November 1987.
74. Hughes, *Pastors and Visionaries: Religion and Secular Life in Late Medieval Yorkshire* (Woodbridge, 1988). Cf. J. Catto, 'Religion under Henry V', in G.L. Harriss, *Henry V: the Practice of Kingship* (Oxford, 1985), pp. 97–116.
75. K. Fincham, 'Pastoral roles of the English episcopate in Canterbury province, 1603–1625', University of London PhD thesis, 1985 [now published as *Prelate and Pastor* (Oxford, 1992)].
76. A. Hughes, 'Thomas Dugard and his circle in the 1630s – a "parliamentary-puritan" connection?', *Historical Journal*, xxix (1986), pp. 771–93, esp. pp. 779–83.
77. R.M. Smuts, 'Public ceremony and royal charisma: the English royal entry in London, 1485–1642', in A.L. Beier, D. Cannadine and J.M. Rosenheim (eds), *The First Modern Society: Essays in English History in Honour of Lawrence Stone* (Cambridge, 1989), pp. 89–93; J. Richards, '"His nowe majestie" and the English monarchy: the kingship of Charles I before 1641', *Past and Present*, cxiii (1986), pp. 70–96; W. Macray (ed.), *Clarendon's History of the Rebellion* (Oxford, 6 vols, 1888), i. 125; F. Heal, 'The archbishops of Canterbury and the practice of hospitality', *Journal of Ecclesiastical History*, xxxiii (1982), pp. 559, 563.
78. K. Sharpe, *English Historical Review*, ciii (1988), p. 207; C. Hill, *Economic Problems of the Church* (Oxford, 1965); Fincham, 'The Jacobean episcopate in provincial society'; Rodes, *Lay authority*, pp. 190–91, 221; Kenyon, *Stuart Constitution*, pp. 135–6; M. Ingram, *Church Courts, Sex and Marriage in England, 1570–1640* (Cambridge, 1987), pp. 365–7 (though he draws different conclusions about Laud, p. 368).
79. M.L. Schwarz, 'Lay anglicanism and the crisis of the English church in the early seventeenth century', *Albion*, xiv (1982), p. 18; cf. Trevor-Roper, 'The church of England and the Greek church', pp. 213–40.
80. A. Foster, 'Church policies of the 1630s', in R. Cust and A. Hughes (eds), *Conflict in early Stuart England* (1989), p. 202.
81. J. Jewel, *An Apologie of the Church of England* (1562), ff. 16v–17r.
82. J. Phillips, *The Reformation of Images: the Destruction of Art in England, 1535–1660* (Berkeley, 1973), p. 141; W. Hunt, *The Puritan Moment: the Coming of Revolution in an English County* (Cambridge, Mass., 1983), pp. 179–80.
83. W. Laud, *Works* (6 vols, 1853), v. 421.
84. Green, 'Career prospects', pp. 112–14; Addleshaw and Etchells, *Architectural Setting*, pp. 118, 141–3.
85. J.G. Hoffman, 'The puritan revolution and the "beauty of holiness" at

Cambridge', *Proceedings of the Cambridge Antiquarian Society*, lxxii (1982–83), pp. 94–105.
86. Green, 'Career pospects', p. 112; Fincham, 'Pastoral roles of the English episcopate', p. 279; S.B. Babbage, *Puritanism and Richard Bancroft* (1962), p. 217.
87. Clifton, 'Fear of Catholics', pp. 71, 75, 124 and ch. 3 in general; C. Hibbard, *The Popish Plot* (1982).
88. S.P. Salt, 'The origins of Sir Edward Dering's attack on the ecclesiastical hierarchy c. 1625–1640', *Historical Journal*, xxx (1987), pp. 21–52. Such an analysis would also fit the evidence in Hughes, 'Thomas Dugard', better than Hughes's principal conclusions.
89. P. Lake, 'Anti-popery: the structure of a prejudice', in R. Cust and A. Hughes (eds), *Conflict in Early Stuart England* (1989), pp. 72–106.
90. This has continued to be an important and lively subject of debate since 1990. P. White, *Predestination, Policy and Polemic* (Cambridge, 1991) and K. Sharpe, *The Personal Rule of Charles I* (1992), esp. pp. 275–402, have amplified in satisfying detail the claims sketched in their papers referred to above. J. Davies, *The Caroline Captivity of the Church* (Oxford, 1992) responds to the claims made here, as does N. Tyacke, 'Anglican attitudes: some recent writings on English religious history, from the Reformation to the Civil War', *Journal of British Studies*, xxxv (1996), pp. 139–67. D. MacCulloch, 'The myth of the English Reformation', *Journal of British Studies*, xxx (1991), pp. 1–19, is a succinct statement of the general interpretation that my paper challenges. K. Fincham (ed.), *The early Stuart Church, 1603–1642* (1993) is a useful collection of essays. The most important recent work includes A. Milton, *Catholic and Reformed* (Cambridge, 1995), on attitudes to the papacy; I. Green, *The Christian's ABC* (Oxford, 1996) on catechisms; K.A. Newman, 'Holiness in beauty? Roman catholics, Arminians and the aesthetics of religion in early Caroline England', *Studies in Church History*, xxviii (1992), pp. 303–12; J.D. Maltby, *Prayer Book and People in Elizabethan and Early Stuart England* (Cambridge, 1998) (though the significance of the petitions of 1640–41 is misunderstood); and (a very important paper) A. Walsham, 'The parochial basis of Laudianism revisited', *Journal of Ecclesiastical History*, xlix (1998), pp. 620–51. Interestingly the focus of current investigation (notably Nicholas Tyacke's and Kenneth Fincham's work-in-progress on what they see as the Laudian altar-policy of the 1630s) is much less calvinist theology but rather liturgical practice.

11
History and Postmodernism

Among the postmodernist charges are that history fails to acknowledge the ambiguous nature of representation, that it endorses the naive belief in the discovery of past reality/truth, that it cannot accept the collapse of signification, that it continues to insist on the myth of disinterested historians, and finally, that it persists in the singular notion of explanation through contextualization based on simple inference.

... the discipline was unavoidably implicated in the present order of society, and could not, therefore, be regarded as a self-effacing, or non-ideological undertaking dedicated to the pursuit of certaintist truth.

The questioning of empiricism as an access to knowledge has become so widespread today as to constitute a forceful provocation to the very concept of history as a separate or licit epistemology.

... the literary post-structuralist movement since the early 1980s has had its greatest impact on the discipline in the rejection of the empiricist submission that language mirrors its objects and thus can adequately represent past reality.

Can we say empiricism has ever legitimately constituted history as a distinctive kind of knowledge? It has probably never been possible for us to study the past and discover its single real meaning. Should we not explore the notion that history as a professional discipline is at best only a representation of itself rather than a genuine past reality that transcends its own act of representation?

What if the past – defined as our knowledge of it – does not exist until the historian writes it?

Our knowledge and understanding of the past (as *found* in the evidence) is in substantial part the product of our own minds.
    (Quotations from Alan Munslow, 'Editorial', *Rethinking History* i (1997).)

All the characteristics alleged to belong to 'the past' belong to us ... whilst we suspect that there may well be a 'real past' (an actual past) metaphorically underlying all our disparate versions of it, we 'know' that that past, that 'real referent', is ultimately inaccessible, and that all we have are our versions; the past as such doesn't exist *historically* outside of historians' textual constituitive appropriations.

... the idea of a past 'in itself' to be studied 'for its own sake' really is a hopeless ambition ... postmodernists know that the past has neither rhyme nor reason in it. That it is unfathomable, sublime, shapeless, formless.
  (Quotations from Keith Jenkins, 'Why bother with the past?', *Rethinking History*, i (1997).)

> ... for Jenkins ... history signifies little more than the symbolic inscription of the past by the historian. It is a dialogue, never a mirror. History is always fabricated, always fashioned, always invented, always literary.
>
> Proper historians think of knowledge as a spectrum ranging from hard, serious literalism at one end to soft, playful, speculative fiction at the other. But this vision must be wrong because we compose and configure our explanations as narratives employing precisely the same figurative devices as those writers traditionally located in the realm of fiction. Rather than a spectrum we should consider referentially as just one option of representation. There are many ways to skin a rabbit, and many ways to study the past. If we view history as a literary composition, as a textual construction rather than a reconstruction, we are not limiting history but emancipating it.
>
> ... the illusion that lies at the heart of historical method – the illusion of recoverable reality.
>
> (Quotations from Alan Munslow, review article, *Rethinking History*, i (1997).)
>
> Works by historians who claim to tell us 'what really happens' can be analysed, and exposed, as artefacts manipulating memory for present-day political purposes.
>
> (Arthur Calder, *History*, lxxiv (1999), p. 567.)

Implicit in all the chapters of this book, as in the general run of historical writing, is the conviction that it is possible to make valid statements about what happened in the past. Here, for example, one chapter has told the story of Sir Thomas Seymour's last years, another has offered an explanation for the fall of Anne Boleyn, and another has explored the role of the nobility in Tudor England. Often the interpretations offered by other historians have been carefully scrutinised and modified or rejected. Underlying such often detailed papers is the belief that some interpretations are nearer the truth – because more solidly grounded in the evidence and because more rigorously argued – than others. On the whole such convictions are much more commonly left unarticulated by working historians than boldly defended: they seem so obvious as not to need explanation. Yet in recent years they have come under attack, as the quotations with which this chapter begins show, and it is that challenge that has prompted the response that follows. It was first conceived as a lecture in a first-year course on Approaches to History, and it is intended above all to draw the attention of fledgling students of history to what seems to me a mistaken and harmful approach to history, and warn them against it. This approach will here for the sake of convenience (and in full awareness of the risks of simplification) be labelled 'postmodernism'. The origins of 'postmodernism' lie not in the work of historians, but rather in other disciplines, particularly philosophy, especially the ideas of Nietzsche and Heidegger, linguistics, especially Saussure, and literary theory, especially Barthes and Derrida. Their ideas have become very fashionable in departments of literature and cultural studies, especially in the new universities. They have been taken up by those who see themselves, in the words of the journal they have established, as *Rethinking History*. Most of the examples given above are taken from those who are not so much historians as would-be philosophers of history who seek to tell practising historians what is wrong with their practice. A few – but so far not many – historians have in recent years been influenced by such ideas; and, at a different level, what is best called a naive nihilism or relativism characterises the assumptions of many students. It may thus be timely for one historian deeply suspicious of 'postmodernism' to set out reasons for such suspicion.

The most immediately obvious fault with this wave of theoretical writing is that its products – especially those from departments of literature and cultural studies – are virtually unreadable. Postmodernist scholars rarely set out their claims in plain and comprehensible language. Twenty years ago the jibe went that sociology was a way of obscurely systematising the obvious. Sociologists, supported by lavish grants, would carry out research that showed, unsurprisingly, that the children of the rich did better – possessed greater lifechances, to use the jargon – than the children of the poor. But at least such studies did, when the jargon was decoded, say something about the real world, however trite. Now, however, the charge of obscuring their meaning by the use of jargon is most aptly brought against postmodernists. It would be a brave reader who claimed to grasp precisely what Saussure or Foucault or Derrida, or works of postmodernist literary theory, were about. Obscurity of expression is not, however, evidence of profundity of intellect: rebarbative jargon does not facilitate precision of thought. If something is worth saying, it is worth saying simply and clearly. It is difficult to see what is gained by the use of modish abstractions such as 'discourse' or 'contextualise' or 'problematise', or 'reconfigure' or 'multivalent meanings'. It is a salutary mental exercise always mentally to rewrite and paraphrase such terms whenever they are encountered in order to see what, if any, meaning is being intended. But should not the reader and listener be spared such effort, if only out of courtesy?

As well as being jargon-ridden, much of what postmodernists in literary theory and cultural studies produce seems to be simply a performance, intellectual pyrotechnics, intended to display the scholar's erudition and range, rather than a serious effort to say something worthwhile and verifiable about its subject. The suspicion is strong that it would say just as much, or just as little, if one added 'not' to each proposition in this kind of performance. Take Simon Schama's *Landscapes and History* for example. To sustain the claim that 'landscape is the work of the mind',[1] Schama juxtaposes a bewildering series of supposed connections. It is tempting to caricature this style of writing. Make some bold abstract claim involving fashionable themes. 'The body is the representation of anger'. Support the assertion by a reference to some obscure work with a portentous title such as *Corporeal Ire* from an obscure foreign university press. Move on to quote in copious detail a description of some violent act – a sixteenth-century example might be the third duke of Norfolk's servants stamping on his wife's breasts till blood ran (he made his women bind me till the blood came out at my finger ends, his estranged wife complained, and they 'pynnacullyt me and satt on my brest till I spett blod').[2] Leap across the centuries and countries. Muse on the parallels with Anthony Burgess's novel *Clockwork Orange*. Seize the chance to switch to the film of the novel. Then switch genres again and discuss the cruelty of Turandot in Puccini's opera. And then leap on to some new abstraction. What is wrong here? A preference for superficial similarities of form over a rounded study of the events, books, operas in their proper context. It would be reassuring to conclude that all this was just a caricature, but that would be complacent. And what of value has been said?

Of course, that postmodern academics in departments of literature and cultural studies write obscurely and impenetrably does not mean that they do not have anything to say. They do. But what they have to say is, it will be claimed here, wrong and damaging. The most important point is that postmodernists deny the possibility of objective truth. To deny truth is not, of course, an intellectual invention of the twentieth century. How we know what we know has exercised philosophers since the beginning of philosophy. The best brief discussion of truth is in St John's Gospel.[3] Jesus is being interrogated by Pontius Pilate.

> Pilate therefore said unto him, Art thou a king then? Jesus answered, Thou sayest that I am a king. To this end was I born, and for this cause came I into the world, that I should bear witness unto the truth. Every one that is of the truth heareth my voice.
> Pilate saith unto him, What is truth?

Postmodernists deny the possibility of objective truth. For them everything is rhetoric, propaganda, invention, opinion, self-fashioning, marketing, spin-doctoring. Truth is no more than what someone thinks or wants to be truth. Some postmodernists hold that there are no authors, only readers: it is, they claim, wrong to suppose that authors write books that express their meaning which is then read and understood by readers. Instead, for them, it is readers that bring their own meanings to what they read. We cannot think except through language – and words have a subtle way of determining our cast of thought; language can never truly represent reality. That obviously prompts subversive doubts about the study of history. If the history we write is simply an exercise in rhetoric, if the sources that historians use are not evidence but simply texts, that is exercises in rhetoric in themselves, which every historian necessarily reads in a different way, then anything goes, everything is equally valid. It is not possible to tell the truth about the past or to write an objective history of the past, postmodernists say; to make such a claim is merely a modern ideological position.

But the postmodernist assertion is simply wrong. There is an insuperable difficulty with propositions such as 'there is no objective truth'. What is the status of that proposition? If it expresses the truth, then there is at least one objectively true statement that can be made, which would seem to undermine the claim that objective truth cannot be found. If that statement is false, then there must be some objective truth. In short, propositions such as 'there is no objective truth' are contradictory, self-refuting. Similarly the proposition that 'all philosophical statements are merely opinions' invalidates itself: does that proposition itself count for no more than a mere opinion? In the same way the claim 'all opinions are equally valid' is implicitly claiming that it is more valid than the opposite claim that 'some opinions are better founded than others': but in claiming greater validity for itself, it is refuting its own proposition that all opinions are equally valid. It is not logically possible to hold both claims at the same time, and yet the first cannot be as valid as its opposite. The same problem arises from the claim that 'there is no such thing as a fixed meaning: meanings are always plural': but if that claim is valid, there is at least one meaning that is fixed. Similarly the claim 'truth is always relative to a particular society' provokes the rejoinder that if it is true, then there is one truth that is always true, and not relative. In just the same way the proposition that 'human beings do not have access to the truth' shows (however unhelpfully), if it is true, that in one important matter, they do. These illustrations in self-refutation make a simple but profound philosophical point, worth emphasising and pondering. A further related consideration may be seen in the curious way that those who deny objective truth and profess to believe that everything is rhetoric none the less see themselves as uniquely unaffected by that rhetoric, believing that what they say in denying objective truth is right, while lambasting as wrong those who uphold objective truth. Yet if they can inoculate themselves against rhetoric, and validly criticise others as wrong, that implies the possibility of seeing objectively. To deny truth is thus logically self-refuting. And truth is implicit in logical reasoning. Mr Smith is either alive or dead. A lecturer is either standing in front of the class or not. It not possible for an historian to be at the same time both delivering a lecture in Southampton and reading manuscripts in the Public Record Office at Kew. To hold that the historian is simultaneously both in Southampton and in London is to descend into absurd contradiction. It is not possible both to assert and to deny the same proposition and continue to talk sense.

Of course, it is a difficult philosophical exercise to prove that we exist and that we know that we exist. There have been philosophers who have denied the existence of the material world. The best answer to their claims was given by Samuel Johnson. When Boswell, his biographer, remarked of George Berkeley's denial of the existence of the material world, it is impossible to refute it, Johnson, 'striking his foot with mighty force against a large stone, till he rebounded from it', answered with unforgettable alacrity, 'I refute it *thus*'.[4] The material world does exist. Anyone attempting to walk through a wall would be unsuccessful, and anyone trying to use force, perhaps by running at the wall, would be lucky to escape injury. Marcel Ayme wrote a marvellous short-story about *Le passe-muraille* – the man who could walk through walls unhindered and unharmed. But that was a story. And the existence of the material world is a salutary reminder that truth is not something that anyone can make up. Some postmodernists have gone so far as to claim that modern scientific and technological knowledge is equally uncertain and relative, a social construct rather than a set of true propositions about the material world, claims recently ridiculed by a physicist, Alan Sokal, who sent an article seemingly endorsing them to *Social Text*, only to reveal after it had been published that it was a hoax.[5]

Postmodernists also appear to deny the difference between form and content. But this is to lose touch with reality. Containers hold liquids, not the other way round. Writers, not readers, write books. A forged £20 note – or for that matter a voucher giving a discount on the next box of detergent – may have the same form as a real £20 note, but even a postmodernist would not fail to see the difference.

Postmodernists, however, profess to deny the distinction between what is true and what is made up. Everything for them is invented (or 'constructed'). Historians, they say, are just telling stories about the past. There may be some set ways of going about doing this, but, postmodernists say, these are like the rules of football and tennis, quite arbitrary, and unconnected with what is being discussed. Postmodernists deny that historians study sources in a search for evidence that bears on the problems they are pursuing. For postmodernists, all sources are simply texts, rhetorical constructs open to a multiplicity of equally valid meanings.

The only response that an historian can make is that this is just tosh. It is indeed true that part of what historians do is to tell stories about the past. Especially when teaching very young children, telling them stories is an excellent way to engage their attention and capture their imagination. But the word 'story' is misleading here since it can mean both a continuous account of a set of events and a fictional account of such events. Historians tell stories in the first of these senses, but not in the second. Novelists consciously make things up. Of course, their stories deal with the human predicament, and their characters cannot but be influenced by their own experiences, but they are not intending to give accurate detailed descriptions of real people. But historians do. Suppose this collection of essays included in a paper about Henry VIII a wholly invented story about, say his fourth wife, the one between Jane Seymour who died in October 1537 and Anne of Cleves whom he married in January 1540 ... It would not be difficult to wax lyrical about the attractions of this fictitious wife – but such a paper would be historical fiction, not history. There is a crucial difference between the writing of history and the writing of historical novels. Historians may not invent their evidence. Would an historian studying Tudor noblemen but disappointed by the lack of revealing personal correspondence throwing light on their political and religious sympathies, or another historian studying early Tudor parliaments but thwarted by the absence of any diary offering evidence for debates, be justified in fabricating such hoped-for but missing 'sources'? Manifestly they would not – because what historians seek to do is to construct their story and their explanations of what happened in the past not on the basis of their fantasies and wishful thinking but from their critical reading of the surviving evidence. Scholarly history rests on sources, as a glance at the critical apparatus of any monograph or article in an historical journal will show. Each detail is backed up by a reference, the point of which is not to parade the scholar's learning but simply to make it possible for others to look at the evidence used and, crucially, to verify it. In October 1536 the fourth earl of Shrewsbury was reimbursed for paying coat and conduct money (travelling expenses) and wages to 3947 men on horseback together with 39 captains and 38 petty captains whom he had raised 'against the rebellions in Lincolnshire and Yorkshire' in October 1536. How is that known? It is not historians' invention. The details come from a statement of account showing how many men were paid how much for varying periods of military service. That document is in the Public Record Office,[6] where anyone can go and read it. If anyone goes to the PRO and checks, they will find that the account does indeed say that the earl of Shrewsbury was reimbursed for raising these men. It is possible to exploit the details further, as has been done in Chapter 1 above, to show how many men Shrewsbury could raise and how quickly – 3654 of them by 9 October (it was on 4 October that he had heard of the rebellion and sent out requests for men to assemble[7]). For many earlier periods of history, that kind of detailed evidence simply does not exist, and consequently historians must rely on myths and fictions. Carefully studied, they nonetheless can be highly illuminating. *Beowulf*, for example, has much to teach about the world and mentalities of Anglo-Saxon warrior nobles. But the value of myths as sources to historians depends on how closely they reflect the realities of the world in which they emerged: it is the extent to which myths (perhaps despite themselves) convey accurate information about the activities and values of the society in which they were made that makes them useful for historians, not the extent to which they are fictions.

The point about the difference between truth and fiction is worth taking further. Suppose someone not only invents something but actually lies – says something known not to be true. Postmodernists would, it seems, deny that that is possible. But suppose a group of students was arrested by the police who then put illegal drugs in their pockets, before then charging them with the possession of illegal drugs: would that not be monstrous? Or suppose one student accused another of plagiarising an essay, or stealing money, or spreading diseases. Postmodernists would have to say that since everything is subjective, those accusations were just points of view, and no better, and no worse, than any other. Others might in such circumstances sympathise with Solzenhitsyn that lying was worse than physical oppression.

Of course, historians do not start from a clean sheet: they bring all sorts of preconceptions with them when they study problems and consider evidence. Any historian's choice of subject on which to research reflects his or her interests and values. But it would be wrong to read too much into that. First, any historian's starting point is not just his or her own interests, but what has been written up till then about the matter he or she is studying. Secondly, what historians do is to find evidence that would throw light on the problems they are studying. What they read is not chosen arbitrarily to reflect their interests and prejudices. They read everything that they can find that is relevant. Moreover, it is a very common experience for historians to find that a hypothesis which they had formulated has had to be modified, indeed discarded, because of the weight of evidence discovered against it.

When historians study evidence, the methods and procedures they use are not arbitrary but closely related to what they are studying. They try to look at everything; they acquire the linguistic, palaeographic and diplomatic skills needed; they subject all the sources relevant to their inquiry to systematic, quizzical and disciplined examination; they look out for what corroborates and what undermines hypotheses they begin to formulate; they read and re-read what other historians have made of the same problems, and often talk and argue with them. Before any historical writing receives a PhD or appears in print in an historical journal or under the imprint of a university press, it is subjected to searching 'peer review' by established specialists. All that is not playing a game but rather following procedures inherent in the field of study. And good historians have always been aware of the complexities of the sources from which they work. They are alive to the possibility of forgery or embellishment. They are acutely aware of the circumstances in which a document was made. They are sensitive to the ways in which language is used. They are willing to tease out meaning from any potentially relevant sources, whether administrative records or novels or buildings.

Postmodernists who deny the possibility of objective truth would deny that such intellectual activity can bear fruit: no one can be certain that they have found the truth. But here they are confusing two different points. The existence of truth is one thing; the ability of humans to grasp it is rather different. But the fact that we as humans must often remain ignorant or uncertain about many things, or that we have often made mistakes in our portrayal of the past, does not mean that there is no truth. If we were God, enjoying divine omniscience, we would know the truth about things. Since we are not God, we have to accept our uncertainty. But that does not mean that there is no truth, just that we cannot be certain of it. Our knowledge as humans is not infinite. We cannot see into other people's hearts and minds and grasp their exact feelings and motivations in the way that God could. As historians studying the past, we have to depend on what evidence survives from the past, incomplete and often opaque. That historians are often engaged in chipping away at tenaciously held beliefs about the past, showing them to be unfounded, does not mean that there is no historical truth, only that some 'grand narratives', to borrow the postmodernists' term, (for example, the marxist theory of economic development, or the protestant narrative of the Reformation, or the Whig interpretation of the rise of parliament), are wrong, or at least misleading, because in crucial respects they are not true, that is to say that what they claim does not correspond to the evidence properly studied. But to unsettle an orthodoxy does not entail the dismissal of the possibility of truth. Moreover, if historians often disagree, and fiercely debate vexed issues, that does not show that history cannot be true. In most such debates there is much that is agreed: disagreements occur over questions on which certainty is always difficult for lack of evidence, for example the question of Anne Boleyn's adultery. But to draw from that the conclusion that there is no truth is unwarranted. Anne Boleyn either committed adultery, as she was accused in 1536, or she did not. As an historian working on what I freely admit is scrappy evidence, I cannot know for sure, although in Chapter 4 I have put forward my reasons for concluding that she did. If we were God, we would know the truth.

Postmodernists claim that because we cannot be certain that we know the truth, all attempts to declare the truth are equally valid or invalid. But that is a further confusion. Just because we cannot be certain does not mean that everything we say is equally worthwhile or equally worthless. It is better to think of a spectrum running from total certainty at one end to total uncertainty at the other. Humans cannot always be totally certain about things – though it is worth pointing out again that there are many things about which we can be totally certain (such as the prospect of injury if we tried to run against a brick wall). But there are degrees of probability and degrees of certainty with which we can grasp things. We can carry out a series of appropriate inquiries and tests and we can reasonably conclude that there is a higher or lower level of probability. That is the way in which scientific and medical research is conducted – and it is simply wrong to deny that much scientific and medical knowledge is certain. In matters historical, there are a great many about which we can indeed be pretty certain. Most historical events are not seriously open to dispute. Henry VIII was king of England from 1509 to 1547. He married six times. During his reign England broke from Rome. The monasteries were dissolved. It is hard to see on what grounds anyone could dispute such points. Someone who claimed that Henry did not exist, or that he died in 1533, or that he never married, or that papal authority continued to run in England, or that the monasteries survived, would be wrong, wrong, wrong, wrong and wrong. A more serious example of such error is to be found in those who deny the Holocaust of European Jews in the 1940s. The Holocaust happened. In no way can that be treated as simply a personal opinion, a text, a discourse, no more valid and no more true than the claim that it did not happen. But once it is accepted that the Holocaust did happen, and that denials of the Holocaust are pernicious untruths, then in turn it must be accepted that it is possible to say that some things are true and that other things are false. And once that step has been taken, the rug has been pulled from under the postmodernist stance that there is no truth, only opinions, and that all opinions are equally valid.

Much of what historians do is to establish what happened, who did what to whom and when, and to determine with what degrees of certainty particular conclusions can be drawn. Doing this is not a low-level activity but rather a foundation for everything else. There can be uncertainty and debate about such points of detail. When did Toby Lowe (the later Lord Aldington) leave Austria in May 1945? The date of his departure – whether on 22 or on 23 May – has been seen as a key detail in deciding whether or not he was directly involved in the expulsion of Yugoslav and Cossack prisoners of war, the issue in the Aldington–Tolstoy libel trial of 1989.

But historians also deal with larger questions that are more complex. In the early sixteenth century England was a catholic country; a century later it had seemingly become a protestant country. How had that shift come about? In the sixteenth century England was predominantly an agrarian society; by the nineteenth century industrialisation had dramatically changed it. How had that change come about? In the twentieth century two world wars occurred: why? Such questions are the stuff of historical debate and it is such matters that are likely to occupy most undergraduate students of history, especially in their first and second years. Such large themes, involving the relationships and interactions of huge numbers of men and women, are obviously more complex and less likely to lend themselves to some simple statement, though one might still conclude (for example) that it was Hitler who was responsible for the Second World War. And the vigour of historical debate does not lend any support to the postmodernist position that all interpretations are equally valid. Manifestly some arguments about the causes of the Reformation, or the Industrial Revolution, or the Second World War are more soundly based on the sources, more intelligently and logically reasoned, than others. Whenever historians criticise each other's arguments, they are implicitly accepting that some arguments are better than others.

Nor are postmodernists right when they assert that claims to truth are no more than expressions of power and self-interest, that historians are simply reflecting their own values and culture when they purport to write about the past. When an historian come across a source, it is of course necessary to ask, who said it and why? But the truth and the validity of a claim is independent of the motives for its expression. Someone who denies the Holocaust may be seeking political power in order to pursue a racist ideology, but that in itself tells us nothing about the Holocaust. What proves that the Holocaust happened is the overwhelming weight of evidence, not the wicked motives of those who deny it now.

Thus far postmodernist claims – especially the denial of truth and the treatment of all opinions as equally valid – have been taken at their own estimation.

Such positions have here been shown to be philosophically untenable: and their applicability in historical inquiry dubious. But postmodernists do not always practise what they appear to preach. For all their claims, postmodernists in their own practice do subscribe to a series of propositions which are not far from claims to truth. Despite denying that authors intend to convey meanings through their writings, postmodernists themselves urge on their readers a very definite position. They claim an intellectual superiority for their own methods and insights, and over scholars such as myself who reject them. Irony and ridicule are their preferred weapons here, much preferred to reasoned argument: instead those who are unpersuaded are mocked as naive and unsophisticated. Postmodernists claim to possess the key to the understanding of political, social and cultural matters. All that is rather odd, given their belief that truth is relative and simply the expression of a current ideology. How can postmodernists tell anyone that they are wrong, or holding untenable positions, or biased, or distorted or old-fashioned? By what criteria can they do this without contradicting their belief in the relativity of truth?

What fundamental social truths do postmodernists tend to espouse? First, they tend to assume that all human relationships, including sexual relationships, even conversation, are relationships of power, zero-sum games, in short an intellectual mercantilism in which participants either win or lose, and that all forms of cultural expression are weapons in such struggles. It is an act of intellectual legerdemain to make such an assumption the starting point in any historical inquiry. It can be no more than a hypothesis that needs testing against the evidence in each case.

Secondly, postmodernists often rely on unarticulated monocausal explanations: class, or gender, or sexuality, or race, or self-interest, or whatever is currently fashionable, is held to be the key to the understanding of everything, so offering a short-cut to learning or virtue: yet something that explains everything explains nothing; and the devil lies in relating general theories to particular events. Postmodernists, however, often seek to deploy the key they claim to have found. They seek to augment what their sources reveal in the desire to tease out their supposed hidden assumptions: they express a conviction that there is always something between the lines and that it is more important than what is on the lines, to the point of often claiming their sources as authority for the opposite of what they appear to say, or for things they do not even mention. But that is a dangerous step on the road to saying that the sources say what those who study them want them to say.

Thirdly, postmodernism is often associated with an extravagantly negative attitude to modern western society, echoing the claims of marxists in earlier intellectual generations, though the case is rarely systematically spelled out, and would seem, as far as material progress goes, to fly in the face of the evidence. There are many features of modern society that are not agreeable. But in terms of scientific, technological and medical knowledge, and economic development, modern western society surpasses those that came before, and remains a model to those outside.

Fourthly, postmodernists tend to disregard the role of individuals and the place of contingency in human affairs, stressing instead vast impersonal forces. In this too they are Marx's heirs. Marxist scholars long emphasised the role of economic factors and played down the role of individual men and women in human development. Obviously the relationship of individuals to the society in which they live is of crucial importance. But the role of individuals is vital to grasp too. A striking illustration is offered by Archie Brown's study of *The Gorbachev Factor*. Brown's emphasis on Gorbachev's personal actions offers a powerful riposte, showing that if someone other than Gorbachev had become General Secretary of the Soviet Communist Party in 1985, the world would now be a very different place. That is not to say that what happened was what Gorbachev wanted or planned, simply to note that individuals matter and that they and their actions can affect the course of events very profoundly.

Oddly, while denying the role of individuals generally, postmodernists highlight and idolise individuals of their own persuasion. High priests of postmodernism – Derrida, Foucault – are invoked as semi-divine authorities and gurus. Postmodernist writing becomes a highly self-referential genre, a modern scholasticism: claims are supported by reference to other gurus, not to evidence. Those who take part often set themselves apart and above the rest of us, a gathered church, superior, exclusive, using a private cant, intolerant, not least of criticism or even questions, and tending to demonise those who are not wholly involved as enemies, or worse, traitors. It fosters a climate in which it can sometimes seem dangerous to voice contrary arguments or to express what one sincerely believes to be the truth, though this is more a disquieting tendency rather than some desperately dangerous immediate threat.

Where does postmodernism come from and why have so many in departments of literature and cultural study followed it? Does postmodernism itself merely reflect the caprices of a particular intellectual generation: is it, for example, no more than the intellectual detritus left by the discrediting of Marxism and the collapse of the Soviet empire? The origins of postmodernism is an intriguing but difficult question. And any answers, however embarrassing, do not in themselves show that postmodernism is wrong. Nietzsche, Heidegger, Derrida, Foucault must be seen in the general context of early and mid-twentieth-century European thought, and that is obviously a large issue. Do the collapse of the Austro-Hungarian Empire in the First World War and the horrors of the Second World War help to explain the rise of nihilist-cum-existentialist philosophies? At a different level, no doubt part of the explanation is psychological. It is interesting that some of the exponents of these approaches were involved in the Nazi regime or sympathetic to Russian or Chinese communism, in short that they were admirers of state power. That does not, to repeat, of itself invalidate these ideas, but they do perhaps appeal specially to admirers of different kinds of strong government. 'Whatever is, is right.' Many of these European intellectuals were men of great learning, but perhaps their approaches have had a particular appeal in an age of mass higher education. Not all of the vastly increased numbers of students have been as qualified and hard working as they would need to be to make their studies worthwhile – and for such students, and particularly for their teachers marking their essays and examination scripts, there may have been some attraction in the notion that all opinions are equally valid, that there is no truth: it makes it possible to give good marks and good degrees to not-so-good students. At a different level, many scholars of literature may have welcomed anything that made their subject seem more 'scientific' and not just a matter of personal feeling: how can emotional responses to plays, poems and novels – the approach of the Cambridge critic F.R. Leavis – constitute an intellectual discipline? Another factor may have been the unwillingness of anthropologists studying the myths of what they have become reluctant to call primitive peoples to criticise, let alone to condemn them. They treated their myths not as demonstrably wrong, though in the right hands capable of revealing a good deal about the lives and values of the people, but as advanced and sophisticated metaphorical representations of their world, that modern anthropologists could decode. It is entirely proper to recognise the achievements of primitive societies, but greater boldness in asserting the superiority of our values, what Harold Wilson once called 'the eternal decencies', would not be amiss. Cannibalism and human sacrifice are indeed wrong, the practice of female circumcision hard to defend. Making such claims is not the mindless imposition of European values on those of a different way of life; suggesting that 'some societies have evolved more complex cultures and modes of organisation than others' is neither racist nor colonialist. After all, as Robert Conquest has pointed out, the proposition that 'all cultures should be treated equally', as the postmodernists would wish, implies that a society that does treat all cultures equally is in their eyes superior to one that does not: once again the postmodernist case, when closely examined, refutes itself.

Instead of succumbing to the postmodernist heresy as presented by the siren voices of modish commentators, students of history should rather reflect on what practising historians actually do. Historians work hard, reading both in the sources and other historians' books and articles. Their ideal is to read everything, to consider anything that might conceivably be useful. They do not knowingly suppress or omit material; nor do they skimp, take short-cuts, or accept someone else's reading without checking. In short, they bring to their work their reasoning and imagination. The greater those powers, the better their history. Moreover historical learning is cumulative: it is not going round in circles, but rising in a spiral. It is not necessarily the case that the newest works are the best – far from it. But collectively, the writings (say) of British historians over the past generation are impressive. As a result we know more and understand better a range of topics. That can be put to a straightforward test. Students should be asked to choose any historical subject; they should then first read what was written about it up to 1950, and then what has been written about it since 1950, and evaluate what has been added to learning and to understanding since then. Such reflection on the practice of historians will confirm the conviction, more often implicit than articulated, that there is a truth about the past. Historians cannot always be certain of it, though they often can, and they recognise in their practice that some accounts of the past are better, because, as the fruit of hard work and imagination, they are closer to that truth, than others.

Notes

1. S. Schama, *Landscape and Memory* (1995), p. 7.
2. *LP*, XII ii 143.
3. John, xviii. 37–8.
4. C. Hibbert (ed.), *Boswell's Life of Johnson* (1979), p. 122.
5. P. Boghossian, 'What the Sokal hoax ought to teach us', *TLS*, 13 December 1986, p. 14. Cf. A. Sokal and J. Bricmont, *Intellectual Impostures* (1999).
6. PRO SP1/110 ff. 67–68; summarised in *LP*, XI 930.
7. *LP*, XI 536–7.

Index

Abbot, George (d. 1633), archbishop of Canterbury 197, 200, 208
Abbot, Robert 196
Act of Appeals (1533) 112
Act of Six Articles (1539) 192
Adamson, Patrick 197
agriculture 37
Aird, Ian 165
Aldington, Lord, *see* Lowe, Toby
Alsop, Jim 4–5
Amadas, Mistress 98
Amicable Grant 1, 17, 23–4, 29, 30–1, 53
Andrewes, Lancelot (d. 1626), bishop of Winchester 196, 200
Angus, earl of, *see* Douglas, Archibald
Anne of Cleves 121, 134, 136
Appleyard, Alice 161
Appleyard, John 163, 164, 166, 167, 168, 171
Appleyard, Robert 161
architecture 3, 175–87
  new houses 175–6, 177–8, 179
  palaces 176–7, 178–9, 180, 183, 185
  styles 179–87
Arminianism 191, 199, 200, 201–9
Arminius 191
Arran, earl of, *see* Hamilton, James
Arundel, earl of, *see* Fitzalan, Henry; Fitzalan, Thomas
Arundell, Charles 168
Arundell, Sir Thomas 31
Ashley, Kate 137, 138, 149
Aske, Robert 27
Athequa, George, bishop of Llandaff 86
Attlee, Clement 129
Audley, Lord, *see* Tuchet, James
Audley, Thomas 112, 113
Ayme, Marcel 221–2

Bacon, Nicholas, Lord Keeper 176, 195
Bainton, Sir Edward 98

Bancroft, Richard (d. 1610), archbishop of Canterbury 199
Baro, Peter 198
Barthes, Roland 218
Barton, Elizabeth 119
Bath, earl of, *see* Bourchier, John
Bayly, Dr 169, 170
Beaufort, Henry (d. 1447), Cardinal Bishop of Winchester 139
Bedford, earl of, *see* Russell, John
Bellin, Nicholas 181, 183–4
Benet, William 66, 73
Bergavenny, Lord, *see* Nevill, George
Berkeley, George 221
Bess of Hardwick, *see* Hardwick, Elizabeth
Bible 115, 196, 220
Biddle, Martin 183
bill of annates (1532) 111
Block, J.S. 51
Blount, Thomas 163, 164, 166–7, 170, 171, 172
Bodiam Castle, Sussex 180
Boleyn, Anne 2, 3, 5, 6, 12, 24, 63, 64
  adultery 80, 82–3, 88–99, 225
  fall of 80–99
  miscarriage 81–3
  relationship with Henry VIII 80–1, 83, 85
  witchcraft accusation 81–2
  Wolsey's fall and 51, 52, 54–5, 63
Boleyn, George (d. 1536), Viscount Rochford 80, 84, 85, 87, 92–4, 96
Boleyn, Mary 90, 94
Boleyn, Thomas (1477–1539), viscount Rochford and later earl of Wiltshire 58, 61
  fall of Wolsey and 51, 52, 54, 73
Bonner, Edmund 70
border regions 32–3
Boswell, James 221

Bourbon, duke of 16
Bourchier, John (1499–1560), second earl of Bath 23
Brandon, Charles (c.1485–1545), first duke of Suffolk 29, 64, 88
   fall of Wolsey and 51, 52, 53, 54, 56–8, 61, 64–5
   house 175
Brereton, Sir William 80, 87–8, 92, 95, 96, 146
Brooke, Willoughby de, Lord, *see* Willoughby, Robert
Brown, Archie 228
Browne, Sir Anthony 86, 90, 176
Browne, Elizabeth, countess of Worcester 89–91, 93, 95
Bryan, Sir Francis 62–4, 86, 96, 116
Buckeridge, Anthony 200, 202
Buckhurst, Lord, *see* Sackville, Thomas
Buckingham, duke of, *see* Stafford, Edward; Villiers, George
Bullinger, Henry 148
Burcher, John 148
Burgess, Anthony 220
Burghley, Lord, *see* Cecil, William
Burghley house 185
Bush, M.L. 29

Calder, Arthur 218
Cambrai, treaty of 68, 72–4
Cambridge University 203
Campeggio, Cardinal 54, 57, 58, 62–5, 70–2, 74
Carew, Sir Nicholas 86
Carey, Lucius (1610–43), second viscount Falkland 207
Carey, Valentine (d. 1626), bishop of Exeter 200
Carles, Lancelot de 6, 89
Carleton, Dudley 203
Carleton, George 200
Carnaby, Sir Reynold 27, 31
Cartwright, Thomas 197
Casale, Sir Gregory 63, 65, 66
Castillon, French Ambassador 121, 122
Catherine of Aragon 67, 71, 86
   death 83, 87, 94
   Henry VIII's divorce from 8, 15, 60, 62
   advocation to Rome 65–7, 69, 71, 74
   legatine court 54, 57–8, 62–5
   Wolsey and 54, 60, 62, 65–7, 74
Catherine Parr 134–6, 137
Cavendish, George 4, 54, 57, 93
Cecil, Sir William (1521–98), Lord Burghley 163, 166, 167, 168, 176, 193, 199
censorship 203
Chapuys, Eustace, imperial ambassador 9, 25, 26, 29, 56–7, 68, 70
   on Anne Boleyn 80–1, 82, 83, 84–5, 87, 92, 93, 94, 97, 98
   on Jane Seymour 83–4, 85
Charles I, King 28, 200
   religious policy 191, 197, 201–9
Charles V, Emperor 25, 72–3, 84, 85, 86–7, 119
Chaucer, Geoffrey 22
Cheke, John 43, 140, 141
Chelsea parish church 180
Cheyney, Sir Thomas 86
Chillingworth, William 202
chivalric culture 7–8
Church of England, *see* religion
Clarence, duke of, *see* Plantagenet, George
Clarendon, Lord, *see* Hyde, Edward
Clement VII, Pope 65–7
Clement, Sir Richard 175, 176
Clerk, John 56, 69, 71
Clifford, Henry (1493–1542), eleventh lord Clifford and first earl of Cumberland 27, 33
Clifford, Henry (1517–70), second earl of Cumberland 27
Clifton, Robin 205, 209
Clinton, Edward (1512–85), ninth Lord Clinton, later first earl of Lincoln 141
Cobham, Nan 89
Collinson, Patrick 200
Colvin, Sir Howard 177

Compton, Sir William (d. 1528) 44, 53, 175
Conquest, Robert 229
Constantine, George 92, 94, 95
Cornwall 23, 24, 32
Cornwall, Julian 38
Cosin, John (d. 1672), bishop of Durham 208
council of the north 33, 118
court, government and 129–32
court of augmentations 110–11, 115, 130
Courtenay, Henry (d. 1538), marquess of Exeter 10, 29, 30, 31, 86
Cranmer, Thomas (d. 1556), archbishop of Canterbury 7, 9, 94, 123, 192
Cromwell, Thomas 5–6, 7, 12, 16, 20, 25, 84, 97, 108–23, 129, 131
    Countess of Worcester and 90
    court of augmentations and 110–11, 115
    dissolution of monasteries and 115–16
    downfall 2, 3, 6, 123
    fall of Anne Boleyn and 86–7, 91, 96, 97
    rebellions and 25
    religious policy and 6, 7, 111–12, 114–16, 192
    Throckmorton's insult and 12
Cumberland, earl of, see Clifford, Henry

Dacre, William (1500–63), third Lord Dacre 27, 33
Darcy, Sir Arthur 26
Darcy, Thomas (c.1467–1537), first Lord Darcy 24, 25, 26–7, 55–6, 59
Daubeney, Giles (1452–1508), first Lord Daubeney 22
Davenant, John (d. 1641), bishop of Salisbury 199, 200
Davies, C.S.L. 6–7, 178
de Carles, Lancelot 6, 89
de Dominis, Marco Antonio, dean of Windsor 200
de Mendoza, Inigo 54–5, 62, 67
de Praet, Louis 16

de Vere, Robert 146
Declaration of Sports 196
Delaware, Lord, see West, Thomas
Denny, Sir Anthony 149
Derby, earl of, see Stanley, Edward
Dering, Sir Edward 209
Derrida, Jacques 218, 219, 228
Devereux, Robert (d. 1601), second earl of Essex 23
Dickens, A.G. 108–9, 115
Dingley, Sir Thomas 13–14, 15
Dispensations Act 113
dissolution of monasteries 115–16, 192
Donne, John 194
Dorset, marquess of, see Grey, Henry
Dorset, Thomas 114
Douglas, Archibald (c.1490–1557), sixth earl of Angus 69
Dowe, Mother 163
du Bellay, Guillaume 68
du Bellay, Jean 55, 59, 62, 68, 179
Dudley, Amy, see Robsart, Amy
Dudley, Edmund 40, 41, 42, 161
Dudley, John (1502–53), earl of Warwick, later duke of Northumberland 23, 139, 151, 161–2, 163
    architecture and 182, 183
Dudley, Robert (d. 1588), earl of Leicester 1, 161
    Amy Robsart and
      death 163, 166–72
      marriage 161, 162, 164
    Elizabeth and 162–3, 165, 166, 172
Dudley Castle, Staffordshire 182, 186
Dugard, Thomas 207

Edward I, King 33
Edward IV, King 21
Edward VI, King 11, 23, 36, 162, 184
    marriage of Catherine Parr and 135–6
    religious policy 191
    Thomas Seymour and 139–41, 147–8, 152
Elizabeth I, Queen 23, 34–5, 36, 83, 176, 184
    death of Amy Robsart and 164, 171–2

Elizabeth I *(cont.)*:
  doubts on paternity of 93, 94
  marriage of Catherine Parr and 135
  religious policy 192, 193–4, 195, 197, 199
  Robert Dudley and 162–3, 165, 166, 172
  Thomas Seymour and 134, 136–8, 148, 149, 151, 152, 153
Elton, Sir Geoffrey 1, 2, 7, 12, 13, 25, 85, 86, 108–23, 129–32
Elyot, Sir Thomas 38, 40, 41, 42, 43, 86
Essex, earl of, *see* Devereux, Robert
Exeter, marquess of, *see* Courtenay, Henry

Falkland, Lord, *see* Carey, Lucius
Ferdinand de San Severino 122
Feria, Count de 163, 165
Fernandez–Armesto, Felipe 4, 5
Field of Cloth of Gold (1520) 177, 180
Fiennes, William (1582–1662), viscount Saye and Sele 205
Fisher, John (d. 1535), bishop of Rochester 8, 120
Fitzalan, Henry (1512–80), twelfth earl of Arundel 168
Fitzalan, Richard 146
Fitzalan, Thomas (1585–1646), fourteenth earl of Arundel 39
Fitzherbert, Anthony 61
Fitzherbert, Sir John 39, 42
Fitzjames, Sir John 61
Fitzwilliam, Sir William (c.1490–1542), earl of Southampton 61, 86, 90, 94
Fletcher, Anthony 203
Flowerdew, Mr 162, 164
Foster, Anthony 162, 166, 170, 171, 172
Foucault, Michel 219, 228
Fourdrinier, Norman 165
Fowler, John 135, 139, 140, 141, 147
Foxe, John 4, 85, 88, 182, 191
Foxe, Richard (d. 1528), bishop of Winchester 182
France
  campaigns in 35
  nobility in 42
Francis I, King of France 64–5, 68, 72, 178, 181
Fulmerston, Richard 39–40

Gardiner, Stephen (d. 1555), bishop of Winchester 3, 7
  architecture and 182–3
  Cromwell and 2, 109, 118
  fall of Anne Boleyn and 91
  Wolsey and 63, 65–6, 68, 69–70, 71–2, 73
gentry 44
  local government and 33–4
  wealth 36, 38
Germany
  Henry VIII's policy on 119, 121
  Lutheranism in 63
Giovanni da Maiano 183
Gloucester, Humphrey duke of 139
Gonson, Mr 121
Gooderick, Thomas (d. 1554), bishop of Ely 152
Gorbachev, Mikhail 228
Gosnall, John 152
government
  court and 129–32
  Cromwell and 108–23, 129, 131
  nobility and 2–3, 4–7, 17, 21–3, 28–9
Grey, Henry (1517–54), third marquess of Dorset, later duke of Suffolk 141, 142, 143, 144–5, 148, 149, 151
Grey, Jane 23, 144, 147, 161, 162
Grey, Richard (d. 1524), third earl of Kent 37
Grey, Thomas 149
Grindal, Edmund (d. 1583), archbishop of Canterbury 193
Guildford, Sir Henry 61
Gunn, Steven 6, 20, 52
Guy, John 5, 7, 51, 109
Gwyn, Peter 3, 29

Haddon Hall, Derbyshire 176, 180
Haigh, Christopher 2, 51
Hales, John 203

Hall, Edward 55, 56, 57, 60
Hall, Joseph 203
Hamilton, James (d. 1575), second earl of Arran 98, 116
Hampton Court 175, 176, 178, 180, 181, 184
Hardwick, Elizabeth (d. 1608), Bess of Hardwick, countess of Shrewsbury 176
Hardwick Hall, Nottinghamshire 175, 176
Harington, John 144, 145, 146
Harlech Castle 180
Harrington, John 26
Harsnett, Samuel (d. 1631), bishop of Norwich 195, 200, 207
Hastings, George (1488–1544), first earl of Huntingdon 24
Heidegger, Martin 218, 228
Henry I, King 22
Henry II, King 22
Henry III, King 28
Henry IV, King of France 200
Henry VII, King 20, 23, 30, 176, 180
Henry VIII, King 1, 108, 225
    Anne Boleyn and 80–99
        relationship 80–1, 83, 85
        witchcraft accusation 81–2
    building 176–7, 178, 179, 180–1, 183, 186
    Catherine Parr and 134
    chivalric culture and 7–8
    court and government 129–32
    Cromwell's government and 108–23
    divorce from Catherine of Aragon 8, 15, 60, 62
        advocation to Rome 65–7, 69, 71, 74
        legatine court 54, 57–8, 62–5
        Wolsey and 54, 60, 62, 65–7, 74
    fall of Wolsey and 51, 52, 54–5, 58, 59, 61–74
    funeral 181
    impotence 93–4, 98
    interpretations of dominance or faction and 3, 4–17, 22, 61–2, 109–10
    Jane Seymour and 5, 80, 81, 83–4, 85, 134
    nobility and 29–30, 36
    religious policy 2, 5, 8–9, 17, 85, 191, 192–3, 194, 195
    Scottish policy 32, 33
Herbert, George 194
Hertford, earl of, *see* Seymour, Edward
Heylyn, Peter 202
Hill Hall, Essex 185
history, postmodernism and 17, 217–30
Hobbes, Robert, abbot of Woburn 96
Holinshed, Raphael 25
Holland, Hugh 30
Holocaust denial 225, 226
Holt Castle 145–6, 147
Hoo, William 85
Hooker, Richard 197
Houlbrooke, Ralph 11
Howard, Henry (d. 1547), earl of Surrey 11
Howard, Thomas (1473–1554), third duke of Norfolk 2, 7, 11–12, 24, 29, 98
    Cromwell and 109, 118
    fall of Wolsey and 51, 52, 53, 54, 58, 61
Howes, Edmund 184
Howson, John 196, 200, 202
Humfrey, Lawrence 38, 40, 41, 43, 44
Huntingdon, earl of, *see* Hastings, George
Hurstfield, Joel 88
Hussee, John 89, 97
Hussey, Sir John (c.1465–1537), Lord Hussey 24, 25–6, 27
Hyde, Mr 162
Hyde, Edward (1609–74), first earl of Clarendon 207

Ightham Mote, Kent 175, 176
inflation 38
Ireland 32, 33, 116
Ives, Eric 2–3, 7, 51–61, 67, 68, 69, 70, 71, 85, 86–7, 109

Jackson, Thomas 98
James I, King 36
    religious policy 195–7, 199–200, 207

Jenkins, Keith 217
Jewel, John (d. 1571), bishop of Salisbury 207
John of Gaunt (1340–99), duke of Lancaster 21, 146
John, King 28
Johnson, Samuel 221

Kent, earl of, *see* Grey, Richard
Kerridge, Eric 38
Ket, Robert 161
Ket, William 161
Kildare, dowager countess of 86
Killegrew, Henry 164, 167
King, John (d. 1621), bishop of London 205
King's College Chapel, Cambridge 180
Kingston, Sir William 6, 90, 91, 95
Kirby Hall, Northamptonshire 185, 186
Knole palace, Kent 180
Knollys, Sir Francis 167

Lake, Peter 197, 200, 201
Lambert, John 122
Lambeth Articles (1595) 199, 202
Lancaster, duke of, *see* John of Gaunt
Langey, Ambassador 68, 73
Latimer, Hugh 150, 182, 184
Laud, William (d. 1645), archbishop of Canterbury 191, 196, 197, 200–2, 204–8
le Sauch, Johann 68
Leavis, F.R. 229
Leicester, earl of, *see* Dudley, Robert
Leland, John 177
Leti, Gregorio 134, 135, 138, 151
Lever, Thomas 167
Lisle, Lord, *see* Plantagenet, Arthur
local government
    gentry and 33–4
    nobility and 31–3
Longleat, Wiltshire 175, 182, 185
lord lieutenancy 35
Lowe, Toby, Lord Aldington 226
Luther, Martin 8, 192
Lutheranism 63, 191, 192

MacCulloch, Diarmaid 201
McFarlane, K.B. 22
Madrid, treaty of 73
Manners, Henry (1526–63), second earl of Rutland 141–2, 145, 148, 149, 151
Manners, Thomas (d. 1493), first earl of Rutland 24
Marcher lords 32–3
Marillac, Ambassador 118
Marney, Sir Henry (d. 1523), first Lord Marney 175, 180
Marxism 227–8
Mary I, Queen 5, 23, 86, 94, 113, 162, 182
    marriage of Catherine Parr and 135
    Thomas Seymour as suitor for 134, 136
Mary Queen of Scots 27
Mendoza, Inigo de 54–5, 62, 67
military, nobility and 35–6
monasteries, dissolution of 115–16, 192
Mont, Christopher 118, 119
Montagu, Lord, *see* Pole, Henry
Montagu, Richard 197, 202
Montaigne, George (d. 1628), bishop of Lincoln, archbishop of York 200, 205
More, Sir Thomas (d. 1535) 16, 59–60, 61, 120
Morrill, John 191
Morton, Thomas 203
Munslow, Alan 217, 218

Neale, Sir John 98
Neile, Richard (d. 1640), archbishop of York 199, 200
Nevill, Charles (d. 1601), sixth earl of Westmorland 27–8
Nevill, George (d. 1535), sixth Lord Bergavenny 61
Nevill, Richard (1428–71), first earl of Warwick 21
Nietzsche, Friedrich 218, 228
nobility 1, 3
    central government and 2–3, 4–7, 17, 21–3, 28–9
    contemporary attitudes to 38–44

continuing power of 1, 20–45
critics of 38–41
decline of 20–1
gentry and 34
local government and 31–3
medieval period 20, 21
military role 35–6
monarchy and 1, 29–33
rebellions and 23–8
royal ministers and 28–9
wealth 36–8
Nonsuch Palace, Surrey 177, 178, 180–1, 183, 185
Norfolk, duke of, *see* Howard, Thomas
Norris, Henry 54, 80, 87, 88, 92, 94–5, 96
Northampton, marquess of, *see* Parr, William
Northumberland, duke of, *see* Dudley, John
Northumberland, earl of, *see* Percy, Henry; Percy, Thomas
Norton, Thomas 195

Overall, John (d. 1619), bishop of Norwich 196, 198, 200
Oxburgh Palace, Norfolk 180
Oxford University 203

Page, Sir Richard 96
Paget, Sir William 149, 184–5
Palsgrave, John 56
Parker, Matthew (d. 1575), archbishop of Canterbury 193, 195
parliament 36, 60, 85, 111
    Thomas Seymour and 140, 141–2, 150
Parr, Catherine 134–6, 137
Parr, William (1513–71), marquess of Northampton 141, 142, 145, 148
Parry, Thomas 138, 143, 144, 149
Parsons, Robert 168
Paulet, George 122–3
Paulet, William (c. 1483–1572), Lord St John, later marquess of Winchester 149
Paynell, Thomas 118

Percy, Henry (c.1449–89), fourth earl of Northumberland 21, 30
Percy, Henry Algernon (1478–1527), fifth earl of Northumberland 31
Percy, Henry (c.1502–37), sixth earl of Northumberland 25, 27, 31, 69, 94
Percy, Henry (1564–1632), ninth earl of Northumberland 37
Percy, Sir Ingram 25, 27
Percy, Thomas (1528–72), seventh earl of Northumberland 25, 27–8, 31
Perkins, William 203
Peto, William 15–16
Petre, Sir William 146
Pevsner, Sir Nikolaus 179, 181
Philip II, King of Spain 162, 182
Picto, – 164
Pilgrimage of Grace (1536) 1, 6, 10, 24–7, 30, 35, 192
Pinkie, battle of (1547) 139
Plantagenet, Arthur (d. 1542), viscount Lisle 61
Plantagenet, George (1449–78), duke of Clarence 21
Plantagenet, Margaret (1473–1541), countess of Salisbury 30, 120
Platt, Colin 181
Pole, Sir Geoffrey 30, 86
Pole, Henry (c.1492–1539), Lord Montagu 10, 29, 30, 86, 151–2
Pole, Reginald (d. 1558), archbishop of Canterbury 8, 12, 29–30
politics
    architecture and 3, 175–87
    as factional struggle, *see* faction
poor laws 114
postmodernism 17, 217–30
Potter, Barnaby 203
praemunire, statute of 51, 59
Praet, Louis de 16
predestination 191, 195, 196, 197, 198–201
privy council 130–2
Prynne, William 202

Quadra, Bishop 163, 166, 167, 168

Rabb, T.K. 178
Radcliffe, Henry (c.1507–57), second earl of Sussex 23
Rastell, J. 40, 41, 42, 44
rebellions 23
    against Amicable Grant (1525) 23–4, 30–1
    Cornish rebellion (1497) 23, 24
    northern rebellion (1569) 27–8
    Pilgrimage of Grace (1536) 1, 6, 10, 24–7, 30, 35, 192
regional councils 33
religion 191–209
    architecture and 182–3
    Arminianism 191, 199, 200, 201–9
    Charles I's religious policy 191, 197, 201–9
    Cromwell and 6, 7, 111–12, 114–16, 192
    dissolution of monasteries 115–16, 192
    Elizabeth I's religious policy 192, 193–4, 195, 197, 199
    Henry VIII's religious policy 2, 5, 8–9, 17, 85, 191, 192–3, 194, 195
    James I's religious policy 195–7, 199–200, 207
    predestination 191, 195, 196, 197, 198–201
Rich, Sir Richard 118
Richard II, King 28
Richardson, John 198
Richmond Palace, Surrey 176, 181
Roberts, Peter 87, 116
Robsart, Amy
    death 1, 163–72
    illness 163, 165–6
    marriage to Robert Dudley 161, 162, 164
Robsart, Sir John 161
Rochford, Lady 93
Rochford, Lord, see Boleyn, George; Boleyn, Thomas
Russell, Conrad 191, 197, 199, 201
Russell, John (c.1485–1555), first lord Russell, first earl of Bedford 31, 32, 138, 148–9

Rutland, earl of, see Manners, Henry; Thomas

Sackville, Sir Thomas (d. 1608), Lord Buckhurst 34
Sadler, Sir Ralph 116, 122
St James's palace 177, 180
St John, Lord, see Paulet, William
Salisbury, countess of, see Plantagenet, Margaret
Samman, Neil 68, 69
Sander, Nicholas 81
Sandys, Sir William (c.1470–1540), Lord Sandys 175, 176
Saussure, Ferdinand de 218, 219
Saxony, duke of 119
Saye and Sele, Lord, see Fiennes, William
Scarisbrick, J.J. 51, 109
Schama, Simon 219
Scotland 32, 33, 139, 152, 208, 209
Selden, John 205
Serlio, Sebastiano 177
Seymour, Edward (c.1500–1552), earl of Hertford, later duke of Somerset and Protector 23, 32, 33, 134, 161
    architecture and 181
    Elizabeth's suitor and 138
    marriage of Catherine Parr and 135, 136
    Scottish campaign (1547) 139, 152
    Thomas Seymour's intrigues and 134, 139, 140, 141, 144, 149, 151, 152
Seymour, Jane 5, 80, 81, 83–4, 85, 99, 134
Seymour, John 137
Seymour, Sir Thomas (d. 1549), Lord Seymour of Sudeley 1, 23
    architecture 182
    downfall 134–53
    Jane Grey and 144, 147
    lands 136, 145–6
    marriage to Catherine Parr 134–6, 137
    as suitor for Princess Elizabeth 134, 136–8, 148

Sharington, Sir William 139, 143, 144, 146–7, 149, 176, 182
Sharpe, Kevin 202
sheep bill (1536) 113
Shelton, Mrs 95
Shrewsbury, earl of, *see* Talbot, George; Talbot, Gilbert
Shute, John 177, 183
Sidney, Henry 168
Simnel, Lambert 23
Skelton, John 29, 53, 116
Smart, Peter 195
Smeaton, Mark 80, 87, 89, 91–2, 93, 95, 96
Smith, – 170–1
Smith, Sir Thomas 185
Smythson, Robert 177, 185
sociology 219
Sokal, Alan 222
Solzhenitsyn, Alexander 223
Somerset, Charles 22
Somerset, Henry (d. 1549), second earl of Worcester 89
Somerset, Protector, *see* Seymour, Edward
Somerset House 181–2, 186
Southampton, earl of, *see* Fitzwilliam, William; Wriothesley, Thomas
Spinelli, Gasparo 183
Stafford, Edward (1478–1521), third duke of Buckingham 29
Stafford, Henry (1501–63), Lord Stafford 39, 61
Stafford, Sir William 90
Stanhope, Anne 136
Stanhope, John 34
Stanhope, Sir Michael 34, 140
Stanhope, Sir Thomas 34–5
Stanley, Edward (1509–1572), third earl of Derby 24, 33
Stanley, Sir William 146
Star Chamber 130
Starkey, David 2, 7, 51, 85, 86, 117, 129–32
Stokesay 179
Stone, Lawrence 36

Stow, John 184
Strype, J. 145
Sudeley, Gloucestershire 182
Suffolk, duke of, *see* Brandon, Charles; Grey, Henry
Summerson, Sir John 180
Supplication against the Ordinaries (1532) 111–12
Surrey, earl of, *see* Howard, Thomas
Sussex, earl of, *see* Radcliffe, Henry
Sutton Place, Surrey 180

Talbot, George (1468–1538), fourth earl of Shrewsbury 1, 24–5, 26, 27, 35, 223
Talbot, Gilbert (1552–1616), seventh earl of Shrewsbury 34–5
Tawney, R.H. 36
taxation
    Amicable Grant 1, 17, 23–4, 29, 30–1, 53
    death of fourth earl of Northumberland and 30
    Wolsey and 56
Temse, MP 111
theatre 203
Theobalds, Hertfordshire 176
Thirty Nine Articles (1563) 194, 198
Thomas, William 42
Thorpe, John 177
Throckmorton, Sir George 12–16
Throckmorton, Michael 12
Throckmorton, Sir Nicholas 168
Thynne, Sir John 182, 185
Torrigiano, Pietro 180
Trevor-Roper, Hugh 204
Trunckey, Robert 183–4
Tryndell, – 168
Tuchet, James (1463–97), seventh Lord Audley, 23
Tuke, Brian 68, 70
Tunstal, Cuthbert (d. 1559), bishop of Durham 118
Turner, William 178
Tyacke, Nicholas 191, 198–201
Tyndale, William 4
Tyrwhit, Robert 145, 149

Umberto de Gambara 62–3
Utrecht town hall 183

Vannes, Peter 63, 65, 66
Vaughan, Stephen 16, 119
Vergil, Polydore 4
Verney, Sir Richard 169, 170, 171, 172
Vernon, Henry 21
Vertot, Abbé de 134, 138
Villiers, George (1592–1628), first duke of Buckingham 202
Vitalis, Oderic 22
Vorstius, Conrad 199
Vyne, The, Hampshire 175, 176

Wales 32, 33, 87–8, 116
Walker, Greg 3, 4, 29
Wallop, Sir John 119, 121
Warbeck, Perkin 23
Warham, William (d. 1532), archbishop of Canterbury 61
Warnicke, R.M. 81, 82–3
Wars of the Roses 20, 21
Warwick, earl of, *see* Dudley, John; Nevill, Richard
Wendon, Rauf 98
Wentworth, Thomas (1525–84), second Lord Wentworth 23
Wernham, R.B. 108, 117, 121
West, Thomas (d. 1554), ninth Lord Delaware, 10–11
West Drayton, Middlesex 184–5
Westminster Abbey 180
Westminster palace 130, 179
Westmorland, earl of, *see* Nevill, Charles

Weston, Sir Francis 80, 87, 89, 95, 96
Weston, Sir Richard 180
Whitby, Prior of 98
White, Peter 198
Whitehall palace 130, 177, 181
Whitgift, John (d. 1604), archbishop of Canterbury 195, 197, 199, 207
Wightman, – 136, 148, 153
Willoughby, Sir Francis 185
Willoughby, Robert (c.1452–1502), first Lord Willoughby de Brooke 22
Wilson, Harold 129, 229
Woburn, abbot of, *see* Hobbes, Robert
Wollaton, Nottinghamshire 185, 186
Wolsey, Thomas (d. 1530), archbishop of York, Cardinal Legate
   architecture and 177, 180, 181, 183
   divorce from Catherine of Aragon and 54, 60, 62, 65–7, 74
   fall from power 3, 6, 51–74
   as King's adviser 5, 16
   nobility's attitude to 29, 53
   treaty of Cambrai and 72–4
Woodford, Robert 205
Worcester, countess of, *see* Browne, Elizabeth
Worcester, earl of, *see* Somerset, Henry
Worden, Blair 203
Wriothesley, Thomas (1505–50), first earl of Southampton 12, 95–6, 145, 176
Wroth, Thomas 140
Wyatt, George 97
Wyatt, Sir Thomas 97, 116, 122

Zagorin, Perez 2